A Behind-the-Scen 

g

Keith Publications, LLC
www.keithpublications.com

Arizona
USA

Visual Eats
A Behind-the-Scenes Look at Modern Italian Cooking

By Enzo Fargione

Edited by Ray Dyson
www.raydyson.com

Cover art by Elisa Elaine Luevanos
www.ladymaverick81.com

Interior photos by Greg Powers

www.keithpublications.com

ISBN: 978-1-62882-011-9

Contact information: info@keithpublications.com
Visit us at: www.keithpublications.com

Printed in The United States of America

Dedication

For those who get up early in the morning,
work on their feet all day long, and go to bed very late at night.

Acknowledgements

My Father Rosario, a man who has always portrayed a tougher image of himself than he actually is.

My Mother Maria Luisa, without her continuous love, passion, support and encouragement I would have never turned out to be the man I am today.

My Grandmother "Nonna" Corradina, because her immense unconditional love for me will last me at least two lifetimes.

My sister Daniela, because even if so different we are so similar and we rebel and excel in the same way.

My beautiful niece Giulia Rubin, one of the greatest and sweetest unexpected surprises of my life, my little Enzina.

My daughter Chiara, the greatest unexpected surprise of my life, capable of inspiring me in so many ways I did not know were possible.

My life's best friend Giorgio Pilati, because every time we are together he makes me feel like I never left Italy, loving me unconditionally without asking anything in return.

My loving soul mate and everyday pride Julia Seneca Saah, the only person who fully understands me with her love, patience and support, and makes me want to be a better man every day.

In Appreciation:

Roberto Donna
My mentor.

Mario Sobbia
My first culinary professor and teacher.

Diane Nine
My book agent, who believed in me at first bite.

Dave Smitherman
My editor, who was able to convert my thoughts into fine print.

Ross De Blois, Ron Tipa and Edwin Livingston
For their continuous support, help, friendship and love, three incredible people who find goodness in every day of their lives.

Robert K Bailey
For his support, help and friendship.

Tom and Maury Byrne
In appreciation for the love, support and constant care for my daughter.

Greg Powers
Because of his talent all the food photographs in this book deliver a realistic and authentic sharp message.

Stefano Pascucci
A unique loving and crazy friend I wish I could spend more quality time with.

Special thanks to:

Ms Phyllis Richman, Ms Lynne Breaux, Mr. Tim Carman, Mr. Tom Sietsema and Mr. Todd Kliman for their time and very valuable contributions.

An incredible thank you to Keith Publications for the trust invested in a chef whose goal was to deliver his personal memories, his knowledge, and the realities of one of the hardest industries out there. Especially to Ray Dyson, who edited this manuscript with care and precision.

Special greetings to my family of Sicilian roots residing in Toronto, Canada, the past 50 years.

A big loving hug and much appreciation go to those who worked side by side with me for the past 26 years believing in the same goals as I did day after day.

In particular:

David Ventura, Lee Vernick, Clinton F. Wheeler III, Elisabeth Barbato, "Oz" Jose Leon, Soo Han, Jeremy Cooke, Fernando Contreras, Michael Fusano, Emanuele Cognetti, Tony Servideo, Aldo Traettino, Ursula Avella, Horacio Chacon, Carl Vitellino, Enzo Febbraro, Lorraine Carleo, Sean Comiskey, Manuel Mathious "Bello," Davide Mazzei "Vecio," Piero Ricchiari, Andreas Brandt, Charlie Saah, Susan Pettis, Daniele De Luca, Francesco Ricchi, George Bogdanovic, Janet Donovan, Michael Palmer for the fantastic portrait cover photo of this book, and my dog Max, a 120-pound American Bulldog who waited by the door for my return from work every single night for the past eight years before he recently passed away.

A special mention for chefs Roberto Donna, Michel Richard, Patrick O'Connell, Robert Irvine and Jose Andres. Thank you so very much for your endorsements, genuine quotes and flattering statements, but mostly for your friendship. You inspire me professionally on a daily basis.

In loving memory of Venanzio Giusti and Karen Cathy, dear coworkers and dear friends.

Reviews and Praise

"I love Enzo's unique vision of modern Italian cooking. He is a creative chef and restaurateur, and shares his passions and challenges for both in this book.
Try his recipe for raw onion salad, crispy and delicious; I love the texture of the onion petals layered with caviar. A purée of anise over a perfectly cooked fish, a rabbit in artichoke prosciutto crépinette, or his pasta with Parmesan parsley foam; all inspire me to dream in culinary Italian."
~ Chef Michel Richard, 2007James Beard Foundation's Outstanding Chef in America Award Winner and author of "Happy in the Kitchen"

"I had the pleasure of meeting Enzo when he was only 17 and at the beginning of his culinary career. I have always admired his talents, his artistic work and enjoyed his friendship. "Visual Eats" tells decades of realistic restaurant stories while its recipes help to spread a better understanding of great Italian cooking across America.
Bravo, Enzo, I'm proud of you!"
~ Chef Roberto Donna, 1996 James Beard Award winner and *Esquire* magazine "Chef of the Year" for 2012

"I enjoyed reading *Visual Eats*! It's a wonderful cookbook and a spot-on approach in telling realistic and funny tales of the restaurant industry. Love Enzo's creativity and his precise details in executing all the featured dishes. His vision of modern Italian cooking breaks away from traditionalism in a fun and playful way while preserving the essence of quality and professionalism. *Visual Eats* is a perfect marriage of words and recipes."
**~ Chef Patrick O'Connell, The Inn at Little Washington, Virginia
2001 James Beard Foundation's Outstanding Chef in America Award Winner and Cook Book Author**

"I love Visual Eats and I love how my friend Enzo is so passionate about Italian cooking. His work and professional commitment has helped elevate food quality in Washington DC for years. This book can inspire and will motivate many people to cook his amazing modern Italian cuisine at home. Enzo is a talented chef and one of the hardest working people I know and I am very proud of him."
Chef Jose Andres, 2011 James Beard Foundation's Outstanding Chef in America Award Winner, Cook Book Author and Time Magazine 2012 One of "100 Most Influential People in the World"

"Reading Visual Eats made me re-live the good old days with a smile. Enzo and I shared memorable days in kitchens across America cooking for charity functions, shared great times in the gym working out and we always shared the same passion for food and wine with infinite joy and friendship. I love the way he tells the stories and the recipes he features in this book: a reflection of his commitment to culinary greatness with mastery and professionalism that leads to his personal approach to modern Italian cooking."
Chef Robert Irvine, restaurateur, TV personality and host of Food Network program "Restaurant Impossible"

TABLE OF CONTENTS

INTRODUCTION 1

CHAPTER ONE 11

CHILDHOOD MEMORIES AND FOOD FACTS

CHAPTER TWO 29

BROTHS AND STOCKS—THE FOUNDATIONS OF FLAVOR

CHAPTER THREE 38

APPETITE OPENERS

CHAPTER FOUR 78

URBAN LEGENDS AND UNUSUAL SATISFYING STARTERS

CHAPTER FIVE 161

SURPRISING SALADS

CHAPTER SIX 200

SUCCULENT SOUPS

CHAPTER SEVEN 238

THE PASTA CHRONICLES

CHAPTER EIGHT 323

TALES OF CULINARY ROAD TRIPS

CHAPTER NINE 359

EVER FELT LIKE A FISH OUT OF WATER?

CHAPTER TEN 396

THE SIMPLE PLEASURES OF THE FLESH

CHAPTER ELEVEN 449

DELICIOUS DESSERTS

CHAPTER TWELVE 493

THE REALITIES OF THE RESTAURANT

CHAPTER THIRTEEN 508

CRITICISMS, OPINIONS AND JUDGMENTS
THE HEAVY HAND OF THE PRESS

INDEX TO RECIPES 528

Introduction

I have friends who hate to get up in the morning and go to work. They dread the idea of getting to their jobs, with the only bright spot being a warm cup of coffee in anticipation of another gray day in purgatory.

Not me! I am indeed the luckiest guy in the world, and I have my dream job. I have wanted to be a chef ever since I smelled my mother's cooking the first time back in Italy.

At the young age of three I got my first taste of cooking. I was all bundled up with an apron and standing on top of an old stool. I felt like an alpinist who had just reached the top of Mount Everest as I stood in front of the kitchen stove waving a wooden spoon. Needless to say, I raised a few eyebrows back then. My mother indeed got very concerned.

I knew right away what the future had set for me. Back in Italy it is so much simpler to be inspired because of the great natural ingredients found everywhere you turn: tasty produce, open-air markets, trailers and carts filled with hundreds of cold cuts, fresh fish, meats, game and fresh cheese selections. The vast selections can be overwhelming, and if you are not careful at the time of ordering you may find you buy more than you want or need, much to the delight of the peddlers.

I have been very lucky to grow up in a place where food and wine are respected equally, as much as the national flag or the national soccer team. That should tell you something about our priorities back home: mangia, mangia (eat, eat) is our motto. As you can imagine, in Italy cooking is an art form, a way of life.

To this day my happiness is a direct result of doing something I love for a living. Imagine if you can also be successful at something you are passionate about. What a great feeling! It does take many years to fully understand how to combine ingredients and mature professionally. It is a never-ending process; if you want to keep growing, you never stop learning, especially when you fail. Every time I have failed I was always able to get back up and move forward with my head up high, as I knew one day it would all pay off if I worked hard enough.

In my early professional years I used to combine wonderful ingredients and colorful elements in surprising dishes with the hope of shocking my guests and the media. I learned it was the wrong approach to genuine cooking, but it taught me a valuable lesson.

Impress yourself with taste and presentation, color and concept. Respect the traditions and respect the ingredients. There is no point in transforming a fresh leaf of basil into a long, rubbery string of nonsense...basil is basil, a leaf is a leaf.
Would you wear fur-lined flip-flops in a snowstorm? What is its purpose?

I am one of the lucky few enthusiastic to go to work, and one of the few who craves to experiment, assemble, combine and test in my kitchen lab at all times. What a wonderful journey! I am forever thankful for it, for all cooking has given me and for all the happiness it continues to bring me.

I believe everyone should be able to present a dish in a very artistic and colorful way: Its concept glamorous, its execution detailed and attentive, its idea unique, but once your guests savor it, the taste should make them forget all about that, and it becomes the equivalent of a leading actor in an award-winning movie. All the elements come together to create a winning combination.

We all know it is very difficult to excel and to recreate that winning taste for each and every dish, and if I knew how to do that I would be the most perfect chef in the world. But I am not; therefore I can only continue to try to be the best possible chef I can be, and continue my search for the perfect combination of color, taste and presentation every single day with every meal I prepare. The good thing is I never give up. The bad thing is that I am never fully satisfied. I have a feeling I will be searching for the rest of my life as I know no matter how happy I am with a dish there is always a better way to do what I do. But that challenge is also what keeps me excited, committed and motivated to do my best. Growing up in Italy was fundamental for my early love and interest in food.

What better food country to live in than Italy? Of course I have a lot of respect for France, Spain, the Asian countries and the Latin Americans, and during the past 27 years of my American life I have learned a lot from them. I love the way Chinese, Mexican food or even pizza have become a way of everyday eating life for American people. Nowadays if you mention the word pizza to an average teenager in the U.S. and ask where it comes from very likely the answer is New York.

That's because this country was able to blend different cultures and traditions into what today is the American way of life. As a new country America was able to offer freedom to any cultures to implement and recreate the original tastes from their homeland and create a new tradition of American food: a blend of flavors. In Europe we have culinary traditions dating back even before the Roman Empire. Those are traditions we are very proud of. We embrace them, we protect them and we preserve them because it is our heritage.

I remember going to the market with my mother, and as a little kid I would see things I thought were magical: fresh fish jumping on ice on the stand, the butcher filling the casings with sausage meat right before my eyes, the warm bread coming out of the oven at the nearby bakery, the live chickens and the caged rabbits sold to you as fresh as they could possibly be. To the grownups I am sure it was just another day at the market, but to me it was a place filled with wonder and it made me want to keep going back.

For years I was a sponge, quietly absorbing all the activity around me. I watched my mother make fresh pasta, cook varieties of ragù, roast meats and fish, and make sauces of all kinds perfect for any occasion. My grandmother sometimes made her famous "ravioli di ricotta col bicchiere" which is ricotta raviolis made with a glass. She would lay the ricotta filling on top of a thin sheet of pasta dough with the help of a spoon, sliding the filling with her finger. Then she would cover it with a fresh sheet of dough brushed with egg wash to make it stick. To form its shape she would use a small glass placed upside down, and by pressing onto the ravioli pocket she would seal the filling. Over the years I have learned to appreciate ricotta raviolis so much I started eating them uncooked, driving everyone crazy in my house. I was a bomb ready to explode.

So it was not much of a surprise when I told my parents I wanted to be a cook. I remember my father looking at me like I was drunk or in need of brain surgery. He was a traditionalist and still very hard-headed. I guess he wanted me to enroll in some sort of engineering school like he did and have a stable life. My mother limited herself by saying, "Really?" but she knew already. She had watched me over the years, and we shared the same passion meal after meal. She had always supported me no matter what, even at a very young age.

My father said, "I don't think it's a good idea. Pick something else." I was 13 at the time and I was a very good soccer player, but following that dream would have driven my family crazy. That's a tough life. I also loved airplanes and often imagined what it would have been like to be a jet pilot or even go to the moon. I was definitely a dreamer, but I was also a realist. In Italy, doing what the family expects has great importance. So in order to make my parents happy I told them I would enroll in the air force. I saw my father's smile stretching like the Joker of the Batman movies. His boy would be a jet pilot. However, two months before enrollment I worked up the courage and told my parents I wanted to get into culinary school and make a career of it. I had to be true to myself and my passion. And so it began. I failed to be a jet pilot and I could not be happier.

To start my professional career I enrolled in a three-year program in culinary school, where I met one of the most influential people in my life, Professor Mario Sobbia of the culinary arts at the Giuseppina Colombatto Culinary Institute in Torino. From this eccentric and always energized man I learned how to let go of the little boy in me and let the man out. It is thanks to him I was able to come to the U.S. I was his first choice when some Italian restaurateurs from San Diego came to town searching for a young cook able to open a restaurant in California. The other very influential man in my professional life was chef Roberto Donna in Washington, D.C.

When I was in school Professor Sobbia used to tell us tales of mythical proportions about how chef Donna had just opened a restaurant in D.C. that was considered the best in all of Washington. The year was 1984, and the restaurant was the famed

Galileo. I graduated in 1986 and that same summer I came to my new home in the U.S. From there my life changed completely. My four-month tenure as a chef in San Diego had given me more disappointments than joy. I was just not really good at recreating lasagna or spaghetti with meatballs or different types of chicken preparations. It was difficult for me to deliver a fake product that was supposed to represent the Italian culinary pride. Soon after, I met Roberto Donna in Washington.

He was looking for cooks for his restaurant, Galileo. I was looking for a new job with possibilities of a stable career while learning as much as I could. Professor Sobbia, in the meantime, had worked as a mediator, arranging my move to the nation's capitol and into Roberto Donna's kitchen. Over the last 27 years I have been strapped to a rollercoaster car of personal and professional emotions as a result of that decision.

While working side by side with Roberto, I watched him become one of the most influential chefs in Washington throughout the early years of the new millennium. In the mid-90s I watched him reach a celebrity status only few have been able to achieve in the U.S. Sadly, I also watched him crumble in the wake of well-publicized legal issues and poor business decisions. But he did put me in business, and professionally he taught me everything he knew. He was always there for me, and during the early years he always protected and inspired me both in the kitchen and out. What a great mentor he was and how lucky I have been. I choose to remember the real Roberto Donna, the way he was until 2005: energetic, impulsive and always meticulously careful in everything he did professionally.

One thing for sure: he deserves credit for the way people are eating in Washington today. Roberto was like a big earthquake when he opened Galileo and everyone in town got the wake up call. Back then he was able to educate Washingtonians about the authentic and traditional Italian ways of eating fresh products, cooked "at the moment," and he never compromised his vision or quality or originality. Mediocrity was not in his vocabulary.

During the past 27 years I had the luck and the privilege to meet very important and influential chefs and service industry professionals across the country, some of whom I share a wonderful friendship today—the late Jean Louis Palladin and Julia Child, the glorious Mario Batali, Patrick O'Connell, Lidia Bastianich, Michel Richard, Emeril Lagasse, Tony May, Eric Ripert, Jose Andres, Charlie Palmer, Todd English, Daniel Boulud, David Burke and Charlie Trotter, Anthony Bourdain, just to name a few.

Sometimes I wonder what my professional life would have been without constant inspiration. I have always been very driven and known exactly what I wanted for my career. I have always volunteered for extra projects, offered my contribution for charity dinners and business trips. I have expanded my knowledge on cooking and business for many years as I have always been eager to learn as much as I could without focusing too much on compensation. The way I saw it I was getting paid with experience; I was meeting professionals I used to read about in cookbooks and food magazines. To me, there was no better payoff. I always figured money and fame would follow naturally.

Imagine me as a young cook traveling all over the country with Roberto Donna and cooking side by side with Jean Louis Palladin or meeting Julia Child and being able to talk to her, to feel the passion she had about food, or going to New York for the James Beard Awards for the first time and mingling with wonderful chefs, chatting with Mario Batali in his legendary orange clogs, shorts and tuxedo top. After working as chef at Galileo for five years all I knew was Roberto's cooking. I felt very proud and thankful, but also very ignorant in so many ways. I was so eager to see different kinds of cooking, different ways of organization and different food concepts.

From then on and into the following 20 years I have experienced a radical professional transformation: it was a very slow process for me, but I was able to open a few restaurants with different chef partners and friends and get my feet wet with all the problems and benefits that owning restaurants bring to the table. The chain of Il Radicchio Restaurants and the fine dining Barolo on Capitol Hill are what I still call today my first diving boards into the pool of ownership. For the first ten years I stabilized: There was very little or no change about the way I was cooking, not very adventurous, but very comfortable between the parameters of what I knew best. Things started to change soon after my move from Washington to

West Palm Beach, Florida, where I was offered the opportunity to open and own a unique new concept: an Italian tapas restaurant called Atrium. So my partners and I sold the D.C. restaurants and I was on my way to the Sunshine State.

I saw things a little differently in Florida. I experimented with unusual and new cooking techniques, with colorful food combination; I took advantage of the local products and especially some of the freshest fish I have ever seen. I learned the concept of the dish is just as important as the taste and its presentation. I experimented so much and so well that on my first review in Florida the *Palm Beach Post* rated Atrium as the best and most innovative new restaurant throughout the Treasure Coast of that year: 2006. That felt good! I followed my dream with guts despite how many eyebrows I had raised. It seemed like my new view of cooking was understood, embraced and appreciated. So why stop there? What are my limits?

I have learned with every passing year I can cook the same dish a little better. I have learned that with every passing year I have higher expectations for myself. I have learned that only through passion, love and dedication can you achieve the best results. Success and fame can destroy your work in a single day if you are not careful, if you are not humble. All of us chefs sometimes forget we are not brain surgeons; we are neither rock stars nor Hollywood actors even if we feel like them sometimes. We scream! We are very temperamental! People say we are strange or act like prima donnas. Sometimes we let ourselves go a little too far, but the only reason why we intentionally do that is because we are full of pride and full of passion. For most of us it is not a job. It is a life mission we take seriously, just as a brain surgeon does. When your work is based on details you cannot take shortcuts. Because you care about what you do you excel. It is your own personal drive. In the end it defines who you really are.

Some people have scarified with passion and with the persistence to learn, and worked long hours because they believed in something greater than a paycheck. Most of the time it does pay off. It all depends of how much you put into it. Dedicated and successful chefs are nothing less than passionate human beings who strongly believe in sending a clear and delicious message to those who are willing to try the results of personal visions and hard daily work.

I remember many culinary trips I have taken over the years, mostly because when chefs travel together to different places it is always an adventure. It's wonderful to be able to share the love for our profession and genuine friendships at the same time. I have taken so many trips in so many cities and places that I have lost count, but some memories are still very much alive: the gossips, the practical jokes we play on each other, the incredibly fun situations and the stories behind the curtains. Seeing us in our daily work environment, customers would never imagine the craziness that goes on between chefs. We are a creative group. I had such a glorious time while writing about those hilarious and awkward situations, and some of those memories I will cherish for the rest of my life as they are all part of a wonderful, long journey.

A confirmation of my new professional vision and interpretation of food occurred when I came back to Washington in 2008 and partnered with Teatro Goldoni Restaurant. The original Goldoni was opened by an old colleague and friend of mine, chef Fabrizio Aielli, right at the turn of the millennium: an Italian restaurant designed by one of the most prestigious and successful architect firms at that time. It had a dramatic décor emphasizing the Venetian Carnival motif with original masks, colorful columns, harlequin-style panels and a glass-enclosed open kitchen facing the main dining room. The restaurant was sold for a record price to a young newcomer from the disco club industry who decided to dive into the business and have some fun with it. I got a call from Teatro about eight months after Fabrizio sold, and I met for the first time the new owner. Despite the fact he was totally inexperienced in the restaurant field and had a hard time following our professional vision, I saw the restaurant's full potential. I understood right away I could express myself at my best while implementing a new version of cooking only if given the freedom and the tools I needed to work with. We entered into a contractual agreement and I started racking my brain. The goal was to become the best Italian restaurant in Washington, D.C., within a couple of years. Back then the restaurant was not making any ratings on any of the local or national lists or magazines and had a very bad reputation of Italian–

American disaster with careless executions while delivering inedible food. Big task! Intriguing! Sold!

An incredible amount of work went into the first year: so many hours, so many days. The hardest part was to deliver the same enthusiasm I had to my coworkers and cooks. I constantly sent a very precise and firm message to everybody that our work was based especially on details. At the end of the first year I started to see gratifying results: we had achieved three-star ratings and we were considered the best Italian restaurant in Washington.

We won the prestigious Rammy Award for favorite restaurant of the year 2009 in D.C., and my publicist, Janet Donovan, had done amazing work for the past few months. We were featured in every possible magazine in D.C., and a few national magazines took interest in us. We managed many TV appearances and I was nominated as one of four chefs to watch in the USA in 2008 by *Esquire Magazine*. I also resumed my visits to the James Beard House in New York as guest chef. Finally we had the respect I worked so hard for.

My cuisine had evolved to new highs and made a dramatic turn forever. Everything was suddenly so clear: It was much easier to work and to achieve great results if I only respected and obeyed the rules of each ingredient. Never change or transform the original taste, but combine it with compatible flavors into visual fun, delicate and tasty concepts that will leave the guest dazzled and at times confused while pleased and fully satisfied. The continuous search for unique tastes and food concepts brought me to create the Chef's Table: a culinary journey through 18-20 courses of innovative, original and unique personalized visions of modern Italian cooking.

It was an elegant table in the kitchen dressed with the finest dining luxury products available on the market: Limoge china, hand-blown glasses, silky tablecloths from France and the finest silverware. The diners often experienced gels, smoke, foams, froths and some gelatins; mostly they would experience the real passion for food and cooking that came from the heart while delivered with enthusiasm and pride. I often approached my customers and guests by saying, "Tonight, my goal is to give you something of mine you can go home with, something to take with you and to create a memory with, a topic of conversation. Something that would put a smile on your face whenever you'll look back and think of this evening and the culinary journey you have taken. If I can do that for you, if you'll be able to remember one thing, just one, then my job is done." The Chef's Table received incredible accolades in a very short time and it was often quoted as "the best fine dining experience in D.C." as well as "the best chef's table in Washington."

My crew and I felt very proud about it, especially because a good 70 percent of our clientele was from out of town and that meant it had become a dining destination for travelers. The table was booked three weeks in advance, five days a week. This is what a lot of chefs dream of: appreciation for your hard work, being able to send a clear message and explain how you see and interpret the wonderful, complex and often-misunderstood culinary world.

In this book I combine personal tales and traveling experiences as well as many of my favorite recipes with cooking techniques that reflect my personal vision of cooking with easy execution. A lot of people are often discouraged about the complexity of a recipe: Too long? Too intricate? Not sure if you can find all the listed ingredients? Those books go back on the shelf and are forgotten. Sometimes it can be a challenge to translate the passion of cooking into words and ideas.

I have been very careful in trying to send the simplest message possible, especially for the more detailed and unusual recipes. I want to make sure even the most unskilled or inexperienced cook could recreate any of these at home and sample something new, uncommon and unique. Mostly, I want to make sure it is going to be a fun process for everyone, having a wonderful time while attempting something different and new without compromising the ultimate goal.

Enjoy your culinary journey.

Chapter One
Childhood Memories and Food Facts

I was born in Torino, Italy, on a very cold and snowy day in January. My father, a very modest, hard headed and traditional Sicilian man, was thrilled to have a boy in the family. My mom was a gentle housewife with patience to spare and an invisible loaded gun in her pocket ready to fire in order to restore order and balance when necessary, an authentic love sheriff. My sister, Daniela, is four years older than me and the unfortunate recipient of my sarcasm and my favored victim throughout my childhood. It was inevitable since she is one of the most passionate intellectuals I have ever met, stubborn and revolutionary in her own way. My grandmother is one of the strongest women I know, now at 95 and counting. She's someone who has been tested by life, continuously. There is a unique bond of love and respect between us and she has been, throughout my life, a wonderful teacher of the simple things, unconditional love and culinary traditions among them.

Ever since I tasted solid food my mom noticed something different about me. I just loved to eat...a lot. I was not one of those kids who refused food or was difficult about it, like my sister. My parents never once had to simulate the noise of an airplane while trying to feed me a meal with a spoon or force me to open my mouth. According to my parents I would cry only if I did not get enough. I was told I have always been very favorable to it. There was never a time I refused food. I always welcomed it with a great smile and a lot of excitement. By the time I was eight months I had my first experience with pasta. Love at first bite. At 16 months I loved my chicken and steak, and started to taste some serious desserts.

After I broke and demolished three highchairs, my parents gave up and let me sit with them at the dinner table just like the big grownup man I said I was. They bought a booster seat and there it began—the table experience that would change my life forever.

Like any other kid I had my preferences for food: I loved pasta, salami, potatoes and chocolate. I was never a huge fan of fish, but my parents were so I tasted it from time to time while being careful of what I would put in my mouth. I had dreams of a giant octopus climbing in bed with me while I slept and attacking me. Or one of the eels my mom used to buy at the market would get away and bite me. She used to buy live eels the size of rattlesnakes.

Whenever I visit my family in Italy and go to the market I rarely see live eels anymore, but I remember back then it was quite a scene even for a young, aspiring chef. The fish lady would catch them with a net, pull them out of the tank and fight with them a few minutes while they would try to escape right under her hands. She would grab the head, squeeze the body and force them into a clear plastic bag with sea salt for a quicker death. Nowadays you only see such a scene on the Discovery Channel or on one of those reruns featuring the crocodile hunter.

Walking back home my mom would ask me to help her carry the shopping bags. For some reason I would always end up with the live eels, and I would feel them moving and trying to escape their deaths. One time when I was five years old I peed in my pants on the way home out of fear. I was so scared I promised myself I would never taste an eel in my entire life. Of course I eventually broke that promise, but as of today I am not too eel friendly. One day Mom came from the market with a bag full of them, and as was her ritual she would open the plastic bag in the kitchen sink and finish them off with a large ladle or cut off their heads with scissors. From that moment on I learned never to mess with her. I cannot recall exactly how or why, but one time a couple of the fugitives got on the floor and started to run from the kitchen into the dining room. I was so scared at first I got up on a chair in panic, but then I started laughing so hard watching Mom chasing the eels all over the room waving a ladle while on her hands and knees talking out loud, "Come here, where you think you're going? Had enough? I can do this all day. Hey, I am talking to you."

That situation seemed pretty normal to me at the age of six. Growing up I often recalled that moment with great joy, mostly because over the years I had developed a crude sense of humor, very sarcastic and very dry. I still imagine what the eels would have said running away from Mom and in response to her comments. "No! You will never catch me. Now I am going to hide under the TV set where you can't see me. Please let me go. I want to live...see? I run faster than you."

When I was a little older I used to leave little messages in the kitchen or on her pillow, scribbled on a piece of paper as a joke, such as, "We are the ghost of the eels you killed! We will get you in your sleep; we want revenge," or "Third annual eel marathon on October 6th. Early enrollment discounts for energetic Mothers!" I was always the comedian in my family and managed to make everyone laugh even in the most awkward situations. This time my Mom, given the eels' incredible display in an effort at avoiding sure death, captured the little creatures instead. They were under house arrest for a couple of days in the refrigerator, and then inevitably ended up on our dinner table with tomato sauce and braised sweet onions.

Before I started elementary school I had a pretty good understanding of what kind of food I liked, what food would put a smile on my face and what made me cringe. Mostly I learned food gave me comfort while keeping me between parameters of safety and happiness. I learned how to try to taste new food only if it looked appealing and safe to me. Well, OK, sometimes I was also tricked into it. Given the fact Mom is a wonderful cook I knew she could take even the most unusual ingredients and transform them into something amazing and spectacular.

I had to be very careful as she loved to buy and cook virtually anything available no matter how strange, unusual or bizarre it might be. Over the years I have seen her coming from the market with such interesting products as calf's brain, beef tongue, tripe, pig's feet, ox tails, frogs, marrow bones and pig's ears, just to name a few. I have seen her make natural gelatin out of pig's ears and eat cheese with live worms in it. (That is considered a delicacy, especially in Sardinia and in the south of Italy.) I have seen her drizzle lemon juice and olive oil over poached calf brain Hannibal Lecter-style and eat barely seared, bloody beef liver slices for her dining enjoyment.

For a while I thought she was a cannibal.

Actually, she was ahead of her time. Think of her as the early female version of Anthony Bourdain in the TV program *No Reservations* on the Travel Channel. Nowadays, ironically, I use most of the above ingredients in my cooking. I learned how to appreciate them and how to cook them in various ways, often with a modern twist better suitable and more enticing for the average skeptical palate...including mine.

One day for lunch I was presented with a steak that was darker than my usual veal or beef so I asked my mom what it was. At first she avoided the question and asked me to try it instead. I knew trouble was coming, but I did anyway. It tasted like dinosaur: gamey, hard in fibers and extremely dense. I had a hard time chewing it and it made me salivate so much I was ready to spit it out. I had goose bumps all over from it. What the hell was I eating? I looked at Mom while she gave me one of those smiles that seemed to say, "Isn't this meat great? Eat as much as you like. I bought it just for you!" She was very good at adding the guilt factor whenever she wanted me or my sister to eat whatever food was in front of us. Mostly because she knew well in advance we would not eat it, but I guess she thought that by adding the guilt we would give in sooner or later.

"What is this?" I asked with a mouth full of half way chewed.

"It's horse meat. Isn't it good? Finish this and tomorrow I will get you some more," she said with a smile.

It was a brain-washing procedure I have always hated. I instinctively spit it out of my mouth. My jaw dropped. Are you kidding me? I would never forget that feeling. I loved horses. Back then in Italy in 1975 there was an American TV show about an untamable black horse from the Wild West called *Fury*. I loved that show because only a little boy, the "rancher's son" who was about my age, had been able to communicate with the horse and to share a bond of love and respect no one else could. He was the only one able to ride Fury.

What an amazing show for a little kid: dreaming about horses and friendship, adventure and the far west. It would air every single evening at 7:30 and I would watch it while having dinner with my family. Needless to say, I was a huge fan of it and I would often fantasize about embarking on adventures riding with my friend and going places while fighting the bad people. The way I saw it, Mom served me a grilled slice of my best horse friend, Fury, and if that was not enough, she was going to get me some more the very next day.

I was traumatized for months.

Wine, like food, is another great passion of mine as it complements and balances any meal; mostly it helps to complete any culinary experience if paired correctly. Back home it's very common to drink a glass of wine with your lunch or dinner. In fact, I had my first wine experience at the age of 4. My father used to enjoy a glass of wine with every lunch and dinner. I remember he was the one who introduced me to it by giving me a taste of it in a glass mixed with a double amount of water. I guess I was mostly intrigued by its color as it was definitely different than my usual water. Nowadays I think of that situation as a funny one, since adding water to wine does not take the amount of alcohol out of a glass, but it just makes it easier to drink, especially for a little kid. Whatever happened that evening, it brought me to want to taste more.

One night my father was enjoying the rest of his wine with some cheese and my sister and I were watching TV while finishing dinner. That night for some reason I did not have my usual wine share, as my dad would color my water glass with a few drops of his wine just to make me happy. I decided on a quick remedy while he was talking to Mom. I grabbed his glass and I drank the whole thing in a big quick gulp, placed it back in front of him, and felt very much happy and satisfied. A few minutes later Dad went for his wine.

"Where is it?" he asked. Then he turned to Mom and asked, "Did you drink it?"

"Daniela did you?" he asked my sister, who always hated any kind of beverages other than water.

"No, I did not," she replied.

I wish someone had a camera back then because this is the time when my father turned toward me and asked the very same question. I was never a good liar, but I knew I would have been in trouble if I had admitted my wrongdoing, so I worked up the courage and shouted a big full NO! There was only one problem: my face was as red as a royal flush, my ears were burning and I had a glued-on smile on my face stretching side to side. To make it worse I started singing so loud I remember neighbors finally knocking on the wall after a good 10 minutes of free concert. At this point they were all laughing so hard and with tears on their faces I would rarely remember another moment where for one reason or another my whole family cried at the same time. My mother told me I passed out and slept a solid 15 hours after she took me to bed that evening.

Of course, over the years I have developed a better tolerance for alcohol, but sadly for me and happily for my current neighbors, my singing days are forever gone.

Another great experience I recall is helping my dad bottle wine in what we call back home a cantina. The cantina is not to be confused with a Mexican eatery, but is a narrow, small, jail cell lookalike located in the underground common basement of any apartment building and used as a storage unit. They are assigned to tenants whenever they move in. Usually to get to your unit you have to walk through a catacomb of dark, humid corridors, usually cool in temperature even in summertime.

We used to store all sorts of things in there, from homemade preserved tomatoes to dry spices and at times salami of any shape and kind, olive oil and canned food. We would also have a fair amount of paper goods and boxes with forgotten towels or useless tools. Italians are savers; they do not throw anything away for at least 30 years as they feel they need to get a good run for their money. Too long for my personal taste, but my father being a traditional Sicilian would customize the cantina to his liking by building shelves, electrical and lighting fixtures and homemade sounding alarms with recorded voices that once triggered would shout something like, "Robbery! Robbery! Someone unlawfully entered unit 305. Call the police at once. Notify the doorman."

That's how my father is. Nothing is good enough unless built and customized to his liking. I remember when I was 12 years old he made me help him re-tile the whole cantina floor as, according to him, it did not match the color of the shelves and walls. Imagine someone hearing the alarm going off: You had better be armed with a pad and pen to write down instructions and know how to chase the intruder away or you would end up having a problem with my dad. He would certainly question you if you did not follow the instructions in the listed order.

He never believed in quality expensive wines. He felt more comfortable with modest and more affordable ones for his everyday use. He would buy small barrels from friends who had a connection with local wine makers. Piedmont is the largest Italian region for wine production; therefore, it only made sense to take advantage of such a local gift and at great prices. In the cantina we had a small hand-bottling device. It consisted of a lever with a pin that would push the cork into a small cavity of the bottle placed right under it. With one quick, stiff motion the cork would get into the top of the bottle gap and seal the flavors in forever.

My father would personally go to the market and buy the corks he needed for that particular wine. He would stop by the store and buy sticker labels, and he would wait for the perfect time to go to work. He was convinced one should never bottle wine when it rains, as the high content of humidity would alter its taste, mostly because the cork would work as a sponge trapping and transferring excess moisture. He also believed bottling during a full moon is an accident waiting to happen. I think he applies the same theory of high and low ocean tides to it. While I agree and support the first, I am unsure about the second and I would have to research to determine if this could only be an urban legend.

We would spend hours in filling the bottles, labeling and sealing them with corks. Tasting was optional. My father would never drink wine unless having a meal, a very smart and healthy philosophy I fully endorse, most of the time. Italians rarely purchase expensive bottles from a wine store for private consumption. It is extremely rare unless for gift purposes. Wine stores are more popular in tourist towns such as Rome, Florence or Venice, and it is not unusual to come across some with incredible inventory and historical vintages. Those are the places, along with gastronomy stores, where tourists are easily enticed to bring home a small piece of our traditions and pride and willing to pay handsomely for it. Italians, instead, cherish those traditions every day mostly because it is our way of life. We know where to buy, how to buy, mostly what to buy and we are not happy unless we get the whole package at a great price.

Just as we are picky eaters, we are picky buyers.

In Italy there are two things people will never sacrifice or compromise: Your daily meals and quality time with your family. In a way some of my best food memories come from the dinner table and from the people around it. This is a place where people gather and where the food becomes the predominant source of happiness and an excuse to linger in good company. Think of it as olive oil, a conduit for the cooking process. Without it you cannot sauté or fry.

It is around the dining table that many problems are discussed and where exciting stories are told. In business, many meetings are held while enjoying a meal. Family celebrations such as weddings, confirmations, graduations and birthdays are hosted at local restaurants. Food is all around us and in many cases food is what brings people together. For example: In Europe when you dine at a restaurant the food plays the leading role even if you are discussing business. In America it is the other way around. Business comes first and it is complemented by the food.

It's funny how in America many business deals are negotiated on a golf course. In Italy there is nothing to negotiate. We are not really big fans of golf and it is not unusual to spend that time at a dinner table, especially on the weekends with a sumptuous meal. We take our time with things we care about, which sometimes comes across as lazy. And in so many ways, we are. I have to admit I do miss that kind of lifestyle at times because it stirs up my daily routine. Sure enough, each time I travel to Italy it takes me a couple of days to get back into it and to fully adjust. Everyone is so laid back, all stores are closed in the afternoon between 1 and 4:30 p.m., and everyone goes home to have lunch with their families. Some take a nap; others enjoy a walk in the park, and a few more a cup of espresso while reading the paper.

They eat anything they want with no worries or concerns for cholesterol, high blood pressure or love handles. Everyone has government-issued health care coverage, monetary benefits and pensions. They retire young enough to enjoy the rest of their lives and strangely enough they live up to their late 80s and mostly in good health. What a life!

In America all we do is work, produce and sell in order to prosper while generating sometimes very stressful lives. I wish we could all slow down a little and enjoy life for what it really is and treasure the little things we have forgotten: a glass of wine, a good conversation, a walk in the park with someone you love, sharing a bite to eat while creating a memory, a simple kiss.

After 27 years I became one of those myself: I run all day, I produce and I stress, but I do not forget my roots or my origins. So I try to create a daily balance between the love for my work and the love for my family, forcing myself to slow down even when I do not really want to. I constantly try. As a matter of fact, usually the only time I sit down to have a meal is when I eat out. Most of my meals are consumed standing up, while I cook or eat out of a to-go box.

My mom would cook different food each day. On weekends we would normally have relatives coming to the house and she would prepare the legendary Sunday meal consisting of 10-12 different dishes, family-style, for everyone to share. It was also customary for the invited relatives to show up with either a couple of dishes they had prepared on their own or with a tray of traditional pasticcini. Those are simply the best one-bite pastries you can have in Italy: a variety of any shape, form, texture and flavor combined in a small taste and mostly available only on Sunday morning at your local pastry shop. Compare them to sweet Chinese Dim Sum and consumed at the end of your 14-course meal, right when you are gasping for air. No matter how full you might be or how uncomfortable your tummy might feel, you will find yourself reaching for them in complete surprise—delicious and dangerously addictive.

It's so much easier to achieve great cooking results in Italy because throughout the country the geological conditions are amazing. I really appreciate, for instance, the produce back home even though they might not look as inviting or as beautiful as the ones we have in the U.S. In fact, they do not look nearly as shiny or as firm, but did you ever bite into a fruit or tasted any kind of vegetable in Italy?

If you have not and you are planning to go, that is worth the price of the airfare alone. Walk into any common grocery store in America, pick a tomato and cut it in half. Unless you come across an exceptional and rare tomato, you feel and experience very little in taste, smell and texture. Now, pick a tomato in Italy, cut it in half, and observe as you run the knife through it; you are suddenly overwhelmed by its pungent smell of sweetness and earthiness. Its succulent pulp feels like a dense flesh, so rich, filled with its natural juice as it slowly drips down your hand.

As you bite into it, you will experience a celebration of flavorful and lingering taste: watering and satisfying while its natural gelatin at the core holds an invitation for you to take another bite. It's natural to me to get so excited by so little. A few years ago while I was in Florence for the first time, my companion and I decided to sample as many restaurants and local dishes as we could. Florence is often considered the most beautiful Italian town with the best food. While I am a fan and a believer Florence is a dream city and to me a second home, I have a bone to pick with those who recently have tried to shake a hundred years of culinary traditions by offering modern molecular interpretations of it while lacking in taste and often disrespecting its traditions. Of course, this is just my personal view, but even for someone like me who is innovative and likes to deconstruct and recreate, I would never alter the taste that was conceived hundreds of years ago, carrying with it traditions and history passed from generation to generation.

Florence cooking offers simple, quality ingredients and wonderful traditions in a stunning historical setting. Each dish has a meaning and a story that comes with it, and almost every recipe can be traced all the way back to the Renaissance time. Going back to the intensity and the simple taste of Italian tomatoes, I will never forget my first experience with Pappa al Pomodoro in Florence (traditional Tuscan tomato and bread soup). We sat down at a local trattoria near Piazza Duomo in a small, tight street on the way to Piazza del Mercato (Market Square).

I ate this traditional soup many times in Washington, mostly prepared by a good friend of mine and ex-business partner, chef Francesco Ricchi, who is a hardcore Florence native and has opened successful restaurants in Washington, D.C., such as I

Ricchi and Cesco Trattoria in the early '90s. His version, prepared with American products, was simply delicious and very rich in taste and colors: bright-red tomatoes with great contrasts of green basil and cracked black peppercorns to finish, and old white bread.

I had never tasted the original soup in Tuscany so I decided to give it a try and ordered a bowl. When the soup arrived I was very confused as it was pink and very light in color. I could not see the basil and it had just a little drizzle of olive oil on top. I thought for sure they served me the wrong item so I called my server and asked him if he made a mistake in delivering my food. He looked at me almost insulted. I could almost hear his thoughts: "Dammed tourists, what did you expect? This is how it's made and this is how it's served." I wondered later how many times this poor guy was asked this very same question every day. What sat in front of me did not look anything like the tomato and bread soup I knew; mostly because there were no tomatoes in it.

Disturbed and obviously disappointed, I felt I was stuck with something I did not really want, but gave it a try anyway. As soon as I brought the spoon to my mouth I froze in surprise. What a revelation! I will never forget that moment. The only thing I could taste was fresh tomato—sweet, ripe and very well-balanced with olive oil and the pungent flavor of the invisible basil that must have been chopped and mixed in it. How could this soup taste so rich of tomato if I could barely see any in it? And all the individual flavors being so tasty and aggressive while perfectly combined in one glamorous final taste? The very next day I went to the market down the street and I bought a few local tomatoes. To my surprise they were just as exceptional in taste and flavor and confirmed my theory that with simple and wonderful ingredients you can make something glorious every single day.

Each time I return to Italy I like to shop at the nearby open market as I love the feeling of being free to sample anything I had missed and to reconnect with original and rare flavors. The perfect analogy, according to my girlfriend, is that it is the equivalent of being a little kid in a huge toy store. She sees my eyes popping out and feels my heart rate elevating to a frenzied state of insanity. I must buy one of each just to try to sample it with my family. Then I go back home and I literally fill my parents' refrigerator with bags of fresh food, driving them crazy as they are usually the ones who end up eating for days since I either eat out trying new restaurants during my stay…or I am on my way back home to the States to try out my new ideas.

Why Can't I Cook Like a Chef?

Basics are everything in cooking. It's similar to construction work: if you do not lay cement between each brick the wall will eventually fall. There is a way to enhance the flavor for everything you cook and there are basic rules we must obey in order to achieve good results. One person's idea or vision is just a small link in the process for the good outcome of a dish. Independently of how simple, difficult or innovative, the cook must apply the laws of flavors and respect guidelines and procedures. But unfortunately there are a lot of young aspiring chefs who are much more concerned with the looks and the architectural aspects of food and often categorize the taste as a secondary element. It is style over substance.

While I respect everyone's vision and interpretation of cooking, I must stomp my foot down and send a clear reminder the most important thing a cook can do is to respect the ingredients for what they are—their taste, their origins and their characteristics. In the past, when I was the head chef at Capitol Hill Barolo Restaurant, I was often approached by young aspiring cooks who just graduated from culinary school. They were mostly looking for hands-on experience, but just wanted a high-paying job.

I particularly remember a young, cocky fellow who walked into the restaurant unannounced, holding his diploma in one hand and a picture book in the other. He was insistent I talk to him at once. While I would usually dismiss such arrogance I decided to meet him instead. I asked my assistant to arrange a table for us and soon after we were face to face. We chatted a few minutes and he introduced himself as the best, most prominent student ever to come out of a culinary program. He had graduated with honors and his picture book was interesting enough to entertain me a while. His plate design and presentations were intriguing, but his combinations of food were just simply vulgar and offensive not only to any possible food lover, but to any possible food eater as well.

How can you possibly combine raw slices of squab breast dressed with grapefruit juice, raw garlic and chunks of kiwi? And what about milk and caramel boiled squid rings turned into a dessert and served warm accompanied by a milk chocolate sauce with spicy hot pepper? While he was trying to convince me I should hire him I was taken by surprise and disgust. My jaw dropped and I started shaking my head feeling I had been set up by some of my friends in a glamorous joke. I was literally looking for the hidden camera, but could not find it. When I finally realized the scenario was very real I had no choice but to ask, "What kind of salary are you looking for?"

"Well," he replied, "you have seen my work. You had a chance to meet me and here is my diploma. I would not consider a position here for less than $65,000 a year plus benefits." Keep in mind this was 1998. Imagine a 22-year-old kid marching into a restaurant with no appointment and demanding a large salary regardless of his inexperience. What a poor display of class, passion and respect. I suddenly realized this was a very sad reality. I shook his hand, saying he was way too good for us. I suggested he empty his cup of knowledge and arrogance, and find a way to refill it with proper culinary wisdom and humility. I can only hope by now he learned how to respect his basic ingredients and hopefully learned how to properly combine them.

Unfortunately, not everyone can be a chef. But not everyone can be a musician, a painter or a good actor either. The curiosity that tickles our souls makes us walk a specific path of interest to a destination only we know is the final one. Like a painter or a singer or any other artists who offers and shares personal insights, chefs too are perfectionists and meticulously attentive in sending the right message. Only an artist can feel the sense of accomplishment in creating something—the visual, the taste, the concept, the sound and execution of any challenge.

When I cook only I can feel full satisfaction. Is the food cooked to correct temperature? Was I able to retain its natural color? Was its taste delivered the way it was intended and how? What can I do to make this dish better? Is its concept and presentation innovative enough while respecting the original flavors and ingredients? How many people would ask themselves these very same questions when cooking out of a cookbook at home while following a recipe?

A passionate foodie will eventually try to cook a few recipes with the main goal to correctly execute those while respecting quantities and cooking times. You will only sample the final taste in the end to achieve satisfaction. Professional chefs have a different way of organizing, executing, proceeding and thinking. And they can be really difficult to work with: some are arrogant, others introverts, few others simply rude or disrespectful. In my young days in Italy I remember comparing a chef's kitchen to a church: a place where you can only whisper and mainly listen and where your opinion is not necessarily appreciated or needed. You must take it all in without questioning just because you believe. But there are also great and wonderful chefs determined to bring awareness and teach those who are inclined and willing to listen.

Almost always, chefs must combine their passion for cooking with its business aspect. Not an easy task, as you can imagine. We must meet deadlines, food and labor costs, and often deal with daily problems that make our job more difficult and very stressful. There will always be situations where a chef cannot fully express himself and make a certain guest happy. One night I received a complaint because I had not shaved enough white truffles on an $80 risotto dish. Unfortunately, chefs are also running a business and we must work within the parameters of our profit margin. I have yet to encounter a diner who is willing to pay $400 for a bowl of rice and a couple of ounces of shaved white truffles. An up-charge is usually offered to satisfy those who want more, but to my surprise I notice many decline. I cannot blame them. It is virtually impossible to accommodate everyone's requests, but while my guests' happiness is my number one priority I am also determined to deliver the most authentic Italian traditions in a more personal and visionary way.

When I was a little boy I was an excellent soccer player and a pretty good painter. I made noise with various instruments for my own entertainment and even wrote a few poems and a small play. It occurred to me that as much as I loved to play and write I would never be good enough in order to become really great in any of those fields. I had to face my limits and respect them. I never felt like that in cooking, though. On the contrary, I was always very motivated and dedicated, eager to learn as much as possible to increase my professional knowledge and build the foundations for what I wanted to become. A few years back during the teaching of a cooking class, a female student asked me a very interesting question: "How many times did you do that incorrectly before you got it right?"

After cooking for many years the basics of our profession drive on cruise control. Experienced chefs rarely burn garlic in a pan or have a sauce stick. We would look at certain food and be able to tell if it is missing salt or determine just by the touch its cooking temperature. After that day, when I am asked a similar question I usually reply by saying it takes a while to fully understand the transformation from raw food into a final cooked product. Taste, color, texture, aroma and temperature: five basic elements no aspiring cook should ever ignore. We all have to make a few mistakes before we make that recipe ours, but once you get it right you should always be able to reproduce it the same way.

In the past 20 years there has been a revolution in the cooking industry. The Food Network has become a part of our everyday life, cooking reality shows have captured the attention of millions and highlighted the importance of our work in an unprecedented way, while creating interest and respect for it. Food magazines paint great profiles while spreading awareness. There are culinary organizations and associations endorsing every aspect of the culinary field. Someone not too long ago has told me chefs are quickly becoming as popular as movie stars.

I find comfort knowing, instead, that more people start to recognize our daily hard work, but we are hardly celebrities, we are food and taste visionaries. Chefs nowadays can achieve better and more precise results when cooking. New tools and devices are now available to simplify even the most elaborate work. There are infrared thermometers and chocolate tempering machines, high temperature-resistant silicon baking molds, tools to instantly freeze and defrost food, sous vide temperature-controlled water circulators, handheld smoker tools, and many types of utensils and high-speed blenders. When I first came to the U.S., none of these were available for us.

We can achieve better results in shorter times and produce better tasting and more appealing food than anyone at home thanks to the tools and organized kitchens now available. I hear comments from my customers such as, "How does he make that?" or "Do you think they buy this or do they make it?" Our success is not just because of advances in kitchen gadgets. We also have years of experience, a touch of confidence, unusual ideas and incredible persistence. Mix all that together and there you have it. Well, let's not forget occasional screw ups.

There is absolutely no pre-made or processed food I serve to my customers. Everything is made in the restaurant and prepared on a daily basis: The bread is baked twice a day and before each lunch and dinner service. So are the breadsticks and focaccias. All the pasta—whether stuffed or colored—is made daily and so are the desserts as well as some cheese, cold cuts and sausages. Where is the pleasure of buying a specific food product where all you have to do is open the bag, drizzle some oil on it and sell it for three times what you have paid for it? Is there a culinary pride in there I do not see? All my life I have always tried to overcome the competition, always tried to make sure everyone knew I made that specific dish by scratch. This, to me, is what being a chef means: offering something only you can make, only you know how to put together.

Signature dishes? "I heard that restaurant serves this or that and the chef presents it in an unusual way." As my publicist would say: "Buzz! Buzz! Buzz! You can't have enough." The reputation builds when people make you a topic of conversation. When a dish is served, people tend to pause and analyze it in detail before they take the first bite. They understand the visual part of a meal is extremely important as it is the very first contact you have with the food and suddenly a first impression is formed—architectural presentation, combination of ingredients and colors.

The second part is the aroma: This is a little tricky as cold preparations are much harder to detect, but for hot dishes it should be a confirmation and an instant approval. I see many of my guests, once they are served, cracking a smile in agreement of what they are seeing followed by a quick whiff of the smell while their eyes widen in surprise. Once they take the first bite and begin to savor it, the entire experience becomes as one. Their heads start nodding in approval, wanting to share their enjoyment either verbally or at times by asking their companion to take a bite from their plate.

This is the moment when a chef becomes proud of his own work and the very same is felt by anyone who is home cooking a recipe or an entire meal when it turns out exactly the way you wanted. It is like you have challenged something and ultimately won the battle. Many times, those who love to cook at home face challenges acquiring prime ingredients. Restaurants can pick and choose food purveyors, products, ingredients, quality and prices. Most of the time food is delivered to us in timely fashion. We take raw material, we portion it, we cook it and we use it on a daily basis. Restaurants even have 30 days to pay for the delivery, making it all much easier to generate profit and to keep the business prosperous.

It's a lot more difficult for those who are willing to cook at home and entertain: the cook has to venture out to shop for specific ingredients at much higher prices for often a much lower quality. For those inclined to recreate a recipe, they are often headed for a good amount of frustration in finding exactly what they are looking for, and because of timeline or geographical restrictions prime ingredients are often substituted with similar types or surrogates. Then the battle begins at home with the preparation and the cooking in a kitchen not as equipped or as organized as the ones in restaurants. After a few hours of dedicated work the meal is ready, and the cook is usually self-critical, offering warnings or explanations for a particular dish. After dinner the cleaning process starts: something I have never been a fan of, but a must and a very tiring chore especially at the end of your working day. That is a lot of dedication.

On my day off I usually dine out and enjoy doing so as much as possible. No meal is too big or too small for me as I am equally happy with a few slices of cheese, cold cuts and a glass of wine or a sumptuous eight-course meal. I love Mexican, Chinese, Thai or Indian in the same way I might like Italian if well-prepared and well-executed. I truly enjoy a meal anytime the simplicity of good basic ingredients is highlighted. Any cuisine prepared fresh and at the moment, with attentiveness to its flavors, deserves to be enjoyed over and over. I rarely cook at home unless we have guests or friends coming over for major holidays. It's very frustrating for me and I guess for a lot of chefs to try to recreate the same taste and well-executed quality dishes in the same way when cooking at the restaurant. I personally do not experience the same joy—different, but not the same. My joy for cooking at home is usually justified by the quality of friends who accompany the event. When a chef cooks at home, he cannot rely on the same burners, the same pots and pans, the same basic stocks or broths. At home we have different ovens and different equipment and mostly a much different environment. We do get a little lost: we love our kitchen routine in every detail.

The difference between choosing to microwave a frozen meal and preparing a multi-course dinner from scratch is only one...passion. It's the passion that makes you spend the whole day shopping, cooking and chopping so you can offer something special, something that comes from you. Not many people understand or fully respect this process and maybe this is why every time I am invited over for a home-cooked dinner, I always accept with great joy and excitement. I know and understand the great rollercoaster of troubles and efforts they have gone through creating it.

I can say with confidence that home cooks work much harder than any chefs in any restaurants, by comparison, if we keep in mind the great troubles they go through to achieve the simple joy of a home-cooked meal.

Chapter Two
Broths and Stocks—The Foundations of Flavor

We often hear about stocks and broths and how important they are. But what are they really? And why are they so important? They take so long to make, can we do without them? My answer is no, absolutely no. Anyone can easily go to the store and buy bouillon cubes for faster usage and in different flavors or use water instead, but why not take the time to make the correct basics for cooking? In the end everything will taste so much better.

Unfortunately, because of the fast-paced society we live in, less-aspiring chefs and home cooks do not tend to dedicate the proper time needed to build the foundation of flavors, therefore skip important and fundamental steps. Why would you go through the trouble of making a risotto from scratch by selecting only the best rice, finely chopping the onions, attentively grating only authentic Parmesan cheese and using only high-fat butter to enhance flavors if you are then using water or bouillon-made stock knowing it will ultimately change the taste of the dish for the worse?

Making a stock or a broth does take time. Its preparation alone can seem almost endless: selecting the ingredients, chopping, combining all the spices and herbs and of course following all the necessary steps for a good outcome. It is much easier to make stocks in the kitchen of a restaurant as the designated pot is usually placed on the back burner of a stove, or in bigger restaurants in commercial stock boilers or in large kettles for hours.

There is, however, a simpler way to recreate all of that by sacrificing just a little extra time in making the basics for any kind of cooking. Then you can deliver the original and wonderful flavors you want, especially at home. There are many chefs and restaurants that make endless amounts of different stocks, way too many in my opinion, and some are created just to confuse you and do not really serve a purpose. Anyone could theoretically use any kind of bones and carcasses to make a stock or any kind of vegetable or fish to create a flavorful liquid conductor. The possibilities are so many that lately I started to see ridiculous recipes for broths and stocks in cookbooks, such as "snails broth" or "chives stock" and even "curled parsley fume."

Fair enough, you could make stocks and broth out of anything, even out of my shoes, but would you use it? Mostly, how much do you really think a parsley fume could enhance the flavor of the dish you are cooking? Then why not use fresh parsley instead and add it at the end for both color and flavor? I am a firm believer that when it comes to basics there are only a few elementary liquid preparations needed in cooking, and I use them on daily basis in my kitchen. Now you can too. They are:

Chicken Broth
Veal Stock Reduction
Lobster Broth
Vegetable Stock

These, in my opinion, are the four basics for cooking, just like air, water, fire and heart. If you want to venture into any other kind of stocks or broths, such as rabbit or venison or shrimp, I suggest using these very basic recipes and eventually customizing them or changing them a little according to its base flavor. For instance, I would use the veal stock reduction recipe base if I want to make venison stock. I would substitute the veal bones and the veal chunks for toasted venison bones and add a few juniper berries. For a shrimp broth I would use the lobster stock recipe by substituting the lobster heads with the equivalent in weight of fresh shrimp heads and shells. It just takes a little imagination and the combinations are endless. Your meals will be much better with just a little preparation.

Anyone can make any of these stocks at home. It is easier and faster than you think. I am aware there are only small quantities used while cooking at home. This is why my recipes will direct you in making just enough for immediate use and a little reserve for later. I suggest transferring the leftover stock in a few small plastic freezing containers with lids, wrapping them well with plastic film to avoid spillage, labeling and dating each container and freezing them once they are room temperature. This way you will have a little extra ready to use anytime and in small amounts to reduce waste.

Chicken Broth

A good, tasty chicken broth should have certain basic characteristics: the flavor of its vegetables, the delicate taste of its white meat, a clear off-yellowish hazelnut color, and it should be cooked on a very low flame, barely boiling and for a long time till all the individual flavors combine into one. Also, a good chicken broth is made by using only cold water. Using warm or hot water will result in a final turbid color and a much weaker flavor. Its taste should be balanced, delicate and with a considerable lingering aftertaste without overpowering your palate while delivering a sense of hospitability for a second sip.

Chicken is without a doubt the most popular bird used for any kind of soup and in many cases its broth becomes the base for many cooking preparations, including fish-based dishes. A curious tip is that a good chicken stock should retain an almost neutral water color, very liquid and clear enough to see through it. So why is it golden or yellow at times?

Two reasons: in the first case the golden color is given by the chicken soup base bouillons (if you choose to go that way, even though you know I do not recommend it) often used for home preparations once combined with water. It is a misrepresentation of how a good broth should be. In the second case, a well-executed broth gives the illusion of a yellowish color as its melted fat floats on top of its liquid while cooking. Also, the presence of the dark-toasted white onions gives not only the needed taste to the soup, but also a slight hazelnut-like shade to the broth. When the broth is ready, we will skim the floating fat and filter the liquid through a fine strainer. Only then does one truly realize a great chicken broth has very little color and an incredibly rich and delicate aroma.

In case of emergency, the only commercial bouillon I endorse is Maggi chicken cubes. I remember a few years back cooking at a charity event in East Sandwich near Cape Cod, Massachusetts, with other celebrity chefs. Among us was the late Jean Louis Palladin. About ten of us were sharing the kitchen while preparing our dish for the evening event. Suddenly we all hear repetitive and loud "f**k" coming from an agitated Jean Louis.

"Hey, are you all right there?" I asked.

"No! I just spilled my chicken broth all over!" and like a madman he left on a golf cart, driving out of the compound and into the streets of Cape Cod. He did not think there was anything wrong with illegally driving a golf cart to the nearby store, sharing the road with cars and trucks in order to save his dish. Jean Louis was like that: determined in his own way, both funny and serious at the same time.

He came back about twenty minutes later with a big smile on his face, holding a few packages of chicken flavor Maggi bouillon cubes in a shopping bag. He quickly made an improvised chicken stock and started to rave about its flavor. I have to say he was right. It was surprising tasty and pretty delicate considering how it was made. Glad to know in case of dire emergencies I have a quick alternative, but it definitely never is a first choice.

Ingredients
5 lbs chicken bones
5 sprigs of fresh thyme
2 stalks of diced celery
4 medium-size diced carrots
3 onions cut in half coin-like
1 tbsp whole black peppercorns
3 each dry bay leaves
2 ounces of fresh parsley
2 tbsp of salt

Directions
Wash the chicken bones under cold water a few minutes, removing all impurities.
Burn the onion halves on an open fire on a burner until they turn black.
Combine the chicken bones and all ingredients together in a large pot.
Cover with COLD water and cook at a very low flame about 3 hours, skimming the fat occasionally.
Taste for salt and correct if necessary.
Remove the floating fat with a large ladle and filter the broth through a very fine mesh.

Once room temperature, keep refrigerated.

Veal Stock Reduction

This stock is the father and the base of many common meat sauces. It is known as "demi glace," that translates from French into "halfway reduced glaze." Even though there might be a thousand versions of demi glace recipes and every restaurant or chef might claim theirs is the real one, the substance of this stock is always based on well-toasted veal bones, a mix of vegetables and fresh herbs, red wine reduction and optional meats.

There are some French chefs I know who even mix in second-grade goose liver toward the end of the cooking process in order to enhance its flavor. Others add truffle juice or white truffle oil or even sautéed mushrooms. The truth is, no matter what book you execute this recipe from you will realize it is always a new and a different one, and mostly customized by authors and chefs to their personal likings and needs.

Since I am no different from any of them, over the years I customized my own recipe that marries well in taste and balance with most meat-based preparations used at the restaurant and at home. Mostly it has a very nice, delicate well-rounded texture and the substance and flavor of its meat is very much present in an almost imaginary way. It is like a liquid steak in your mouth, full of flavor you just cannot bite into.

It is not as easy as it might seem to make a great veal stock: if the bones are toasted just a few minutes more their burnt flavor is transferred throughout the liquid. Too many fresh herbs and you will taste the vivid bitterness while overpowering it. My veal reduction is a product of patience and respect. Some people think a stock-making process is also a recycling one and an opportunity to clear up leftovers from the refrigerator. Be very careful of what you add to any stocks or broth as it will change the taste and possibly ruin the process. My suggestion is to stick to the recipe and you will always be on safe ground.

I like to reduce my veal stock three times before I filter it. This way I maximize the flavor and I get the best out of each ingredient, especially the sautéed chunks of veal and bones that are full of proteins. Once filtered, I reduce it again by almost half and I choose to add black truffle juice and peelings to round up its taste while making it richer in flavor. Once ready, its consistency should be like thick syrup, dense, brown and incredibly aromatic. After being refrigerated, this stock should turn into a very hard gelatin easy to be scooped out in needed quantities and because of that its refrigeration shelf life almost triples. For home use, please follow the same procedures for the chicken broth: divide into small containers, wrap, label and freeze the extra for future use.

Ingredients

10 lbs roasted brown veal bones cut in medium chunks
1 lb canned plum tomatoes
1 bunch of fresh rosemary
1 bunch of fresh sage
1 bunch of fresh thyme
2 oz dry porcini mushrooms
3 stalks of chopped celery
2 chopped white onions
3 chopped medium-size carrots
1 tbsp whole black peppercorns
3 each dry bay leaves
1 mashed garlic head
2 tbsp salt
2 liters dry cooking red wine
½ cup olive oil
15 oz of cubed veal neck meat
2 oz of canned black truffle peels and shavings in its juice (optional)

Directions

In a large, hot sauté pan sear the veal cubes with a little oil at a very high flame until crispy.
Transfer it to a larger pot with all the ingredients except the bones, truffles, tomatoes and the wine.
Cook ten minutes, add the bones and the wine and divide the liquid in half.
Add the tomatoes and fill the pot with warm or hot water, boil under moderate flame.
Divide the stock by half and refill the pot again with water to the top.
Repeat one more time and divide again by half.

When the stock is reduced by half for the third time, taste for salt and filter through a fine mesh strainer.
Move the filtered liquid into a medium-size pot, empty the truffle peels and juice and reduce by half under moderate-to-low flame.
Taste for salt again and filter one more time.
Once room temperature, transfer it to a refrigerator.

Lobster Broth

This is the most delicate broth of the four listed. By using only raw lobster heads and by simmering it for only twenty minutes, we are able to capture the true aromatic and light taste of the crustaceous. I am a big fan of this broth because it makes a great base for a fish soup or shellfish-based pasta preparations, an excellent broth for a fish risotto or a great liquid conductor for baked style fish.

Unlike chicken or veal stock, I choose to boil this broth only for twenty minutes. I realized its fishy taste is stronger than it first appears, therefore once used in preparations such as risotto it will reduce more and its taste turns too overwhelming and way too strong. This is why I tend to use fewer lobster heads than needed and by cooking it to a light flavor the real taste of the lobster will come out through the cooking process. Also, it will remain delicate and well-balanced.

Some recipes call for fresh tarragon. I like tarragon as it marries very well to almost any fish preparations, but I personally prefer to exclude it from my broth as I think its strong anise/lemony taste turns this preparation way too aromatic and way too exotic. For those who would like to see the difference, please add about one ounce of tarragon (fresh only) to the recipe.

Ingredients
5 raw lobster heads
2 gallons of water
5 stalks chopped celery
5 medium chopped carrots
5 dried bay leaves
4 medium chopped white onions
4 tbsp salt
1½ tbsp whole black peppercorns

Few sprigs of fresh thyme
1 whole dried anise star

Directions
Combine the lobster heads and all the ingredients together in a large pot.
Cook under moderate-to-high flame until it starts boiling.
Lower the flame to moderate-to-low and simmer no longer than 20 minutes.
Taste for salt and correct if necessary.
Remove the floating impurities and filter the broth through a very fine mesh.
Once totally room temperature, keep refrigerated.

Vegetable Stock

What can I say about a vegetable stock? Does anyone actually use this? You would be surprised how many customers request it because of their dietary restrictions. This stock is substituted for the three listed above, whenever possible, in order to accommodate even the most unusual requests. In the U.S. there are many more vegetarians and vegans than we might realize. So why not create an excellent alternative to fish and meat and give them an opportunity to enjoy a great meal without sacrificing flavor?

I also prefer a rich and well-balanced vegetable stock to a chicken broth for preparations such as vegetable risottos or any kind of garden-based soups. It is very easy and quick to make an elegant and flavorful alternative to a chicken noodle soup preparation. The noodles or any other kind of pasta would cook very well into it as its starch will blend throughout the cooking process, making it thicker in consistency. I only use fresh-cut vegetables and I like to sear them first with a little olive oil in order to blend all the flavors together and get some color and taste out of them.

You will notice halfway through the recipe process I pass some of them through a food mill and put its purée back in the pot for additional cooking. This is a way to really enhance its flavor as it is so much more difficult to achieve great taste out of any kind of vegetables than it is for meats or fish. The filtering process is equally as important: when passing this stock through a very fine mesh (or even better, a cheese cloth) make sure to capture the veggie purée, letting only the clear liquid through it.

Ingredients
5 medium diced carrots
10 diced stalks of celery
2 whole roasted garlic heads cut in half coin size
4 medium diced white onions
8 medium diced fresh tomatoes
2 bunches of fresh Italian parsley
6 large diced fresh Portobello mushrooms
4 medium diced bell peppers
5 medium diced zucchini
2 large diced fennel bulbs
2 lbs of chopped fresh spinach
2 each dried cloves
3 each dried bay leaves
1 oz dry porcini mushrooms
2 tbsp salt
2 tbsp whole black peppercorns
¼ cup extra virgin olive oil
3 gallons of water

Directions
In a stock pot sauté all the listed ingredients (except the tomatoes) with the oil at moderate flame about 10 minutes, making sure the vegetables do not pick up excessive color.
Add the tomatoes and the water and boil at moderate flame about 30 minutes.
Remove half the vegetables and purée them through a food mill.
Return the purée to the stock pot and into the liquid and cook again till it reduces almost by a quarter.
Taste for salt and correct if necessary.
Filter the stock through a very fine mesh.
Transfer into refrigerator once it reaches room temperature.

Chapter Three
Appetite Openers

How many times have we said "no, thanks" to a tray of passing hors d'oeuvres because we are either lacking of appetite or because whatever was offered did not look appealing enough to tantalize our palates and curiosity? Everything tastes better when we are hungry because then we are easily open and more inclined to try a new kind of food in order to satisfy our brain and our stomachs. A few years back I noticed that passing tasting bites can be very boring and unattractive at cocktail receptions unless the guest is hungry, so I decided to completely transform the nature of what cocktail food is all about and I started thinking "what if?"

What if I create wonderful and exciting miniature one-bites that not only look amazing, but are also tasty, elegant and unique in their concept and presentation? Something that would leave a mark and create a memory, miniature food that is almost irresistible. Even when you are not hungry it evilly tempts you until you finally give in. All of us have experienced at least once the overdone and over served bruschetta, canapé, cheese platter or marinated olive.

Enough of that! I wanted to make sure each guest would pay attention and genuinely enjoy the food that was served while delivering a snapshot memory to take with them, just like another virtual business card to add to their collection for the evening to be mentally filed for future needs. They are commonly known as "amuse-bouche" or "hors d'oeuvres." I call them instead Appetite Openers! My first goal is to open my guests' appetites, to surprise them with a little unexpected extra, and to prepare them for a wonderful meal while directing them down a path of great expectations.

Most of the Appetite Openers listed here are served to my customers just before they are handed the menu, or they are served at cocktail parties. It is a wonderful way to begin a meal and a unique way to deliver a shocking gastronomic overture. This makes for a genius first impression. Some are very simple and easy to make, others might require special tools such as silicone molds or pastry accessories that can be easily purchased at specialty food stores such as Sur la Table or William-Sonoma.

Other recipes might call for a high-speed blender or for lollipop sticks and Chinese ceramic spoons. No worries! Sometimes you can substitute a high-speed blender and regular spoons for home use. With quick research and a little shopping online, you will be able to find and purchase almost any of the same professional culinary gadgets we use at the restaurant. Then you can reuse them as many times as you like.

Remember when we were kids and Mom use to tell us, "Don't play with your food"? Well, I always did and I always will. I like to create an illusion and offer a concept of a dish that visually appears to be something it really isn't. I love to combine ingredients and colors and form unusual presentations; mostly I love to shock while respecting the identity of the food itself and protecting its original taste and flavor.

For instance: gelato lookalike cornets served on ice cream trays with marinated salmon belly with crispy fennel and caviar. An eggshell filled with a Gorgonzola cheese panna cotta with candied celery. And what about a square seared tuna loin dusted with anise and black pepper resembling a lollipop?

The key is to have fun while cooking and to produce something original and different. But what I really love is to see the expression on people's faces once they are offered a sample from a passing tray, and more so to see how the food breaks up conversations and disrupts their trains of thought, redirecting their attention to a new topic: the food they are eating.

Infused Salts and Olive Oil Tasting

In my opinion any food served to a guest, whether if in a restaurant or at home, should look absolutely attractive, sexy, elegant and colorful. Even the simplest ingredient such as salt should be able to tantalize the guests' palates, spark curiosity and look remarkably inviting when making an entrance on the table. Appetite Openers are considered small bites, a prelude to your meal and they are usually prepared in a way to make a great first impression on the diner. I feel the same way about olive oil and salt tasting.

Even though it is more of an American thing rather than an Italian one, dipping your bread in a side dish filled with olive oil and salt has become almost a ritual for diners in most Italian restaurants across the country. I love great olive oil and I love salt, but I think there is a better way to experience the quality of our oils or salts for tasting as a pre-meal. Therefore, it did not take long for me to come up with an array of infused salts and a variety of exceptional regional olive oils and marry them all in one plate. I chose the perfect rectangular plate hosting six square openings for three varieties of salts and three different olive oils. I selected three extra virgin olive oils from the regions of Liguria, Tuscany and Sicily, and I paired them with in-house infused salts: dehydrated Ligurian black olives, Chianti wine and crispy basil. The infused salts create a great presentation on a plate and carry the flavors of the region from which the olive oils are produced. They are very easy to make and they last forever. Remember to preserve them in an airtight glass jar for longer shelf life.

Basil Infused Salt

Ingredients

1 small box of 8.5 oz of Maldon salt
2 oz of large fresh basil leaves
1 cup of blended oil for frying

Directions

To Fry the Basil Leaves

Bring the oil to 350 degrees temperature.

Carefully drop in just a few leaves at a time, pushing them down with the help of a perforated long ladle spoon until crispy and still bright green. I suggest standing on the side of the sauté pan for protection as the basil leaves will release water once in contact with the hot oil.

Remove the leaves from the oil and rest on deli paper.

To Mix

In a medium-size mixing bowl combine the salt and the crispy basil leaves.

With both hands, crush the basil leaves to a fine, powder-like consistency, mixing with the salt.

Black Olive Infused Salt

Ingredients
1 small box of 8.5 oz of Maldon salt
2 oz of pitted Ligurian black olives

Directions
Place the black olives on a sheet pan over a silicone baking mat and dry in hot oven at 200 degrees about 4 hours or until they are completely dry.
When cooled, crumb the olives in a food processor.
Spread the olive crumbs on a new sheet pan and place in oven again about 1 hour at 250 degrees.
In a medium-size mixing bowl fold the olive crumbs with the salt very gently with a rubber spatula in order not to break the salt crystals.

Chianti Infused Salt

Ingredients
1 small box of 8.5 oz of Maldon Salt
4 oz of Chianti red wine

Directions
Place the salt on a small sheet pan over parchment paper and spread evenly.
With the help of a spoon, spread the red wine on top of the salt until it is all covered and stained with the wine.
Set aside in a dry place and gently stir the salt once a day for the next 4 days or until the wine is completely evaporated and dry, leaving the crystals with a bright, intense flavor and color.

Deconstructed Sicilian Green Olive Poppers

As a kid I used to spend lengthy summers at our beach house on the Mediterranean. It is fair to say I grew up learning the best of the Northern (Piedmont) and Southern (Sicily) Italian culinary traditions. I love the abundance of the local Sicilian products, the freshness and the simplicity of how they are used and employed in the kitchen by the locals for daily home use.

Capers grow wild on the roadsides and are forgotten on the ground. Olive trees of any kind adorn the local plazas in sunny little towns with their massive presence and splendor, and many varieties of olives are hand-picked, seasoned and preserved in so many different ways it is not unusual to find street vendors selling cones of some of the best tasting marinated olives for only a few pennies.

The flavor of a Sicilian green olive is recreated in this recipe in a gelatin-like texture without its pit, on a spoon and with a crunchy contrast of oven-dried cherry tomato with few drops of extra virgin to better transport its taste to the palate. It is very explosive and dense, but also delicate and aromatic at the same time. To deconstruct the olives we would need to extract the juice with the help of a high-speed blender and use a flexible non-stick half-sphere silicon mold to freeze the olive purée. To transfer the juice into the spheres, I recommend using a professional sauce gun; however, this can be easily substituted with a small water pitcher for pouring purposes.

Ingredients

1½ cups green olives juice
4 gelatin sheets
½ cup whipped cream
A few hard cherry tomatoes small/medium

Directions

For the Green Olive Juice

With a small knife discard the pit out of the pulp of each olive.
Transfer the pit-less green olives into a high-speed blender and add a few leaves of fresh crispy basil, a few golden toasted garlic chips, extra virgin olive oil, cracked black peppercorns and abundant preserving juice of the green olives.
Blend it all at high speed into a thick liquid.
Add a few more basil leaves if necessary for a greener color.
Transfer the liquid to a very fine strainer and collect only the liquid, discarding the pulp. Measure 1½ cups and set aside.

For the Poppers

Warm the gelatin sheets previously soaked in cold water with 3 or 4 spoons of cold green olive juice.

Directions

Place the shot glasses in a hotel pan over a sheet of parchment paper or a thin rag in order for the glasses not to tilt or move during the cooking process.

In a blender combine all the ingredients, mixing a few seconds at low speed as we do not want the heavy cream to whip.

Pour the mix into the shot glasses ¾ full and bake in water in a hotel pan about 30 minutes at 275 degrees.

Make sure to cover the hotel pan with 3 or 4 layers of plastic wrap before baking.

At such a low temperature the plastic will not melt, but it will seal onto the edges of the pan, creating the steaming process we need.

Once ready, they should be delicate but firm.

Remove from the water and let them cool.

Merlot Reduction

In a small pot reduce by more than half a liter of red wine with a stalk of chopped celery, 2 chopped carrots, 3 chopped shallots, a few black peppercorns, a few broken pieces of dried porcini mushrooms, a small sprig of rosemary and a few leaves of sage.

Filter the reduced liquid and set aside.

Merlot Red Wine Caramel

Ingredients

1 cup sugar

¾ cup very well reduced Merlot red wine

2 garlic cloves hand mashed

½ cup crushed fillets of canned Italian plum tomatoes

Pinch of salt and white pepper

A small sprig of fresh rosemary

Directions

At low flame toast the crushed garlic and the sugar in a small pot till the sugar turns golden and is mostly melted.

Add the tomato, the rosemary and the wine reduction at once and let it reduce about 10 minutes.

Add salt, pepper and reduce till ½ of its original volume.

Remove from fire and set aside a few minutes.

Pass the mix through a fine meshed cone, making sure to push through as much of the tomato pulp as possible.

Set aside to cool.

To Serve
Using a broiler, pass the shot glasses under high heat a couple of minutes until a nice golden and crispy crust forms on each custard. With the help of a small spoon or a plastic squeeze bottle, adorn each top with a small quantity of the wine caramel, making sure to cover the entire top surface.
Decorate the top with a small fried basil leaf or with small sprigs of fresh rosemary.

Anise Dusted Tuna Lollipops

These savory bites are not only wonderful to eat, but also great in concept and to look at. The tuna squares pretend to be something they are not and with the help of the anise crust and the lollipop sticks they really attract attention whether being served across the room or at the table.

I like to use sushi-grade tuna as I only sear the outside part of it, leaving the inside very much raw for its bright color contrast and to balance the upfront spicy taste of the anise pepper dust. I use the bagna cauda sauce to connect all flavors into one. Bagna cauda is a Piedmont regional dipping sauce made of garlic, anchovies and olive oil. It is commonly consumed in the winter, served hot in tea-light terracotta pots accompanied by a variety of raw and cooked vegetables for dipping.

I decided to twist the original recipe a little and to create a cold version of it, making it a dense and very fine velvety sauce to complement the taste of the tuna while creating an explosive sensation right at the first bite. The lollipop sticks can be purchased online, mostly from candy supply companies. Be sure to buy 4-inch-long ones to create elevation and credible resemblance.

Black Peppercorn Anise Dust

Ingredients
1 cup whole black peppercorns
7 bay leaves
2 tsp ground cumin

2 tsp ground coriander
2 tsp fennel seeds
3 garlic cloves peeled
½ cup dried star anise
1 tbsp oregano dry
1 tbsp sweet paprika

Directions
Mix all ingredients together in a bowl.
Grind through coffee grinder till fine dust.
Discard all bigger pieces and small chunks left from grinding.
Keep in a glass jar or plastic container covered with a lid.
Do not refrigerate.

Bagna Cauda Sauce

Ingredients
15 cloves of cleaned and peeled garlic
1 cup of milk
6 oz can anchovy's fillets in oil or salt
¼ cup extra virgin olive oil
2 oz heavy cream

Directions
Place the garlic with the milk in a small bowl and refrigerate overnight.
The next day cook the milk and garlic until extremely tender at a very low flame.
Add the anchovies and the extra virgin olive oil and keep cooking at extremely low flame about 15 to 20 more minutes.
Add the cream and cook for 5 more minutes.
Remove from fire and let it cool.
Transfer to high-speed blender till very fine and smooth.
Refrigerate once cooled.

For the Tuna
It does not take much tuna to make a few of these lollipops. The important thing is to choose a very lean, thick steak with no fibers or fat.

With a very sharp knife cut the loin in long, rectangular, thick strips approximately 6 inches long and 1-by-1 inch thick perfect squares. One strip will make about 5 lollipops.
Roll the strips in a little olive oil and then into the anise dust to cover it lightly.
Sear the strips at high flame in olive oil about 6 seconds on each side, lightly salt them and remove from heat. The outside part should be crispy, leaving the inside part almost cold.

To Serve
Discard the tips of each strip and slice about 5 one-inch thick squares out of each seared loin.
Spear the lollipop stick through each tuna square from the top making sure it stays straight, giving both balance and the desired optical illusion.
With the help of a plastic squeeze bottle, adorn each lollipop with a big drop of the bagna cauda sauce right on top of each tuna square, a little crystallized salt and decorate with either a few fried capers or fried micro basil leaves.
Serve at room temperature.

Gorgonzola Panna Cotta Eggshells

This is one of the most visual Appetite Openers of the list. I really like how its concept brings out the complexity of each ingredient and their simplicity at the same time. We take very simple ingredients that combine very well together, such as Gorgonzola cheese and celery, and we make them all fit in an eggshell by applying different cooking techniques. The speck adds taste and smoky flavor, and the polenta cracker offers a crunchy and neutral element to clean the palate after each scoop. (If you cannot find speck, you can substitute it with Parma prosciutto.) There are many chefs who love to use eggshells and fill them with dessert custards or many other salty and savory preparations and present their creations on fancy ceramic pedestals or silver egg holders to add importance to the dish. Because of the complexity of this dish, I often distress it by serving it in their original and rustic-looking egg cartons.

For this dish we need to cut the top of each egg with an egg cutter tool. After emptying the eggs, wash them very well and set them upside down till the inside is completely dry. Use your finger to reach inside, scrape and remove the film at the bottom of each egg. Make sure to use only Italian Gorgonzola cheese. Do not be tempted to use American blue as this is way too salty and too sharp. For the polenta crackers you can use instant polenta, or better yet if you have any of the organic white corn from Anson Mills.

I serve these with a colorful ice cream plastic tasting spoon because of the size and weight. So next time you are in a gelato store and you plan to make this recipe, remember to ask for a few spoons along with your cone. You will find these eggs to be delicious to eat and extremely fun to handle: the candied celery gives that sweetness and gummy taste to contrast the crunchy speck and the polenta cracker. And it combines very well with the sharp taste of the Gorgonzola panna cotta.

Gorgonzola Panna Cotta Cream

Ingredients

¾ tbsp of granular powder and unflavored gelatin
1 tbsp of cold water
½ qt heavy cream
5 oz sour cream
1 pinch of salt
1 pinch white pepper
6 oz Gorgonzola cheese cubed and without the skin

Directions

Mix the gelatin in water and bloom 5 minutes.
Bring the cream to boil with the salt and the white pepper.
Add the Gorgonzola cheese, stirring constantly about 30 seconds and then turn the flame off.
Continue stirring with a whisk until the cheese is completely dissolved.
Set aside for 5 minutes.
Stir in the bloomed gelatin.
Once melted, pass the mix through a fine strainer and cool to room temperature.

Place the sour cream in a medium-size bowl and add the Gorgonzola cream a little at a time while mixing with a whisk, mixing to a silky texture.
Transfer the liquid into a sauce gun or a carafe.
Line up the empty eggshells on their serving cartons.
Pour the panna cotta mix into each one of them up to ¾ of their capacity.
Transfer to a refrigerator for at least 3 hours until firm.

Candied Celery

Ingredients
4 oz of only the green part of celery, thinly cubed
½ cup sugar
1 tbsp lemon juice
1 bay leaf
1¼ cup water
1 pinch salt

Directions
In a small pan, at moderate flame, combine all the ingredients and simmer about 1 hour or until the celery is completely cooked and candied and the liquid is reduced to a thick light caramel.
Set aside to cool and then transfer to a small sheet pan or a large plate.
Once at room temperature, collect the candied celery cubes and its liquid and combine it in a small glass jar or plastic container with a lid and keep refrigerated.

For the Crunchy Speck
We can compare speck with a smoky, spiced, cured air-dried prosciutto. It has an incredible, delicate, smoky flavor and it is very popular and commonly used in Italy, but unfortunately not as much in the U.S. Back home we use it for many preparations while cooking because of its distinctive taste and flavor. We often serve it thinly sliced to be consumed as cold cuts.
For the eggshells we would need a few thick-cut slices in order to create small cubes.
Transfer the cubes into a pan with very little butter and cook the speck crispy in its own fat at moderate flame.

Remove the speck from the pan and place it on a large plate with absorbing paper and cool to room temperature.

Polenta Crackers

Ingredients
2 cups milk
1 tbsp sugar
1 tbsp salt
¾ cup polenta
¼ cup of water
2 tbsp extra virgin olive oil
1 cup all-purpose sifted flour

Directions
In a large bowl combine the milk, water, sugar, salt and oil, mixing well with a whisk.
Add the polenta and the sifted flour, mixing carefully to avoid lumps.
Divide the mix onto 3 different half sheet pans over silicone baking mats.
Cook in the oven about 45 minutes to one hour at 275 degrees.
Remove from oven after a nice gold color and cool to room temperature before breaking to desired shapes by hand.
Store in a sealed plastic container to preserve freshness.
These crackers are also wonderful to serve along with cold cuts or cheese.

To Serve
The eggshells must be served at room temperature along with all their components in order to fully appreciate their natural flavors.
Never serve these cold out of the refrigerator.
Line up the eggs, the speck, the celery, and the polenta crackers.
Optically divide the egg into 4 parts and reserve each section for a specific ingredient.
Place a small teaspoon of the candied celery on one side, a small teaspoon of crispy speck cubes on the other.
Stick a long strip of the polenta cracker into the custard coming out of the shell for elevation and finish by placing the tasting gelato spoon in the last remaining section of the eggshell.
Serve immediately and watch for your guest's reaction.

Fava Bean Stuffed Tempura Zucchini Blossoms

This is a wonderful example of a vegetarian delight. In the spring and summertime I love to use zucchini blossoms as they are unique in taste and texture. I often stuff them with a variety of food options that complement well in taste and originality while taking advantage of the current season offerings. I love to stuff them with goose liver mousse and serve them with white truffle shavings and a Port wine glaze, sometimes until the first two weeks of October or whenever still available.

In warmer months I love to create seafood foams using fresh Maine lobster or rock jumbo shrimp. I discovered that by using a very light and customized tempura batter and by frying at 385 degrees I was able to fully capture the delicate taste of the stuffing while preserving the crunchiness of the blossoms for a few extra minutes before they lose their texture.

For this recipe I went for a vegetarian option and decided to use fresh fava beans to create a very delicate and upbeat Appetite Opener. We need a few of the freshest medium-size zucchini blossoms possible, some fresh fava beans previously poached in salty boiling water for just about two minutes and peeled out of their skin, and a tempura batter. Be careful not to over-poach the fava beans as we are aiming for a very bright color and a crunchy texture. I like to serve the crunchy blossoms by cutting their tips diagonally to show the stuffing's bright color, passing them around in small disposable bamboo cones for easier handling. Depending on the season I love to adorn the Openers with fine julienne sprinklings of summer black truffles for both edgy taste and color contrast.

Fava Bean Stuffing

Ingredients
2 cups fresh fava beans poached and peeled
5 large leaves of fresh basil
1 tbsp ground Parmesan Reggiano cheese
Pinch of salt
Pinch of white ground pepper
1 tsp of white truffle oil

1 tbsp extra virgin olive oil
1 tbsp as needed vegetable stock reduction

Directions
Combine all ingredients in a high-speed blender till a smooth and dense paste.
Add a little extra vegetable stock if needed, making sure the stuffing keeps a dense consistency.
Taste for salt and pepper and adjust if necessary.
Transfer the mix to a disposable pastry bag and place in the refrigerator to rest about 2 hours.

Tempura Batter

Ingredients
3½ oz all purpose flour
3½ grams fresh yeast
½ tsp baking soda
5½ fluid oz beer

Directions
Dissolve the fresh yeast into the beer with your fingers.
Whisk in the flour and the baking soda a little at a time, making sure not to form any lumps.
Store in refrigerator 15-20 minutes before using.

To Serve
Set up the oil at 385 degrees hot.
Stuff each zucchini blossom with the fava bean purée, making sure to seal the top by twisting the hanging petals together.
Remove the tempura from the refrigerator and stir well before dipping the stuffed flowers in it completely.
Shake excess batter out and lay in hot oil one at a time.
Make sure to cook evenly on each side by flipping them with the help of a large perforated spoon.
Cook till golden crisp.
Remove from oil and place on absorbing paper.
Sprinkle with crystallized salt and with the help of a serrated knife, gently but firmly cut across the tip of the blossom diagonally.
Place the stuffed jewels upright and sprinkle the open top with julienne summer truffles if desired.

They should be served immediately and consumed while still hot and crispy.

Cornets of Marinated Salmon and Crispy Fennel

These lookalike gelato cones are very popular in some of the fine dining restaurants across America, but very few make them worthwhile and memorable. I rarely make mini cornets that are not stuffed with seafood. I choose to do so because by experimenting for both crispiness and taste I discovered the perfect balance in flavor between the cornet and its toppings.

I started to experiment with those a few years ago and I have changed the recipe of the tulip cones depending on the intensity of the local fish. In Florida, I used to make a less-sweet tulip batter because of the freshness and the delicate taste of the everyday fish. In Washington, D.C., I find the seafood to be a little more intense and upfront in taste so I make a sweeter and more peppery tulip batter for a better edgy contrast. I love to use fresh salmon belly because of its fat and texture, but I often play with tuna, scallops, fresh branzino or other fish that would marinate and combine well with the sweet taste of the cones.

To make the cones we need a plastic stencil with two-inch-diameter circles, a silicone baking mat, small aluminum cones to roll the cooked tulips on them, and a small offset spatula for easier spreading. The salmon belly should be diced in very small cubes and matched in size by the crispy fennel. Use only the tender part of the fennel, discarding the outside leaves. I use a ratio of two-parts salmon to one-part fennel, and I marinate them just before serving in order to preserve their original taste, but also to ensure a delicate and balanced outcome.

Remember to stuff the cones only at the last second and just before you serve them as the moisture of their stuffing will make the cone soft after only five or six minutes. I love to serve them in a mini gelato cone stand; the ones used at the restaurant have four compartments and the cones present upright and majestically decorated in a way to give the illusion of real mini ice cream treats.

Cornets Tulip Mix

Ingredients

4 oz egg whites
4½ oz powdered sugar sifted
2¼ oz all purpose flour sifted
2.5 oz melted butter
2 generous pinches ground black pepper

Directions

Whip the egg whites to stiff peaks.
Delicately whisk in the sifted flour, the pepper and the sugar, making sure not to form any lumps.
Gradually add the melted butter and incorporate in a silky and smooth thick paste.
Refrigerate for one hour.

To Make the Cornets

Preset the oven at 325 degrees.
Lay the silicone baking mat of a half sheet pan and on top of it the plastic circles stencil.
With the top of a small offset spatula, spread a thin layer of the tulip batter mix into each circle.
After covering them all, remove the stencil and bake in hot oven a few minutes. This is a very delicate step because we want to make sure the batter is not totally cooked, but still lightly golden in color and easy to be bent and modeled on the aluminum cone right after they come out of the oven.
We only have 4-6 seconds to roll each one of them before we make a new one, so with the help of a small spatula remove only one circle from the sheet pan and model it quick on the aluminum cone.
Bend it and roll it on a working table, quickly forming a cone shape before it cools off and hardens.
Discard the cone and repeat the same step for each circle still hot on the silicone baking mat.
If the resting circles cool excessively and they turn too hard to model or bend, just place them back into the oven for a minute till the butter softens again.
Once cold keep the cornets on paper and in a sealed plastic container away from moisture.

Depending on the humidity in your kitchen these cornets might keep crispy and fresh as long as one week or as little as a couple of days. Do not ever refrigerate.

Salmon Belly and Crunchy Fennel Marinate Mix

Ingredients

6 oz salmon belly diced in very small cubes
2 oz fresh fennel cubes diced same size as the salmon
1½ tbsp extra virgin olive oil
Generous pinch of salt
Generous pinch of ground white pepper
1 tsp lemon juice
1 tbsp minced chives
½ tsp finely chopped shallot

Directions

Place the diced fennel and salmon in a small bowl.
Add the rest of the ingredients and fold in well.
Taste for salt and pepper and adjust if necessary.

To Serve

With the help of a teaspoon fill each cone with the salmon fennel mix.
Decorate each cone with a small drop of sour cream and a small quantity of caviar. I like to use California Osetra type for both cost and taste, but any other kind of caviar will do.
Finish decorating each cone with fresh dill.

Salty Goose Liver Spoons and Green Tomato Marmalade

I grew up disliking livers of any kind. It was only when I came to the States that I started to understand and appreciate goose liver. We use to cook it at the old Galileo in many ways, mostly seared and accompanied by fruits and at times with fresh porcini mushrooms and black truffles. I have developed a taste for it and become a big fan after I tasted it at Jean Louis Palladin's restaurant at the Watergate Hotel one night. From that moment on I felt the drive and the need to explore and to learn different techniques in order to cook it properly.

One of my favorite ways to cook goose liver is to poach it in a reduction of sweet wine for a couple of minutes at a very low flame and to serve it as cold appetizer with many different components. Thomas Keller at The French Laundry in California makes a similar and wonderful preparation called Torchon. He too marinates the liver overnight in milk in order to soften the fibers and to give a more delicate taste, then he serves it mostly with fresh fruits. Make sure to de-vein the goose liver with a small knife and to properly remove all films and membranes.

We need cheesecloth to shape the liver in, and a long and narrow small pot for fish poaching to better fit our roll while cooking. After cooking the liver, I like to take a quarter of the poaching liquid and reduce it down to a glaze in order to enhance the flavor of the dish when I serve it.

This recipe is very complex, delicate and demanding. If we cook the liver 30 seconds too long we will compromise its texture. If the liquid is boiling too hard, excessive fat will melt out of the liver, compromising its final taste. If not rolled or tied properly, it will break apart while cooking. Goose liver is one of the most difficult foods to cook and I have learned in the past that, unfortunately, if we consider how expensive it is, the only way to learn how to prepare it is to screw it up a few times, and to make sure we acknowledge our mistakes and correct them while implementing reliable solutions. In my personal case, in my younger professional years I got yelled at a lot. I got called a few unpleasant names and if I remember correctly I got hit in the head with it once. It is safe to say I have acknowledged my mistakes all right.

This Opener is just a jewel in taste, presentation and concept. It always raises a lot of eyebrows when served and has an explosive taste factor combining the sweetness of the green tomatoes, the salty taste of the infused Chianti salt, and the unique and gamey sharp taste of the goose liver. All these individual elements come together as one and produce and intense and lingering fireworks show in your mouth.

Prosecco/Port Wine Stock

Ingredients
1½ liters inexpensive cooking white Port wine
1½ liters Prosecco wine
2 pinches salt
1 tbsp whole white peppercorns
A small sprig of rosemary
A small sprig of thyme
A few leaves of sage
2 medium carrots chopped
2 stalks of celery chopped
4 shallots chopped
1 tbsp granulated sugar
2 bay leaves
½ cinnamon stick

Directions
Combine all ingredients in a medium-size pot and boil down to a total of 1½ liters of liquid.
Filter once cold

Goose Liver Roll

Ingredients
1 medium goose liver B grade
½ gallon milk
½ cup granulated sugar
2 shallots chopped
1 small sprig of thyme
1 small sprig of rosemary
4-5 few leaves of sage
Pinch of salt

Directions
Split the liver apart with both hands and remove all veins with a small knife.
Whip the sugar and salt in the milk and transfer to a small compact container along with the goose liver, shallots and the herbs.
Marinate in the refrigerator for 24 hours or at least overnight.

Remove the marinated liver from the liquid and wait till it reaches room temperature and is soft enough to be modeled.
On a working table unwrap a few layers of cheesecloth and by applying pressure, roll the liver in the cloth forming a roll of about 2-3 inches in diameter.
Make sure it is very tight and compact.
Tie both ends of the roll with a string while twisting hard.
Gently tie the center of the roll hard enough to keep its original shape and to create support while cooking.
Transfer the roll to the gently simmering Prosecco and Port wine stock.
Immerge the roll completely and cook no longer than 90 seconds.
Remove the roll and set aside to cool.
Transfer the roll to a refrigerator, turning it over every 5 minutes, discarding the excess liquid.
When slightly cool but still soft enough to be shaped unwrap it from the cloth and delicately transfer it to plastic wrap.
With both hands roll the liver back and forth by holding the two ends, shaping the roll into a tight small log.
Refrigerate for at least 8 hours before using.

Chianti Red Infused Salt

See recipe in Appetite Opener chapter.

Green Tomato Marmalade

Ingredients

1 lb seedless green tomato fillets
9 oz granulated sugar
1 lemon juice filtered of seeds
1 grated lemon peel

Directions

Poach the tomatoes in boiling water a couple of minutes.
Remove the peel and with a knife slice the outside fillets discarding the whole core and seeds.
Weigh 1 lb of green tomato fillets and set aside.
In a medium-size pot combine all the ingredients and cook about 20 minutes at moderate-to-low fire, stirring occasionally.
Remove from fire and rest for a few minutes.

With the help of kitchen tongs or cooking twisters, place the warm tomato fillets into a proper preserve glass jar and top with a little bit of the cooking liquid.
Seal the jar and rest upside-down till room temperature.
Store in refrigerator and wait 24 to 48 hours before using.

To Serve
Cut small ½-inch poached goose liver cubes, place one on each serving spoon and flavor them with a small drop of the Prosecco/Port glaze right on top.
Micro-cube a few fillets of the green tomato marmalade and with the help of a teaspoon place a small quantity on top of the poached liver.
Sprinkle the top with a little red wine infused salt and decorate with fragments of fried basil leaf for color and crunchiness if desired.
Make sure to serve immediately, not too cold, and at near-room temperature.

Deconstructed Dirty Vodka Martini

This is a classic example of how the twisted mind of a chef works when he gets way too bored or when he is not cooking. One day while I was waiting for my table in a high-end restaurant in San Francisco, my girlfriend Julia and I were watching a gentleman sipping his dirty vodka martini at the bar. It was quite amusing to see how he would spill some of his drink each time he reached for the olives, dipping his fingers inside the glass. I started thinking (and maybe a little too hard since Julia noticed the evil culinary light bulb going off in my head).

When I came back to D.C., I experimented with transforming the martini drink into a semi-solid Appetite Opener. I deconstructed the whole drink down to a bite-size spoonful, preserving its original taste while only changing its consistency. The hardest part was finding a way to solidify the vodka. I used the deconstructed Sicilian green olive poppers recipe to recreate the dirty olive taste and transformed the martini drink into a gelatin cube. Remember to put aside some of the original salty green olive water they are usually preserved in.

This recipe will not satisfy your hunger, but I wanted to include it in this book because it is a clear example of how chefs often think outside the box. This makes it a fun bite, a shocker, and definitely a new and original way to enjoy your dirty martini without spilling a single drop. When I serve this dish, customers often ask me, "What should I eat first? The olive or the martini?" My answer is always the same: "Enjoy it the same way you would consume a real one."

Ingredients
½ cup distilled water
¼ cup unflavored vodka
1 tbsp green olive preserve water
2½ gelatin sheets
2-3 drops lime juice
2-3 drops Martini & Rossi white dry vermouth

Directions
Bloom the gelatin in cold water and set aside.
Whisk in the vodka with the water, the filtered preserve olive water, the lime juice, and the vermouth.
Melt the gelatin and add to the vodka mix, whisking well but delicately, and pass through a very fine mesh to remove lumps.
Place the mix in the small, cubed silicone mold compartments and freeze till solid.
Remove from freezer take out of the molds making sure not to chip the corners.
Store in refrigerator on deli paper covered with plastic wrap.

To Serve
I like to serve this in a very small two compartments dish.
Remove the martini cubes from the freezer, pop them out of the ice tray onto a plate and transfer them to a refrigerator about 20 minutes in order to regain their gelatin consistency.
You'll notice that during the defrosting process the cubes will leave some liquid on the bottom of the plate. This is quite normal. Just remove them from the excess liquid and place them face up on each plate.
Sprinkle the top with few flakes of the red wine-infused Maldon sea salt to give both taste and color contrast and optionally, a very small leaf of micro mint.

On the opposite side dish compartment, place a green olive popper and decorate it according to its recipe, but without the cherry tomato chip.
Serve immediately with a small spoon.

Regional Italian Oyster Shooters

Everybody loves shooters. They are the symbol of hard parties and younger crowd, college years, fun times and irresponsibility. In my younger academic years I never experienced what the wild campus life is all about so I thought to go back in time and create delicious symbolic reminders of simple euphoria for those who have. Alcohol would have been the logical choice, but since food takes stage here, I decided to blend the idea of party time with a fine dining experience. The result is a fun and unusual way to consume freshly shucked oysters in a shot glass, dressed with a variety of micro delicious ingredients that symbolize authentic regional Italian cooking.

I love Blue Point oysters, but any other type will do if you choose to substitute them with your personal favorites. We will need some shot glasses, an oyster knife and each oyster would have to be shucked at the moment to ensure freshness. This means we have to prepare all the ingredients for each individual glass ahead of time and ready to be assembled. Four of the region styles I chose for their unique ingredients are Piedmont, Ligurian, Sicilian and Roman.

Ingredients for each Piedmontese shot glass
1 tsp micro diced fresh porcini mushrooms
1 tsp micro diced Parmesan Reggiano cheese
1 tsp micro diced fresh celery hearts
A couple of drops of natural white truffle oil
A sprinkle of cracked white peppercorns
A couple of drops of extra virgin olive oil

Ingredients for each Ligurian shot glass
1 tsp micro diced poached potatoes
1 tsp micro diced poached baby string beans
3-4 each toasted pine nuts
2 each micro diced pitted Ligurian black olives

½ tsp of pesto sauce
(Pesto sauce recipe)
A few drops of extra virgin olive oil
A sprinkle of cracked black peppercorns
1 tsp paper-thin sliced scallions

Ingredients for each Sicilian shot glass
1 tsp small baby capers
1 tsp paper-thin sliced scallions
2 slices of roasted garlic chips
1 tsp micro diced cherry tomatoes
A sprinkle of powdered hot red pepper
A sprinkle of fennel pollen or 3-2 cracked fennel seeds
2-3 drops of extra virgin olive oil
A sprinkle of cracked black peppercorns

Ingredients for each Roman shot glass
1 tsp crispy pan-seared micro cubed pancetta
1 tsp micro cubed roasted artichoke heart
A few drops of extra virgin olive oil
A sprinkle of cracked black peppercorns
1 tsp paper-thin sliced scallions
2-3 small leaves of micro basil

To Serve
Line up the shot glasses and place a shucked oyster in each one. For each shot assemble the appropriate regional ingredients listed above.
You could serve these on a tray for individual consumption or as a set of four for the most adventurous ones.

Milk Chocolate-Coated Olive Oil Mousse Lollipops

How far can our imagination take us? Mostly, how far can we let it go while implementing, changing or re-purposing a culinary idea? This next Opener is a classic inexpensive dish with very simple elements. When I was a little kid in Italy I used to love merenda, the typical afternoon snack between lunch and dinner and at playtime and homework sessions that makes every little kid happy. It usually consists of a sweet snack based on pastries, cake or even gelato. I have great memories of coming home from soccer sessions and running to the kitchen to fix my own succulent snack. I used to slice some leftover bread from lunch, pour just a little olive oil on it, and with a knife I would dig in the Nutella jar and spread as much chocolate as possible, topped with just a little sprinkle of salt.

Many times I used to sit back while watching cartoons on TV and eating my snack with a big smile on my face. The chocolate would smear all over my lips while creating a new smile that would stay with me a long while after.

I wanted to share this wonderful food memory with my customers, but how could I possibly propose a simple snack such as bread and chocolate on my fine dining menu? I destroyed it and re-constructed it in a more elegant and shocking way that delivered the original idea and its taste, but created in a completely different setting. The result is a mousse of extra virgin olive oil and sea salt coated with milk chocolate and sprinkled with focaccia bread crumbs and accents of edible gold leaves in a shape of a lollipop. I have created the mousse using a flavorless powder called maltodextrin. This is made from cornstarch, and while all starches would thicken in water, maltodextrin thickens in fat. By gradually adding olive oil to it we will obtain the desired paste consistency we need to form a few little marble-size balls. The milk chocolate adds a great sweet contrast to the salt and oil and the focaccia crumbs the crunchiness we need for contrast. I like to spackle some accents of gold leaf on it to give the importance it deserves.

At first, when you crack into the center you would taste the salt and the olive oil. Your mouth eventually will warm the extra virgin by releasing its strong and pungent flavor. At this point the chocolate taste will rise, balancing all the flavors together into a new explosive one. This is an unusual and elegant way to open your appetite, preparing your palate for the next course while shaking up your taste buds.

Ingredients
1 cup maltodextrin
1/3 cup excellent quality extra virgin olive oil
1 big pinch fine sea salt
2-3 oz milk chocolate
1 tbsp focaccia bread crumbs

1 or 2 edible gold leaves
1 sprinkle of crystallized salt
6-inch-long lollipop sticks

Directions
In a small bowl combine the maltodextrin, the olive oil and the salt till it thickens to a soft paste.
With your hands form a few small balls about ½ inch in diameter and place them on a large plate and on deli paper.
Spear a lollipop stick right on top of each ball all the way through them.
Place the lollipops in the freezer for at least two hours till solid.
Melt the milk chocolate at very low temperature in a small plate or bowl.
Dip each frozen lollipop into the melted chocolate, coating the olive oil mousse by gently spinning out the extra chocolate.
Quickly dust the lollipop with focaccia crumbs while the chocolate is still soft.
Remember, the mousse is frozen; therefore it will take only a few seconds for the chocolate to solidify.
Sprinkle with just a small pinch of crystallized salt and place upright to rest on a different plate over deli paper.
Place in refrigerator about one hour till firm and the olive oil mousse regains its original soft consistency again.

To Serve
Remove the lollipops from the refrigerator and let them sit out for a good 6 minutes.
Spackle little bits of gold leaf on each one and serve at near room temperature.

Parmigiano Leaves and Artichoke Mousse

I love the combination in taste of Parmesan cheese and artichokes. Nowadays we can find fresh artichokes year-round and take advantage of their natural flavor whenever we want. I find these two flavors to be very strong when combined together, and if not matched properly and attentively the results can be way too explosive and overpowering. It is very important in this case to taste the raw products before we cook them in order to determine the right proportion based on their original taste. In wintertime the local artichokes are strong in taste and a little more fibrous. In summer the imported ones are more delicate and tender, but a little shy in taste.

The cheese will almost always overpower the taste of the artichoke; therefore, I love to use this next Opener mostly in wintertime when I can easily balance the taste between the two in a more equal and delicate way. This recipe is intricate and if not executed carefully it will turn into a disaster. Use only 100 percent Parmesan Reggiano as only this cheese has the right amount of natural fat that will melt to a point to form the tuiles. Grana Padano or Parmesan surrogates will let you down in a way you will waste not only your time but also your money. To execute these properly it takes some practice, patience and time.

There are two ways to make these: served plain as a snack or in this case accompanied by a mousse of artichokes. In the first scenario we will need some grated Reggiano, a cast iron pan and a little butter. Using very little butter in the pan, drop a few tablespoons of grated cheese apart from one another in the pan and spread them in small circles as flat and uniform as possible. When the cheese melts it will turn a light golden color. With the help of a small knife and the back of a wooden spoon, lift each tuile and serve immediately while warm and crispy, possibly with a flute of champagne. The consistency of this one is very delicate and very fine, almost transparent.

In the second case we will need the help of a silicone baking mat, the oven and a very small shot glass to shape the tuile into a small curved basket in order to better host the artichoke mousse. Its consistency is more rustic and hard and more aggressive in taste. I like to decorate these Openers with red beet chips because of their color and delicate taste. Enjoy making these and remember to be patient.

To Make the Tuiles

Preset the oven at 325 degrees.

In a sheet pan and on a silicone baking mat form 2 to 2½-inch flat circles of grated Parmesan Reggiano, making sure each one is proportionally distant from another by at least 4 inches.

Bake in hot oven a few minutes until golden.

Remove at once and with the help of a small offset spatula transfer each tuiles to a small upside-down shot glass in order to form the wanted basket shape.
Remove only when completely cold, being very careful not to break it as it is extremely delicate.
Place on deli paper and in dry area. Do not refrigerate.

Artichoke Mousse

Ingredients
½ tbsp of grated Parmesan Reggiano cheese
4 fresh peeled and cleaned artichoke hearts
1 tsp minced garlic
1 or 2 pinches of salt
1 or 2 pinches of ground white pepper
6 large fresh basil leaves
4 spoons extra virgin olive oil
½ cup of vegetable stock or chicken broth
1/3 cup of heavy cream
1 large shallot

Directions
Thinly slice the artichoke hearts and sauté in a hot pan with only two spoons of oil, garlic, sliced shallot salt and pepper.
When sautéed golden add the stock and cook for a few minutes at low flame till the liquid is almost gone.
Add the cream and reduce a few more minutes.
Now add the basil and remove the pan from the stove.
Transfer the mix to a refrigerator and let it rest till cold.
Combine the Parmesan cheese with the cooked artichoke mix and transfer to a high-speed blender, pouring the rest of the oil into it a little at a time till the desired mousse consistency is formed.
Place the mousse into a disposable pastry bag and refrigerate.

For Decoration

Ingredients
1 small red beet
A few leaves of micro basil
Crystallized salt

Directions
Peel the red beet and make very thin slices by using either a mandolin or a slicing machine cutting coin size.
Set the oven at 180 degrees and place each red beet slice flat on a silicone baking mat.
Cook in hot oven about 2 hours.
Remove the chips from oven and let them cool completely.
With the help of a small spatula transfer each chip to a plate over deli paper.
Sprinkle with salt.
Fry the basil leaves in hot oil for few seconds, remove and place on deli paper to dry.

To Serve
Remove the artichoke mousse from the refrigerator and set it out till it reaches room temperature.
Line up the Parmesan leaves on a serving tray.
Squeeze a small coin-size puff of artichoke mousse on each leaf.
Decorate by placing small pieces of red beet chips on top of the mousse and with small crispy fried micro basil leaves.
Serve immediately.

Spoons of Solid Spinach Foam and Deconstructed Clam Broth

Imagine a miniature instant shellfish soup, all its elements deconstructed and grouped in a small Chinese spoon, revived at the very last second by a warm squeezed clam juice out of a pipette right before consuming. What comes in mind is..."just add water" or "space food." This recipe surely sounds like it, but it is not. This is a great tasting bite because is very flavorful, elegant and unique in its own way. By cooking the clams only a few minutes, we are able to keep them soft and juicy up until the time of serving. All other components are cooked in different methods and reassembled as one in a deep-dish style spoon to better host the liquid. I personally love the way the caper berry slice influences this Opener since it combines the tastes of the clam, the spinach foam and the candied tomato into one unique taste.

Solid Spinach Foam

Ingredients
½ qt heavy cream
4 eggs
4 oz goat cheese
12 oz sautéed fresh spinach
1 clove of roasted garlic
Salt
White ground pepper

Directions
First sauté the fresh spinach with olive oil, salt, pepper and a little minced garlic, then make sure to let it rest in a small colander in order to drain all the excess water.
Weigh 12 oz of drained sautéed spinach and transfer into a high-speed blender along with all other listed ingredients and mix well till fine and smooth.
Pour the mix in each square silicone mold compartment and cook in hot oven at 300 degrees about 15-20 minutes.
Remove from oven and let it rest.
When at room temperature, transfer the mold to the refrigerator till completely cold.
Delicately remove the solid spinach cubes from the mold, place on deli paper and cover with plastic film.
Keep refrigerated.

Candied Cherry Tomatoes

Ingredients
A handful of small cherry tomatoes peeled from their skin
A few sprigs of fresh thyme
3 garlic cloves hand-mashed
1 pinch of salt
3 pinches of sugar

Directions
Set the oven to 180 degrees.
Drop the tomatoes in boiling water a few seconds, remove them and set aside.

Peel them at room temperature with a small knife and remove excess water.
In a small bowl combine the tomatoes with salt, sugar and the hand-mashed garlic, mixing well.
Transfer in a small sheet pan on silicone baking mat, making sure to distance the tomatoes.
Cover with a few sprigs of fresh thyme and dry in hot oven about 2-2½ hours.

For the Clams
Cook a handful of very fresh, little neck clams in a covered pan a few minutes only with a little extra virgin olive oil, a pinch of oregano, garlic, crushed hot pepper, salt, ground black pepper, basil leaves and a few spoons of water.
Cook at very low-to-moderate flame just until the clams open.
Remove the pan from the stove and transfer its content to a new container to rest.
In a new small container filter the clam juice through a very fine mesh and delicately shuck the cooked clams in it.
Make sure the juice covers them entirely, keeping them soft and moist.
Do not refrigerate.

To Serve
Line up the ceramic Chinese spoons and all the ingredients ready to be assembled and combined at room temperature.
With a small sharp knife cut a ½-inch small cube of spinach foam and place in the middle of the spoon.
Cut a coin-size slice of caper berry and place flat on top of the spinach cube.
Warm the clams in their juice and with the help of small cooking tweezers place a single warm clam on top of the caper slice.
Cut in half a small candied cherry tomato and place face down on top of the clam.
Decorate with a drop of extra virgin olive oil, fried micro basil leaf and a sprinkle of cracked black peppercorn.
Capture some of the warm filtered clam juice in a small plastic pipette and place it inside the spoon away from the foam, resting on the handle.

When serving this Opener, instruct your guests to squeeze the warm juice on top of the deconstructed spoon, creating a flavorful balance of solid food and liquid to be combined in one bite.

Ham and Peas in a Toothpaste Tube

It is not every day that while having a meal at your favorite restaurant you are served a toothpaste tube. When I was in Europe about four years ago I was shocked by a restaurant in London that served me a small tube filled with a blueberry pie paste as the pre-dessert course. I hated its taste as it was bland and not very flavorful, but I loved the idea so much I decided to implement it in my restaurant with a tasty filling and as an Appetite Opener instead of a pre-dessert.

It does not really take much to make an impression or to create shock value. Usually the concept of a dish, if well-created and executed, does just that. But in this case it is the vehicle and the idea that really delivers a punch. In order to make this work in the U.S., I needed to fill the tubes with a very familiar and delicious paste to win over the skeptics so I opted for comfort food: ham and peas. Initially, I also tried with campfire beans, a pasty version of macaroni and cheese and a few other starchy vegetables, but none of them delivered the taste or effect I was looking for.

After you taste the ham and peas paste on a warm brioche, you forget entirely where it comes from as its delicious, familiar taste delivers such an incredible level of satisfaction you could probably even serve it with a real toothbrush.

Special Tools Needed
(Available at www.jbprince.com)
Fillable aluminum tubes with caps
Filling grid for tubes
Tube crimper pliers

Ingredients
¾ lb of fresh or frozen English peas
¼ medium-size sweet white onion, sliced
1 big shallot, sliced
2 small garlic cloves, sliced

3 slices of Parma prosciutto, cubed
1 tbsp of butter
6 leaves of fresh basil
½ cup chicken broth
Pinch of ground white pepper
Pinch of salt
½ cup heavy cream
1 sage leaf chopped
1 tbsp of extra virgin olive oil
Micro greens

Directions
In a medium-size pot golden the prosciutto, the onions, shallots and garlic with butter and sage until well-colored.
Add the peas and stir for a couple of minutes, then salt and pepper.
Add the chicken broth and at low-to-moderate flame reduce to half the liquid.
Add the heavy cream and reduce by half as well.
Remove from stove, taste for salt and pepper, add the basil and stir well.
Transfer to high speed blender, add the extra virgin olive oil and mix till a very smooth, liquefied green paste.
Ice bath chill, and store in a disposable pastry bag.

Brioche
Please see recipe from Cold Starters for Poached Goose Liver Fantasy (Page 112).

To Assemble
On a working table place the empty toothpaste tubes upside-down in each slot of the filling grid.
Fill them up to ¾ of their capacity in order to leave some room from the top for easier sealing, making sure to shake each one of them to get rid of any possible air pockets.
With the crimper pliers, press firmly at the end of each tube, closing and folding each end.

To Serve
At the restaurant we serve this Appetite Opener on a small narrow rectangular plate in order to better host the tube and the brioche. However, you can serve this any way you like.

Cut the brioche in strips of about 4 inches long by 2 inches wide and about ¼-inch thick.
Toast in oven till lightly golden and place on a serving plate.
Sprinkle the brioche with crystallize salt, cracked black peppercorns and a few drops of excellent extra virgin olive oil.
Decorate with just a few leaves of colorful micro greens and serve while still warm with the pea's tube next to it.
Instruct your guests to unscrew the cap, and squeeze the paste right on top of the brioche.

White Chocolate/Black Olives Square Bites and Gorgonzola Cream

This is a very unusual combination of flavors, but to my biggest surprise all the ingredients combine perfectly well to a very well-balanced message that pops in your mouth and lingers more than you expect, pleasantly. The sweetness of the white chocolate offsets the strong taste of the Gorgonzola in a way that creates a sort of sweet and salty taste. There is no doubt even lighter cheeses need a sweet counterpart to be better appreciated, but in this case I was missing a single element for taste that would combine them all. I found it in black olives oddly enough, but bull's eye!

As skeptical as I was, I realized all these ingredients together create a superb and delicate taste full of sweetness swirls, salt and cream with a sharp edge of a very common and simple element such as black olive. The surprise is in the taste. You could even customize its sweetness for those who are not great fans of blue cheeses for a lighter version. In this case, add a single drop of chestnut honey right on top of the miniature sandwich and the sharp taste of the Gorgonzola will "almost" disappear.

For the Black Olives

Place the black olives on a sheet pan over a silicone baking mat and place in hot oven at 200 degrees about 4 hours or until they are completely dry.
When cooled, finely crumb the olives in a food processor.
Spread the olive crumbs on a new sheet pan and place in oven again about 1 hour at 250 degrees.
Store in an airtight container.

For the White Chocolate Squares

Temper the white chocolate and spread on acetate sheet evenly with an offset spatula.
Cool for a couple of minutes and sprinkle some of the olive crumbs on top of the chocolate.
Cut into small ¾-inch squares while still a medium-soft texture.
Transfer the chocolate to the refrigerator till solid, then collect each square and set aside.

Gorgonzola Cream

Ingredients

4 oz creamy Gorgonzola cheese
1½ gelatin sheets
¾ cup heavy cream
Salt
Ground white pepper

Directions

Set the gelatin sheets in cold water a few minutes.
Cut the cheese in small cubes and warm over hot bath in a metallic bowl along with ½ cup of the cream.
When warm and soft, blend in the cheese into a cream with the help of a whisk and add the soft gelatin, making sure it does not form any lumps.
Set aside for ten minutes.
Transfer the mix to a small counter mixer, add the rest of the cream and run about 30 seconds.
In an ice bath and with the help of a rubber spatula, chill the mix till firm and transfer to a pastry bag.
Use immediately while still creamy and before it hardens.

To Serve

On a serving plate lay as many chocolate squares as desired.
Pipe a dime-size of Gorgonzola cream in the middle of each square and finish by placing one more on top, creating miniature sandwiches for one-bite enjoyment.

Chapter Four
Urban Legends and Unusual Satisfying Starters

In the previous chapter I mentioned the importance of opening the appetite, how to stimulate the palate and how to awake the senses. Many think appetizers, soups or salads are an optional part of a meal; especially in the U.S. some people are inclined to consume only a single dish in order to satisfy their hunger and nothing more. That is eating, not dining. Back home appetizer, soup and salad course are a very important part of any meal and the foundation of culinary traditions that define Italy as a gastronomic wonderland.

Over the past 27 years of my "American life" I have noticed incredible cultural changes among restaurant patrons. I remember clearly when I first came to Washington, D.C., my then-boss and restaurant manager Savino Recine (co-founder of the original Galileo Restaurant on P Street) complained daily about guests who did not know how to properly eat Italian. I remember Savino lamenting especially about how difficult it was to persuade a guest to try a soup or an appetizer before consuming the main dish. He told me the average American was happy by ordering simply one thing, the bigger the better, the one item on the menu with the best value, combined with many other garnishes and ingredients.

A clear example is a dish that once was (and still is) served across America in retro-style Italian restaurants. Veal parmigiana is served with overcooked sides of spaghetti with highly reduced tomato sauce that looks and tastes more of tomato paste, steamed broccoli or other vegetables. I hate this retro version of Italian food, mostly because many of the dishes widely popular in America are unknown in Italy and they deliver a wrong message of authenticity. We all know about chicken parmigiana, fettuccine alfredo, spaghetti and meatballs, cheese manicotti or stuffed pasta shells. Some of the above are the products of the first Italian immigrants who came in the late 1800s and at the turn of the new century. They were poor and starving and they had very little to feed their families with so they combined their food in one plate, not by choice, but by necessity.

Later on Italians started to produce cold cuts with American products—prosciutto, salames, coppa, even mortadella that was originally created and produced in a town called Bologna, and because of its mispronunciation over the years it has become widely known to Americans as baloney. However, the bologna widely available in stores is a completely different product from what we have in Italy. Because of the lack of quality meats and financial struggling, many of the original quality cold cuts turned out to be different products altogether: some of them completely new to Italians. One of those is the pepperoni everyone loves on pizza. This is supposed to be a reproduction of the spicy southern salame with red wine and garlic that was very popular in Sicily, Calabria and in some areas of the Campania region. Back home we could compare it to a salamino piccante.

Italians started making their own sausages using lower quality pork meat with lesser taste. They increased the amounts of garlic, wine and spices used for the marinating process and gave a spicier bite to the salame, hoping for a higher quality product. Dry aged, this was an instant success used at first for home consumption, then for retail, and sold in street carts along with fruits and vegetables. Pepperoni started to be so popular that someone saw the potential to produce it in large quantities and to distribute it across the States by changing its original recipe just enough to produce large profits. I challenge anyone to go to any grocery store or pizzeria in Italy and ask for pepperoni. They will look at you stunned as they would have no idea of what you are talking about. With that in mind, next time you are in a pizzeria in the U.S. that advertises "imported original pepperonis from Italy," please have a good laugh for me.

In later years, when the first Italian restaurants opened their doors they offered a variety of cold cuts as appetizers and starters, including the now American-Italian pepperoni and bologna as well as main course dishes that would combine meat, pasta and vegetables for a value meal much more appealing to the American taste. There has been a cultural shift in the past few years and a willingness to try new food, to evolve in quality, to learn traditions and proper ethnic etiquettes, to participate in cooking classes, to learn about ingredients and food altogether. That has given us chefs and restaurateurs the chance to succeed in different and more bizarre restaurant concepts and in delivering unusual and original products.

The explosion and success of the Spanish tapas restaurants confirms the above statement. The internationally acclaimed chef Jose Andres has brought a lot of that to the U.S., and he has educated and introduced Americans to what small plates and variety is all about. For lack of better words, most of what he serves in his restaurants is a variety of food in appetizer portions.

I remember when Jose opened his first Jaleo restaurant in D.C. We talked about tapas and the firsthand experience he had while working with mastermind chef Ferran Adria at El Bulli restaurant in Spain. Jose had learned so much working under him and was eager to introduce a new and different way of eating across America. Jose is a driven man equally funny in the kitchen and out. He is a friend I have shared many laughs with, in addition to a few poker games and a couple of culinary trips. I am very happy for all the success he has had over the past few years as I know how hard he has worked for it. Today he is a successful chef who co-owns a few tapas restaurants in the Washington, D.C., area, in California, Las Vegas, and San Juan, Puerto Rico. He also hosts his own TV cooking show on PBS, "A Taste of Spain."

But appetizers are much more than simple tasting: they are the start of a meal, an introduction that paves the way to culinary satisfaction. For us Italians, appetizers are just as important as pasta. Growing up in Italy, it was very common to top our dining table with at least 8-12 different kinds of appetizers for a Sunday lunch and find ourselves tasting from each plate before we started the meal. This process, at times, lasted for more than two hours, especially when we used to have guests coming over to the house, such as relatives or particularly my aunt Enza from a nearby town called Vercelli in Piedmont.

My aunt Enza is a great cook. She would prepare dishes out of the simplest ingredients, and they would all look wonderful and taste divine. Her son, my cousin Massimo, basically shared everything with me. We were like siblings up to the age of 17. He would take me to the kitchen whenever we would visit on Sundays, and he would show me the wonderful plates his mom had prepared for all of us. I remember my mother working extra hard in the kitchen every time my aunt and cousins would come over on the weekend to spend the day with us. It was like a culinary challenge that for the past 40 years has shown how well these two phenomenal housewives could cook: a long-running, silent cooking contest. Whenever we would spend the night over in Vercelli, usually on a Saturday, the four of us (Massimo, his sister Luisella, my sister Daniela and I) would raid the fridge right before bedtime. Armed with a single spoon we would sneak in the kitchen, open the refrigerator and virtually taste one of each, leaving handwritten notes delivering messages such as, "The tasting gang has hit again!" It was almost like we had a "license to taste." The best part of it was that no one would ever get upset the next day. My aunt would see it as a great compliment to her cooking and hard work.

Over the years I have treasured all the great food memories and I have cherished the wonderful tastes of the imaginary mile-long menu that has stretched for the past four decades. I have learned that all the great traditional classic dishes are almost impossible to reproduce in a different country and especially when separated by an ocean. I have tried so hard to recreate all the flavors that had moved me as a child, and with that I try to create a great memory for everyone to treasure. I was never really happy with the end result as it would only bring temporary joy to my palate and weak excitement in my heart.

With my always-evolving culinary drive, armed only with my hard head and frantic motivation, I realized I needed to deliver novelties from my kitchen while creating the "wow factor" in taste and presentation, even with appetizers. With the evolution of the American palate and a better understanding of the foreign culinary traditions, there comes the willingness to adopt a different way of dining and therefore a respect for the very menu my guests order from. Because over the years the dining procedures have stretched from consuming a single plate to multi-course tasting meals, the inventiveness of a chef and the creation of new dishes has become a "must factor" in any respectable kitchen and restaurant. Consequently I have opted for a new, colorful and less traditional way of indulging and tempting my customers into ordering more soups, appetizers, salads and even desserts to complement their meals: by creating curiosity and uniqueness on a plate.

All the following recipes are fruits of imagination, tradition, taste, playfulness and inventiveness. They are a mixture of textures from liquid to solid, from smoking techniques to air flavoring methods, and they all combine into one final taste while delivering the "wow factor" I continuously look for each time I step into my kitchen. Some recipes are a modern approach to Italian classics such as the deconstructed buffalo mozzarella offered in an unusual and creative concept. Others are modern versions of personal food memories created with a twist such as the veal carpaccio on a cold marble slab.

Then we have fantasyland where all the ingredients gather and mingle together like during school recess when we go back to our classes dressed with colorful costumes awaiting the final bell to rush to the amusement park for a day of pure fun. The four-minute smoked branzino carpaccio, the dry-wet minestrone soup, the Italian sushi rolls, the tomato terrine Popsicles or the deconstructed ratatouille salad—they all reflect the fun I had while creating and perfecting these tasty recipes. A great amount of irony is delivered on each plate along with the delicious food. As long as I continue having fun while working, the kitchen will always be my favorite playground.

Cold Starters

When I talk about cold appetizers people often mistake its meaning and concept: the word "cold" sometimes discourages diners to order and consume those preparations, especially in wintertime. I have heard comments such as, "Who would want to start their dinner with a cold dish while it's freezing outside?" There are many restaurants that do not respect their ingredients. Some pre-portion their salads and appetizers and keep a good number of ready to be served orders in the refrigerator to minimize labor and to expedite service. Some others keep berries and tomatoes refrigerated during the entire dinner service and, consequently, they are consumed ice cold by their customers.

When we bite on ice-cold food, we only taste 50 percent of its flavor. It causes discomfort in our mouths and rejection from our palates. Our brain tells us the temperature difference between our mouths and the food is way too great, and it sends alert signals causing us to question whether we really want to consume such a cold dish. Cold appetizers should be always served at room temperature with only few exceptions. Only at room temperature are we able to fully appreciate the taste and the flavors of food. And only at room temperature are we able to create a comforting feeling in our mouths in order to truly enjoy and fully appreciate the food we are eating. I encourage anyone to keep any kind of vegetables, herbs and fruits out of the refrigerator as long as possible during service, and to allow time for any of these delicate ingredients to reach the right temperature before being served to your guests.

Canvas of Modern Style Vitello Tonnato

What a perfect example of an old-country dish reinvented to a modern version while respecting its original taste and ingredients. This is a traditional meager and simple cold appetizer from the Piedmont region using nothing more than overcooked, sliced, poached veal topped with a sauce made of mixed canned tuna, anchovies, capers and mayonnaise. It is a spectacular and comforting plate filled with memories that captures my attention each and every time I travel back home. When I revisit a traditional dish with the intent to modernize it I ask myself if I should dare mess with it. I twist things all the time, respectfully. I can destroy a dish and re-propose it with a few twists for the new and modern market trend, applying the latest available cooking techniques and presentations. I may stray away from traditional methods in search of a modern and very visual impact, but there is one thing I never change: its taste.

It is my cooking philosophy to be respectful of the original taste at all times. I can change its visual presentation and alter its concept, add a few new ingredients or adorn a particular dish with added flavors; however, the original taste must stay the same. I decided to create a "canvas" because I can cast different colors and because of the way I lay out all involved ingredients, just like a painter does in his studio. On my take of the Vitello Tonnato there are a few added flavors such as the lemon zest for lighter freshness and black truffles for a more important and flavorful approach to the dish.

The sauce is represented in the veal stuffing with the tuna mix while the mayonnaise is deconstructed with visible poached slices of quail eggs and excellent quality extra virgin olive oil drizzled on the paper thin slices of toasted bread. Caper berries are simply sliced and placed upside down for crunchiness and flavor while the roasted red pepper froth marries taste with modern cooking techniques. It is easier to make than it sounds, mostly it is one of those dishes you really have fun putting together. It tastes absolutely delicious, and it makes a glorious entrance on any table.

Poached Veal

Ingredients

2½ lbs of veal top round, cut in half, lengthwise
½ tbsp of whole black peppercorns
2 bay leaves
1 stalk of celery
1 medium-size carrot
1 white onion
Few sprigs of fresh thyme
Few sprigs of fresh sage
1 cup of white wine vinegar
Salt
Water

Directions

With the butcher string tie the two pieces of veal tight and set aside.
Fill a medium-size pot with water.
Add the herbs, salt, bay leaves and the black peppercorns.
Dice the carrots and celery and add them to the pot.
Add the vinegar and salt as well.
Peel the onion and stick 3 toothpicks through it to hold it so that it does not fall apart while cooking.
Bring the pot to boil for 5 minutes.
Now add the two pieces of veal and boil them about 15-20 minutes.
Take the veal out of the liquid and cool for 10 minutes.
Wrap them with film and refrigerate for 4 hours.

Tonnato Sauce for Stuffing

Ingredients

4 boiled eggs
1½ lb of canned tuna in olive oil
Juice of 2 lemons

3½ tbsp extra virgin olive oil
4 tbsp capers
2 pinches of white pepper
2 pinches of salt
2 fillets of canned anchovies in oil
1 tsp of chopped Italian parsley
½ tsp of minced garlic

Directions
Combine all ingredients in the food processor till a dense, fine paste.
Adjust for salt and pepper.
Refrigerate.

Additional Ingredients
A few slices of fresh winter black truffle
1 tsp of infused black truffle oil
Maldon Salt crystals
A few leaves of fresh mache
2 quail eggs
A very small piece of two-day old white bread loaf
1 lemon
A drizzle of excellent extra virgin olive oil
A few whole caper berries

Roasted Red Pepper Froth

Ingredients
2 medium-size red bell peppers
3 cups of chicken broth
Ground white pepper
5 grams of powder lecithin
½ tsp of minced garlic
¼ tbsp of olive oil
1 pinch dry oregano
Salt

Directions
Roast the peppers in the oven at 400 degrees, set them in a mixing bowl covered with plastic film for one hour.
Peel the peppers and remove the seeds and set aside.

Place the red pepper fillets in a high-speed blender and add the salt, pepper, oregano and garlic.
Purée till very fine and silky.
In a small pot combine the pepper purée with the broth and simmer until there is a quart of total liquid.
Set aside and cool to room temperature.
With a small handheld immersion blender combine the lecithin with the liquid, filter through a fine mesh and set aside till serving time.

For the Quail Eggs and the Toasted Bread
Hard boil the quail eggs, peel them and set them aside in the refrigerator till cold.
Slice the quail eggs as thin as possible, coin-size, making sure to keep the yolk intact in a whole bi-color slice.
With the help of a meat slicer or a mandolin, shave the bread paper thin in slices no longer than 1 inch, sprinkle with salt, black pepper and generous olive oil and toast in a warm oven at 300 degrees till golden.

To Serve
Thin slice the veal (approximately 8 medium slices per order) and place face-up on a working table.
Pipe in a touch of tuna mix lengthwise across each slice and with the palm of your hand roll them up close.
On a rectangular, wide plate or on a large square one, place two rolls of the stuffed meat on top of each other, forming a cross on four different areas of the plate symmetrically and perfectly distanced.
Place a few leaves of mache around the plate as a bed for all other ingredients, filling the empty spaces with lengthwise sliced caper berries, face-down and a few slices of toasted bread.
Drizzle with truffle oil, extra virgin olive oil, cracked black peppercorns and crystallized salt.
Zest some lemon peel all over and delicately adorn the canvas with the coin-sized slices of quail eggs and with a few generous shaves of winter black truffles.
Froth the liquid red pepper and place a few teaspoons of it around the dish for color and taste.
Serve immediately.

Four-Minute Smoked Branzino Carpaccio in a Cigar Box

This is a fun and delicious starter that always satisfies because of its concept, taste, presentation and shock value even if you are not a seafood eater. If you are looking for a "wow factor" this is definitely it. Over the years I have become a cigar lover and consequently I saved many of the empty wooden boxes for both decoration and prestige, but when they started to pile up I decided to use them as vehicles for quick tableside smoking preparations.

I place a small plate in the cigar box with the thin slices of branzino and I dress it with all its fixings. Then I light three or four applewood smoking chips and while burning I set them in a small ramekin bowl inside the box next to the marinated fish plate. I blow the fire out, causing the chips to smoke, and I close the lid immediately, trapping the fumes inside. It takes approximately four minutes to serve this dish and by the time it is presented in front of the guest and its lid opened only a gentle puff of smoke unleashes, stimulating the guest's appetite.

There is not enough time to change the taste of the branzino while smoking; however the fumes pick up the taste of the mushrooms, the garlic chips and the citrus dressing, combining it all in one delicate and very aromatic flavor. I love to make this dish especially in spring and summertime because of the quality of the mushrooms available such as porcini and morelles. In colder months they can be replaced with chanterelles and portobellos. Make sure to use the right size bowls and dishes to place inside the box, otherwise they may not fit inside so the lid can close properly.

Special Tools Needed
1 small flat rectangular plate
1 cigar box
1 very small tea candle bowl
3 or 4 small applewood smoking chips

Ingredients for one Carpaccio serving
2-3 oz fresh fillet of Mediterranean branzino fish
½ blood orange medium-size
1 medium-size morelles or a small porcini mushroom or both
1 scallion

4 crispy-fried golden garlic slices
A sprinkle of crystallized salt
A sprinkle of cracked black peppercorn
3 sprigs of pea shoot tendril micro greens
Few drops Tuscan extra virgin olive oil

Directions
With a very sharp knife cut the branzino into paper thin slices and lay them flat, close to each other on the rectangular plate until the entire surface is covered.
Sprinkle with salt and cracked pepper.
Drizzle the citrus dressing liberally all over the fish.
Dress the Carpaccio with the roasted garlic chips and the thinly sliced scallions.
With a small sharp knife peel off the orange and cut two little segments out of it, slice them in half, and place them on the Carpaccio as well.
Slice the morelles very thin (coin–size) or in case you are using fresh porcini mushrooms have crispy slices no thicker than a few millimeters.
Place them on the Carpaccio and finish decorating with the pea shoot tendrils for color and crunchiness.

Citrus Dressing

Ingredients
Few drops lime juice
Few drops lemon juice
Few drops orange juice
Little zest of lime, lemon and orange
Salt and white pepper
1 oz Tuscan extra virgin olive oil

Directions
With a whisk combine all the fruit juices in a small bowl.
Add the salt, the pepper and the olive oil.
Whip vigorously till dense and store in refrigerator.

To Serve
Place the Carpaccio plate inside the cigar box on one side.
On the other side place the small tea candle bowl.

Drizzle the fish with extra virgin olive oil.
Light up the wooden chips till they are fully in flame.
Transfer the burning chips into the tea candle plate and blow the fire out, causing them to smoke.
Close the cigar box and serve immediately while the fish gently smokes inside for 4 minutes.
Open the lid in front of your guests, allowing the smoke to puff out of the box.
Remove the tea candle bowl with the charcoals before consuming the dish.

Le Bijou 1922

Italian Sushi Rolls

This is a typical "fun to look at, great to eat" appetizer. This is the Italian version of sushi rolls wrapped in Parma prosciutto on the outside with a filling of marinated goat cheese, crunchy poached asparagus and roasted slices of portobello mushrooms. With a bamboo sushi mat I shape the rolls the same way we would with real sushi, by applying pressure on each turn. Because of the softness of the goat cheese, all the other ingredients sit inside the roll firm, and I keep it stored in the refrigerator in plastic wrap up until the last second. At the precise time, I slice the roll in half first and then in half again, creating six identical pieces of fake sushi (discarding the end tips). Make sure to clean your sharp knife after each cut as the goat cheese will stick to the blade and it will transfer on the roll on your second cut, creating a visible mess. Once the rolls are set upright you will notice how the green color of the asparagus and the dark tones of the portobello give a wonderful contrast with the white of the goat cheese. I serve this dish with chopsticks and pickled carrot shaves resembling Japanese ginger and with a small sushi soy sauce dish where I pour the balsamic vinegar dressing for dipping.

When I first had the idea for this dish I was determined to serve it as a salad. As a matter of fact I serve it with a few leaves of baby arucola, and after a few orders I have noticed my guests having great fun at the table, passing around pieces of the Italian sushi as if they were real Japanese rolls. They would dip each piece in the balsamic dressing and they would eat the fake ginger without really eating the salad. This is when I realized it was accepted more as an appetizer than a salad. This is one rare preparation where I keep it stored in the refrigerator until the last second as I need it as firm as possible to slice through it. By the time the rolls are cut and the plate is decorated with each of the needed ingredients, your guests will enjoy this dish at the temperature it was intended to be consumed. To make this dish as authentic as possible, I often serve it on Japanese ceramic trays with traditional settings.

Balsamic Vinegar Dressing

Ingredients

½ cup of balsamic vinegar

½ cup of extra virgin olive oil
½ cup of vegetable seed oil
Pinch of salt
Pinch of white ground pepper

Directions
Blend all ingredients in a high-speed blender until forming a creamy and thick sauce.
Adjust with salt and pepper.
Store in refrigerator in a plastic squeeze bottle.

Pickled Shaved Carrots

Ingredients
1 medium-size carrot
1½ oz white wine vinegar
1 mashed garlic clove
Small pinch of salt
Small pinch of white ground pepper
4 or 5 yellow mustard seeds, each

Directions
Peel the outside part of the carrot and discard it.
With a potato peeler shave the carrot in multiple layers all the way to its core.
In a small bowl combine all the ingredients together and marinate the shaves for at least 2 days before using.
Keep refrigerated.

Marinated Goat Cheese

Ingredients
1 lb goat cheese at room temperature
2 tbsp of extra virgin olive oil
2 tbsp of heavy cream
¼ tsp minced garlic
Small pinch of oregano
Small pinch of salt
Small pinch of white ground pepper
Small pinch of crushed hot pepper flakes

Directions
Make sure the goat cheese is at room temperature.
Mix all ingredients by hand with a rubber spatula or small firm whisk until they are all combined together in a smooth, silky paste.
Place the mix into a disposable pastry bag and transfer it to a refrigerator for a couple of hours.

Sushi Rolls

Ingredients for one roll
5 slices of Parma prosciutto
2 green asparagus
3-4 slices of portobello mushrooms
2 oz marinated goat cheese
A few slices of extremely thin cut Yukon Gold potato

Directions
Place the potato slices flat on top of a silicone baking mat and brush them with melted butter and a sprinkle of salt.
Bake in oven at 180 degrees until crispy golden.
Quick poach the asparagus in salted water al dente and set aside.
Slice the head of a portobello mushroom creating 3 or 4 slices not thicker than ½ inch each and sear crispy in hot pan with a spoon of olive oil, salt, pepper and a touch of garlic.
Lay a single sheet of plastic film on the bamboo mat covering its whole surface.
Vertically lay the slices of prosciutto on top of the film one by one in order to create a solid sheet with no visible gaps.
Horizontally spread the goat cheese across the prosciutto applying pressure with your fingertips, creating a strip of about 1-inch wide and 6-7 inches long.
Place the asparagus and the slices of portobello on top of the goat cheese side by side.
Now gently, but firmly turn the mat until forming a solid roll squeezing on each turn.
The roll is now formed and automatically wrapped in plastic film.
Refrigerate for at least two hours.

Lemon Dressing

Ingredients
The juice of 1 lemon, filtered
Little zest of lemon
Salt and white pepper
1 oz extra virgin olive oil

Directions
With a whisk combine the lemon juice in a small bowl with the salt the pepper and the olive oil.
Whip vigorously till dense and store in refrigerator.

To Serve
Remove the Italian sushi from the refrigerator and quickly slice it with a sharp knife into 6 pieces of equal size and place them on a square or long cheese-like plate.
Gently shake the bottle of balsamic vinegar dressing from the fridge and pour some of it in a small soy sauce bowl and place next to the rolls.
With your fingers, pinch a few slices of the pickled carrots and squeeze the liquid out of it, making sure no mustard seeds are present, and place on the plate.
On each roll, spike in half potato crisp making sure it sits upright creating elevation and crunchy contrast.
Serve with few leaves of arucola salad with a little of the lemon dressing and with chopsticks.

Chicken Livers Terrine with Crunchy Almonds Cocoa Nibs and Vin Santo Gelatin

Some of the typical flavors of Tuscany are concentrated and displayed on this dish highlighting a perfect balance between sweet and salty. The dense and velvety taste of the chicken liver terrine marries well with its sweet counterparts, rounding up the taste into an explosion of different flavors and textures, leaving the palate fresh and clean for a second bite. Making the terrine is the easy task. If you follow the recipe it will take you to a wonderful and flavorful spread. There are so many recipes out there, too many, that I have decided to make my own and customize it to my liking. It took me a couple of tries to perfect it as I was looking for a dense, deep taste with an easy execution and a rich yet delicate outcome.

What requires attention is the rosemary and garlic bread in the raising process. So be careful not to let the dough rise too long as it could jeopardize the final outcome. To bake properly it means to reach the perfect balance between rising and cooking, so do not get discouraged if your loaf will not turn out perfectly light the very first time you try. It takes some practice and understanding to excel in the baking world.

The most important tip for this recipe is about the "dusting" procedure with the cocoa nibs and the toasted almonds. There are many different kinds of nibs on the market. Choose the ones with very small grains and not too bitter in taste as they could turn out to be overpowering. Also make sure the almonds are toasted just right and not too much as they release a very bold and aggressive taste if they stay in the oven too long. It has happened in the past while preparing this dish that too much pressure is applied on the cube at the time of "dusting," consequently changing the shape of the cube, making it look almost deformed. In order to prevent that, gently spread a very thin film of extra virgin olive oil with your finger to facilitate the sticking process.

Make sure not to apply too much nibs or almonds as our goal is to add just a little taste and crunchiness to the terrine and not to change its taste entirely. I love to spread it on my toasted rosemary and garlic bread as all the tastes come together, leaving a happy and satisfied smile on my face. I get even happier when after each bite I savor the Vin Santo gelatin that cleanses my palate and leaves me with a sweet-salty aftertaste, reminding me how precious and wonderful simple Tuscan ingredients can be.

Chicken Liver Terrine

Ingredients
1½ lbs chicken livers
2 medium sliced shallots
½ small carrot diced
½ stalk of celery diced
½ small sprig of rosemary chopped

2 sage leaves chopped
2 bay leaves
1 garlic clove minced
¼ lb butter
Salt and white pepper
2 oz sliced and then finely minced pancetta
½ oz dry porcini mushrooms soaked in ½ cup of water
¾ cup heavy cream
3 fillets of anchovies
3 eggs
1 cup Prosecco wine
½ tbsp of ground white pepper
¾ tbsp of salt

Directions
In a small brazier cook the celery, carrots, shallots, garlic, the herbs and the bay leaves with the butter for few minutes.
Add the minced pancetta, the anchovies, the chicken livers and the soaked and squeezed porcini mushrooms chopped up in small pieces preserving the soaking water.
Cook until the chicken livers are crispy and stick to the bottom of the pan.
Add salt and pepper.
Pour in the wine and the filtered porcini mushrooms water.
Reduce by 3/4 and set aside.
While still hot pass the mix to a food processor and place the mix into a bowl.
Let cool a few minutes and then stir in the eggs and the heavy cream, gently mixing with a spatula, and place in a high-speed blender till fine paste.
Bake in a stainless steel pate mold in water at 275 degrees about one hour.
Refrigerate overnight before removing the terrine from the mold.

Vin Santo Gelatin

Ingredients
1½ liters of Vin Santo wine
2 small carrots diced
½ white onion diced
1 tsp whole black peppercorns

½ sprig of rosemary
3 small leaves of sage
¼ cup sugar
1 bay leaf
½ orange peel
½ lemon peel
4 gelatin sheets

Directions
Place all ingredients in a large stock pot (with the exception of the gelatin sheets) and reduce the liquid by half.
Remove from the stove and set aside for 15 minutes to cool.
With the help of a spoon stir in the gelatin sheets previously soaked in cold water and mix well till dissolved.
Filter the liquid through a very fine mesh and store in a rectangular deep plate in the cooler until firm.

Rosemary and Roasted Garlic Bread

Ingredients
2 tbsp olive oil
½ cup warm milk
2½ cups all purpose flour
½ cup whole wheat flour
1½ tbsp finely chopped fresh rosemary
4 roasted garlic cloves
½ cup warm water
½ tbsp salt
1½ tsp dry yeast

Directions
In a small mixing bowl use your fingers to dissolve the yeast in the warm water and milk.
Let it rest for 15 minutes.
Add the oil, the flours, the rosemary, the whole roasted garlic cloves and the salt, and with the paddle attachment mix gently at low speed.
Mix for a few minutes and change the paddle with the hook attachment for better kneading.
Mix at medium speed till the dough is smooth and elastic.
Remove from mixer.

Place the dough on oiled plate covered with plastic wrap and let it raise in warm area till it doubles in size.
Remove from the plate and gently shape in a small ball, being careful not to press on the dough too much to preserve its original softness.
With a knife make a cross-like incision on top of it and let it rise again about an hour.
Set the oven at 400 degrees and bake about 30 minutes.

To Serve
Toast some whole almonds in the oven and once cold crush them down by hand.
Sift the almonds, discarding the smaller crumbs, retaining only the bigger pieces the size of small pea halves.
Lay them on a plate and set aside.
Pour some roasted cocoa nibs on a separate plate.
Cut a 1½-inch cube out of the chicken terrine and dust each side by gently pressing with your hands on the almonds and on the cocoa nibs, alternating sides to have a different color on all 6 parts.
Place the two-colored cube on a square or round plate.
Cut the Vin Santo gelatin into small ½-inch cubes and place all around the terrine, decorating the dish in symmetry with a few optional micro greens corn shoots.
Toast a couple of small rosemary-garlic bread slices and serve while still warm.
Optionally, decorate the plate with toasted crushed pistachio and pistachio dust.

Marinated Wild Alaskan Salmon with Liquorice Froth

Italy meets America!

I have heard so many comments about this dish as the combination of hardcore American and Italian products often creates skepticism and loud reactions from first-time diners. The skepticism stops after the first bite. Alaska and Italy have very little in common, but I was able to tie the traditions and the natural local products of two different worlds in a crispy and innovative taste combined by a single ingredient: liquorice.

The American elements are the wild Coho or the Sockeye salmons and the pink grapefruit. The Italian counterparts are crispy shaved fennel, baby arucola and Sicilian green olives. The combinations of these ingredients make a refreshing and crispy appetizer, especially because of the silky, dense and flavorful taste of the salmon. I like to slice it with a sharp knife as thin as I can. Then I lay the slices flat on a large plate and I marinate them for at least three hours. Alaskan wild salmon is very deep and velvety rich therefore it does not need strong or excessive extra flavors: for example I do not even use lemon juice in the marinating process. The fennel, once shaved and combined with the arucola, is the taste bridge to the fish. The Sicilian green olives shock your palate and it rounds outs the wild taste of the salmon with a sharp edge, creating continuous interest at each bite. The grapefruit works as a neutral refreshing ingredient.

So where does the liquorice fit in all of this? It is hard to find good liquorice in the U.S. As little kid I used to go to the tabaccaio store (a small store where tobaccos, office products and candies are sold) to buy some of the most flavorful and sharp liquorice I can remember. In the past few months I have looked so hard for a similar product and I finally found it in Darrell Lea, a company that produces great soft liquorice out of Australia with no added artificial colors or artificial flavors. Their liquorice is as good as it comes, dense and pasty. However it is a little too chewy to combine it with our delicate appetizer so I decided to add its flavor in the form of interesting, airy froth.

By combining an intense and rich liquorice "broth" with lecithin (a natural powdery soy bean emulsifier) we create the base for a firm and light froth. Once whipped it has about 45 seconds before it disintegrates, therefore it must be added at the very last second before serving. The liquorice ties all the flavors together.

Overall I would say the function of the liquorice makes a more complete and better-tasting dish while delivering that unusual and delicate kick. For those who are still skeptical I suggest you to taste it without the froth first, and then with it.

You be the judge of it.

Marinated Alaskan Wild Salmon

Ingredients
About 3-4 oz of Coho or Sockeye salmon fillet
2 tbsp of extra virgin olive oil
A tbsp of finely chopped spring onions
Pinch of cracked black peppercorns
Pinch of crystallized salt
A very small pinch of juniper berry dust (optional)

Directions
With a sharp knife cut a few slices of either Coho of Sockeye wild Alaskan salmon paper thin.
Lay them flat on a plate and season them with the extra virgin olive oil, the finely chopped spring onions, the pepper, crystallized salt (and if you would like a more sharp and upfront taste a very small pinch of juniper berry dust).
Flip the slices over and repeat the marinating procedure on the other side.
Cover with a plastic film and refrigerate for at least 3 hours.

Liquorice Froth

Ingredients
3.5 oz of Darrell Lea soft black liquorice
1 qt of vegetable stock
8 grams of powder lecithin
Pinch of salt
Directions
With a sharp knife cut the liquorice logs into thin slices and combine them with the stock in a medium-size pot.
Add salt and simmer at very low fire about a half hour until the liquorice is completely melted, stirring occasionally.
The broth should never boil, releasing a pungent smell; its taste should be very strong and slightly salty.
Set aside to cool.
Once at room temperature combine the lecithin and the liquid with the help of a small immersion blender, making sure not to form any lumps.
Filter through a fine mesh and refrigerate.

Arucola Fennel Salad

Ingredients
3 Sicilian green olives
A few baby arucola leaves
2 oz of shaved crispy fennel
3 segments of pink grapefruit each cut in 3 pieces
2 tsp of lemon dressing
A few small sprouts of white liquorice fennel micros

To Serve
Take the marinated salmon out of the refrigerator at least 15 minutes before serving.
With a small knife peel a few small wedges lengthwise off the green olives, discarding the pit.
Slice each wedge into thinner pieces and set aside.
Toss the fennel and the arucola leaves with the lemon dressing and place in the middle of an elegant small bowl or a deep glass plate.
Decorate the salad with the grapefruit segments and the green olives.
Roll each salmon slice with your fingers, making sure to form gentle and delicate loose logs.
Place each of them on top of the salad apart from one another and in different angles while preserving the needed elevation for the salad and while forming symmetry for an elegant and colorful presentation.
With a small hand immersion blender froth the liquorice mix by tilting its wide container to create an optimal angle for the tip to move in and out of the liquid, causing it to bubble. The froth will form and accumulate quickly, but it is very important to make sure to froth a little extra in order to give a firm consistency.
Rapidly decorate the appetizer with the stiff froth, placing at least 2 or 3 full tablespoons of it right on top.
Finish by adorning the dish with a few sprouts of white liquorice fennel micro greens right on top of the froth.
Serve immediately.

Cold Stone Veal Carpaccio

It was fascinating to watch the young teen behind the counter playing with the ice cream on a cold marble table, combining chocolate chips, M&Ms and crushed Oreo cookies into a new, improvised flavor right under the curious and entertained eyes of waiting guests. My daughter Chiara and her soccer teammates had incredible smiles painted on their faces drooling in anticipation of tasting this customized treat I found unappealing and messy. But I loved the concept and I start thinking: How could I adapt this idea into my cooking and make it mine? Mostly, how can I deliver a "wow factor" in concept, presentation and taste using the same basic elements?

After a few days and a few different experiments I called my friend Vladi, who works for a marble company. I commissioned several 10x10 marble slabs one-inch thick and asked him to drill three individual holes on one side about two inches apart. I purchased some miniature bamboo cones online, I placed the marble slabs in the freezer, and I went to work. The idea was to play with basic ingredients while making the diner's own dish right before their eyes.

By mixing the given components on a cold marble slab, you create an unusual and modern version of Piedmontese veal Carpaccio. Once all the ingredients are in place, the concept is recreated with a fun and delicious twist. Add and mix as you please. The final taste will not change. It is very important to dice the mushrooms, the Parmesan cheese and the cardoons very small as they go inside the cones and need to be served at room temperature, as well as the marinated veal Carpaccio cubes. This last one is previously pressed into a small butter cup in a shape of a small tower.

Place the curved Parmesan tulip under the un-molded veal only at the last second as it is very fragile and could easily break. Place the quail egg yolk on top of the veal and shower it with black truffles slices. I like to serve this dish immediately in order to avoid temperature changes and possible water condensation on the marble slab. I often compare this dish to a puzzle where all the pieces are assembled together forming a complete picture only when the very last component is put in place.

Whenever possible I also love to substitute the black truffles with the white ones in the fall. In this case marinate the veal with the white truffle oil instead of the black and enjoy a good shaving right on top of the Carpaccio before serving. For the lemon dressing, follow the same steps of the recipe by changing the black truffle oil with the white one.

Veal Carpaccio

Ingredients
2½ oz veal fillet cleaned of fat and fibers and diced in ¼-inch cubes
1 tsp of natural black truffle oil
A pinch of crystallized salt
A pinch of cracked black peppercorns
1 tsp of hazelnut oil
1 quail egg yolk
A few slices of fresh black truffles
½ tbsp of toasted hazelnut halves
1 oz of assorted micro greens

Directions
Set aside the hazelnut halves, the quail egg, the truffles and the micro greens till serving time.
With a sharp knife dice the veal fillet in cubes not bigger than ¼ inch and marinate it in a bowl with the hazelnut and the truffle oils only.
Avoid adding any salt or pepper or it will compromise the sturdy consistency of the veal tower.
Push the cubes into an aluminum butter cup or even a tall espresso one, pressing well.
Place in the refrigerator covered with plastic wrap.

Parmesan Cheese Tulips

Ingredients
4 oz egg white whipped to stiff peaks
5 oz powder sugar
2 oz and a full tsp of AP flour

2.5 oz melted butter
½ cup of grated Parmesan Reggiano cheese
Pinch of salt

Directions
In a small bowl, using a rubber spatula gently fold the stiff peak egg whites with the sifted flour, the sugar, ¾ of the grated Parmesan cheese and the salt.
Add the melted butter a little at a time making sure not to form any lumps.
Let the mix rest in the refrigerator for at least one hour before using.
With the help of a stencil and a silicone baking mat, form a few small rectangular strips of about eight inches long and 1½-inch wide.
Sprinkle the remaining quarter of Parmesan cheese right on top of each tulip and bake in hot oven at 325 for a few minutes till light golden color.
Remove from oven and with the help of a small offset spatula rapidly curve the tulips over a wine bottle to form a half shape circle showing the dusted bits of Parmesan cheese on the outside part of it.
When cool, store in an airtight container over deli paper.

Black Truffles Lemon Dressing

Ingredients
2 tbsp of lemon juice
2 tsp of natural black truffle oil
Little zest of lemon
Salt and white pepper
1 oz extra virgin olive oil

Directions
With a whisk combine the lemon juice in a small bowl with the salt, pepper, the olive oil and the truffle oil.
Whip till dense and store in refrigerator in a plastic squeeze bottle.
Before using remember to shake vigorously.

Balsamic Vinegar Glaze

Ingredients

1 liter of balsamic vinegar
1 very small sprig of rosemary
2 leaves of sage
1 small chopped shallot
1 tbsp of honey
Pinch of salt

Directions

Combine all ingredients in a small pot and boil down at moderate fire until it reduces to about a quarter of its original amount.
Filter through a fine mesh and set aside till room temperature.
Transfer to a refrigerator and in a plastic squirt bottle.
The reduction, once cold, should be very thick and pasty just like the consistency of watered-down ketchup.
The best way to test is to squirt some out of the bottle and check for thickness: if it runs excessively it needs to be reduced more.
(Remember this is now a reduction and extremely rich in taste, therefore I suggest using it in very small quantities, and to squirt it through a very fine tip in order to limit excessive amounts that could change and overpower the overall taste of the dish.)
Make sure the reduction is at room temperature before using as it could be difficult to squeeze it out of the squirting bottle if cold out of the refrigerator.

Bamboo Cone Stuffing

Ingredients

½ oz finely cubed poached cardoons
½ oz finely cubed fresh porcini or chanterelles mushrooms
½ oz finely cubed Parmesan Reggiano cheese

Directions

For the Cardoons
Pick only the tenderest stalks, and peel out the thick fibers with the help of a small knife.
Cut it in 2-3 shorter pieces and poach them for a couple of minutes in salty boiling water. Remove the cardoons and cool naturally at room temperature.

Cut in very small cubes and set aside.

For the Mushrooms
Clean the mushrooms with a damp cloth and remove all impurities. Cut into small cubes identical in size as the cardoons and set aside.

For the Parmesan cheese
Before dicing the cheese in matching cubes as the previous two ingredients make sure to remove it from the refrigerator for at least 3 hours.
This procedure will allow you to easily cut into it in desired shapes at softer room temperature.

To Serve
Remove the marble slab from the freezer and wipe it well with a dry towel.
Place it on a working table with the 3 holes on your left.
Quickly place 3 small bamboo cones into each hole, standing upright.
Fill them top to bottom with the dice mushrooms, the cardoons and lastly the Parmesan Reggiano cheese all at room temperature.
On the opposite top right side place a small ceramic ramekin and fill it with the assorted micro greens.
Right below it place vertically a ceramic Chinese spoon and fill it up with the black truffle lemon dressing.
From top to bottom squirt a zigzag stream of balsamic vinegar reduction right on the middle of the marble between the cones and the spoon and ramekin.
With a quick gesture place the marinated veal tower in the middle of the dish on top of the balsamic glaze, top it with a sprinkle of crystallized salt, a pinch of cracked black peppercorns and with a fresh quail egg yolk.
Decorate the dish with a few toasted hazelnut halves and a good shave of the truffles right on top of the veal.
Lastly, delicately place the end tip of the Parmesan cheese tuile under the veal tower, making sure it curves toward the bottom part of the dish while held up by the weight of the meat.
Serve quickly and let the fun begin by combining all the ingredients together on a cold marble slab.

Deconstructed Buffalo Mozzarella

Making fresh mozzarella from cow milk whether in a restaurant's kitchen or at home is not as difficult as it seems. Anyone with a little enthusiasm and patience could do it and have some fun with that. It all comes down to three essential steps: selecting the right curd, pinpointing the accurate water temperature for curd melting, and kneading and stretching the cheese mass into small, uniform, elastic balls. But making fresh mozzarella from buffalo milk in the U.S. is practically impossible. I often laugh when I dine out and read on a restaurant menu, "in-house-made fresh buffalo mozzarella," as I know the only place on Earth it can be produced is in the south of Italy's Campania/Neapolitan region.

In Italy the water buffalo graze free in designated areas where the pasture is optimal and controlled and their milk is collected at least once a day for either mozzarella or ricotta cheese production. The milk is never shipped anywhere else outside Italy and its production is local only. Only then is the mozzarella exported all over the world, and because it is so delicate and perishable it can only be shipped out by overnight freight to ensure its freshness at its arrival. The combination of production costs, shipping and the monopoly of it makes its price tag very high. This product can be compared to the white truffles of Alba as it has the same characteristics of uniqueness and prestige.

Personally I love to eat it plain and at room temperature with just a drizzle of extra virgin olive oil and a sprinkle of salt in order to fully taste its delicate and unique milk flavor. A lot of people dress it with balsamic vinegar, but it is a big mistake as the balsamic is way too strong and acidic and it covers the taste of the milk. If you serve it as a caprese salad, make sure to dress only the tomatoes and place the mozzarella on the side of the dish away from the balsamic.

As much as I love this glorious cheese in all its simplicity, I decided to twist it in a new concept offering a new version and in a new shape while preserving its characteristics and traditions. This is a wonderful and very delicate summer dish that takes advantage of the juicy and ripe cherry tomatoes available in so many colors and flavors and of the freshest basil around. The balsamic gelatin provides a delicate and sweeter taste that complements the buffalo mozzarella as during its cooking process most of its vinegary taste transforms into a much milder and more appealing flavor.

I deconstruct the cheese using a high-speed blender, some of its preserving water, called in Italian "acqua di governo," salt, gelatin and a little extra virgin olive oil to create an already dressed cube ready to eat. With the help of a flexible square silicone mold approximately 1½ inch, I pour the liquid mix into it and freeze it until solid enough to be shelled out in one perfect cube. I simply decorate it with fried crispy basil leaves set upright to give the dish elevation, taste, color and crunchiness. It is beautiful to look at as I use various types of colored cherry tomatoes, delicate to eat and its unusual concept always generates great compliments and admiration.

Deconstructed Buffalo Mozzarella Cubes

Ingredients
6 oz fresh buffalo mozzarella cut in small cubes
¼ cup of water from the mozzarella
½ tbsp of granular gelatin unflavored
½ tbsp of extra virgin olive oil
Pinch of salt
Pinch of ground white pepper

Directions
Bloom the gelatin in 1½ oz of cold water and set aside.
In a small pan gently warm the preserving mozzarella water, but make sure not to overheat it, remove from the stove and whisk in the gelatin until dissolved.
Set aside till room temperature.
In a high-speed blender mix the mozzarella cubes, the extra virgin olive oil, the white pepper and the salt till liquid.
Filter the mozzarella water and the gelatin mix and combine it in the blender with the other liquid mix.
Blend till smooth and very fine, taste for salt and pepper and pour the mix in the cubed silicone mold compartments.
Cover with either parchment paper or plastic wrap and freeze until solid.
Shell the cubes out and place them on a plate on top of deli paper.

Cover again with plastic wrap, transfer to the refrigerator for a few hours until completely defrosted.

Balsamic Vinegar Gelatin

Ingredients
4 oz vegetable broth
12 oz balsamic vinegar
1 tbsp unflavored granular gelatin
Pinch of salt
Pinch of ground white pepper
1 tbsp of honey
¼ sprig of fresh rosemary
2 leaves of fresh sage
½ tbsp of olive oil
1 garlic clove mashed by hand

Directions
Bloom the gelatin with 3 oz of cold water and set aside.
In a small pan golden the garlic with the oil, the rosemary and the sage.
Add the honey and caramelize for a minute or so.
Pour in the balsamic vinegar first and 15 seconds later the vegetable stock, the salt and the pepper.
Reduce it down to approximately ¾ of its original quantity at moderate fire.
Remove from the stove and set aside about 15 minutes.
Now whisk in the bloomed gelatin and filter through the fine mesh.
Cool the mix in an ice bath, stirring constantly.
Transfer it to a low square container with high borders (a plate would do) and refrigerate for at least one day covered with plastic film.

Additional Ingredients
Small cherry tomatoes of at least 5 different colors all in the same size
A few large fried crunchy basil leaves
A few drops of extra virgin olive oil
Crystallized salt
A few fresh oregano micro green leaves
Cracked black peppercorns

To Serve

Make sure all the ingredients are at room temperature before starting the plating process with the exception of the balsamic gelatin.

Use either a round or a square plate.

Dry the mozzarella cube of excess water and place it off-center on the plate.

With a very sharp knife cut a thin strip of balsamic gelatin 3½ inches long by ½ inch wide and place it right on the side of the cheese cube.

Slice all 5 tomatoes in half and use only one quarter of each and a different color to plate the dish.

Place each quarter right on top of the gelatin strip covering the entire surface lengthwise.

Dress them with a sprinkle of crystallized salt, extra virgin olive oil and decorate each tomato with a small fresh oregano micro leaf.

Drizzle a little oil on top of the cube along with crystallized salt and crushed black peppercorns.

Stick a couple of leaves of fried basil on top of the mozzarella creating elevation and serve within 3 minutes.

Poached Goose Liver Fantasy

I personally love this dish for its presentation and for the way it eats. It has very little logic as at first glance it displays different, colorful ingredients on a solid red wine caramel strip, nothing out of the ordinary. But then if we take a closer look we discover an incredible array of different textures, food temperatures and flavors that if consumed individually would make this dish extremely boring. The revelation is in the taste once each component is combined like an explosive wakeup call creating one of the most complete and flavorful experiences ever. The first bite is a shocker!

From the second one on, it is a circus act and that is when the show really begins. The goose liver is served at room temperature, the balsamic gelato sits on top of the hazelnut texture and the crunchiness of the Florentine creates a great sweet-salty contrast. The caramel ties all the ingredients together and finally the warm crispy brioche offsets the cold temperature of the gelato. It is shockingly tasty and extremely delicate with different flavors popping up in your mouth, forcing you to the next bite and creating deep sadness once it is all gone.

The Cremona Mostarda adds an interesting flavor to the goose liver, providing a tingling sense of satisfaction. The mostarda is nothing but whole pieces of fruits cooked in syrup for hours and once tender and caramelized, a strong essence of mustard is added to the mix. Originally from the town of Cremona, it is very common in Italy and it is often used to accompany boiled meats or used at times in pastry recipes. This is definitely a different way to enjoy goose liver as the saltiness and the sweetness of its ingredients create an incredible sensation in your palate.

Buckle up!

Poached Cremona's Mostarda Goose Liver

Ingredients

1 medium-size goose liver B grade (approx. 1 lb)
½ gallon milk
½ cup granulated sugar
2 shallots chopped
1 small sprig of thyme
1 small sprig of rosemary
4 leaves of sage
Pinch of salt
5 oz mostarda di Cremona fruits dried from their preserving syrup and sliced thin
A few assorted micro green leaves to decorate the dish
Pinch of crystallized salt

Directions

Split the liver apart with both hands and remove all veins with a small knife.
Whip the sugar and salt in the milk and transfer to a small compact container along with the goose liver, shallots and the herbs.
Marinate in the refrigerator for 24 hours or at least overnight.
Remove the marinated liver from the liquid, wait till it reaches room temperature and soft enough to be molded.
On a working table unwrap a few layers of cheese cloth and, by applying pressure, roll the liver and the slices of the mostarda di

Cremona together in the cloth forming a roll of about 2-3 inches in diameter.
Make sure it is very tight and compact and the mostarda is spread evenly.
Tie both ends of the roll with a string while twisting hard and firmly.
Gently tie the center of the roll hard enough to keep its original shape and to create support while cooking.
Transfer the roll to the gently simmering Prosecco and Port wine stock.
Immerge the roll completely and cook no longer then 90 seconds.
Remove the roll and set aside to cool.
Transfer the roll to a refrigerator turning it over every 5 minutes, discarding the excess liquid.
When slightly cold but still soft enough to be shaped unwrap it from the cloth and delicately transfer it to plastic wrap.
With both hands hold the two ends and roll the liver back and forth, shaping the roll into a tight smaller log.
Refrigerate for at least 8 hours before serving.

Prosecco/Port Wine Stock

See the Salty Goose Liver Spoons recipe in the Appetite Openers chapter.

Cabernet Red Wine Caramel and Cabernet Reduction

See the White Corn and Reggiano Custard recipe in the Appetite Openers (Page 44). Substitute the merlot wine with a good, robust cabernet and follow the recipe precisely.

Salty Hazelnut Florentines

Ingredients

3.5 oz butter
5 oz sugar
1½ oz glucose/honey
1½ oz heavy cream
7 oz toasted and ground hazelnuts
1 oz AP flour sifted
Zest of ¼ of a lemon
1 big pinch of salt

Directions

In a small pot combine the butter, the sugar, the glucose, the cream, the salt and the lemon zest.

Bring the mix to a boil at moderate fire, stirring occasionally.

Remove from the stove and quickly whisk in the sifted flour and the ground hazelnuts, mixing well and uniformly, making sure not to form any lumps.

Transfer the mix into a different container and set aside till room temperature.

Refrigerate for at least 3 hours.

Place a silicone baking mat on a sheet pan and set the oven at 325 degrees.

Roll a few small balls the size of cherry tomatoes and place them on the mat spaced about 3 inches apart.

Press the top of each ball down with the palm of your hand, flatting them a little in order to better facilitate and speed up the cooking process.

Bake about 6-8 minutes until golden.

Remove from oven and cool.

Remove the Florentines with the help of an offset spatula and delicately store in airtight container over deli paper.

Toasted Hazelnut Texture

Ingredients

2 cups of non-toasted hazelnuts

3 rounded tbsp of sugar

4 pinches of salt

2½ tbsp of Frangelico Liqueur

Directions

Set the oven at 200 degrees.

In a mixing bowl combine all the ingredients and quickly transfer to a small sheet pan over a silicone baking mat.

Spread the hazelnuts evenly covering the whole surface.

Bake for approximately one hour till very dry and toasted.

Remove from the oven and cool to room temperature.

Place the hazelnuts in a food processor and reduce to a granular texture.

Adjust for salt and sugar.

Store in an airtight container.

Brioche

Ingredients
10 oz AP flour sifted
4½ oz soft butter
2 eggs
3½ tbsp warm milk
3 tbsp sugar
2½ grams fresh yeast
Pinch of salt

Directions
In a small glass dissolve the fresh yeast into the warm milk with your fingers and set aside a minute.
Combine all the ingredients, including the yeast/milk mix in a mixing bowl with the paddle attachment, and mix gently at low/moderate speed about 15 minutes till it forms an elastic, smooth paste.
Place parchment paper into a buttered metallic brioche mold in order to cover its entire surface and host the brioche mix.
Once the dough is in place move the mold in a warm area and let it rise for at least a couple of hours or until it doubles in size.
Bake in hot oven at 480 degrees for the first 12 minutes, then lower the oven temperature and continue baking about 20 minutes at 400 degrees.

Balsamic Vinegar Gelato

Ingredients
½ qt milk
½ qt heavy cream
½ lb granulated sugar
10 egg yolks
1 cup balsamic vinegar reduction

Directions
In a small bowl mix the sugar and eggs till foamy.
Boil the milk and heavy cream and set aside about 10 minutes, then stir in the balsamic vinegar reduction.
Combine the whipped eggs and sugar with the milk and balsamic while still warm.

Strain through a fine mesh and cool completely before freezing in the gelato maker.

Balsamic Vinegar Reduction
Makes 2 cups

Ingredients
1.2 liters balsamic vinegar
½ cup honey
½ vanilla bean

Directions
Combine all ingredients in a medium-size pot and reduce by half at low/moderate fire.
Filter the mix and store in refrigerator once cool.

To Serve
I like to use a long white cheese-style plate for this preparation so that each ingredient can be properly lined up in different areas. Visualize the plate divided in 3 symmetric sections as each of them will host (on left, center and right) different food groups and ingredients.
Squeeze a solid string of cabernet wine caramel in the middle of the plate from one end all the way to the other dividing the plate in half, and then place it in front of you horizontally. We will build our dish from left to right placing each ingredient right on top of the caramel sauce in order to create a linear and elegant presentation while the sauce will hold the ingredients in place.
Cut a half-inch-thick slice of poached goose liver with a wide blade knife and place it flat on the very far left of the dish.
Cut a slice of the brioche of about 3 inches by 1½, warm it up in the oven till crispy, and place it right in the middle of the plate. On the far right we will group a tablespoon of the toasted hazelnut texture and we will place a small ball of the balsamic gelato right on top of it.
Stick one of the hazelnut Florentines into the gelato, creating the illusion of a half moon shape.
Quickly decorate the dish with a few micro green leaves and a gentle sprinkle of crystallized salt on the goose liver.
Serve immediately.

Tomato and Eggplant Popsicles with Basil Gelatin

Tomato. This is one of the most common and satisfying ingredients in existence. For us Italians, tomatoes are synonymous with pride, joy and something we just cannot do without in our daily diet. This recipe reflects simplicity with a twist or, as someone once said, "An intricate way to best enjoy the taste of a simple fruit from the garden."

I love to make this dish in the summertime as tomatoes are widely available and at their best in flavor. Select only vine ripe, a little softer than the ones we would normally use for a salad and preferably organic. What makes this dish glorious is the combination of its three basic ingredients: ripe tomatoes, high quality extra virgin olive oil and crystallized salt. Use a medium-size metallic mold to build the terrine, preferably deep and rectangular to better create the shape of a Popsicle once it is molded. The seared eggplant slices add wonderful flavor, but I use them predominately to wrap and to hold the terrine in place. I use the goat cheese in very small quantities to connect all the tastes together.

In order to assure firmness during the plating process I use no salt to marinate the tomatoes to prevent excessive water release and to make sure each cut slice stays intact for easy handling. The wooden sticks are easily available online and inexpensive. They are easy to handle and they create a realistic illusion for our purpose. Once at room temperature we dress our Popsicle with olive oil and salt only. The balsamic glaze plays a small role in this dish and it is used mostly for decorative purpose. The basil gelatin instead primes the palate to receive the taste of the tomatoes. In fact I suggest consuming the whole gelatin cube first. Once your mouth is bursting with basil flavor, enjoy your terrine: the taste lingers in your mouth and marries with the tomatoes in a very delicate way bite after bite.

Ingredients

Approximately 7 lbs medium-size vine ripe tomatoes
3 pinches of dry oregano
3 pinches of cracked black peppercorns
¾ lb fresh goat cheese

3-4 medium-size eggplants
3 tbsp of extra virgin olive oil to marinate the tomatoes
3-4 tbsp of olive oil to sear the eggplants
Salt for the eggplants
1 tsp of minced garlic
A few micro leaves of fresh basil for decoration
A few flat wooden Popsicle sticks about 4 inches long
Some balsamic vinegar glaze stored in a plastic squeeze bottle
(See Page 102 for recipe from Cold Stone Veal Carpaccio)
Crystallized salt to finish

Directions
Blanch the tomatoes in hot boiling water a few seconds, and with the help of a small knife peel the skin.
Cut the tomatoes in half and remove the seeds and the core with your fingers.
Squeeze by hand, removing the excess water, and sit them face down on a perforated pan over a towel.
Place a new pan of the same size on top of the tomatoes and press them overnight until most of the liquid is gone.
Peel the eggplant and with the help of a slicer machine create large, very thin slices.
Sear them in a hot pan with the olive oil until translucent on both sides, but not colored.
Add salt and pepper and place them on a tray apart from one another over absorbent deli paper.
Refrigerate overnight covered with plastic wrap.
In a small bowl mix the goat cheese with ½ tablespoon of the extra virgin olive oil until smooth solid paste and form a few small balls half inch in diameter by rolling them under the palms of your hands.
Place in the refrigerator overnight as well.
The next day fold the inside of a metallic terrine mold with plastic wrap, making sure it sticks well on the sides and bottom, and leave an excess of at least 3 inches of it hanging over its sides for later wrapping.
Place each slice of the cooked eggplants inside the mold covering the entire inside surface, overlapping each slice by at least half inch in order to ensure a durable and firm protecting wrap for the tomatoes.

Make sure to have at least two inches of excess eggplant hanging over each side of the mold as we will have to fold it over when we finish creating the base of our terrine by sealing it.
Remove the tomatoes from the refrigerator and squeeze each one of them by hand to rid of the excess water.
Transfer them to a medium-size bowl and dress them with the remaining extra virgin olive oil, the oregano, black pepper and the minced garlic.
It is now time to stuff our terrine.
Place the first layer of marinated tomato halves covering the entire bottom.
Press them down with your hands and place a few goat cheese balls on top of them in no particular order or distance.
Repeat these steps until the mold reaches its capacity and gently fold the excess hanging eggplants on top of the tomatoes sealing the terrine.
Wrap the excess plastic following the same steps as above, press down again and transfer to the refrigerator with a weight on top of it, applying pressure overnight and giving the tomatoes the time to settle and take form.
The terrine should sit for at least 24 hours before attempting to remove from the mold and serve.

Basil Gelatin

Ingredients
2 oz basil leaves
24 oz vegetable broth
1½ tbsp unflavored granular gelatin
1 pinch of salt

Directions
Bloom the gelatin with one ounce of cold water and set aside.
Bring the vegetable stock to a boil, add the basil leaves, salt, and remove from the fire.
Sit for a minute or two until the basil leaves turn into bright green color, then quickly blend at high speed till completely liquid and foamy.
Pass the mix through a fine mesh and set aside.
Add the gelatin to the warm basil liquid and mix with a spoon until dissolved.

Pass the liquid again through a fine mesh and transfer to a small wide container or a square deep plate, cover with plastic wrap, and place in the refrigerator about 5 to 6 hours.

To Serve

Remove the terrine from the refrigerator and flip the mold upside down on a cutting board.
Slowly unwrap only the desired amount needed and remove the excess water collected overnight.
With a large blade knife, discard the first end piece of the terrine.
Now firmly cut a slice no wider than one inch and set aside.
Make sure the outside eggplant wrap stays in place and that it holds the tomato stuffing tight.
It is important to cut the slice when the terrine is very cold and firm, but it should always be served at room temperature to better enjoy the delicate taste of the tomatoes.
Move the terrine to a serving plate and lay it flat on one side.
With absorbing paper remove any excess water.
Make an incision with a small, sharp knife all the way through one of the end sides and place the wooden stick in it creating the illusion of a Popsicle.
Once at desired temperature, pour some extra virgin olive oil on it, a generous amount of crystallized salt, and decorate with a small sprig of micro basil.
Cut a cube of basil gelatin one-half inch and gently place it on one side of the plate.
To finish, for both taste and color, serve the Popsicle within a circle of balsamic vinegar glaze squeezed out of a plastic bottle and finish by decorating the dish with a few of the micro basil leaves right on top of it in circular pattern.

Hot Starters

To me, hot appetizers can be compared to a road trip. You are driving and suddenly get lost. You have no idea where you are going, you have no GPS or maps, and you need to pull over and to ask for directions. I got lost many times ordering from menus where choices are scarce in main dishes, but abundant in starters. That leaves me disoriented, undecided and confused. I need an exciting prelude to pave the way to my main dish. I need directions.

Starters open my appetite and often help me make the right decision when selecting a main dish. Even though there are no culinary rules or set guidelines, there is a realistic connection between starters and main dishes I wish more people would explore. I enjoy starting my meals with at least one or two appetizers, and then I feel ready to enter my culinary trip and indulge all the way to dessert.

I love to sample different varieties and I prefer hot starters to cold ones even in summer time. Whenever I get stuck in main dish decisions I often order an extra appetizer and suddenly it all makes sense. Hot starters are nothing more than miniature main dishes, samples of colorful combinations of ingredients, tastes and concepts, and at times they are personal visions of abstract canvas on a plate. How many times have we found ourselves reading a menu and saying, "Sure, I'll share that with you" or "I was just looking at that. Interesting. I think I'll try it." Having an appetizer does not mean cheating on your main course, but indulging in the proper way to start a meal by helping to fully receive and appreciate your main dish. Think of it as an assigned escort who accompanies you from your limo to a red carpet social event. Now you are ready to start your journey with class.

My vision of hot starters combines textures, ingredients and flavors under one big umbrella of tasteful concepts. It is not that difficult to create a wow factor even when the expectations are high. It is very important to carefully choose the proper vehicle to deliver the food we are serving with elegance and inventiveness along with its taste. Mostly, it has to be practical for its consumption. Imagine lobster bisque served in a soup bowl: ordinary. Now imagine the same lobster bisque served in a cappuccino cup with a spoonful of milk froth while creating the illusion a cappuccino is being served. Add a few lobster croquettes in it for a crunchy surprise and suddenly the same ordinary bisque has become new, classy and innovative.

Since the possibilities for hot starters are infinite, for this book I chose only a few different ones by ingredients and execution. Mostly I wanted to make sure everyone could recreate these even at home while presenting them differently and still following its precise concept. Most of these recipes were created and customized while taking advantage of seasonal products such as fresh peas, porcini mushrooms or truffles; others while following a curious and imaginative drive taking advantage of a personal momentum and vision. In some recipes ingredients can be substituted with similar ones if out of season or if difficult to find: mushroom for mushroom, red wine for red wine or even cheese for cheese. Whatever the substitution may be, the goal is to keep the taste and flavors of the dish the way it was intended to be consumed and as original as possible. This is why I suggest trying the recipe first before applying any desired changes and do not forget to always serve hot appetizers on warm or hot plates in order to keep consistent hot temperatures until the last bite is consumed.

I hope you enjoy these as much as I do.

Green Peas Cappuccino and Goose Liver Custard

This is a very creative and wonderful springtime preparation that combines vivid colors and an incredible marriage in flavors and textures. If you like goose liver and if you like peas, this is a dish that will satisfy and impress in every possible way. It is very simple in its preparation and it is very easy to make at home. The goose liver custard is baked in the cappuccino cups at a very low temperature and cooked like brûlée to create flavor and a crunchy separating layer from the pea soup. The crunchy leeks add crispiness and texture to the dish while the porcini powder and the foam complete the illusion of a real coffee treat.

In Italy a cappuccino is often consumed with a side pastry such as cookies, fruit tortes or even sweet strudels. It only made sense to me to complete it with a salty version of a strudel filled with ricotta and fontina cheese and fresh porcini mushrooms. I like to see how my guests handle the whole concept of it almost as if they were savoring a real cappuccino. Some dip the strudel into the cup, absorbing the pea liquid. Some alternate a bite and a spoon of the custard. Others stare at it a few minutes, then crack a smile in admiration and with a convinced look they arm themselves with the spoon and start their culinary journey.

Green Peas Cappuccino

Ingredients

1¼ lbs cleaned fresh peas
3 heads of finely sliced shallots
4 leaves of chopped fresh sage
2 sliced garlic cloves
2 oz pancetta cut in two pieces
3 oz butter
½ cup heavy cream
8 basil leaves
½ tbsp of natural white truffle oil
Ground white pepper
Salt
1½ cups of chicken stock

Directions

In a medium-size pan combine the sliced garlic, the sliced shallots, the chopped sage and the chunks of pancetta with the butter at medium fire until translucent.
Add the fresh peas and cook for 5 minutes, adding the salt and the pepper.
Add the chicken stock and cook about 8-10 minutes at moderate heat.
Now add the cream and cook an additional 5-7 minutes.
Remove from the stove; add the basil leaves and the white truffle oil.
Discard the pancetta from the pan and run the mix in a high-speed blender until very fine and velvety.
Adjust for salt and pepper.

Goose Liver Custard

Ingredients

½ lb goose liver B grade de-veined, cleaned and cut in small cubes
½ qt heavy cream
4 eggs
Ground white pepper
Pinch of salt

Directions

In a high-speed blender combine all the ingredients together and blend until perfectly smooth.

In a hotel pan, lay out the cappuccino cups over a layer of parchment paper in order to create stability, and pour the mix in each one only to half of its capacity.

Fill the pan with warm water around the cups and all the way up to ¾ of their height while being very careful not to spill any water into them. If that accidentally happens, you must discard.

Cover the hotel pan with 3 or 4 layers of plastic wrap perfectly sealed.

Place the pan in a hot oven and bake about 20-25 minutes at 265 degrees.

When ready remove the cappuccino cups from the pan and water and set aside to cool.

Porcini and Fontina Strudel

Ingredients

2 oz Aosta fontina cheese cut in very small cubes
7 oz ricotta cheese
6 oz sautéed fresh sliced porcini mushrooms
1 egg
3 tbsp grated Parmesan Reggiano cheese
Pinch ground nutmeg
Pinch salt
Pinch white ground pepper
1 egg and a splash of water for wash
A few sheets of frozen phyllo dough
1 tbsp of extra virgin olive oil
1 tbsp of fresh chopped basil
½ tsp of minced garlic

Directions

In a small pan sauté the fresh porcini mushrooms with the extra virgin olive oil, the garlic and the fresh basil, salt and pepper until crispy.

Set aside till cool.

In a small bowl mix the ricotta cheese with the parmesan, the egg and the cubed fontina.

Add the sauté porcini, salt, pepper, nutmeg and with a rubber spatula fold well before placing the mix in a pastry bag.
Lay 3 sheets of phyllo dough on your working table, one on top of the other, cut an opening in the pastry bag of about ¾ inch wide and from left to right in one motion squeeze out the mix, forming a long round tick string on top of the sheets.
Roll into a medium-size, long cigar shape, sealing the ends with a light brush of egg wash.
Wrap the roll tightly with aluminum foil and deep fry it for 6 minutes at 375. You could also bake the rolls in the oven at 400 degrees without the aluminum about 5 minutes, but be careful as the dough tends to crack and flake.
Remove from the stove or oven and set aside.
Before serving, place the roll in the oven for a minute till crispy, and then slice it diagonally with a bread knife, creating a small roll of 1½ inch in length.

Crunchy Leeks

Ingredients
2 medium-size fresh leeks
¼ cup of corn starch
2 cups of blended oil to fry
Salt
White pepper

Directions
With a sharp knife discard the top (green part) and select the white part only for this preparation.
Cut the leeks lengthwise in very thin julienne style and wash under cold water to remove the dirt and all impurities.
Once clean dry on a towel and place them in a small bowl with the corn starch, mix well.
In a strainer shake off the excess starch as our goal is to have only a very light coat to preserve the taste and create crunchiness during the cooking procedure.
In a pan bring the oil to 350 degrees and add a small handful at a time, frying to a crispy consistency while preserving their natural green color.
Place them on deli paper and sprinkle with salt and white pepper.
Keep in warm place or, once cool, in an airtight container.

Froth and Decorations
A sprinkle of granulated sugar
A sprinkle of dry porcini mushrooms powder
A few sprigs of fresh pea shoot micro tendrils
Chilled milk for the froth

To Serve
Place the saucer and the hot cappuccino cup on the desired serving plate.
Sprinkle a little sugar on the goose liver custard as you would for a crème brûlée and with the help of a pastry torch caramelize the top till crispy.
Allow a few minutes for the sugar to cool, creating a hard coating, and with a carafe gently pour in the hot pea soup leaving a half-inch space from the top of the cup.
With a cappuccino machine steam the chilled milk into firm froth and top each cup with a generous spoonful on one side only.
Quickly sprinkle it with the porcini powder giving the illusion of cinnamon or chocolate dust while on the other side of the cup gently place a few crunchy leeks.
Place the warm strudel upright on the same serving plate as the cappuccino and decorate it with a few micro green pea tendrils, a drizzle of olive oil and a few cracked black peppercorns.

Winter Poached Duck Egg and Crunchy Stuffed Sage Leaves

This is typical comfort food, or at least for me, as fall and winter are my favorite seasons. Growing up in a northern town like Torino I was able to appreciate the best of what Piedmontese cuisine had to offer in the colder months. I remember venturing with my friend Giorgio into the woods of the nearby hills after a lengthy bike ride looking for mushrooms in a London like foggy day. We were both teenagers and full of energy. The ducks were singing their way around us and the noise of silence from the sky would often make us look up for the first snowflake to drop. After a couple of hours of fun we would return home with a bag full of mushrooms, and I would cook them for us both under my mother's vigilant eye, having the time of our life. It is virtually impossible to recreate the same happy memory so I decided to reinvent a modern version of the food that surrounded our happy times instead.

I like the balance of the poached egg with the crispy texture of the mushrooms. The Port wine reduction is a wonderful bridge for flavors and combines very well with the sharp taste of the cheese in the crunchy sage leaves. The incredible aroma of this very humble but luxurious dish comes from the earthy black truffle slices that somehow combine each and every single ingredient into one glorious Piedmontese gourmet journey.

I prefer using duck eggs instead of chickens as they are denser in the yolk and have a deeper and intense velvety taste. The most difficult part is to poach them correctly. If you have never done this before, prepare yourself for some disappointments as it takes a little practice and a few eggs to understand the dynamic of it. Once you master the egg poaching procedure, you will realize this is a very simple dish to prepare as all the other steps are very basic. Once you cut into the egg, its yolk will run across the plate, transporting flavor and substance. Do not be shy about helping yourself do what in Italy we call scarpetta: scraping the plate clean of the leftover sauce or juice using a piece of bread as the vehicle to transport it to your mouth.

Now that is comfort!

Ingredients

1 large duck egg
½ tbsp of finely chopped chives
1 small hat of Hen of the Woods mushroom
A few shaves of dense winter black truffle
2 tbsp of fresh pancetta cut in small cubes
Salt
Ground white pepper
1 tsp of natural black truffle oil
Assorted fresh micro greens to decorate
2 tbsp of Port wine reduction sauce
Crystallized salt

Directions

Sauté the pancetta cubes in a small pan till very crispy, discard liquid and set the cubes aside on deli paper in warm place.
Discard the mushroom stem, and clean from impurities with a damp towel.

Dip it in the tempura batter and deep fry a few minutes till crispy, salt and pepper it and set aside, keeping warm.
Bring the poaching water to temperature; gently crack in the duck egg on one side of the pan and rapidly, with the help of a couple of spoons, hold the egg together till the hot water cooks the first external coat protecting its liquid center.
Let it simmer about two minutes, with a perforated spoon remove from water and set on a clean cutting board.
With a small knife carefully cut all the strings and extra parts off the egg to restore its original oval shape.
Set aside on a plate covered with plastic wrap for a minute before serving.

Poaching White Vinegar Water

Ingredients
2 cups of water
2 tbsp of white wine vinegar
Pinch of salt

Directions
Place all the ingredients in a small pan and bring to boil for a couple of minutes.
Lower the fire and keep at a light gentle simmer for poaching.

Crunchy Stuffed Sage Leaves

Ingredients
6 large size sage leaves
2 tsp of soft Taleggio cheese
1 cup of blended oil for frying
½ tbsp of flour

Directions
Make sure all the sage leaves are approximately the same size.
Blanch them in hot salted water for a few seconds in order to get rid of the bitter taste until they turn to a bright green color.
Remove from water and lay them open on a plate to cool and dry.
Spread a generous quantity of soft Taleggio cheese on 3 leaves only.

Place the other leaves on top of them applying pressure and creating "sandwiches."
Press gently on the edge of the stuffed leaves trying to seal them as much as possible in order to avoid the cheese coming out during the cooking process.
Dust the leaves with flour and cook them quickly in the tempura batter.
Fry in hot oil till golden crispy on both sides.
Set aside on deli paper and sprinkle them with a little salt.

Tempura Batter
See the Fava Beans Stuffed Tempura Zucchini Blossoms recipe in the Appetite Openers (Page 52).

Port Wine Reduction Sauce

Ingredients
½ liter of Port wine
½ small diced carrot
½ stalk of diced celery
½ small diced onion
2 pieces of dry porcini mushrooms
1 tsp whole black peppercorns
½ sprig of rosemary
½ sprig of sage
½ sprig of thyme
1 small diced shallot
1 bay leaf
¼ liter of veal stock reduction

Directions
Place all ingredients in a small pot and reduce the Port by half.
Add in the veal juice, bring to boil and reduce by half again.
Filter and keep refrigerated.

To Serve
I like to serve this dish in a curved bowl or deep plate so the sauce stays in place while hosting the other ingredients to show off their textures and colors.
Place a couple of spoons of the hot Port wine reduction right in the center.

Place the cooked chanterelle mushrooms in the middle on top of the sauce and facing up.
Carefully set the poached egg on it firmly, making sure it does not wobble or move.
Season the egg with a few drops of black truffle oil and the chives, salt, the crispy pancetta cubes, a pinch of crystallized salt and a good shave of fresh black truffles.
Serve immediately after decorating the dish with a few micro greens and the still crunchy stuffed sage leaves.

Aromatic Shellfish Broth in an Eggshell

Sometimes if you want to get noticed you need to scream out loud. That certainly applies to this dish. I find it to be a real challenge to make a tasty fish soup any day of the week, even a bigger task to make a shellfish one. However, a quick shellfish broth with a great taste and elegant presentation can be a real head scratcher. There are so many good fish soup recipes out there. Some are more elaborate and suited for traditional Sunday meals involving 20 different kinds of fish, and others are much simpler for a quick last-minute supper.

The outcome of a fish soup is based on two basic elements: the knowledge of combining different types of fish that marry well together, creating one great final taste, and the ability to properly time each piece's cooking temperature. What we have here is not your typical fish soup, but an intelligent way to combine tasty shellfish in a broth as an appetizer. I like this dish because each piece is cooked at the right temperature and because it is very tasty and presented in an impressive way.

Why a duck egg? Well, first of all what is a shellfish broth doing in an eggshell to begin with? It does not belong there. The shell holds the temperature well, it creates interest and shock value, and the shrimp looks like it is trying to escape from the egg. Some have compared it to an alien peaking out its spaceship. There is no logical reason why I use an eggshell for this appetizer except I really like it. I prefer the duck egg because it is a little bigger than the chicken and I can fit in all the ingredients more comfortably.

Since this is a quick soup I decided to include ready-made fixings at the time of serving, such as the basil gelatin cube and the chopped chives, crystallized salt and the cracked black peppercorns. They all add great aroma and flavor once combined. To complete the dish for both tradition and taste I squeeze in the last-minute extra virgin olive oil with the help of a disposable plastic pipette. Do not think of this as a food toy, but as a very delicate and tasty appetizer, easy to make and with a bang of presentation, just like a loud scream.

Ingredients
1 very large duck egg
1 head of fresh jumbo shrimp
1 medium-size sea scallop cut in 4 pieces
3 small calamari rings
2 little neck clams
1 small mussel
1 small shucked oyster
The tip of a tsp of minced garlic
Small pinch of dry oregano
Small pinch of hot crushed red pepper
¾ cup of lobster stock
½ tbsp extra virgin olive oil
1 tbsp of finely chopped canned San Marzano tomatoes
Salt
Ground white pepper

Directions
Place the egg in its carton to create stability and with the help of an egg cutter snip the top to create an opening of a little over one-inch diameter.
Empty the shell and carefully wash it under cold water to properly clean the inside, removing its film and all impurities.
Place the eggshell back in its carton upside down and let it dry.
Peel the shrimp off its shells, leaving the head and the tail attached, and set aside.
In a small sauté pan color the garlic with the extra virgin olive oil, the clams, the mussel and the calamari rings for less than a minute.
Add the oregano and the hot pepper and simmer only a few seconds before stirring in the freshly chopped tomato.
Add the lobster stock, salt and the white pepper and simmer at low fire covered with a lid for a couple of minutes until the mussel and the clams open their shells.
Now add the shrimp and remove the clams and mussel from the pan and set aside on a plate covered with plastic wrap.
Add the scallops and the oyster and cook less than a minute.
Remove the oyster, the scallop pieces, the calamari rings and set aside in the same plate with the clams and mussel. Keep covered.
Taste the broth and correct with salt and pepper if necessary.
Remove the shrimp as well and set aside with the other shellfish, keeping the plate covered with plastic.

With the help of a fork, crush down the bigger pieces of tomatoes in the broth and mix well.

Basil Gelatin
See the Tomato and Eggplant Popsicles recipe in the Cold Starters chapter (*Page 117*).

Serving Tools and Ingredients
Ceramic egg holder
1 plastic pipette filled with excellent quality extra virgin olive oil
Assorted long stem micro greens for decorations
½ tsp of finely chopped chives
A small cube of basil gelatin of about ½ inch
1 serving tsp to host the basil gelatin cube and the chopped chives
Crystallized salt
Crushed black peppercorns

To Serve
Fill the plastic pipette with the extra virgin olive oil and set aside.
Place the eggshell upright on the ceramic egg holder.
With the help of fine, long cooking tweezers remove the clams and the mussel from their shells and place them inside the egg.
Transfer in the scallop pieces, the calamari rings and the oyster as well.
Leave the shrimp wrapped under plastic on the plate in a warm place.
With the help of a sauce gun or a small carafe, pour some of the hot broth inside the eggshell on top of the shellfish, making sure the liquid does not spill over the outside part of the egg, staining the white shell.
Leave about ½ inch from the top for the shrimp and the other ingredients.
Carefully insert the shrimp inside the shell among the other shellfish pieces, making sure it sits straight with its whole head coming out of the egg.
Quickly insert the long stem micro greens inside the shell next to the shrimp, creating elevation.
Transfer the egg set to a serving plate and serve along with the olive oil pipette and a teaspoon with the chives, the basil gelatin cube and a pinch of crystallized salt and a pinch of cracked black peppercorn resting on top of the basil cube.

Stir the teaspoon in the egg and complete by squeezing in the pipette with the extra virgin olive oil, creating instant aroma and delicate, sharp taste.

Warm Wild Venison Carpaccio

Many people often ask me why I consider this appetizer a hot dish instead of a cold one. I like to think because the venison fillet has been seared, the chanterelles mushrooms are served hot and the venison slices are served at room temperature, this dish should be categorized as a hot one. Better yet, a warm appetizer. The combination of the venison slices and the hot mushrooms, along with the other ingredients deliver a warm and satisfying sensation to the palate. It is warm, gamy, pungent yet round and delicate in its aftertaste. The combination of the porcini powder, the presence of the chocolate and the sherry vinegar give the meat a unique and satisfying balance. The halved blueberries, the Parmesan shaves and the black truffles are all fundamental ingredients for an explosion of flavor without altering the original taste of the venison.

But what really makes this dish extraordinary and different are the hot slices of the crispy mushrooms that melt in your mouth once combined with the rest of the dish. It is a wonderful way to start your meal on a cold day. To serve I like to use a long rectangular plate, but a classic round one will do as long as all the ingredients are placed on the Carpaccio symmetrically and apart from one another, creating a delicate visual balance in presentation. I love to finish this dish with a few leaves of Ruby Queen micro greens as they marry the taste of the venison, the chocolate and the porcini powder. If you are unable to find Ruby Queen, I suggest using a few pea tendrils in substitution for taste and color.

Ingredients
1 small, cleaned, peeled and very fresh wild venison tenderloin
4-5 large wild blueberries
A few shaves of 30-month-aged Parmesan Reggiano cheese
1 or 2 medium-size very firm chanterelles mushrooms
Pinch of salt
Pinch of crystallized salt
Pinch of cracked black peppercorns
Pinch of ground white pepper

1 tbsp dry porcini powder
½ tsp chocolate powder
1 each of small sprigs of rosemary sage and thyme
1 small garlic clove
1 small shallot head
1 tbsp of very fine sifted bread crumbs
1 egg for egg wash
1 tbsp of excellent sherry vinegar
A few winter black truffles shaves
1 tsp of natural black truffle oil
1 tsp of extra virgin olive oil
A few crumbs of shaved dark chocolate
A few leaves of Ruby Queen micro greens
1 tbsp extra virgin olive oil

Directions

On a small plate combine the porcini and the chocolate powder, mixing very well.

On a different plate prime the venison fillet with ¼ tablespoon of extra virgin olive oil and coat it completely with the mixed powder. Set aside.

In a small pan pour the remaining ¾ tablespoon of olive oil along with the mixed herbs, the shallot, and the garlic and bring the oil to hot temperature.

Remove the herbs from the pan before burning and quickly sear in the venison a few seconds, making sure it is perfectly crispy and seared uniformly.

Sprinkle a pinch of salt and ground white pepper and set aside to cool.

Once cool wrap the seared venison fillet in plastic film, twisting real tight on each end, and place in the freezer till completely solid.

Trim the chanterelles mushrooms, pass them in egg wash and bread crumbs and set aside.

Slice each blueberry in half coin-size, from a small block of dark chocolate shave a few layers, crumble them with a teaspoon and set out at room temperature.

Make sure to remove the venison from the freezer at least 10-15 minutes ahead of time in order to slice it easily when putting the dish together.

To Serve

Cut very thin slices of the venison with the help of a meat slicer overlap the slices to cover the entire surface of a rectangular plate.

Pour the sherry vinegar on the Carpaccio and spread it evenly with a spoon, drizzle on the black truffle oil and the extra virgin.

Sprinkle with crystallized salt and cracked black peppercorns.

Place each half of blueberries on the Carpaccio, spaced apart and face up, showing the inside green center.

Fry the breaded chanterelles till golden and crispy, slice them when still hot and place them on the Carpaccio in symmetry.

Quickly place the black truffle slices and the shaves of Parmesan with the help of cooking tweezers and dust with a little dark chocolate crumbs.

Finish decorating with a few leaves of Ruby Queen micro greens and serve while the mushrooms are still very hot.

Crunchy Monkfish Liver Custard with Lemon-Honey Preserve

I am aware this recipe may be a little unusual, but the plain truth about this dish is, well…it is so delicate and so very delicious. Personally, I am not a huge fan of monkfish and I am not a huge fan of liver either, but I realized that by stimulating my creativity in cooking I also stimulate and educate my palate each time I make something new and different. This custard is very light in taste, smell and texture. If you use the freshest liver available on the market I can guarantee you there is almost no way to detect what you are about to eat is made of fish products. Do not get tempted to use canned or frozen substitutes as it will jeopardize both texture and taste. Most of the time when I serve this dish at the restaurant I instruct the server not to describe it or to reveal its ingredients until after the first bite is taken. The only visible ingredients are the artichoke chips and the lemons. The rest is a mystery.

There is always a lot of skepticism whenever uncommon food is served such as innards or even wild game. Imagine going to dinner at a traditional Chinese restaurant that serves tendons, pig intestines or duck feet. Even though they are part of a long-respected culinary tradition and delicious in their own way, I bet they may not be a first choice for dinner by the average Western customer. Today, in popular tasting menu restaurants I can serve anything I want as long as I am happy with the final result, taste, concept and presentation.

A few years back I was in Sicily visiting my family at the beach house. Coincidentally, chef Roberto Donna was in Sicily at the same time vacationing in a nearby town. I invited him and his family over for lunch and later on we drove to a small village called Marzamemi near a town called Pachino, where the world-renowned ciliegino cherry tomatoes are produced and where my father lived most of his youth. Our goal was to visit a popular store called Campisi, specializing in typical Sicilian products as well as local tuna and tuna part products: from dry eggs bottarga to smoked tuna, from preserved tuna cheeks to tuna prosciutto called mosciame. At Campisi, chances are if you name it, they have it.

What a great afternoon we had: I felt like a kid in a toy store. Then I suddenly stopped in front of a basket displaying vacuum packed tuna products, off-white in color and plastic in appearance. We looked at each other smiling, and then I shouted, "This can't be! You've got to be kidding me!" The package read "dried and preserved tuna sperm." After verifying it as authentic along with its quality and origins with the store's owner, Paolo, we went to the cashier armed with a unique product and very dangerous minds. About a month later I asked Roberto if he ever used the tuna sperm we brought back from Italy. Laughing like a possessed child he told me he served it grilled and drizzled with lemon juice and olive oil to the then *Washington Post* food critic Phyllis Richman as one of her testing menu courses at his then-restaurant, Laboratorio. I still shake my head fifteen years later as I am writing this.

The custard's caramelized top gives a unique taste marrying the sour lemons and the sweet chestnut honey, while the artichoke chips add great contrast and create a diversion in texture. I love to use powders only in certain dishes where the flavor, as well as the color, can really be appreciated. In this case the parsley powder has a wonderful balance in the whole dish. It adds that surprise kick and makes the dish come alive because of its bright green color. You will be so surprised with the end results that you will find yourself serving it to your guests just to see if they can guess what they are eating…as a tease.

Monkfish Liver Custard

Ingredients

12 oz of very fresh monkfish liver cut in small pieces of about one inch
½ tbsp of small capers
2 fillets anchovies
½ big diced shallots
½ tbsp fresh chopped thyme
2 cloves of sliced garlic
Salt
Ground white pepper
2 tbsp of extra virgin olive oil
2 tbsp dry white wine
½ qt heavy cream
5 eggs
1 tbsp granulated sugar to caramelize at serving time

Directions

In a medium-size sauté pan sear the monkfish with the garlic and the shallot for a few minutes.

Sprinkle with salt and pepper.

Add the capers, the anchovies, and the fresh thyme at once and mix well for a couple more minutes.

Add the wine and reduce almost entirely, leaving just a little liquid in the pan.

Remove from the stove and with the help of a food processor reduce to a paste.

Transfer the mix to a high-speed blender, add the eggs and the heavy cream, and liquefy until almost foamy.

In a hotel pan line up small ramekins or small plastic cups over deli paper and fill them with the custard mix.

Cover the pan tightly with 3 layers of plastic film and bake in warm water bath at 230 degrees about 25 minutes.

Once ready remove the ramekins from the water and set aside to cool.

Sliced Lemons and Chestnut Honey Preserve

Ingredients

4 big hard lemons
5-6 tbsp hot chestnut honey
1 tbsp small capers
½ medium-size peeled garlic clove
½ medium-size peeled shallots
3 tsp of kosher salt
Pinch of ground white pepper
8 tbsp of sugar

Directions

The biggest task in this recipe is to eliminate the bitter taste of the lemon's white spongy part that can potentially ruin our work. I realize no matter how hard I try there is always going to be a little of it left in anything that involves fresh whole lemons. Since I could not solve the problem entirely, I decided to limit the damage by poaching the whole lemons in syrup first. This step eliminates the bitter taste of the lemons by almost 40 percent. An extra 30 percent is eliminated during the second blanching with the sliced lemons

and an additional 10 percent during the curing process. The remaining 20 percent is balanced with the sweetness of the honey.
In a small pot make syrup out of a combination of 9 cups of water, 6 spoons of sugar and a teaspoon of salt, boil down to ¾ and plunge in the whole lemons, boiling them about 7-8 minutes.
Slice the shallot and the garlic paper thin and set aside.
Quickly fry the capers, the shallot and the garlic slices till crispy and transfer them to deli paper to dry.
With the help of a slicer machine cut the four blanched lemons in paper-thin slices, discard the seeds and the end parts.
In the same small pot where we previously cooked the lemons, bring the syrup to a boil and blanch the lemon slices about 30 seconds.
Remove from the water and lay them on a tray.
Once at room temperature cure the slices with the remaining 2 tablespoons of sugar and the 2 teaspoons of salt.
Cover with plastic wrap and place in the refrigerator about 2 days.
Transfer the lemons in a small bowl with the cooked capers, garlic, shallot and the white pepper.
Pour in the hot chestnut honey and with a rubber spatula gently fold in till mixed.
Fill a small glass jar, top with the leftover honey, and seal the top.
Turn the jar upside-down till it cools to room temperature, and then place in the refrigerator for at least 6 days.

Artichoke Chips

Ingredients
Whole artichokes
Blended oil for frying
Salt
Ground white pepper
Lemon juice

Directions
Clean the artichokes entirely by removing all leaves and the inside at the core.
Brush them quickly with lemon juice in order to prevent oxidation and with the help of a slicer machine shave them paper-thin lengthwise, including the stem.
Pre-heat the oil at 375 degrees.

Dry the slices with a towel, removing all the excess water, and quickly fry them till crispy, preserving their natural color as much as possible.
Set the chips aside on deli paper to absorb the oil.
Sprinkle with salt and pepper and once at room temperature preserve in airtight container.

Garlic Chips

I love garlic as it is a basic element in Italian cooking and a much-needed natural ingredient for many regional style recipes. I would consider sinfully marvelous the wonderful aroma of the barely seared garlic with olive oil and rosemary and the delicate fumes that releases while opening everyone's appetite. I often sear them together in hot oil and purposely walk through the dining rooms of my restaurant while the pan is still sizzling, earning the undivided attention of my dining guests. Because of its pungent taste and smell, garlic should generally be used in small quantities and in a very conservative way.

One way to convert garlic into a more delicate and more useful component, especially for cold preparations, is by slicing it thin and frying it into crispy chips or shaves. This way it is much more appealing in taste and texture and can be used to decorate cold preparations without overpowering or changing the food's original taste. I love to shave it paper-thin and watch it crumble in weightless crisps once fried. It is indeed a very delicate alternative to sauté garlic. I often use them as a vehicle of flavor for hot preparations such as instant sauces or as flavor correction tools for soups and deconstructed dishes.

Directions
Slice the raw and peeled garlic cloves paper-thin using a very sharp small mandolin or a hand truffle shaver.
Bring the oil to temperature 350-375 and quickly fry the chips until golden.
Remove from the oil and rest on deli paper.
Sprinkle with a little salt and transfer to airtight container once cool.

Parsley Powder

Ingredients
½ lb fresh Italian parsley
Pinch of salt
Pinch of ground white pepper
1 garlic chip

Directions
Place the fresh parsley in the dehydrator till completely dry at low-medium setting (if you do not have one you can substitute it by using a microwave oven at low temperature, but be careful not to burn it).
Grind the dry parsley with the salt, the white pepper and the garlic chip, mix well and sift it through a fine mesh.
Keep it in a jar or into an airtight container.

To Serve
Remove the jar with sliced lemon preserve from the refrigerator and set it out at room temperature.
On a round or a square plate, place the hot custard off-center.
Dust the custard with a little sugar and with the help of a pastry torch caramelize the top.
Let the sugar harden and then top with a few artichoke chips, creating elevation.
On the side of the custard place a couple of slices of the preserved lemons and sprinkle with crystallized salt.
Decorate the plate with a few drops of extra virgin olive oil, the parsley powder and adorn the lemon slices with a few leaves of micro parsley.
Preferably serve the custard warm to hot, but never excessively hot.

Butter Roasted Baby Octopus in Spicy Orange Caramel

This is a classic example of how you can convert an existing recipe into your own. A couple of years back on one of my trips home I called an old friend and culinary schoolmate of mine, chef Alfredo Russo—Alfredino to his friends. I remember back in school he had a completely different vision of cooking from the rest of us. He excelled in the kitchen and he was always motivated to learn by working in nearby restaurants even just for a day or for the pleasure of it (without pay) simply to learn. Alfredo nowadays is the owner and chef of "Dolce Stil Novo," a wonderful restaurant on the outskirts of Torino in a small town called Venaria at La Reggia, and the proud recipient of one Michelin star from the prestigious guide. I loved one of the courses he cooked for me: seared octopus with raw polenta canned corn sauce and chopped Sicilian capers.

When I came back in the U.S., my wheels started spinning and I decided to adapt his idea and create a similar dish that would satisfy both my ego and my palate. It did not take long to create a similar raw polenta sauce and I opted to use baby octopus instead because of their tenderness. I felt the dish was missing important and creative elements; it was not complete. Or at least not to me. I made a caramel out of orange juice and spicy Sicilian hot pepperoncino. I fried the capers instead of chopping them, and because I thought the dish needed a little extra crunchiness I baked a few polenta crackers to marry the taste of the sauce.

I love the combination of poaching the baby octopus first and cooking them crispy in butter later as they retain a wonderful and delicate buttery flavor and the small tentacles turn real crunchy. The spicy caramel combines all the ingredients with fruity notes of orange, and the crispy capers and basil leaves add taste and colors to the dish. I thank Alfredo for the idea and I wish him continued success with his restaurant, his future projects and his career.

Ingredients
2 lbs fresh baby octopus
High fat butter
Salt
Ground white pepper
1 carrot
1 stalk of celery
½ white onion
3 halved lemons
2 bay leaves
½ cup of white vinegar
1 or 2 crispy fried basil leaves
½ tbsp of fried small Sicilian capers
1 wine bottle cork

Crystallized salt
Cracked black peppercorns
1 tsp of excellent quality extra virgin olive oil

Directions
Stick a few toothpicks into the onion to hold the leaves together during the poaching process.
In small pot combine salted water and the vinegar, the celery, the carrot, the halved lemons, the onion and the bay leaves.
Boil about five minutes, and then add the cork. (The cork is used as a spongy filter that softens the fibers of the octopus during the cooking process. Note to the skeptical: try to cook an octopus without a cork and then with it. As strange and weird as it might be, the octopus will be much more tender if cooked with the cork. I have no explanation of why that is, except it works.)
Now add the octopus in the water and boil for approximately one hour till completely cooked.
Remove them from the water and place them on a plate, cover with plastic wrap immediately while they are still hot and set aside.

Sweet Raw Polenta Sauce

Ingredients
7½ oz canned sweet cooked corn including its preserving water
1 spoon of extra virgin olive oil
Pinch salt
Pinch white pepper
¾ tbsp honey
½ spoon grated Parmesan Reggiano cheese
1 roasted garlic chip

Directions
Combine all ingredients in a high-speed blender about a minute until reduced to a very fine semi-liquid purée.
Taste and correct for salt and pepper if needed and filter the sauce through a fine mesh.

Spicy Orange Caramel

Ingredients

1 cup sugar
¾ cup freshly squeezed and filtered orange juice

Directions

In a small pot golden the sugar evenly.
Add the orange juice at once and cook at moderate flame about 10 minutes.
Once the sugar has melted completely remove from the fire and set aside a few minutes.
Filter the caramel through a fine mesh and set aside to cool.
Transfer the mix to a plastic squirting bottle and into the refrigerator.

Fried Basil Leaves

I love basil! People often say you are not a real Italian if you do not like basil. Well I am a real Italian all right as I love basil so much that if there was a basil-scented shampoo out there I would use it in the shower every morning. I cannot imagine cooking a tomato sauce without fresh basil or having a simple mozzarella and tomato dish without its accompanying flavor, or imagine a classic Neapolitan-style pizza just out of the wood-burning oven missing fresh hand-cut basil leaves. That could be compared to a national disaster, a state of emergency, a sin that would hardly be forgiven. However, in cooking all likes and dislikes must be respected.

In Italy there are so many different types of basil and many of them in different shapes and with different flavors thanks to the many different geological conditions of the turf it grows on. A perfect example is the basil from the Liguria region: a unique and unmistakable Riviera jewel that grows mostly in baby stages. Its leaves are very small and packed with an incredible aroma and taste, so strong the locals only use this particular Genovese type to make their world-renowned pesto sauce with local pine nuts, locally grown garlic and of course local Ligurian-produced extra virgin olive oil.

Believe it or not, the traditional use of cheese in their pesto sauce is optional as its flavor and taste is nearly perfect using only the natural ingredients from the garden. I was stunned when I first heard of it as I have been making pesto all my life using only the greatest Parmigiano and the best pecorino. This urban legend was confirmed by an old friend and colleague of mine who worked for me at Il Radicchio restaurant in Georgetown in the mid 1990s, Giorgio.

When I first tasted the cheeseless pesto made only with Ligurian products I was unable to tell if it had cheese in it. As a matter of fact it tasted so rich and so smooth it completely satisfied my expectations. Giorgio is a very proud hardcore cook: born and raised in the Liguria region he returned home after working in the U.S. for a couple of years for the love of his land. Nowadays he shares his time by growing olives, producing local olive oil and cooking at a restaurant he opened near Genoa a few years ago.

I like to fry larger leaves as I use them in many preparations to transport flavor to food or as decoration. Often, during the cooking process the leaves turn brown in color. Do not get discouraged, it means the oil is way too hot and not only are you losing color, but also a lot of flavor. Pick the leaves one by one and mostly of the same size to ensure consistency in cooking time. Dry with a towel and only fry a few at a time in order to avoid changes in oil temperature. Make sure to cook uniformly in order for the leaf to lose all the water and for the oil to seal in the flavor and the color. The end result should be a perfect basil leaf chip with a very bright color, crunchy and full of flavor.

Directions

Bring the oil to 350 degrees temperature.

Carefully drop just a few leaves at a time into the hot oil, pushing them down with the help of a perforated, long ladle spoon until ready. I suggest standing on the side of the sauté pan for protection as the basil leaves will release water once in contact with the hot oil, causing it to pop out.

Remove from the oil and rest on deli paper.

Transfer to airtight container once at room temperature.

Polenta Crackers
See the Gorgonzola Panna Cotta Eggshells recipe in the Appetite Openers (Page 48).

To Serve
Use a warm pasta bowl or a deep plate in order to keep the sauce in place.
Cut the baby octopus in half and cook in a small pan with abundant butter till crispy.
Sprinkle with white pepper and set aside.
Place a couple of spoons of the warm raw polenta sauce in the center of the plate and delicately stack the crispy baby octopus on the sauce, drizzle a little orange caramel on top in circular motion and sprinkle the fried capers on top.
Break the basil leaf in a few smaller pieces and decorate the octopus.
Finish by surrounding it with two-inch-long polenta crackers.
Drizzle with very little extra virgin olive oil, cracked black peppercorns and crystallized salt.

Marinated Roasted Heart of Lamb

I never thought I would appreciate lamb heart as much as I did for this recipe. The idea to turn an unusual food source into a delicacy has always fascinated me. I was extremely skeptical the first time I proposed this dish on the menu, but to my surprise orders started to flock to the kitchen, leaving me baffled and amazed. The heart is a tough muscle and it retains a lot of blood, but once marinated, properly roasted and finely sliced, it becomes extremely tender, very delicate and flavorful in taste. The combination with the goat cheese sauce along with pungent ingredients such as black olives and roasted garlic create a perfect and aggressive taste balanced by the sweetness of the sun dried tomatoes and the aromatic fresh rosemary.

In fact this is a very humble dish with very basic ingredients; therefore I needed to provide an important stage for its visual credibility. That is how I came up with the crispy potato ring: it serves as a vehicle to host and present the heart to the guest, edible, crunchy in texture, made out of simple ingredients as well, but elegant and delicious at the same time. Be patient when frying the potato ring for the first time. It takes a little understanding and practice as the starch will often make the potato stick on the ring mold.

Ingredients
1 medium-size fresh heart of lamb
2 cloves of mashed garlic
1 peeled and halved shallot
1 sprig of rosemary
1 sprig of sage
1 sprig of thyme
½ cup of olive oil
Crystallized salt, a drizzle of extra virgin olive oil and optional micro green leaves at serving time

Directions
To prepare for the marinating process, use a sharp knife to discard the heart's extra trimmings of fat and slice it into two perfect halves. Dry the extra blood with a towel, trying to absorb as much as possible, and set both pieces in a small deep container such as a small square plastic bowl.
Pour in the olive oil, the garlic, the shallot and the herbs.
Mix well and rest in the refrigerator about 4 or 5 days covered with a lid or plastic wrap, making sure both pieces stay completely under the oil.

Goat Cheese Sauce

Ingredients
Excellent creamy goat cheese
The equivalent of ½ tsp of fresh chopped rosemary
4 paper-thin fried crumbled garlic chips
Veal stock reduction
1 large sun dried tomato half cut in small fine strips
¼ tbsp of butter
5 pitted whole Liguria black olives
Heavy cream
Salt
Cracked black peppercorns

Directions

In a small pan reduce by half the veal stock with the garlic chips.
Add the goat cheese and with the help of a spoon dissolve it into the sauce until a fine velvety paste with no lumps.
Add the heavy cream, the salt and the cracked black peppercorns along with the butter and cook a few seconds until dense and creamy.
Add the sun dried tomatoes, rosemary and black olives only at the end in order not to overpower the taste of the goat cheese and to keep their colors bright and alive.
Use the sauce right away.

Crispy Potato Rings

Ingredients

1 large, long baking potato
Blended oil for frying
Salt
A stainless steel ring mold of about 2 inches high and 2½ inches in diameter

Directions

Peel the potato and slice it into a paper-thin strip approximately 7 inches long and 2 inches high.
Rapidly wrap it around the ring mold overlapping one end by at least one inch over the other end in order to create a big enough grip to keep it closed with the kitchen tong while frying. The starch of the potato will work as natural glue keeping the two overlapped ends sealed.
Make sure the oil is set at 375 degrees and with the help of a kitchen tong grip tight without breaking the potato strip on the ring and immerge into the oil till crispy and golden.
Once ready, set aside on deli paper and wait until completely cool.
With the help of a tip of a small knife, carefully remove the ring mold from the potato crisp in one piece making sure not to break it, salt it and keep in warm place until ready to serve.
You could make a few of them ahead of time if you wish, in this case make sure you cook them a little crispier and keep them in an airtight container.

To Serve

Remove the heart halves from the oil and the blood, and set out to room temperature.

In a hot sauté pan sear the two halves with the marinating garlic, shallot and herbs for a few seconds on both sides till crispy and well-colored. (Do not use any additional oil to sauté as the marinated heart will have enough on it to be seared properly.)

Sprinkle some salt and cracked black peppercorns and transfer in hot oven about 2 to 3 minutes at 425 degrees.

Make sure not to overcook the heart as ideally it should be served medium rare.

Remove from the pan and set aside on a cutting board.

With a very sharp knife, cut the heart into very thin slices as wide as fingers.

Let it sit a minute, allowing the excess blood to run out of it and to settle properly.

In the middle of a flat warm plate, place a couple of spoons of the goat cheese sauce making sure to arrange the olives and the sun dried tomatoes mostly on the side of the dish in a circular pattern, leaving enough room for the crisp potato ring to be set right in the middle.

Place the potato crisp on the plate and gently place the heart slices inside it, creating a delicate stack.

Finish by placing a couple of garlic chips on the lamb, sprinkle with crystallized salt and drizzle lightly with a very good extra virgin olive oil. You can also decorate with fresh rosemary needles or tender micro greens.

Serve immediately.

Gratinée Oysters with Crunchy Pearls by the Sea

This hot appetizer is incredibly tasty and is a stunner in presentation. There are many different types of oysters and all categorized by their geographic origins such as Pacific, Flat Europeans or Belon, Japanese Kumamoto and Atlantic also commonly referred to as Virginica or Eastern after the area where they are cultivated. Each oyster has its own degree of salt and I mostly like to use Atlantic oysters above all, such as the mild salted Caraquet. I also like the Pine Island because of its fruity finish, therefore well balanced to the salty taste of the prosciutto for this particular recipe.

Most of the time, however, I use the Blue Point as they are always available in the Washington area and always very fresh. I love the combination in taste of the mascarpone, prosciutto, scallions and the oyster. The shellfish are baked a couple of minutes and then gratinée only a few more seconds, leaving them soft, juicy and moist. The caper froth provides taste, but also a foamy visual creating elevation on the shell and a delicate contrast as if the oyster was covered with bright green seaweed. The black pearl is the equivalent of a cherry on a cake: the crunchy sphere coated with semolina flour contains the semi-liquid caviar center that bursts in your mouth with sharp flavor and makes the oyster real in all its natural elements.

I thought it would be great to create a natural stage of their habitat to serve these shellfish on. I did a little research and got in contact with a Virginia plastics manufacturer and explained exactly what I needed. He built a few tempered glass see-through boxes by the dimensions of 10 inches long by 4 inches wide and 1½ inches high. Then, before he sealed the top, we filled them with some sand, mini-shells and seawater from Sicily I brought back from my beach house, and filled them by ¾ of their capacity. Once sealed, we recreated the visual appearance of underwater life. While the sand moves and uncovers the sea shells, the water creates the appearance of a small wave. To serve, I place a few strings of fresh seaweed on top of the box and the oysters on top of it. That makes a very realistic yet elegant ocean stage everyone seems to enjoy and remember.

The hardest part is to make the caviar pearl. It takes a little practice and patience to create a perfect pearl as you must work very fast with all the ingredients in order to prepare it at frozen temperature. If the pearls are not at frozen stage throughout this preparation, the final result will definitely be jeopardized. Once you scoop the pearls out and coat them with egg wash and semolina, quickly re-shape them and place them back in the freezer to harden again. It is very important to have the oil ready at the correct temperature, then remove them from the freezer and only then cook a few at a time, ensuring proper execution. If you leave the pearls out of the freezer for too long before frying, they will pop and break during the cooking procedure.

Ingredients
10 fresh Atlantic oysters
About 7-8 spoons of mascarpone prosciutto cream depending on the size of the oysters

Directions
Carefully open the oysters with the proper knife and save their liquid in a small cup to be used for the caper froth and the caviar pearls later.
With the help of a tablespoon, detach the oysters from their shells, but leave them on; this way it will be so much easier to handle at the table while eating.
Set aside.
Set 7 to 8 spoons of the mascarpone prosciutto cream at room temperature and gently cover each oyster with a thick layer of it. Spread uniformly on the entire surface, wrap with plastic film and place in the refrigerator to rest.

Mascarpone and Parma Prosciutto Cream

Ingredients
1 lb mascarpone cheese Galbani
1 egg yolk
Salt
Ground white pepper
4 oz of Parma prosciutto thinly sliced and cut in small tiny strips
2 small, finely chopped spring onions

Directions
In a mid-size bowl whip the egg and combine the mascarpone cheese at room temperature with the prosciutto, the salt and the pepper till all ingredients are mixed into a semi-soft paste.
Add the chopped spring onions and mix well.
The cream can be used right away to top the oysters, but at times, depending on the quality, if the mascarpone cheese texture is too soft you might want to set the cream in the refrigerator about an hour till firmer.

Caper's Froth

Ingredients

5 oz of finely chopped capers
1½ qt of vegetable stock
10 large leaves of fresh basil chopped
Ground white pepper
8 grams of powder lecithin
Pinch of salt
The liquid saved from the oysters

Directions

In a small pot combine the vegetable stock, the capers, the white pepper, the salt and some of the liquid from the oysters.
Simmer, not boil, until consumed down to a quart of total liquid.
Taste for salt, add the basil leaves and set aside to cool about 5 minutes.
Blend the broth till fine and liquefied. (Both the capers and the basil will give a nice bright green color to the liquid that will show later in the froth.)
Set aside to cool completely.
Once at room temperature combine the lecithin into the liquid with the help of a small immersion blender.
Filter through a fine mesh and refrigerate the liquid until use.

Crunchy Caviar Pearls

Ingredients

2 oz of inexpensive caviar
½ cup of fine semolina flour
1 egg and a little water for egg wash
2 tbsp of filtered water from the oysters
4 tbsp heavy cream
Blended oil for frying
1 tbsp of high fat butter
½ cup of fine sifted AP flour
1 tbsp of vodka

Directions

In a small pan combine the butter with the water of the oysters, the gin and the heavy cream and reduce till half of its original quantity at low to moderate fire.

Set aside for 25 minutes to cool and stir in the caviar.

Transfer into a high-speed blender and liquefy completely, filter and place in a small, rectangular (but wide) container covered with plastic film in the freezer about 4 or 5 hours till solid.

On your working table line up the sifted flour, the fine semolina and the egg wash.

With a ¼-inch diameter melon baller, scoop out tiny frozen caviar pearls and one at a time pass them through the flour, the egg wash and finally through the semolina, making sure each pearl is perfectly sealed.

Place the pearls on deli paper and return them to the freezer covered with plastic film until ready for use.

To Serve

Place a couple strings of fresh seaweed on the see-through glass box.

Bake the oysters about 3 to 4 minutes at 400 degrees, pass them through a salamander/broiler for a few seconds until lightly colored.

Place the oysters on the glass box lengthwise on top of the seaweed, making sure they are set and firm on the plate.

Fry the pearls quickly in hot oil at approximately 385 degrees until golden.

Place a pearl on each oyster.

With the help of a hand blender whip the caper liquid and place a spoonful of froth on each oyster.

Serve immediately while gently shaking the glass box to create the illusion of a wave.

Vegetarian Caviar Tin

This is a wonderful vegetarian alternative to the usual grilled vegetable platters or the overdone pastas with tomato sauce offered to vegetarians when dining out. Unfortunately, vegetarians are often limited to poor quality selection. Vegetarians should not feel slighted in their choices when ordering from a respectable menu as nowadays many wonderful restaurants provide alternatives to meat and fish that will make a steak eater insanely jealous. I created this recipe because one evening I overheard a lady complaining how rare it is to find a quality vegetarian appetizer when dining out. Motivated by pride and a willingness to prove her wrong, I went to work. I wanted to create a vegetarian dish with an incredible wow factor that would elevate the importance and the quality of each ingredient to a level of glamour. I wanted to make it especially tempting to those who would usually discard a vegetarian option when selecting from a vast quality menu. If I could entice a regular diner to select a meatless or fishless dish, then I knew for sure my creation was going to be a winner among vegetarians.

The result is a combination of flavors, textures and colors hosted in a simple round aluminum tin that gives the impression of a sinful and sumptuous caviar treat. The different textures of the vegetables play off each other and give a sense of individualism, while the red beet couscous deliver the optical illusion of the caviar and gives substance to the dish. Perhaps, the single most important ingredient is the Taleggio fondue. This is what combines it all into one glamorous taste, delivering a delicate message of quality, unity and satisfaction for the palate to enjoy, or as one of my customers simply stated, "It's like having a circus in your mouth!"

Enjoy the show!

Vegetarian Tin

Ingredients
A small handful of fresh baby asparagus
2 oz of toasted Israeli couscous
1 medium baby red beet
1 fresh sage leaf
3 cups of vegetable stock
1 medium shallot
1 medium fresh porcini mushroom
4 tbsp of very fine sifted bread crumbs
1 egg for egg wash
1 tbsp of finely chopped Vidalia onions
½ small garlic clove
2 tbsp of high fat butter
1 small fresh cauliflower floret

½ tbsp of grated Parmesan Reggiano cheese
1 tsp of corn starch

Tools
1 caviar tin of approximately 3½ inches in diameter and 1½ inches high

Directions
Wash the red beet, place in a small metal baking pan with half cup of water, seal the top with aluminum foil, and bake at 350 degrees about one hour until completely cooked and tender.
Once cool, peel and cut in small pieces.
In a small sauté pan golden one tablespoon of minced shallot with one tablespoon of high fat butter and the chopped sage, add salt and pepper.
Add the chopped red beet and stir together for a minute.
Add ½ cup of vegetable stock and simmer about 5 minutes or until the liquid reduces by half.
Transfer to a high-speed blender and liquefy.
In a small pot cook the Israeli couscous with the remaining vegetable stock, ½ tablespoon of butter, a pinch of salt and white pepper.
Place the couscous in a small pot at moderate fire with enough red beets purée to give a bright purple color.
Mix well with a spoon, reducing down the liquid like a risotto.
Remove from the stove; add ½ tablespoon of grated Parmesan cheese and ½ tablespoon of butter, mixing vigorously to form a creamy and pasty consistency.
Blanch the baby asparagus in salted water a few seconds and very al dente and set aside.
Clean the porcini mushrooms and cut them in thin slices of approximately 2 inches long.
Pass the mushrooms through the egg wash, add the bread crumbs and fry them golden crispy, add salt and white pepper, set on parchment paper and store them in warm dry place.
In a small pan combine ½ tsp of extremely fine chopped shallots with 1 tsp of high fat butter, cook the shallots transparent and sauté the asparagus sliced diagonally in short ½ inch pieces for a few seconds only.

Add a half tablespoon of vegetable stock, salt and white pepper, and reduce almost completely. (Our goal is to keep their bright green color and their crispiness intact.)
Set aside.
With the help of a small mandolin, shave the shallots paper thin and dust with the corn starch, shake off the excess flour and fry them till golden and crispy.
Salt, pepper and set aside.

Taleggio Fonduta

Ingredients
2 oz of soft Taleggio cheese
4 tbsp of heavy cream
A pinch of ground white pepper
1 egg yolk
½ tbsp of AP flour

Directions
Cut the Taleggio cheese in small cubes, place in a small bowl, add salt and pepper and top it with the heavy cream.
Set in the refrigerator for 24 hours.
The next day bring the bowl to room temperature and stir in the flour mixing gently by hand and making sure not to form any lumps.
Place the bowl on top of a boiling pot of water at moderate to low fire, occasionally stirring the mix until perfectly melted.
Remove from the water bath and mix in the egg yolks vigorously. (We should have a semi-thick paste consistency.)
Set aside in a container to cool, and then transfer to the refrigerator covered with plastic wrap.

To Serve
Remove the caviar tin lid and place on your serving station.
Lay the crispy porcini mushrooms slices on the bottom covering the entire surface.
Cover the mushrooms with a generous spoon of the Taleggio fonduta, followed by the baby asparagus, pressing down gently, making sure the tin is as compact as possible and uniformly spread out in layers.
Top with the hot couscous and fill up all the way, scraping off the excess, giving the impression of a bright red and firm caviar tin.

Sprinkle the top with a little grated cauliflower and place the crispy shallots right in the center, creating elevation, and decorate with a few green micro leaves for a colorful presentation.
Serve with the top lid placed on the side of the tin, hanging from the rim.

Chapter Five
Surprising Salads

How can a common salad find the importance and the appeal it deserves on a restaurant menu alongside more desirable items such as meats, fish and pastas? Are salads considered bountiful plates of field greens or just simple appetizer dishes, an intelligent alternative to main course or dessert options?

In Europe salads are pretty much what they ought to be: field greens to accompany your main dish, usually on a smaller side plate for your enjoyment while cleaning your palate after every few bites and rarely consumed as appetizers or as main dishes. Americans embrace the concept of a salad in a completely different way. Here, a salad is usually customized to the needs of the diner. It's fixed and tossed with fish, meats, cheese and fruits, and is offered as an intelligent alternative to a cold appetizer or at times as a dessert option at the end of the meal. Frankly, the possibilities are endless.

Catering companies and large chain restaurants have invented countless types of salads over the years, introducing them to the public with various flavors mostly designed for speed, but not for comfort, and with an "all in one" meal concept. It is not unusual to find eight to ten different items in a simple salad. I remember once I purposely ordered an Indian chicken curry salad with apples, cranberries, toasted walnuts, slices of Asiago cheese, scallions, cilantro, pumpkin seeds and yogurt all tossed with field greens. I did this out of curiosity. It was served with a slice of warm bread and I remember thinking with a smirk on my face if I would have asked for a scoop of vanilla ice cream in it I would have had a five-course meal right there for $8.95 and all in the same bowl.

Nowadays these are one of the many alternatives to a sit down meal and they are sold in stores, restaurants, supermarkets and even by street food carts, but do we really know why? What comes to my mind is time and money. If a quick 20-minute salad can substitute a 45-minute multi-course sit down lunch and be more affordable, then why not? Italians can be picky eaters. They do not care about the time spent around a table as long as the meal offers quality and variety, but they also have a much easier schedule than what we have here in the U.S. Life in Europe is simpler, slower and possibly better for the human soul.

Americans in general are not picky eaters, but they can be once they understand and value their food, their wines and the wonderful natural products and resources this land has to offer. A passionate diner will eventually become an educated one. In many years spent away from home I learned to appreciate how important a simple salad can be. As a little kid I never gave importance to leaves of greens as my passion was pasta. Why would I care about a plate of simple and unattractive lettuce dressed with olive oil and vinegar when I could have lasagna, gnocchi, fettuccine or a sumptuous risotto every day of the week instead?

Salads were never a meal option for me, but I was taken by total surprise once I discovered how popular they were on menus of many restaurants across the country and often offered as a multi-course choice. That was an incredible cultural shock. But with cultural shock comes education of the mind and in this case education of the palate. My "virginity" was taken one day when I found the courage to order a Caesar salad topped with a grilled, sliced Cajun-style breast of chicken.

That day I was neither very hungry nor in good company, therefore food did not play an important role for me as I remember ordering that dish mostly out of politeness. When the food arrived my plate looked like a classic example of food mediocrity lacking basic respect for the culinary laws I grew up with…up to that moment. To my surprise the Romaine leaves were crispy, the dressing light and tangy, the chicken grilled to perfection, moist and with a wonderful balance in spices and salt. Even though the chicken was a little too hot in temperature to be sitting on top of the salad I was incredibly surprised in learning sometimes rules do not necessarily apply. That revelation instantly opened a new professional door leading me to a path that until that moment was completely unknown to me.

I was 18 then and suddenly my salad eyes were opened. I had never experienced up to that moment a salad tossed with meats or fruits. I started to appreciate salads more and more with each passing year, and I think it was then curiosity started knocking at my professional door. Over the past years I have created many different salads and featured them on many menus as items of gastronomic desire alongside meats, fish and pastas, giving them the respect I think they deserve.

I wanted to especially tempt non-salad eaters with unusual and attractive options of curiosity and with combinations of ingredients and concepts that would tantalize the taste buds and the mind. A salad does not have to be just a salad: forgettable or unimportant or a side dish living in a main course's shadow, unappreciated, unworthy and unappealing. Even a salad should be glamorous in all its splendor and simplicity: a revelation for the palate and mind that should open many more avenues and aspects of dining, from its look to its taste and freshness.

I decided to include just a few of the ones I really love because of the unique way I have created them. Some reflect basic Italian traditions, others a more complex research of the taste with unusual and seasonal combinations. Some are winners for taste, final satisfaction and concept, and some by mistake and a few more by an occasional flash of genius.

Roasted Artichoke Hearts on Roasted Bell Peppers Carpaccio

This is a classic example of revised and re-arranged simplicity. A humble roasted artichoke on stage for a monologue, with his sidekick bell peppers Carpaccio alongside with all its fixings. I am a firm believer simple dishes with simple ingredients often need more care and attention than more complex ones. There are no tricks here: select the freshest artichoke you can get your hands on and the best quality peppers you can find, and transform them into culinary classics with pride and basic cooking steps. This is a general rule I apply to all my cooking.

When I used to spend my summers in Sicily as a young boy I remember the long days around my relatives, who are humble land and farm workers. My cousins and I used to walk to the nearby beach through entire fields of grape vines, vegetables and fruit trees, and on our way back after a few hours of fun we would smell the fumes of the roasted peppers, artichokes and other vegetables cooked on wooden charcoals as our mothers prepared lunch.

I remember watching the peppers slowly cooking till crispy and juicy and the artichoke leaves falling apart once roasted. They would peel the peppers and dress the fillets with just a little olive oil, garlic and sea salt, accompanied by roasted slices of artichoke heart and chopped basil leaves. The artichokes were so meaty and intense in flavor I remember thinking I could have eaten just that as a meal and be fully satisfied for the day.

This is a re-creation of my Sicilian summer memories in a personal version with a little twist in presentation and concept. Once the peppers are roasted, make sure to place them in a small bowl while still hot and to cover it with plastic film. The heat from the peppers will create a vacuum-like condensation effect and it will make the skin much softer and easier to peel. This technique can be used for all bell peppers and is proven successful; however, if all you have in hand is green peppers, then you must place them directly into a paper bag hot off the grill or oven, close and rest about 30 minutes. The paper bag will work as a filter and it will delicately and slowly help to separate the skin from the vegetable.

This is the only way you will be able to successfully peel an entire green pepper. I love to use a black olive sauce or dressing with this dish as it marries very well with the taste of the artichokes and the peppers. If you are unable to find Ligurian olives, try the Greek Kalamatas as an alternative.

Ingredients
1 whole artichoke
1 small red bell pepper
1 small yellow bell pepper
1 medium caper berry
2 tbsp of extra virgin olive oil
½ tbsp of chopped Italian parsley
2 small chopped basil leaves
1 tsp of minced garlic
Pinch of salt
Pinch of cracked black peppercorns
Pinch of ground white pepper
2 meaty fillets of anchovy
1 tbsp of small non-pareilles capers
½ cup of dry white wine

½ cup of vegetarian stock
Pinch of dry oregano
A few leaves of Italian frisée salad
Pinch of crystallized salt
8-10 large leaves of artichoke chips
4-5 garlic chips
A few fresh leaves of micro green oregano
1 lemon

Directions

Clean the artichoke, removing all the leaves until only the heart remains; remove the fibrous choke at the core with a spoon and with a small knife slice just enough tough green fibers of the stem, leaving it intact and attached to the heart of the artichoke. Quickly rinse in cold water and thoroughly cover the whole artichoke with the lemon juices to prevent black color oxidation.

Place in a small deep aluminum baking pan sitting with the stem upright and combine one tablespoon of extra virgin olive oil, ½ tablespoon of capers, one fillet of anchovy, the vegetarian stock, ½ tsp of minced garlic and the white wine.

Sprinkle a pinch of salt on the artichoke and a pinch of the white pepper only in the liquid, cover the pan with aluminum foil making sure to seal it tight on the edges of the pan and bake in a hot oven for approximately 10 minutes at 400 degrees until completely cooked, but very much al dente.

Remove it from the pan and set aside. If you are not serving the artichoke the same day, use the cooking liquid as a preserving component to store it in. This is a wonderful way to keep it fresh and juicy for a few days.

Place both peppers in hot oven about 15-20 minutes at 375 degrees until completely roasted or if you are going to use the grill make sure they cook at high temperature, turning them over often until ready.

Once cooked place them in a small bowl, cover with plastic film and set aside about 30 minutes.

Peel, rinse the peppers and cut them in very thin strips of about 3-4 inches long.

Place them in a strainer about 15 minutes to get rid of the extra water.

In a small bowl combine the peppers with the remaining spoon of extra virgin olive oil, a pinch of dry oregano, half tsp of minced

garlic, the chopped basil leaves, the chopped fillet of anchovy, the chopped parsley, the remaining half spoon of small capers, the salt and a pinch of cracked black peppercorns.
Toss well with your hands and marinate for at least 8 hours.
Keep refrigerated.

Artichoke Chips and Garlic Chips
See the Crunchy Monkfish Liver Custard with Lemon-Honey Preserve recipe in the Hot Starters (Page 139).

Black Olives Dressing

Ingredients
1 cup balsamic vinegar
¾ cup blended oil
1 ¼ cup extra virgin olive oil
Pinch of salt
Pinch of ground white pepper
½ cup puréed Ligurian black olives

Directions
Combine all ingredients in a high-speed blender for a couple of minutes until the mix is velvety and smooth.
Taste for salt and pepper.
Transfer to a plastic squirt bottle and store in refrigerator.

Tools
1 round aluminum mold of about 4½ inches in diameter

To Serve
Set the artichoke and the marinated peppers out to room temperature before serving.
Select a chilled large white oval plate and make sure to have all the needed ingredients ready.
Divide the serving plate in 3 sections in order to build our salad: on the far right place the round mold with a couple of scoops of marinated peppers in it and with the help of your fingers gently spread them out evenly till completely flat, giving the appearance of an even sheet.
Twist the mold off and remove.

On the round peppers Carpaccio place the large leaves of artichoke chips one at a time creating elevation.

Baby Arucola White Asparagus Scorzone and Piedmontese Hazelnuts

This is perhaps one of my favorite summer salads. It is very light and delicate, but very flavorful and complete in taste and expectations. I particularly like how it blends very simple ingredients together, creating a unique aftertaste that lingers a long time, giving you a refreshed light feeling. The blood oranges, the arucola leaves and the Parmesan cheese are the strong flavors, the uncommon ones such as the summer black truffle Scorzone, the white asparagus and the Piedmontese hazelnuts are three elements that blend into a "wham" taste that delivers a punch.

Sometimes you do not have to look very hard to find the right combinations of flavors. I remember putting this together by improvising an alternative course for one of my tasting menus. It was a last minute thing. I quickly assembled a few ingredients between the dietary parameters given to me by my frantic guest when she insisted on having a "neutral course with a dazzling kick"...whatever that meant. I believe it was July. I had plenty of summer black truffle Scorzone and enough crispy white asparagus to spare. In a few quick steps I managed to make my guest happy and was able to deliver what she was looking for.

Indeed it takes so little to make people happy and by doing so I felt I got a great reward by creating a winning new tasting concept. The hazelnuts from Piedmont are by far the best in the world: their taste, smell and texture are indescribable and truly amazing. They are mostly used in pastry recipes and occasionally for salty preparations such as this one. Remember to shave the Scorzone very thin and only at the last second or it will not retain its crispy texture.

Ingredients
6 medium white asparagus
2 oz of baby arucola leaves
2 tbsp pancetta cut in medium-size cubes
1 tbsp of Piedmontese hazelnuts

1 blood orange
A few shaves of fresh summer Scorzone black truffle
A small block of Parmesan Reggiano cheese for shavings of about 2-3 oz
Salt
Ground white pepper

Directions
In a hot oven toast the hazelnuts till golden and set aside.
Once cold gently crush them into medium-size pieces.
With a very sharp knife peel the orange and cut out the segments, place in a small container and set in the refrigerator.
Cut the ends of the asparagus, peel the skin off and boil them in a small pot with salted water for a few minutes only. Make sure they are completely cooked and tender, but still crunchy to the touch.
Set aside to cool naturally and then place in the cooler covered with plastic wrap.
Roast the pancetta cubes in a small pan till crispy, discard the cooking fat and keep in warm place until serving time.
With a damp towel clean the black truffle Scorzone and remove the outside impurities with the help of a clean soft toothbrush if needed.
Tip: *Having the Parmesan cheese at room temperature before serving makes it much easier to shave in larger thin pieces without it breaking or crumbling.*

Black Truffle Hazelnut Balsamic Dressing

Ingredients
¼ cup balsamic vinegar
1 tbsp of natural black truffle oil
½ cup of extra virgin olive oil
¼ cup of hazelnut oil
Small pinch of salt
Small pinch of ground white pepper

Directions
Place all ingredients in a high-speed blender and form a velvety thick dressing.
Taste for salt and pepper.
Transfer to a plastic squirt bottle and store in refrigerator.

To Serve
On a chilled white square plate line up the poached white asparagus, evenly cut log-style, and place right in the middle. Dress with a few drops of the balsamic dressing, sprinkle a few crushed hazelnuts and a few crispy pancetta bits.
Set aside.
In a separate bowl dress the baby arucola leaves with the truffle dressing, the crushed toasted hazelnuts and the pancetta.
Create the first layer of the salad by placing a few leaves at a time on top of the asparagus, leaving the tips visible for presentation. Alternate a few orange segments, a few slices of Scorzone and the Parmesan cheese shaves.
Repeat this step two more times in order to have a delicate multi-layered, colorful salad.
Finish coordinating shavings of Scorzone and Parmesan cheese by placing the final segments of blood oranges apart for visual balance and presentation.

Grilled Watermelon, Shaved Fennel, Toasted Almonds and Castelmagno Cheese

I am sure not everyone has had grilled watermelon as a salad before, and I am sure there is a lot of curiosity and skepticism about this unusual dish, but the skepticism dies after you try: then you are hooked. In Italy we enjoy watermelon as summer refreshment after a meal or as a snack on a hot day at the beach. This fruit cannot be compared at the same level of importance to an apple or a pear, and it is often dismissed in the culinary world as it is used only for smoothies, bar drinks or as a secondary ingredient. I personally love it; and especially its delicate and floral taste that lingers in your palate a few seconds before it disappears.

When I used to spend my summers in Sicily at my beach house it was customary for us to pick up a watermelon on our way home from the beach and to enjoy it the same evening after chilling it in the refrigerator a few hours. I remember complaining about its sweetness because it was filled with incredibly dense sugar pockets, way too sweet for my palate. But unfortunately that is a great problem Sicily has: the extremely hot temperatures during summertime enhance the development of an unusually high content of sugars in most of the local fruits.

My mother always told me I was way too critical about food throughout my young years, but in a good way. I always voiced my opinion about it. I always appreciated it and always critiqued it no matter what the food was. Yes! I was a pain in the butt even at a young age. One day while having lunch I alternated a bite of thin crispy fennel with one of watermelon. Until that moment I never realized how similar they were in texture and how much of the same aromatic taste they shared. But 25 years later, when by mistake I had done the same thing, a light bulb went on and this time I explored their similarities in depth and decided to combine these two delicate tastes into a new one.

I grilled the watermelon and made it a base for my salad. Then I shaved the fennel paper thin and combined it with a very delicate but dense cheese from the Piedmont region called Castelmagno. I added yellow cherry tomatoes for colorful presentation and texture. However, the salad was missing a way to tie all the ingredients together. It missed a neutral component that would blend the other flavors into a common one. I found the answer in toasted almonds.

Almonds add crunchiness and texture, but mostly add an insisting and unusual taste that marries very well with the watermelon. By blending almond paste and almond oil in the lemon dressing I was able to create a combination that worked as a bridge, giving access to the fennel and to the grilled watermelon in great balance. This is a very unique and refreshing salad, and I can guarantee you that after you taste it you will never look at a watermelon the same way again.

Ingredients

The heart of a sweet and ripe watermelon
1 small crispy fennel bulb
6-8 whole almonds with the skin
5-6 small and ripe yellow cherry tomatoes
2-3 medium-size scallions
1½ oz of fresh Castelmagno cheese
½ tbsp of extra virgin olive oil
Cracked black peppercorns
Crystallized salt
A few Italian parsley micro leaves
The tip of a teaspoon of minced garlic

A few leaves of black opal basil micro greens (optional)

Directions

Bake the almonds in a hot oven till perfectly toasted and set aside.
Slice the cherry tomatoes in half and wash the scallions under fresh water.
From the heart of a ripe watermelon cut a slice of the dimensions of approximately 7 inches long by 2½ wide and ½ inch thick.
Set it on paper towel sheets to absorb all excess water on every side.
Turn the grill on at very high temperature.
Brush the watermelon slab with the extra virgin olive oil and rapidly mark both sides on the hot grill.
Do the same for the scallions and set in the refrigerator about 20 minutes.
With the help of a meat slicer machine, shave the fresh fennel in crunchy paper-thin slices and set aside covered with a moist towel.

Almond Oil Dressing

Ingredients

¼ cup blended oil
½ cup extra virgin olive oil
¼ cup almond oil
Pinch of salt
Pinch of ground white pepper
½ cup of filtered lemon juice
½ oz of soft, moist almond paste

Directions

Dissolve the almond paste with your fingers in very small pieces and combine with all other ingredients in a high-speed blender about a minute until forming a creamy, velvety dressing.
Taste for salt and pepper.
Filter through a cheesecloth and discard the few lumps created during the blending process.
Transfer back to the blender for a few seconds again.
Store in a small plastic squirt bottle and refrigerate.

To Serve
In the middle of a chilled rectangular plate lay the grilled strip of watermelon at room temperature and sprinkle a little crystallized salt, black peppercorns and some almond dressing.
In a small bowl toss the fennel shaves with a little almond dressing, the minced garlic and half of the micro parsley leaves and delicately place on the entire watermelon surface, creating a very light and "fluffy" lookalike layer.
Place the yellow tomatoes on top of the fennel, coordinating for symmetry and visual balance, and repeat with the toasted almonds and the charred scallions cut in thin strips about 2 inches long.
Decorate with the remaining micro parsley leaves and small irregular pieces of the Castelmagno cheese.
Finish with a little more dressing, a sprinkle of crystallized salt and cracked black peppercorns and place a few optional leaves of black opal basil micro greens on top.

Roasted Vidalia Onions Liquorice and Smoked Tuna Shaves

Not too long ago I was in my hometown in Torino visiting my family, and as ritual my better half and I had dinner with my childhood friend Giorgio and his wife Paola at the famous nearby restaurant Combal Zero owned by chef Davide Scabin, who is considered the "Rebel Chef" in Italy for his innovative imagination and personalized approach to cooking. He retains a solid spot in the San Pellegrino world's best 50 restaurants list year after year and his restaurant is currently the proud recipient of two stars from the European Michelin guide.

Ironically, Davide and I attended the same culinary school in Torino in our younger days, but in different classes and with different culinary professors. We both remember, however, bumping into each other passing through the school kitchens every now and then, sharing a joke with our common classmates or lurking around the building waiting for the final bell to ring the end of class. Small world!

At that specific dinner he served a roasted red onion from Tropea, the southern Italian region of Calabria. This is one of the sweetest red onions in the world and is the onion with the lowest lachrymal factor and renowned all over Europe for its unusual sweet and mild flavor. I really enjoyed that course because it featured liquorice essence, a very unusual ingredient not very common or widely used in Italian cooking. In the U.S., I have enjoyed making a similar roasted onion salad for years using the delicate sweet taste of the Vidalia jewels from Georgia, but it has never occurred to me to combine it with liquorice until I tasted Davide's version.

When I came back home I realized after a few tastings that if used in small quantities the liquorice essence marries perfectly even with a different type of sweet onion. My original version is both delicate and sharp in flavor and well balanced, but in order to add the liquorice I had to make some changes. For my salad I roast the onions very al dente as I love their crunchy texture when combined with the wine vinegar and the salty taste of the smoked tuna. I make a very light sweet mustard sauce as a vehicle to combine those two different flavors and a sprinkle of cracked black peppercorns for aromatic after-bite. By combining the liquorice essence I have reduced the amount of smoked tuna, the cracked black peppercorns and the vinegar, and added the grappa. I have transformed my original savory and sharp salad into a more aromatic and delicate one. I also find the polenta-caper cracker brings a much needed component to the dish and sets the stage in your palate, especially when combined with the optional taste of the caviar.

I like this revised version much better than my original one as it has a unique lingering aftertaste and is more complete in its concept. I thank Davide for the idea. He has become a national celebrity and the co-host of a popular cooking show in Italy called "La Terra Dei Cuochi." It is always nice to see him every time I visit home and dine at his restaurant, or whenever he visits me at my restaurant in Washington, D.C.

Ingredients
1 large size Vidalia onion
The tip of a teaspoon of finely minced garlic
A few strings of chopped chives
½ tbsp of grappa
1 large tbsp of white wine vinegar
A few shaves of excellent smoked tuna from Sicily
1 small tbsp of extra virgin olive oil

5 pieces of Darrell Lea dark soft eating liquorice
1 tsp of excellent Ossetra or Sevruga caviar
1½ tbsp of golden-sweet mustard dressing

Directions
Roast the onion (with its skin) in hot oven at 350 degrees till al dente, and set aside to cool.
Cut the liquorice in very thin slices and place in a very small pot with half cup of water under very low fire till reduced by half and completely melted into an aromatic and dense dark liquid.
Filter and preserve.
With the help of a meat slicer machine shave 3 pieces of smoked tuna and set aside on parchment paper.
Peel the roasted onion and part its leaves in size of approximately 2 inches by 3 and place in a medium-size bowl.
Dress the onion leaves with the minced garlic, the wine vinegar, a little salt, the extra virgin olive oil, the grappa, and the finely sliced fresh chives.
Toss together.

Golden-Sweet Mustard Dressing

Ingredients
1 tbsp of chestnut honey at room temperature
2 tbsp of gold Dijon mustard with seeds
1 tbsp of white wine vinegar
Salt
Ground white pepper
½ tbsp of sour cream
A few drops of lemon juice

Directions
Whisk together all the ingredients in a small bowl till a smooth and uniform pasty dressing is formed.
Refrigerate.

Capers Polenta Crackers

Ingredients
1 cup milk
½ tbsp of sugar

½ tbsp salt
¼ cup and a tbsp of polenta
2-3 tbsp of water
1½ tbsp of extra virgin olive oil
½ cup of AP sifted flour
½ cup of small nonpareilles capers
5 fresh basil leaves

Directions

In a large bowl, whisk in the milk, water, sugar, salt and oil.
Add the polenta and the sifted flour, mixing carefully to avoid lumps.
In a blender purée the capers with the basil and a touch of olive oil until a fine paste and combine with the flour polenta mix.
Transfer the contents of the bowl in a full sheet pan over a silicone baking mat.
Cook in the oven about 45 minutes to one hour at 275 degrees.
Break them into desired size only after completely cooled.
Preserve in an airtight container over layers of parchment paper.

To Serve

You can use any size plate for this salad as it fits perfectly in a pasta bowl, in a rectangular cheese plate or even on a large flat square one. I like to use a large square one as I would rather build my salad horizontally than vertically because it gives me more imaginative power and room to create a mosaic-like presentation.
Brush a thick strip of mustard dressing across the plate right in the middle, about 3 inches wide.
Roll 3 slices of the smoked tuna and place one in the middle of the plate and on top of the mustard strip, the other two on both sides next to it.
With cooking tweezers pick one onion leaf at a time, and place each leaf alternatively on the smoked tuna, dressing each layer with some liquorice essence, creating 3 different piles.
Finish by drizzling more liquorice and Frantoio oil, and top with a sprinkle of chopped chives.
Adorn with 3 slices of the crackers and with one more slice of the smoked tuna on top of each onion pile, creating an elegant visual balance.

Deconstructed Ratatouille Honey Lemon Mint and Gelatin Tomato Cubes

This is a personalized version of a French classic, but in different shapes, concept and temperature. I love a good ratatouille, especially when it is served warm and with a hot crispy baguette. This salad has all the elements and ingredients of the French classic, but it is so different in execution and at the same time a lot more beautiful and elegant in presentation. I have designed this salad after a trip to Paris where I was served a very hot ratatouille on a very hot summer day. Even though I loved it, what really bothered me was eating a scorching hot appetizer on a day where the thermometer reached 90 degrees at lunchtime. Mostly, why did they serve it so hot when it is usually served warm or cold?

My revised version highlights its delicacy in a much lighter way without sacrificing the taste or basic ingredients in a more appealing presentation while preserving its traditions. I use three different sizes of melon ballers to carve the vegetables into perfect round shapes, and I combine toasted slices of black olive bread to connect the individual flavors to the marinated roasted peppers that sit on the bottom of the salad. Another basic ingredient for the Ratatouille is tomato. That plays a very important role in the original version, delivering taste, color and structure while transporting its flavor throughout the dish with a velvety thick balance among all other vegetables.

In this case the honey mint dressing delivers balance, but I still decided to include the tomato in a completely different way and texture: small gelatin squares. These juicy soft bites burst with flavor and a dense, delicate balance. The salad is built and presented within a circle of thin cucumber slices wrapped around a metal mold and served under a thick "brush stroke" of light, golden, sweet mustard dressing. The salad per se is very flavorful and complete, so opt to use the mustard dressing depending on your personal taste. Remove the metal mold only before serving to assure stability and balance and feel free to decorate the top with a few fresh micro greens of your choice.

Ingredients
½ zucchini
1 small Yukon potato
½ small eggplant
1 medium-size carrot peeled
2 small red cherry tomatoes
2 small yellow cherry tomatoes
1 small cucumber
1 small red pepper
1 small yellow pepper
4 small cooked sweet-sour pearled onions
Pinch of salt
Pinch of ground white pepper
Pinch of cracked black peppercorns
Pinch of dry oregano
About 3 cups of vegetable stock
3 tbsp of white wine vinegar
2 bay leaves
A few tomato velvet cubes
Assorted micro greens to decorate the salad
Tip of a teaspoon of minced garlic
1 leaf of fresh basil chopped
1 slice of toasted black olive bread cut in round shape
1 clove

Tools Needed
3 melon ballers of the following sizes: 15 mm bowl round 5/8", 22 mm bowl round 3/4" and a 28 mm bowl round 1-1/8" (small, medium, and large)
1 round aluminum mold of approximately 4 inches in diameter and at least 2 inches high

Directions
Place both peppers in a hot oven about 15-20 minutes at 375 degrees until completely roasted.
Once cooked place them in a small bowl, cover with plastic film and set aside about 30 minutes.
Bring the vegetable stock to a gentle boil with 2 tablespoons of white vinegar, 2 bay leaves, the clove and a little salt; simmer a few minutes.

Using the smaller melon baller carve a few pearls out of the carrot and set aside.
With the medium-size baller carve pearls from the zucchini and the eggplants, and with the large baller repeat this step for the potato.
Make sure to separate each vegetable group in different containers as they all have different cooking temperatures.
Turn up the heat under the simmering vegetable stock and bring to a vivid boil.
Cook the zucchini first about 30 seconds until bright green, set aside and let it cool naturally. (It is absolutely discouraged to use cold water to chill the vegetables as we want them to preserve the acidic taste acquired during the boiling process.)
Now cook the potatoes until completely tender and set aside.
Repeat this step for the carrots and for last the eggplants cooking for 2-3 minutes or until tender.
Peel and rinse the peppers, cut them in strips of about 3 inches long by 2 inches wide and strain the extra water a few minutes.
Toss the peppers with a touch of the honey-lemon dressing, salt, cracked black peppercorns, oregano, the basil and the minced garlic.
Marinate the peppers for at least 8 hours.
With the help of a meat slicer cut very thin strips out of the cucumber lengthwise and set aside.

Sweet Sour Pearled Onions

Ingredients

1 lb of pearled onions
2 tbsp of honey
¾ cup of white wine vinegar
2 bay leaves
Pinch of salt
Pinch of ground white pepper
1½ tbsp of sugar
2 cloves of garlic mashed
¾ cup of vegetable stock

Directions

Blanch the pearl onions in hot water a few seconds to better peel off their skin.

In a small hotel pan combine all the ingredients together and mix well, then add the onions.
Seal the top with aluminum foil, pressing tight on the edges, and bake in hot oven at 375 degrees for approximately 18-20 minutes depending on the size of the onions.
When al dente but translucent, remove the foil and let the pan cool completely.
Remove the onions and place in a smaller container, filter the cooking juice and combine with the onions again to preserve.
Keep refrigerated.

Honey Lemon Mint Dressing

This recipe needs the leftover cooking juice of the sweet-sour pearled onions.

Ingredients
4 oz of pearled onions cooking juice, filtered
½ tbsp honey
1½ tbsp sugar
5 leaves of fresh curly mint
Juice of 1½ lemon
Pinch of salt
Pinch of white pepper
A tip of a teaspoon of minced garlic

Directions
In a medium-size pan at low fire, golden the honey and the sugar together.
Add the liquid from the onions, salt and pepper and reduce by a quarter of its volume.
Filter the juice and cool in an ice bath.
Place the juice in a high-speed blender with the mint leaves, the garlic and the lemon juice.
Blend till it thickens, taste for salt and pepper and refrigerate in a small plastic squirt bottle.

Tomato Velvet Cubes

Ingredients
3 oz vegetable broth

9 oz of juice from fresh ripe tomatoes
1 tbsp of tomato paste
1¼ tbsp of unflavored granular gelatin
2 cups of tomato purée
Pinch of salt
Pinch of ground white pepper
Pinch of dry oregano
4 basil leaves

Directions
Bloom the gelatin with one ounce of cold water and set aside.
Combine the tomato juice with the vegetable stock, salt, pepper, oregano tomato paste and bring to boil. Now add the basil leaves and cool for 8-10 minutes.
Stir in the gelatin until completely dissolved.
Filter the liquid through a fine mesh and add the fine tomato purée, transfer to a small wide container or a square deep plate and place in the refrigerator about 4 hours till solid.
Cover with plastic wrap.

Golden-Sweet Mustard Dressing

Ingredients
2 spoons of chestnut honey at room temperature
1 spoon of gold Dijon mustard with seeds
Salt
Ground white pepper
½ spoon of white wine vinegar

Directions
Whisk together all the ingredients in a small bowl till a smooth and uniform pasty dressing is formed.
Refrigerate.

Black Olive Bread

Ingredients
6 grams dry yeast
¾ cup of warm water
¼ cup of olive oil
1 oz of black olive paste

4½ oz of Ligurian black olives pitted
1 lb of all purpose flour
2 pinches of salt

Directions by mixer
Stir the yeast into bowl with the warm water and let the liquid stand for 10 minutes in order to revive the yeast.
Add the olive oil, the pitted olives, the flour, the olive paste and the salt.
Mix at low speed with the hook attachment until the dough comes together, first about 30 seconds at higher speed, then again at lower speed about 3-4 minutes.
Remove the dough from the mixer and place into an oiled and deep container covered with plastic wrap.
Let it rise till it doubles its original size.
Roll the dough forming two fat loaves and place on a sheet pan over parchment paper, cover with plastic film and let it rise one more time in a warm area.
Once the loaves have doubled in size, sprinkle with a little flour and bake at 350 degrees about 20-25 minutes.

To Serve
Serve this salad on a rectangular chilled plate or on a large square one.
Cut a thin, but wide slice of the black olive bread of at least 5 inches wide and lay it on a cutting board.
Take the round aluminum mold we will use to assemble the salad in and place it on top of the bread slice.
Hold the mold firm with one hand and with the other cut the bread, keeping the tip of a small knife close to the inside rim in a circular motion.
Toast the round slice and set aside.
Cut several small cubes out of the tomato velvet gelatin of approximately ¼ inch size and keep refrigerated until the last minute.
With a wide pastry brush apply a generous stroke of the golden-sweet mustard dressing across the plate and delicately place the ring mold on top of it right in the middle.
Fold the cucumber slices around the inside rim and place the toasted bread slice on the bottom, creating a nest for the salad.

Place a few strips of the marinated bell peppers on top of the toasted bread, creating a nice flat base.
In a small bowl combine 4 pearled onions, 4 zucchini balls, 4 potato balls, 6 carrot balls, 4 eggplant balls, the 4 cherry tomatoes and a squirt of the honey-lemon mint dressing, salt and pepper if necessary.
Mix well and place a spoon of the mixed vegetables inside the mold on top of the peppers.
Lay in a few tomato gelatin cubes, one more spoon of pearled vegetables, more tomato cubes, more vegetables and finish by placing a few more tomato gelatins in symmetrical way on top of the salad spaced apart for visual balance.
Decorate the top with little micro greens of your choice creating elevation and contrast.
Shake the salad a little to make sure all the vegetable balls are sitting in place and balance them with your hands and fingers if needed.
In one quick motion and with both hands remove the metal mold, twisting away.
Tip: *Always serve this salad at room temperature, never chilled.*

Roasted Baby Beets Mache Goat Cheese Gelato Morelles Texture and Lacquered Leeks

This is a very different way to appreciate these little vegetable roots. Personally I am not a big fan of beets, but I do love the baby ones when cooked crispy and al dente and mostly if combined with citrus, goat cheese and delicate greens for a savory light dish. I used to serve this salad in a quite simple way: sliced roasted beets, crumbled goat cheese, orange segments, mache and artichoke chips. It is true I get bored easily, but after a good run with that successful and tasty combination I decided to pull both ends of the string and dissolve the knot to an absolute flat and restart from zero. To me it is always intriguing and challenging to re-construct or re-create a dish, especially from any of my past menus.

It is a way to continuously challenge myself to stay sharp and updated with the ongoing and always evolving culinary industry, to feed my passion for cooking and the need of those who come to expect higher levels of culinary concepts when dining at my restaurant. I needed a crunchy, savory texture to base my new salad on and found the answer in a combination of dry morelles mushrooms and caramelized almonds that elevate the taste of the baby beets in a very delicate way while combining the flavors of the citrus.

I have been often tempted to experiment with "salty gelatos" made of soft, creamy cheeses, but never found the right inspiration to make it fit into an acceptable combination. In re-building this salad it has been the perfect opportunity to develop a gentle and sharp texture that would smoothly complement and fully integrate with all other ingredients. The result is a velvety gelato that clears your palate with a kick, invigorating your taste buds. The Sicilian orange segments contribute with refreshing bits to the hearty morelles, while the lacquered leek coins are a new fun way to combine flavors and crunchiness.

Ingredients
Pick a variety of baby beets of about 2 inches in size and possibly all different from each other in colors and in taste.
For this salad I like to use the following whenever available:
1 small baby golden beet
1 small baby candy stripe beet or chioggia beet
1 small baby white beet
1 small baby red beet
1 small baby purple beet
1 scoop of creamy goat cheese gelato
A few sprigs of mache salad leaves
Segments of 1 Sicilian-style Tarocco orange
Crystallized salt
Cracked black peppercorns
Ground white pepper
A drizzle of excellent extra virgin olive oil
A drizzle of citrus dressing
6-8 lacquered leek coins
1½ tbsp of salty morelles mushroom texture

Directions
Wash the beets, wrap them in aluminum foil and roast in hot oven at 350 degrees for approximately 30 minutes or until they are completely cooked, but still al dente.

Peel them delicately while still warm with a small knife and set aside.
Wash the mache, dry its leaves and remove the bottom roots, place in a small bowl.
Cut the segments out of the Sicilian orange, leaving them whole and ready to use at room temperature.

Citrus Dressing
See the Four Minutes Smoked Branzino Carpaccio in a Cigar Box recipe in the Cold Starters (Page 87).

Creamy Goat Cheese Gelato

Ingredients
½ qt milk
½ qt heavy cream
4 oz of granulated sugar
8 egg yolks
Pinch of salt
Pinch of ground white pepper
12 oz of excellent creamy goat cheese at room temperature

Directions
In a small bowl mix the sugar and eggs till foamy, then add the goat cheese gradually until a smooth paste.
Boil the milk and heavy cream with the salt and pepper and set aside about 10 minutes.
Combine the goat cheese mix with the milk while still warm, gently stirring with a whisk.
Strain through a fine mesh and cool completely before freezing in the gelato machine.

Lacquered Leeks Coins

Ingredients
1 large size leek
3 cups of vegetable stock
Pinch of salt
Pinch of white pepper
2 spoons of honey
1½ tbsp of sugar

Directions

Cut the greens and roots off the leek stalk down to a piece of about 5 inches long.

Soak in cold water about a day and rinse a few times, discarding all the remaining sand.

Bring the vegetable stock to boil with one tablespoon of honey, sugar, salt, pepper and simmer about 15 minutes al dente preserving its bright green color.

Remove from the liquid and set aside to cool.

Discard half the cooking stock, add the remaining honey and place back on the stove reducing the liquid by ¾.

Filter and chill on ice bath.

Roll the leek into plastic wrap while still warm, twisting both ends till firm and tight and transfer to a freezer till solid.

Set the oven at 250 degrees and place a silicone baking mat on half sheet pan.

Remove the roll from the freezer and let it sit at room temperature about 20 minutes till softer and easier to cut through it.

Remove the plastic and with the help of a meat slicer cut a few paper thin coins, placing them flat on the silicone baking mat spaced apart from one another.

Brush a very small layer of the sugary stock reduction on each coin and bake in hot oven about 2-2½ hours or till they are completely dry and crispy.

Sprinkle with crystallized salt and with a small spatula delicately remove the warm leeks and store on deli paper.

When completely cold, transfer to an airtight container to better preserve their crispiness and taste.

Almonds Morelles Texture

Ingredients

6 oz of fresh morelles mushrooms
2 espresso beans
1 tsp of white peppercorns
1 tsp of black peppercorns
3 large sage leaves
1 shallot sliced in half
1 garlic clove sliced in half
2 oz of dry porcini mushrooms
½ cup of almonds

3 tbsp of sugar
2 tbsp of water
½ tsp of salt

Directions
Clean the morelles mushrooms with a wet towel removing all impurities and place them in the dehydrator along with the sage leaves, the shallots and the garlic for a few hours till perfectly dry.
Toast the almonds golden and set aside.
Combine the sugar and ½ teaspoon of salt with the water and cook at moderate fire till the sugar melts into a golden-brown caramel.
Quickly mix in the almonds and stir well with a wooden spoon to a thick mix with very little caramel left in the pan, pour it over a silicone baking mat, flatten it with the spoon and cool completely at room temperature about 2 to 3 hours.
In a high-speed blender combine all the ingredients and reduce to a crumbly rough texture.
Taste for salt, adjust as needed and preserve in airtight container or in a glass jar.

To Serve
A slate stone plate would fit this salad perfectly for a very visual and dramatic presentation, but any other chilled white plate would do as well.
With a spoon drag the morelles texture across the plate end to end creating a base for our salad.
Dress the mache leaves with a little citrus dressing and place them irregularly across on top of the texture.
Cut the beets vertically in half and set them across the salad face up, coordinating for colors, visual balance and presentation.
Drizzle just a few drops of the extra virgin olive oil on each of them and lightly sprinkle with crystallized salt.
Decorate the dish with the orange segments and the lacquered leek coins set upright.
Drizzle the whole salad with a few drops of extra virgin olive oil and cracked black peppercorns.
Scoop out the creamy goat cheese gelato and place it delicately on one end of the salad on top of the texture.
Serve immediately.

Smoked Baby Spinach Crunchy Lobster and Scallops with Fresh Porcini Mushrooms

There are myths about great things happening by mistake. This is one of them! One day while in the kitchen I noticed a bowl of spinach was left out on top of the convection oven. No idea why as it did not belong there, but when I picked it up I noticed the oven's door was opened just enough to let the motor run and the inside fumes escaped toward the bowl. Staring at the useless greens, I was extremely surprised when I noticed how quickly they absorbed the scent of the roasting veal bones and even more when I brought a few leaves to my mouth to taste how incredibly fast they changed their original taste.

I started wondering if it was possible to properly smoke salad leaves and to combine them with game or even seafood for a different and revolutionary salad. I found a way to cold-smoke the spinach with the help of a commercial handheld smoking gun that allowed me to deliver flavor to the greens in a matter of minutes. By pairing tempura-style lobster and scallops to this dish I was able to find a clever connection of substance, giving the smoked greens glamour and taste. The salmon roe is a sharp addition and serves to better connect the greens to the seafood and cleans the palate from the smoky scent after each bite, marrying well with the crispy porcini slices.

I decided to use shallots and vinegar to better spread the seafood flavor as well as a second unusual sidekick dressing that really connects it all: Saba. The best way to explain Saba is that of a reduced balsamic without the taste of the vinegar. Saba is the sweet reduction of grape must, comparable to the same must used for the balsamic vinegar, except cooked down further to about one third its original volume and aged for two years in oak and chestnut barrels. The result is sweet, syrupy and rich in taste of the Trebbiano or Lambrusco grapes. The Saba is also excellent with desserts and on top of gelatos when used in small quantities.

At the restaurant we usually serve this salad covered with a see-through glass dome and trapped smoke, then we remove it only at the last second, tableside and in front of the customer for a very visual and dramatic presentation. This salad always receives many comments in appreciation even though I think sometimes it looks a lot more like an Addams Family dish.

Ingredients

3-4 oz of baby spinach leaves
½ live lobster
2 large size Diver scallops
1½ tbsp of Saba
1 tbsp of excellent salmon caviar roe
2 small fresh and very hard porcini mushrooms
Pinch of salt
Pinch of ground white pepper
A few sprigs of Magenta Lace micro greens
Crystallized salt
Cracked black peppercorns

Tools Needed

A handheld smoking gun with hickory wood chips/dust

Directions

In a medium-size salad bowl place the baby spinach, cover with two layers of plastic film, sealing the edges completely and tightly. With a small knife make an incision in the center of the bowl in the plastic large enough for the smoking gun's tube to pass through. Load the gun with the chips and smoke the spinach a few minutes, forming an intense and thick cloud.

Remove the tube and seal the top with one more layer of the plastic, shaking the spinach well enough to ensure the smoke has uniform access through it all.

Place the bowl in the refrigerator about 2 to 3 hours.

In boiling and salted water poach the whole lobster about 3 or 4 minutes and set aside.

Once cold carefully remove it from its shell, keeping the claws intact and in one piece.

Cut the tail in half lengthwise, keep half for our preparation and refrigerate the other half, tail and claw.

Slice the half tail in 4 pieces, diagonally, and the whole claw in half making sure to remove the cartilage from it.

Slice the scallops in half coin-size and on a clean towel dry them completely from the excess water, set on parchment paper.

With a damp towel carefully clean the porcinis removing all impurities, keeping the mushrooms whole as we will later slice them lengthwise, keeping both the stem and the cap in one piece.

Tempura Batter

See the Fava Bean Stuffed Zucchini Blossoms recipe in the Appetite Opener (Page 52).

Shallots Vinegar Dressing

Ingredients

½ cup of stone ground seed mustard
½ cup of mayonnaise
½ tbsp of extra virgin olive oil
Salt
Ground white pepper
¼ cup of finely chopped shallots
2 tbsp of white wine vinegar
2 tbsp of vegetable stock
¾ tbsp of dry porcini powder
¼ cup of finely chopped chives
½ tbsp of honey

Directions

Blend all ingredients together in a high-speed blender about a minute until a creamy paste is formed.
Taste for salt and pepper and store in refrigerator.

To Serve

Slice the porcini very thin lengthwise by meat slicer or by hand, keeping both the cap and the stem attached in one whole piece.
In a medium-size bowl toss the baby spinach with a little dressing, and then add the porcini mushrooms delicately mixing with your hand.
Prepare the tempura batter and set aside at room temperature.
Bring the oil to 375 degrees ready to be used.
Dip the scallops and the lobster into the batter and gently shake off the excess.
Cook for a minute or two till golden and crispy, then place on parchment paper and sprinkle with salt and white pepper.

There are a few ways we can build this salad: on a pasta bowl, on a rectangular cheese plate or on a round/square flat one, however the most important thing is to assemble it quickly as the hot tempura seafood will sit on the bottom and in direct contact with the spinach leaves.
Lay the crispy seafood on the bottom of the plate and drizzle half the Saba on top, repeat with crystallized salt and cracked black peppercorns, then place the smoked spinach and the porcini salad on top of it a few leaves at a time in order to create a delicate elevation.
Drizzle the remaining Saba on the leaves; place the salmon caviar across or on one single spot depending on the serving plate and finish by decorating the top with vivid red Magenta Lace micro greens.

Creamy Tomino Treviso Radicchio Endive White Truffles and Barolo Quince

It would be easy to label this salad "Piedmontese" because of the white truffles and the Tomino cheese, but because the Treviso radicchio from the Veneto region plays an aggressive role along with the aged balsamic vinegar from Reggio Emilia I like to think of this dish as a gastronomic mosaic of exceptional regional ingredients. It would be so nice to be able to shop throughout Italy, filling up my basket with only the best products each region has to offer and put together an incredible dish. This is a different kind of salad, where all the components do not necessarily marry with one another, different tastes, textures, and origins. Just think of the anchovies paired with the poached quince or the shaves of milk chocolate with the cheese...enough to raise an eyebrow or two.

However, once combined the result is explosive and full of flavor, yet delicate, arrogant and it leaves an unmistakable mark on everyone after the first bite is taken in. The creamy Tomino cheese is served as a small flan with traditional regional accents of spiciness and tomato in clear gelatin. Because of their bitter tastes, the radicchio and the endive are combined with sweet ingredients such as chocolate, toasted walnuts and small cubes of Barolo poached quince to neutralize their aggressive taste and to create an acceptable balance for the anchovy dressing and the aged balsamic vinegar.

The 25-year-old balsamic is the fruit of a dedicated craftsmanship: to obtain such prestigious vinegar it takes a lot of work and a quarter century of slow aging via consecutive transfers in various barrels made of aromatic woods like oak, chestnut and juniper. Its delicate and complex taste perfectly marries many varieties of cheeses, salads and desserts and is considered a luxury for those who know how to appreciate and respect it. The white truffles complete the dish in taste and prestige, marrying perfectly well with all the present ingredients.
This is a luxury salad with expensive and very strong flavors, an autumn delight that will make you crave more for the rest of the year until truffle season will come by again. Enjoy this salad on a gray rainy day while feeling the first chills of winter and accompanied by a glass of red wine and when possible, with popping logs burning in the fireplace.

Ingredients
3 medium Treviso radicchio leaves
6 baby Belgium endive leaves
3 walnuts shelled
Shaves of Alba's white truffle
A small 1 oz block of milk chocolate
½ medium-size Barolo poached quince
1 creamy Tomino flan
A few drops of 25-year-old balsamic vinegar
A few drops of lemon juice
A few drops of natural white truffle oil
A few small leaves of micro celery

Directions
Toast the walnuts in hot oven, scrape the peel off and set aside.
Peel and cut the Barolo poached quince no bigger than ½ inch cubes and set aside at room temperature.
Slice the Treviso radicchio diagonally in leaves of approximately 2½ inches long, repeat this step for the endive keeping each tips intact.
With a small mandolin, slice a few shaves of milk chocolate and keep refrigerated.

Barolo Quince

Ingredients
1 medium-size quince
2½ cups of Barolo wine
1 cinnamon stick
Pinch of salt
Pinch of ground white pepper
1 tbsp of brown sugar
2 tbsp of honey
1 clove
1 star anise

Directions
In a small bowl combine the honey, the sugar, salt, pepper, the clove and the star anise.
Whisk well till the sugar is dissolved and the honey blended into the liquid and pour into a very small container, peel the quince and submerge the whole fruit in it completely.
Marinate in the refrigerator for 4 days.
Set the oven at 375 degrees, wrap the quince in aluminum foil and slowly cook al dente about 30-45 minutes depending on the size.

White Anchovies/Walnut Dressing Sauce

Ingredients
3 oz of marinated white anchovies in oil
6 garlic cloves peeled and cleaned
½ cup and 1 tbsp of milk
1½ tbsp of extra virgin olive oil
1 oz of heavy cream
1 tbsp of walnut oil
1 oz of toasted walnuts

Directions
Place the garlic with the milk in a small bowl and refrigerate overnight.
The next day cook the milk and garlic until tender and at a very low flame.
Add the anchovies and the extra virgin olive oil and keep on cooking at extremely low flame about 15 minutes.

Stir in the cream and cook 5 more minutes.
Remove from fire and cool about half an hour.
Add the walnut oil and the toasted walnuts, and then transfer the sauce to a high-speed blender till very fine and smooth.

Creamy Tomino Flan with "Electric" Gelatin

Ingredients
4 oz fresh creamy Tomino cheese from Piedmont
3 tbsp of heavy cream
1 tsp of extra virgin olive oil
Pinch of salt
Pinch of ground white pepper

Directions
Crumble the Tomino cheese in a bowl at room temperature and with a whisk temper in the cream to a smooth solid paste.
Add the olive oil, the salt and the pepper.
Pipe the creamy cheese into small round molds of approximately ¾ inch of diameter and 2 ½ inches high leaving a little room to later accommodate a thick layer of the "electric" gelatin.
Refrigerate till firm.

"Electric" Gelatin

Ingredients
The tip of a teaspoon of hot red pepperoncino powder from Sicily
1 gelatin sheet
½ cup of sugar
¼ cup and one tbsp of water
1 mashed garlic clove
½ cup of crushed fillets of canned Italian plum tomatoes
Pinch of salt

Directions
On low flame toast the mashed garlic with the sugar in a small pan till melted and golden.
Add the tomato and the water at once and reduce about 8 to 10 minutes.
Add salt, the pepperoncino dust, remove from fire and set aside a few minutes.

Squeeze the gelatin from the water and stir it in with a spoon.
Pass the mix through a fine mesh cone making sure to push through as much of the tomato pulp as possible.
Set aside to cool, and then transfer to a plastic squirt bottle.

To Apply the Gelatin to the Flan

Gently squirt a layer of the electric gelatin on top of the Tomino cheese flan about ¼-inch thick.
Delicately shake the mold a little to level the liquid and return to the refrigerator until firm.

White Truffle Oil

This is what many chefs call "smart luxury in the kitchen." There are many white and black truffle oils on the market, but only a few are natural, organic, infused, made only with ripe truffles and without any chemicals. Many producers augment their product with a chemical compound or synthetic aromas that mimic the truffle's taste, making it more potent but less refined, overpowering and at times nauseating.

For a natural and aromatic product only truffles in their ripest stage are used, as just before dying they emit a potent odor many like to preserve in extra virgin olive oil. A few years ago a discovery was made that most truffle oils are fake: their flavor is enhanced with chemicals. There were heated debates among restaurateurs and food enthusiasts across Europe. Many organizations and traditionalists stepped forward to discourage the production and the consumption of such oils: one of them was Carlo Petrini, founder of the globally known food movement called Slow Food.

Slow Food began in Italy in 1986 to resist and contest the opening of fast food chain outlets such as the famous McDonald's in Rome near the Spanish Steps in 1989. This was a protest against big international business interests, not a particular company. The organization grew and expanded to include more than 100,000 members with liaisons in 132 countries. Each national and international group has a leader who is responsible for promoting local artisans, local farmers, and local flavors through regional events such as wine tastings, farmers' markets and food tasting fairs.

Nowadays the Slow Food movement has offices in Switzerland, Germany, United States, France, Japan, Chile and England, with headquarters in Torino, Italy. Many publications are put out by the organization, in several languages and in several nations, and in the U.S. the movement made its presence felt with the quarterly magazine *The Snail* until 2009. Slow Food is also responsible for the world's largest food and wine fair event, called Salone del Gusto in Torino, that takes stage every two years and hosts thousands of visitors and food aficionados from all over the world with tastings, seminars and educational programs of natural food and wine resources.

I first met Carlo at one of my former restaurants in Washington, D.C.—Barolo on Capitol Hill. Slow Food was in the U.S. for the first time ever to officially launch the movement on the American market. I believe it was in the late spring of 1998. Thanks to my dear friend and then-publicist Karen Cathy, who recently and sadly lost her battle with cancer, we were able to host the event and secure a prime national spotlight. What an honor it was: we set up the ceremony in our largest private room, which soon filled with journalists, politicians, officials and a couple of celebrity chefs.

The ceremony was followed by a four-course sit down dinner for media and politico invitees only. Everyone took their seats and started reading the menu program we had set for them. One of the courses read, "Roasted fillet of Chilean sea bass with fresh porcini mushrooms, pearled Yukon potatoes, truffle oil and shaves of summer black truffles." Carlo Petrini stood up wearing his trademark red sweater, left the room and requested my presence in private. I met him by the hostess stand. I noticed he had a disturbed look on his face as he paced up and down the hallway with sharp, synchronized moves. When he touched his beard, for a split-second he reminded me of Dustin Hoffman in the movie *Rain Man*.

"Enzo, I'd like to see the bottle of the truffle oil you're using this evening," he said.

When the bottle arrived he took a few seconds to read the back label, then he started lecturing me about the chemicals in the truffle oils and how unhealthy they are. He waved his finger in my face for at least five minutes as if he was directing traffic, explaining how and why the use of such products were against his culinary principles and why they clashed with the Slow Food movement's credo. What a lesson! I felt very small and very stupid as I should have anticipated such a problem when composing the event's menu. The truth is I did not think about it. After his return to Italy, Carlo decided to take it a little further, writing an article for a local newspaper recalling the incident in detail, mentioning my name, the restaurant, and criticizing the whole evening as a success, but full of "obstacles of basic principles."

Even if his actions were inappropriate and a bit disrespectful, I thank Carlo for that lecture because it opened my eyes and made me further appreciate simple and natural ingredients. Since then I only use natural infused oils or make my own whenever the season allows it. Here is a very simple recipe to make a natural infused one, but remember to give the oil the necessary time to fully mature and use it in small quantities only.

Also, if purchasing truffle oil carefully check the label and look for the words "infused with truffles." Any descriptions like "truffle flavoring" or "truffle extract" indicates the product is synthetic and in any of these cases put it back on the shelf.

You can learn from my mistake.

Ingredients
1 oz of ripe white truffles, truffle scraps or truffle pieces
3 cups of excellent, mild and fruity extra virgin olive oil

Directions
Clean the truffles from all impurities using a damp towel and a soft toothbrush without any direct contact with water.
Cut them in smaller pieces in order to better and more efficiently spread the aroma.
Combine the oil and the truffles in a small jar or in a bottle with plastic gaskets to prevent air exposure.
Depending on the quality of the truffles and their aromatic strength, infuse the oil for at least 3 months, gently shaking on a weekly basis.
Test the oil by smelling its aroma first and then by its flavor.

To Serve

Remove the cheese flan from the refrigerator, out of its mold and place it in a corner of a cold large plate for at least 10 minutes until it reaches room temperature.

Strike a spoon of the anchovies-walnut dressing across the plate to the opposite corner diagonally, starting at the base of the Tomino cheese flan: we will build our salad right on top of it lengthwise.

Toss the radicchio and endive leaves with just a few drops of lemon juice and truffle oil, very little salt and ground white pepper.

Alternate the leaves one by one, laying them across the dressing.

Crack the walnuts in half and place them symmetrically on top of the salad leaves.

Place the Queen cubes on the endive leaves only; sprinkle each of them with crystallized salt and decorate with a small leaf of micro celery.

Drizzle a few drops of the aged balsamic vinegar, place a few shaves of milk chocolate across the salad and finish with white truffles shavings.

Chapter Six
Succulent Soups

Soups are liquid indulgences, comfort zones, luxurious sidekicks and pretentious main dishes. But soups can be a very fulfilling course as well, and at times they just work as business cards to introduce the meal you are about to consume. They set the pace and expectations. The varieties of soups are like stars in the sky: each and every ethnic group in the world has adopted soups as a significant part of their meals and they play a very important role on a daily basis.

In Asian countries soups are just as important as rice and available in many varieties and forms. Vietnamese soups are among the tastiest, flavorful and aromatic. French soups are the most elegant and refined while American soups take advantage of local products and historical foreign influences of the past such as a classic clam chowder or the wonderful Louisiana gumbo. But what about the Italians?

All our soups were crafted by necessity: by the poor people of the Renaissance times, by the great Roman Empire to feed its troops, by legendary explorers to fight the cold on long journeys or by those who were not able to afford meats or fish to feed their families and had to find suitable alternatives in a mix of vegetables and pasta liquid meals. I would categorize Italian soups originally as rustic and unrefined. With time our soups went through changes thanks to the ingredients imported from the New World and defined themselves as they are known today—minestrone, pasta e fagioli or Tuscan pappa al pomodoro, just to name some of the most popular ones.

Think of a poor, starving family in Tuscany in the 1600s: tomatoes and basil were abundant, stale bread was common in any home. Combine those ingredients with water and boil for a very humble soup known today as pappa al pomodoro. This famous tomato and bread "thickness" populates many Italian restaurant menus across the country. What used to be a necessity today is a luxury and has become a $15 bowl of rustic tradition.

I rarely order soup when I dine at an Italian restaurant. That's because Italian cuisine is so rich in so many other appealing options. I would order a luxurious risotto any day of the week or a homemade fresh pasta dish instead. However, when I dine at French restaurants, soups are abundant and always part of my meal by choice. Soups are just like any other course of an extensive meal, and even though in our Italian repertoire they get a little lost and overshadowed in terms of importance, the only way to elevate them to center stage is the way they are presented—their concept, visuals and, mostly, taste. In other words they need to be interesting and extremely appealing in order to entice a diner to choose them instead of a different item on the menu.

Italian cooking traditions are sacred and very little can be changed, but there is always a way to offer a different vision of a tradition that has defined an entire country for centuries by using new cooking techniques, and with smart and accurate ingredient pairings. I opted to make my Italian soups more interesting and a lot different from the way they originally are and to recreate them in such ways as to be better noticed and appreciated, at least in my restaurant.

Chilled Honeydew Purée with Roasted Lobster and Spicy Sicilian Pepper Gelatin

Who wants to eat warm soup in hot summer days? Every time I think of soups I picture cold winter days and rainy evenings in the fall, sitting at the dinner table warming up with a robust and comforting liquid meal. Cold soups were new to me; in my early days in culinary school all I learned about was the classic tomato gazpacho. I have to admit soups in Italy are categorized as rustic and only as an optional part of a meal: fish, meat, pastas, appetizers and even desserts benefit from much higher respect of importance and priority in consumption.

The French, since they lack pastas as an alternative in a meal course, have naturally elevated the importance of their soups to a level of respect as high as classic entrées such as their Orange Duck. They have always combined their soups with three or four additional ingredients to make them richer and more of a complete course. They have created settings and stages with combinations worthy of praise due to presentation, execution and taste.

Sometimes I think soups for the French are like brain surgery for doctors, so attentive and so detailed to make even the most skeptical diner an avid fan and admirer.

Nowadays, as a converted skeptic I fully admire the endless possibilities in creating varieties of soups in different concepts and presentation. The real task for me was to create a cold preparation worthy of the same respect and attention as the hot ones since they are generally and almost entirely consumed in summertime, mostly to offset the hot temperatures. It is very rare to achieve a balanced comfort zone with cold soups as it is much harder to deliver chilled satisfying flavors. In my opinion, whoever orders a cold soup must be a real soup lover, therefore he or she should be rewarded with a far superior quality product that exceeds expectations in taste, presentation and concept.

I always thought there was a strong connection in taste between a honeydew melon and roasted lobster. I have always been confident I could come up with an acceptable balance between the two with the help of other complementary ingredients. The result is this delicate and very tasty fine jewel. I only select the ripest melon, liquefy the pulp and elevate its taste with unusual kickers such as Midori liqueur and Cointreau. It is very important to serve this soup at room temperature and not chilled to highlight the connection in taste with the roasted lobster and to fully acknowledge the spiciness of the pepper gelatin. You will realize the fresh thyme is perhaps the strongest connector between the soup and the lobster with neutral refreshing accents of the sour cream and the lemon segments. The caviar delivers importance to the dish and mostly an insisting and sharp combining taste.

Ingredients
3½ lbs of ripe honeydew melons pulp peeled and seeded
¼ tsp finely minced garlic
3 tbsp of Midori liqueur
2 tbsp of Cointreau liqueur
Salt
Ground white pepper
1 tbsp of sour cream
A sprinkle of cracked black peppercorns
A drizzle of excellent extra virgin olive oil

The leaves of a sprig of fresh thyme
5-6 spicy Sicilian red pepper gelatin cubes
1 lobster claw meat and ¼ lobster tail of about 1 lb in size
A sprig of fresh chervil
A tsp of Sevruga caviar
Crystallized salt
Crumbled pocket bits of one lemon segment
1 tsp of olive oil
1 garlic clove peeled and mashed

Directions

Dice the melon pulp very small and run in a powerful high-speed blender till completely liquefied and very smooth in texture.
Place it into a large mixing bowl and delicately, by hand, whisk in the minced garlic, salt, white pepper, the Midori and the Cointreau. Taste for salt and pepper and set in the refrigerator for a couple of hours.
Boil the whole lobster in salted water a few minutes.
When warm, remove the shells and by carefully cracking the claw open, remove the inside meat intact and whole for presentation.
Peel the lemon with a small sharp knife and carefully cut out a couple of segments and set aside.

Spicy Sicilian Pepperoncino Gelatin

Ingredients

½ tsp of spicy Sicilian pepperoncino dust
½ cup of hand crushed canned plum tomato fillets
1 cup of roasted, peeled and finely chopped bell red pepper
24 oz vegetable stock
2 tbsp of unflavored granular gelatin
½ tbsp of extra virgin olive oil
1 garlic clove mashed
5 leaves of fresh basil
Salt
Pinch of ground white pepper

Directions

Combine the gelatin with 3 ounces of cold water, bloom and set aside.

Sauté the mashed garlic with the extra virgin olive oil till golden, then add the fillets of tomatoes, the chopped peppers, salt, the Sicilian pepperoncino and the basil leaves.
Simmer a few minutes at moderate fire, and then add the vegetable stock.
Bring to boil and simmer about 6 to 7 minutes longer, remove from the stove and set aside for about 15 minutes.
When warm, discard the basil leaves from the mix, taste for salt, add the ground white pepper and gently stir in the gelatin with a whisk till completely melted.
Transfer the mix into a high-speed blender till fine and smooth in consistency, then in an ice bath for less than a minute to cool completely.
Quickly place the mix in a wide, high-sided plate before it solidifies, cover with plastic wrap and refrigerate about 4 to 5 hours.

To Serve
In a small hot pan sear the lobster claw and tail with the olive oil, the mashed garlic and a few leaves of thyme.
Add salt, white pepper and set aside.
In a room-temperature serving bowl, strike across a tablespoon of sour cream, creating a wide strip as a base to accommodate all the other ingredients.
Slice the lobster tail in 4 pieces diagonally and place them across the sour cream along with the whole seared claw.
Remove the pepper gelatin from the refrigerator and cut out a few cubes of about ½ inch each, place them along with the lobster, the lemon bits and the caviar making sure they are all set symmetrically for visual balance.
Sprinkle with the crystallized salt and the cracked black peppercorns.
Drizzle with extra virgin olive oil and the fresh thyme leaves and finish decorating with the fresh chervil.
Once the plate is presented the soup is poured in the bowl (never directly on top of the decoration).

Wet/Dry Minestrone and Stinging Nettles Pesto Broth in a Coffee Press Pot

Minestrone is possibly the most well-known and popular soup in Italy. It is a combination of the freshest available vegetables on the market, cooked and served in every region and in every home. If you walk through the open-air markets in Italy, you would find stands selling fresh, mixed and diced vegetables in bulk ready for easy buying and easier cooking. Minestrone is an Italian culinary institution that carries tradition and history all the way back to the early Roman times.

Back then, it was a completely different soup from the one we know today: the Roman army used to feed minestrone to its troops marching throughout Italy and beyond using only leftover vegetables and spelt flour cooked into porridge. It was a meager necessity dish that combined turnips, chick peas, beans, asparagus, lentils, cabbage and onions and in lucky days some meat, and provided fuel for the soldiers in the form of a thick semi-liquid meal. After Christopher Columbus introduced potatoes and tomatoes in Europe, those two ingredients were added to the minestrone recipe.

There are variations in every region and the original recipe customizes itself with local products: in the region of Liguria and especially around the Genoa area, it is custom to add a spoon of pesto sauce in the hot soup right before serving. The idea is genius as pesto marries perfectly well to the soup, providing taste and color. Around the area of Milan, it is often "colored" with a few strings of saffron, while in the Venice area minestrone is at times changed into a seafood and shellfish vegetable meal. But what is minestrone really? It's a combination of mixed vegetables cooked together in liquid where some are freshly cut and others are dried and revived by water. Because of it I came up with the idea to instantly "force combine" a minestrone soup where dry and fresh vegetables come alive in the same bowl using only hot liquid as the flavor conductor and a visual vehicle that makes all of this happen in an instant: a glass coffee press pot.

This dish is divided in two specific parts: the first is a bowl containing a tower of multiple fresh-cut and lightly cooked mix vegetables topped with a stack of mix dry ones sitting on tasty, thick Cannellini white bean purée that will help thicken the soup once the liquid is poured in. The second is an instant infusion coffee pot where I combine fresh herbs with roasted shallots, garlic cloves, ripe cherry tomatoes and a revolutionary pesto sauce made with stinging nettle leaves and basil.

The hot stock is poured into the pot and once pressed it infuses the liquid with all other ingredients, creating a very tasteful and colorful base broth. The liquid is then poured directly on top of the vegetables in the right quantity to mix it into a semi-thick soup just like regular minestrone, and then stirred with a spoon by the guest.

Wet Minestrone

Ingredients
1 small Yukon potato carved in small pearls with a small size melon baller
2 tbsp of dry Cannellini beans
1 small zucchini cut in small cubes of ½ inch
1 medium-size carrot carved in small pearls with a small size melon baller
1 tbsp of dry Borlotti beans
Salt
Ground white pepper
¼ cup of hot vegetable stock *(Recipe: Page 36)*
2 bay leaves
1 tbsp of extra virgin olive oil
The tip of a teaspoon of minced garlic

Directions
In separate containers soak the Borlotti and the Cannellini in water overnight.
The next day boil them separately with bay leaves till tender and set aside.
While still hot transfer the Cannellini beans to a high-speed blender and combine with the extra virgin olive oil, salt, white pepper, the hot vegetable stock and the minced garlic until a smooth and tasty paste.
Boil the pearled potatoes and the carrots in separate, salted water; repeat this step for the zucchini, cooking only 20 seconds.

Make sure the vegetables are cooked entirely while retaining their natural bright colors. Cool naturally at room temperature (avoid washing them under cold water or in ice bath to preserve their original taste).

Dry Minestrone

Ingredients

A few artichoke chips *(Recipe: Page 142)*
A few red beet chips
A few crunchy yellow beet chips (Recipe: Page 249)
A couple of fried basil leaves *(Recipe: Page 147)*
A handful of crunchy Vidalia onions
A small handful of fried crunchy leeks *(Recipe: Page 125)*
5 garlic chips *(Recipe: Page 143)*
5 candied cherry tomatoes *(Recipe: Page 69)*

Directions

Gather all the dry vegetables in separate containers so they are ready to be assembled at the necessary time.
Keep at room temperature.

Crunchy Vidalia Onions

Ingredients

1 big Vidalia onion
2 cups of blended oil for frying
1 tbsp of corn starch
Salt

Directions

Peel and slice the onion paper-thin and place in a small bowl with the corn starch.
Mix well discarding the extra starch, leaving only a thin velvety layer on the onions.
Set the oil at 375 degrees and cook only a few slices at a time till golden and crispy.
Place on deli paper and sprinkle with salt while still warm.
Preserve in airtight container.

Stinging Nettles Pesto

Ingredients

5 oz of fresh baby stinging nettle leaves
10 leaves of fresh basil
1½ tbsp of grated Parmesan Reggiano cheese
1 tbsp of toasted pine nuts
½ cup of extra virgin olive oil
2 small garlic cloves
Salt
Ground white pepper

Directions

Blanch the nettle leaves in salted water, drain and set aside till cool.
In a high-speed blender combine all the ingredients, drizzling the oil a little at a time until creating a fine green paste.
Remove from blender and refrigerate.

For the Coffee Press Pot

Ingredients

1 sprig of fresh thyme
2 cloves of roasted garlic
1 clove of roasted shallot sliced in half
4-5 ripe cherry tomatoes sliced in half
2 tbsp of stinging nettle pesto
1 small sprig of rosemary
2 cups of boiling hot vegetable stock *(Recipe: Page 36)*

Directions

In a medium-size French coffee press pot, combine all the ingredients for presentation with the exception of the broth.

Tools Needed

1 medium-sized melon baller of 22 mm bowl round 3/4"
1 round aluminum mold of approximately 3 inches in diameter and at least 2 inches high
1 medium-size French coffee press pot

To Serve

In a heated serving soup bowl place a spoonful of Cannellini bean purée in the center of the plate and spread gently in a circular motion, creating a round, thick layer.

Place the metallic mold on top of the purée in the middle; lay the poached potatoes, then the zucchini, the Borlotti beans and finish with the carrots.

Firmly press all the ingredients down with the help of a small glass and remove it by gently twisting.

Combine all the ingredients for the dry minestrone on top of the flan, start by laying a few beet chips flat on top of the carrots.

Continue with the dry basil leaves, the artichoke chips, the garlic chips, the leeks and the onions in no particular order, making sure to give the appearance of a light, delicate and elevated structure.

Place the candied cherry tomatoes around the flan, sprinkle with cracked black peppercorns and crystallized salt.

Drizzle with extra virgin olive oil and set aside.

Fill the coffee pot with the hot vegetable stock and with the help of a spoon stir the pesto with the broth creating a vivid green color.

Present the bowl to your guest tableside; press all the ingredients through the coffee filter delicately but firmly in order to release their flavor.

Once combined, pour the soup on top of the vegetables, creating instant minestrone.

Pumpkin/Amaretto Soup Chestnuts Raviolini Parmesan Foam White Truffles and Encapsulated Extra Virgin Olive Oil Teardrop

This silky recipe is a circus of textures, temperatures, colors and flavors. Because of the limited availability of the white truffle season, this soup can be executed only for a few weeks out of the year. However, you could always substitute the white truffles with the black ones in the winter months and with black summer Scorzones right after spring, making it available year-round. Surprisingly, what makes it interesting and unusual is the combination of the butternut squash with the sweet amaretto cookies. Whenever my guests read the soup description on the menu for the first time, there is always a comment or a stare filled with surprise and skepticism. The same goes for the spinach raviolini filled with chestnuts and Savoiardi cookies, a fundamental element for success in this dish.

I choose butternut squash instead of pumpkin as I find its pulp a lot milder in taste and easier to work because it has fewer fibers, therefore more delicate. I add amaretto cookies at the end of the cooking process to round up and edge the otherwise boring soup, creating diversity, taste and a one-of-a-kind aroma. In Italy it is not unusual to pair amaretto cookies with meats, pastas or soup. Most recipes that call for these cookies are about 200 years old and originate almost entirely from the Emilia Romagna region in the Bologna area, even though the cookies were first crafted and baked in a small northern town near Milan called Saronno, and sent to courts all over Italy for local nobles and authorities. This is where the famous amaretto liquor gets its name. It was just a matter of time when cooking ideas started evolving and creating the first recipes employing amaretto in preparations for desserts, soups and game.

I twisted this soup and personalized it with my vision and ideas, preserving its original taste and respecting its origins and traditions. The addition of the chestnut-filled spinach raviolini to the soup is a comfort factor that brings taste to the dish. The Parmesan foam adds a very unique and distinctive edge in an unusual texture that melts into the hot soup instantly, while the encapsulated extra virgin olive oil is a delicate visual attribute for presentation until the sugar melts, freeing the oil and adding to the overall taste.

It is a glorious soup, completed by the unmistakable flavor and fragrance of white truffle shavings. This is indeed one of my favorite soups; especially when I go overboard shaving white truffles all over it for my personal consumption…sometimes I love to indulge. Can you blame me?

Ingredients
2.2 lbs of butternut squash peeled cleaned and cut in one inch cubes
2 small white onions sliced
2.5 oz amaretto cookies
7 cups of chicken broth
1.5 cups of veal stock reduction
2 oz of pancetta or the end part of a Parma prosciutto
4 oz of butter
¼ cup of extra virgin olive oil
3 sage leaves finely chopped
2 sprigs of fresh thyme without the stem
3 garlic cloves mashed
Salt
Ground white pepper
2 tbsp of olive oil
1 tsp of natural white truffle oil
White truffle shavings

Directions
In a large pot roast the pancetta piece with the olive oil.
When crispy add the butter, the onions and the garlic, the chopped herbs and cook till translucent.
Mix in the butternut squash, the salt and pepper, the broth and stock and simmer at moderate fire till the squash starts to dissolve and is completely cooked and the liquid reduced by 1/3.
Turn the fire off and discard the pancetta from the soup.
With the help of a whisk, mash in the amaretto cookies and finish with the extra virgin and truffle oil.
Taste for salt, pepper and correct if necessary.
Purée the soup with a handheld immersion blender first, then transfer to a high-speed blender till extremely fine and velvety.

Chestnut Raviolini

Spinach Pasta Dough

Ingredients

1 lb of AP flour
½ tbsp of salt
1 tbsp olive oil
½ cup of spinach powder
5 eggs

Directions

In a mixer with the hook attachment combine all the ingredients together until it is a smooth and elastic pasta dough.
Wrap with plastic film and set in refrigerator for a couple of hours.

Chestnuts and Savoiardi Cookie Filling

Ingredients

1 lb of chestnuts peeled and cleaned
2 sage leaves finely chopped
1 oz of butter
Salt
Ground white pepper
3½ oz of dry Savoiardi cookies
¼ cup of grated Parmesan Reggiano cheese
½ tbsp of natural white truffle oil
1 qt of milk
Egg wash for the raviolini
2 tbsp of flour for pasta making/dusting
1 sage leaf and half tbsp of butter for sautéing the pasta
A few micro yellow corn shoots

Tools Needed

1 press mold for miniature-size ravioli
1 edged wheel pasta cutter
1 small rolling pin

Directions

In a medium-size pan simmer the chestnuts with the milk, the butter, the sage, salt and pepper.

Cook at low flame until the chestnuts are dissolved and at least 40 percent of the liquid is reduced.
Remove from the stove and immediately mash in the Savoiardi cookies with the help of a whisk, then add in the Parmesan cheese and the truffle oil.
Run the mix in a food processor while still warm to a very smooth and thick paste with no lumps.
Transfer to a disposable pastry bag and rest about two hours at room temperature before using.
Dust the ravioli mold with flour and lay a thin sheet of spinach pasta on top of it.
Brush with egg wash and squeeze the chestnut stuffing in each compartment.
Place another sheet of dough on top, press with your hands first, then with the rolling pin applying pressure until completely sealed.
With a quick motion flip the mold upside-down on the table and release the pasta from the ravioli press.
Dust with flour and cut through the edges with the cutter wheel, creating individual raviolini.
Transfer to a small sheet pan with parchment paper dusted with flour, cover with a towel and place in the refrigerator.

Parmesan Cheese Foam for Siphon

Ingredients
½ qt of heavy cream 40 percent fat
¼ qt of whole milk
1½ cups of grated Parmesan Reggiano cheese
Salt
Ground white pepper

Tools Needed
1 siphon of one quart capacity and 2-3 $CO2$ tank chargers

Directions
Combine the milk and heavy cream in a small pan with salt and pepper and bring it to 140 degrees temperature.
Whisk in the Parmesan cheese until completely dissolved.
Filter the mix through a fine mash and refrigerate.
When cold transfer the liquid into a siphon.

Add 2 CO_2 tank chargers and test the foam for consistency, add one more CO_2 tank if needed.
Keep refrigerated.

Encapsulated Extra Virgin Olive Oil Teardrops

Ingredients
4 oz deco malt
2-3 tbsp of water
Excellent sharp extra virgin olive oil
Crystallized salt

Directions
Melt the deco malt and water to 145 degrees in a small pot.
Remove from stove and set aside.
A few minutes later test the sugar for density.
Blow a sugar bubble using a hollow medium-size stainless steel cannoli mold.
Dip it into the sugar, retaining a sugar film on the edge, blow delicately onto a silicone baking mat and delicately pour the extra virgin olive oil in it.
Rapidly close by pulling and twisting upward, forming a teardrop shape, blow on it to cool the solidifying sugar.
Store the drops in airtight container over deli paper.

Tip: *The teardrops have a shelf life of just about one day.*

To Serve
Warm up the soup and set in a small serving carafe.
Cook the raviolini in a large amount of salted water and sauté them lightly with sage and butter.
Divide the plate into 3 sections and place the raviolini in one, leaving room for the other 2 components.
In the second section gently squeeze the parmesan foam out of the siphon, creating the equivalent in size of a large golf ball and decorate the top with micro yellow corn shoots.
In the final section add the tear drop, sprinkle with crystallized salt and present the dish.
Shave the white truffles in the bowl, and then delicately pour in the hot soup.

White Asparagus Cream Goose Liver Capunet Black Truffle-Tomato Trifle and Parma Napoleon

This is not your typical vegetarian asparagus soup, but a combination of flavors and a visual assembly of colors using simple ingredients and transformed into complex components making this recipe a winner. Chefs have cooked green asparagus soup forever and in many possible ways. It has been done and re-done to the point it has become boring, and frankly I too got tired of it over time. So I explored a new way to revive its interest using only white asparagus as a smooth silky liquid conductor to bring other flavors together such as the roasted goose liver capunet, the Parma prosciutto Napoleon and the tomato trifle.

Individually, all the above elements are stunners in rich taste and quite frankly overwhelming for any palate once combined in a single plate. This is where the white asparagus liquid comes in and steals the show. I cooked this soup preserving only its original flavor in the simplest way. I used potatoes for starchiness, heavy cream to better transport the flavor, and onions and garlic for a lighter taste connection. The result is a flavorful liquid that tones down the rich taste of each component assembled in the bowl, making those compatible with each other and extremely delicate.

Additionally, I have used raw San Marzano tomatoes with black truffles to further distress the intensity of the dish, but at the same time creating a very unusual and refreshing new flavor: as a matter of fact no one pairs truffles with tomatoes. And no one should. But I was able to break the rule in a way that stunned all my culinary beliefs. This combination does not work on its own, but it excels in taste and functionality when combined with the white asparagus soup.

Make sure to properly drain the tomatoes and to chop them only by hand, with a butcher knife. You will get tempted to use a blender or an electrical chopping device, but in this case it would only ruin your work as the tomatoes would release water forever, making it impossible to combine with the diced truffles in a tartar-like consistency.

Ingredients
6 oz of pancetta in one slice
1 medium-size onion sliced
2 garlic cloves sliced
1 medium-size Yukon potato thinly sliced
2 qt of chicken broth
Salt
Ground white pepper
¾ cup heavy cream
6 oz butter
2.5 lbs white asparagus peeled and sliced

Directions
Carefully slice the tips of the asparagus from the stack and save them whole and intact in a separate container for later use.
In a medium-deep pan crisp the pancetta with the butter, then add the onions, the garlic and the potatoes and cook at medium flame for a few minutes.
Add the sliced asparagus, the salt and the white pepper, stirring with a spoon to make sure the asparagus does not get color.
Pour in the chicken broth and cook the soup about 15 minutes on low-moderate flame.
Stir in the heavy cream and simmer about 8 more minutes at medium-high temperature.
Remove the pancetta, taste for salt and pepper and set aside about 15 minutes to cool.
Transfer the soup to a high-speed blender till fine and smooth.
Quickly blanch the asparagus tips in boiling salted water very al dente and set aside.

Goose Liver Capunet

Ingredients
Goose liver
2 Savoy cabbage leaves
Salt
Ground white pepper
1 micro yellow corn shoot
1 thin slice of Parma prosciutto

Directions

Cut a 4-inch long piece of goose liver approximately 1-inch thick.
Sear it in a hot pan quickly with salt and pepper and set aside.
Trim the Savoy cabbage leaves into 6-inch squares, blanch them in salted boiling water for a few seconds, then lay them flat to cool.
Roll the seared liver in the Parma prosciutto slice, cut in 4-inch squares.
Place the cabbage leaves on top of each other, add white pepper and place the goose liver on one end of it, rolling it into a small cannolo by folding both ends just like a burrito, sealing properly for cooking.
Bake in hot oven with a tablespoon of chicken broth, covered with aluminum foil approximately 5 to 6 minutes at 400 degrees.
Remove the roll from the pan and set aside, covered with plastic film.

Black Truffle-Tomato Trifle

Ingredients

1 lb of excellent San Marzano canned tomatoes
A few shaves of black truffles
1 tsp of natural black truffle oil
Crystallized salt
Ground white pepper
½ clove of minced roasted garlic
1 tsp of extra virgin olive oil
1 very small fried basil leaf
1 fresh basil leaf chopped at the moment right before using

Directions

Chop the black truffle slices to miniature cubes and set aside.
Strain the tomatoes about one hour, then with your fingers remove all the seeds and return the fillets to the strainer for another 30 minutes till all the extra water is completely washed out.
Dry the tomatoes on a large towel and transfer to a cutting board.
With a butcher knife, chop the fillets by hand to thick and dry chutney and place in a small mixing bowl.
Add the minced roasted garlic, the white pepper, the minced truffles, the oils, the chopped basil leaf and mix well with a spoon.
Set in refrigerator to marinate for a day.

Parma Napoleon

Ingredients

2-3 large Parma prosciutto slices
3 oz of white asparagus peeled and finely sliced
½ tsp of extra virgin olive oil
¼ cup of chicken broth
2 tbsp of heavy cream
½ tsp of natural black truffle oil
¼ shallot minced
The tip of a teaspoon of minced garlic
A few black truffle slices
½ tbsp of butter
Salt
Ground white pepper
A few small micro green leaves for decoration

Directions

Lay the prosciutto slices on a cutting board and cut out about 8-10 1½-inch squares.
Lay them on a silicone baking mat and bake until crisp in hot oven approximately two hours at 230 degrees.
With a small spatula delicately transfer the prosciutto squares to a plate on deli paper.
In a small sauté pan golden the garlic and the shallot with the butter at low flame, add the sliced asparagus, the broth, salt, pepper and cook for few minutes.
When reduced add the heavy cream and cook at low flame till most of the liquid is gone.
Set aside for 5 minutes.
Transfer the mix to a high-speed blender while still warm, add the black truffle oil and the extra virgin and if necessary add a little extra heavy cream to a thick and velvety white paste.
Set aside till room temperature covered with plastic film or set into a small disposable pastry bag for better handling.

To Serve

Remove the tomato trifle from the refrigerator and set to room temperature.
Place the goose liver capunet on a cutting board, unwrap the first outer cabbage layer leaving the goose liver only with the inside

one, cut out a piece of approximately 1½ inches long exposing the roasted liver stuffing on both ends.
Divide the bottom of a warm soup bowl in 3 sections for presentation purposes: on the first one set the goose liver roll upright, sprinkle the top with a few salt crystals and stick the micro green corn shoot in it for decoration.
On the second one, with the help of a couple of small tablespoons, shape a quenelle out of the tomato trifle, place a small fried basil leaf on top of it and sprinkle with crystallized salt.
On the third one we will build the prosciutto Napoleon.
Choose 5 Parma square chips; squeeze a pea-size amount of white asparagus purée placing it directly on the plate.
Lay the first square on top of it flat, pressing firm to make sure it sticks solid to the plate.
Squeeze a coin-size purée on top of it, followed by a slice of black truffle and again one more squeeze of the asparagus purée.
Top it with a prosciutto square, pressing delicately but firmly enough to settle the first layer of the Napoleon.
Repeat this step 4 more times and finish, decorating the top with a drop of the purée, a few micro green leaves, a slice of black truffle and a couple of the blanched asparagus tips.
Decorate the bowl with a few more asparagus tips, present it to your guest and pour the hot asparagus purée right in the middle of the plate.

Smoked Tomato Bread Soup with Roasted Shrimp and Crunchy Vidalia Onions in a Glass Vase

The most commonly asked question about this soup is, "Is this a deconstructed version of the Tuscan pappa al pomodoro?" Not exactly. Certain traditions should never be changed or altered, but embraced and protected for what they are: glorious elements of gastronomic history. If we look closely, however, we notice similar components of the pappa al pomodoro that would justify the above question: tomatoes, focaccia bread, basil, extra virgin olive oil and cracked black peppercorns. But what I really wanted to do is to combine an instant soup similar to the wet/dry minestrone soup recipe listed in this same chapter.

When I cook I have the need to visualize, and I have noticed customers love to see the magic happening right before their eyes as well. So I opted for a see-through glass vase as a food vehicle to bring this soup alive at the table. The idea is to combine all the ingredients in a glass vase and to pour the hot smoked tomato broth in it, creating a flavorful and unique taste. I love the way the soup marries with the roasted shrimp and the crunchy Vidalia onions. The focaccia croutons will eventually disintegrate, thickening the soup to a Tuscan bread and tomato-like consistency.

Another basic element in this recipe is the extra virgin olive oil squeezed on top of the ingredients by a plastic pipette right before the broth goes in. It spreads its taste quickly and balances the pungent smoky aroma of the tomato, making the whole dish a lot more delicate.

Ingredients for Serving Vase
6 fresh large head of shrimp
5 garlic chips
4 fried basil leaves
5 small ripe cherry tomatoes sliced in half
Cracked black peppercorns
Crystallized salt
1 tbsp of excellent extra virgin olive oil
1 tbsp of olive oil
A small handful of crunchy Vidalia onions
8 focaccia croutons
Pinch of dry oregano
Pinch of crushed red hot pepper
1 bamboo pick for bar cocktails 4 inch long
1½ cups of smoked tomato broth

Tools Needed
1 small plastic disposable pipette for extra virgin olive oil
1 square glass serving vase approximately 5 x 5 inches high

Smoked Tomato Broth

Ingredients
1 qt of vegetable stock
½ cup of smoked tomato paste
6 fresh basil leaves
Salt

Ground white pepper

Directions
Simmer the vegetable stock a couple of minutes.
Whisk in the smoked tomato paste, salt, pepper and the basil leaves.
Remove from the stove and set aside about one hour, stirring occasionally.
Filter the smoked tomato broth through a very fine strainer and taste for salt and pepper.
Keep in airtight glass container to preserve the smoky flavor.

Smoked Tomato Paste

Ingredients
Tomato paste

Directions
Place the tomato paste in a smoker with soaked applewood chips about 3 hours at very low temperature, stirring the paste well frequently.
When ready, preserve in airtight container or in a glass jar.

Crunchy Vidalia Onions
See the Wet/Dry Minestrone and Stinging Nettles Pesto Broth in a Coffee Press Pot recipe on Page 206.

Focaccia Bread

Ingredients
0.3 oz of dry yeast
1.3 cups of warm water
2 qt of room temperature water
1.3 oz of extra virgin olive oil
2.6 lbs of all purpose flour
2.6 lbs of hi gluten flour
1.3 oz salt
1.5 tbsp of crystallized salt

Directions by Mixer

In the mixing bowl stir the dry yeast in the warm water and let stand about 10 minutes.

Add in the room temperature water, the olive oil and mix it all with the hook attachments for a few seconds.

Add flours, the salt and mix at moderate speed for one minute until all ingredients come together.

Change to faster speed and mix about thirty seconds, then again at lower speed for additional 3-4 minutes to create elastic dough.

Remove from bowl and place it in a warm area covered with a towel and let it rise about an hour or until it doubles its original size.

Transfer to a full-size sheet pan with only half of the extra virgin olive oil; stretch the dough to fit the pan and set aside to rise again until it doubles one more time.

When ready, gently brush the remaining oil throughout the whole surface of the focaccia and sprinkle abundantly with the crystallized salt.

Cook in hot oven at 350 degrees for approximately 20-25 minutes.

Focaccia Croutons

Cut the crust out from at least a 3-day old focaccia.

Use only the center white part of it and cut a few ¾-inch cubes.

Set the oven at 250 degrees.

In a plate, generously drizzle the croutons with extra virgin olive oil and sprinkle them with just a touch of crystallized salt.

Transfer to a small sheet pan over a silicone baking mat and place them symmetrically distanced apart from each another.

Bake till lightly golden and completely dry.

Preserve in airtight container.

To Serve

Fill the plastic pipette with extra virgin olive oil and set aside.

In a small pan sauté the 6 shrimp with the olive oil, the oregano, the hot pepper, and the mashed garlic clove until crispy.

Arrange 3 of the cooked shrimp in the bamboo skewer and cut the others in 12 pieces discarding the heads and tails.

In the glass vase mix the halved cherry tomatoes, the garlic chips, the focaccia croutons and the diced shrimp.

Sprinkle with crystallized salt and cracked black peppercorns, adorn with the fried basil leaves, place the crunchy Vidalia onions,

and on one side of the vase set the bamboo skewer with the roasted shrimp.
Now, stick the pipette filled with extra virgin olive oil in the onions for visibility and elevation.
Serve the glass vase, squeeze the oil out of the pipette and pour the hot smoked tomato broth on top of the ingredients.

Chestnut Soup, Buffalo Ricotta Flan, Duck Sausage, Port Wine Glaze, Poached Quail Egg

The very first time I tasted a chestnut soup was at the Watergate Hotel in Washington, D.C., by the hands of chef Jean Louis Palladin at his restaurant in 1989. Back then he was already a legend and his restaurant a destination for international gastronomes. If I recall correctly, back then there was a young and talented French cook working in his kitchen by the name of Eric Ripert, nowadays chef and owner of the nationally respected restaurant in New York City, Le Bernardin, and a television celebrity.

Jean Louis was indeed a very hard person to work for as well as very demanding in the kitchen, and at times even on a personal basis. He was as talented as he was unpredictable. Tales of this man are legendary, odd and quite unreal, and I have personally witnessed many situations in various culinary trips where he was funny, crazy, comical and wild, all in a 30-second window. The wind usually takes longer to change its direction than it took Jean Louis to change his mood.

The first time I was invited to see his kitchen I noticed at the end of the cooking line a visibly damaged wall: it was chipped all over and it looked like someone had purposely hit it with a hammer, marking it deeply. When I returned to my table, I asked my server (who I personally knew) what had happened.

He explained, "The wall in the kitchen is damaged because of the chef. At times when a cook puts up a dish that is not perfectly executed or it does not meet the chef's approval, he throws it across the kitchen and against the wall, breaking the plate as a statement for everyone to see."

Back then, his line cooks needed helmets instead of chef hats. There are urban legends of chef Ripert occasionally quitting his post out of desperation, and more of Jean Louis following him to the changing room, begging him to put his apron back on and return to work.

I have experienced the same in my beginning days with Roberto Donna at Galileo restaurant with very unfair and at time abusive situations. As a little boy with no legal papers I was ordered to obey and perform almost anything asked of me for the good and the glory of the restaurant, including behind the line pushups on the kitchen floor in the middle of the service as punishment. I was a very driven and dynamic boy, and I have always carried out any tasks in the best possible way even in the extreme or in the most unprofessional situation. Back then I liked working out so I did not really mind adhering to a "kitchen military regime," but others did not share the same enthusiasm. As a matter of fact each and every one of my fellow co workers returned to Italy within a year of their arrival.

Regardless of those experiences, or perhaps because of them, my chestnut soup has become excellent, light, hearty and absolutely stunning. With the passing years I have developed a way to combine delicate ingredients to elevate the taste of the chestnuts to a more complete and round flavor, creating a worthy stage in the bowl to better host such glorious soup. My version reminds me a lot of Jean Louis, but I have to be honest when I say his was one of a kind.

The buffalo ricotta cheese flan is delicate and sharp, and with the crispy shallots it helps to combine the reduction of port to the velvety taste of the chestnuts. The roasted duck sausage brings substance and importance to the dish as well as flavor while the poached quail egg highlights diversity, texture and surprise.

Ingredients
2 lbs and 12 oz of peeled and cleaned frozen chestnuts
4.5 oz of speck sliced paper thin
2 medium-size Vidalia onions sliced
4 garlic cloves mashed
2 shallots peeled and sliced

1 medium-size carrot thinly sliced
1½ sprigs of rosemary chopped
1 sprig of sage chopped
1 large Yukon potato peeled and thinly sliced
6 oz of high fat butter
1 qt of veal stock reduction
2 qt of chicken broth
3 oz of dry porcini mushrooms
2 cups of heavy cream
1 tbsp of natural white truffle oil
Salt
Ground white pepper

Directions
Soak the porcini mushrooms in plenty of water and set aside.
Cut the speck in long strips first, then in small bits and sauté crispy in a medium-size pot with the butter.
Add the sliced onions, the garlic, the shallots, the chopped herbs, the carrots and the potatoes.
On medium flame stir occasionally until the onions are translucent, add the chestnuts and combine stirring for a few minutes.
Add salt and pepper.
Chop the porcini mushrooms and filter their soaking water, add them both in the mix with the veal stock and the chicken broth, cooking until it reduces by half.
Now add the cream and simmer for an additional 8 to 10 minutes in order to fully blend with the liquid and to transport the flavor.
Remove from stove, whisk in the truffle oil and liquefy in a high-speed blender till extremely fine and smooth.
Taste for salt and pepper, correct if necessary.

Buffalo Ricotta Flan

Ingredients
½ cup of very fresh buffalo ricotta cheese
2 small eggs
1 pinch of ground nutmeg
1 tsp of natural white truffle oil
¼ cup of grated Parmesan Reggiano cheese
Salt
Ground white pepper

1 cup of heavy cream

Directions

Squeeze the excess water from the buffalo ricotta with a damp towel.

Beat the eggs in a bowl with the nutmeg, the salt and white pepper, then add the ricotta cheese and mix with a spoon.

Transfer the mix into a high-speed blender; add the Parmesan cheese, the heavy cream and the truffle oil.

Run for a few seconds until all ingredients are mixed to a thick liquid consistency.

Butter and fill a few 2 oz metallic molds or aluminum melted butter cups to ¾ of their capacity.

Bake in a water bath at 325 degrees for approximately 20 to 25 minutes.

When ready, remove them from the water bath and set them aside to cool.

Duck Sausage

Ingredients

20 oz of pork butts cleaned
2½ lbs of duck meat
½ tbsp cracked black peppercorns
¾ cup of ice water
1¼ tbsp salt
1 sage leaf finely chopped
1 tsp of minced garlic
1 tsp of sugar
½ tsp of grounded cumin
Salt preserved pork casings

Directions

Clean the pork butt and the duck meat by removing all the cartilage and excess fat, dice in small cubes and combine all the above ingredients together mixing well.

Set in the refrigerator for 24 hours.

The next day grind the meat with the small knife attachment and set aside.

Rinse the salt out of the casings with cold water a couple of times and make a few small sausages 3 inches in size using a sausage stuffing machine.

Port Wine Glaze
See the Port wine reduction sauce recipe from Winter Poached Duck Egg and Crunchy Stuffed Sage Leaves in the Hot Starters (Page 126).

The only difference between the port glaze and the port sauce from the above recipe is timing: cook the port sauce a little longer until it reduces down to thicker consistency.

Remember to use only in very small quantities as the glaze is now richer in taste and it would easily overpower any of the combined ingredients.

Poached Quail Egg

Ingredients
1 very fresh quail egg
1 cup of poaching white vinegar water
Crystallized salt

Directions
Bring the vinegar water to a boil, turn down the flame and simmer about 3 minutes.
Gently crack in the quail egg on one side of the pan and rapidly, with the help of couple of teaspoons, hold the egg together till the hot water cooks the first external coat, protecting its liquid center.
Simmer about a minute and with a perforated spoon remove from water and set on a cutting board.
With a small knife carefully cut all the extra strings off the egg and extra parts, restoring its original round shape.
Set aside on a plate covered with plastic wrap upon serving.

Tip: *There is also a simpler way to poach a single quail egg without going through the trouble of keeping it together through the cooking process. I do not really suggest it as first option because this method leaves the egg tasteless, but it will keep it together for easier cooking. To do this:*

> *Cut a square piece of film wrap about 4-5 inches, delicately drop the quail egg in it without breaking the yolk and pull the 4 corners up, twisting them together to create a tight pocket for the egg.*
>
> *Tie it down with a small string and poach it in simmering boiling water through the plastic a minute or two.*
>
> *When ready, cool completely before unwrapping.*

Crunchy Sage Leaves

See the Winter Poached Duck Egg and Crunchy Stuffed Sage Leaves recipe in the Hot Starters (Page 126).

Refer to the above recipe to make the crunchy sage leaves even though these are not stuffed with Taleggio cheese.

Follow the same steps, skipping the stuffing part and fry each one dipped in the tempura batter.

Keep in an airtight container.

Crispy Shallots

Ingredients

1 medium-size shallot cleaned and peeled
1 tsp of corn starch
1 cup of blended oil for frying
Salt
Ground white pepper

Directions

Slice the shallot paper thin and place into a small bowl mixing with the corn starch, then shake off the excess in a strainer leaving a very light coat on it.
In a pan bring the oil to 350 degrees and slowly fry golden crispy.
Place on deli paper and sprinkle with salt and white pepper.

Keep in warm place until serving or in airtight container when cool.

To Serve
Roast the duck sausage and set aside.
Warm up the port wine glaze and place about a small spoon of it in the bottom of a warm serving bowl on one side only.
Next to it place the warm ricotta flan and top it with the crispy shallots.
Slice the duck sausage thin and place 3-5 slices next to the port glaze fan-style.
Lay two crunchy sage leaves in the remaining empty spot of the dish and delicately place the warm poached quail egg on top of them.
Sprinkle the egg with crystallized salt and drizzle the whole plate with very little extra virgin olive oil.
Serve to your guest and pour the hot chestnut soup in the bowl.

Artichokes Purée, Black Olives Froth, Artichoke Flan, Farro Roasted Garlic Cracker and soft Pecorino di Pienza Croquettes

This is an incredibly simple soup and one of the most delicate and richest in flavor. This is a dream come true for artichoke lovers. It is structured with five basic elements: the artichokes purée, the black olive froth, the artichoke flan, the farro roasted garlic cracker, and the fried soft pecorino cheese from Pienza, a small Renaissance town in the province of Siena in Tuscany, located between the wine areas of Montalcino and Montepulciano. Here the locals still produce amazing quality cheese in the exact way they did 100 years ago, made almost entirely by hand and exclusively with ewe's milk: a wonderful and very sharp cheese. But this is not a Tuscan soup, rather a collaboration of Tuscan and Lazio region local products as the best artichokes and the tastiest farro come from the Roman areas.

Mostly this is my interpretation of an artichoke soup with garnishes and combining ingredients with different textures. I really wanted to deliver the velvety and intense taste of the artichoke in many ways and forms, and to have a crunchy balance that ultimately comes from the farro and garlic cracker as well as from the cheese croquettes. Ever since I can remember my mother used to pair black olives with artichokes whether it was a soup or salad, grilled, roasted or boiled plain artichokes: the marriage was great and so was the combination of colors, but as little boy I got tired of it quickly. I always thought there were too many black olives on my plate and of course I was encouraged to finish everything served in front of me every time and with no exceptions. So I decided to remedy the situation by throwing the unwanted black olives from the balcony in my room whenever I was able to sneak a few in my pocket. That was one way to recycle. I was definitely a pioneer of my time.

I guess my indirect traumatic experience brought me to make quick adjustments in my culinary career, so when I created this soup I decided to include the black olive taste in the form of froth, more elegant and more delicate in taste. Besides, it is so much harder to throw black olive froth out of a balcony...and definitely much safer. As matter of fact this is a much lighter alternative, unexpected and colorful.

The combination in taste between the artichokes, the black olives, the farro cracker and the soft pecorino croquette is phenomenal. But when you eat too much of a good thing it soon becomes boring in taste, so I included a caramel made out of Merlot wine that serves to cut the taste between the artichoke purée and the cheese while breaking the eating routine of the overall taste creating enthusiasm at each bite.

Ingredients

4 whole large artichokes
1 large shallot peeled and sliced
4 garlic cloves peeled and sliced
3 tbsp of extra virgin olive oil
3 qt of vegetable stock
10 leaves of fresh basil
Salt
Ground white pepper
Cracked black peppercorns
1 cup of heavy cream
1 juicy lemon

Directions
Peel and clean the artichokes completely down to the heart, remove the choke from the core and coat with the lemon to prevent oxidation.
Slice them very fine and set aside for a few minutes.
In a deep sauté pan crisp the artichokes with half of the extra virgin, then add the garlic and the sliced shallots and cook a couple of minutes till the garlic turns golden and the shallots translucent.
Add salt and white pepper, the vegetable stock and simmer until the artichokes are dissolving and the liquid is reduced by half.
Now add the heavy cream and simmer about 4 to 5 additional minutes.
Remove from stove, set aside about 5 minutes, then add the basil and stir well until it releases its bright green color.
Taste for salt and pepper and add some more of excellent extra virgin olive oil.
Rapidly transfer the hot soup to a high-speed blender till extremely fine and smooth and ideally chill in an ice bath to preserve the color and to stop the cooking process.

Artichoke Flan

Ingredients
A few artichoke chips for decoration *(Recipe: Page 142)*
The purée of 2 fresh large artichokes (about 3 oz of liquid purée)
1 tbsp of olive oil
Salt
Ground white pepper
4 leaves of fresh basil
1 tsp of minced garlic
4 oz of heavy cream
½ tbsp of grated Parmesan Reggiano cheese
2 eggs
4 tbsp of vegetable stock
½ shallot thinly sliced
½ tbsp of extra virgin olive oil.

Directions
Clean the two fresh artichokes down to the heart removing the leaves, the choke and by trimming the stem.

Slice them very thin and sauté crisp with the garlic, the shallots the olive oil, salt and white pepper.
When colored and golden add the vegetable stock and reduce at very low flame until the slices are fully cooked, but still retaining a little liquid.
Add the basil leaves and the extra virgin olive oil, mix well with a spoon and transfer to a high-speed blender with one or two ice cubes to stop the cooking process and to preserve the bright color.
Add the grated Parmesan cheese and blend to a very fine velvet liquid to approximately 4 oz of total artichoke purée.
Add the eggs and the heavy cream, a pinch of salt and one more pinch of the white pepper, and blend gently for a few seconds only until the ingredients are mixed together.
In a small 2- or 3-inch-deep baking pan line up some parchment paper at the base.
Place a few of 2-inch-high small round baking ramekins or stainless steel forms of about 1½ to 2 oz capacity on top of the paper and coat the inside of them with cooking vegetable spray.
Fill each ramekin cup only up to ¾ and fill the pan with one inch of water to cook in water bath.
Seal the baking pan with 3 to 4 layers of plastic film wrap, making sure to properly seal the edges, and bake in hot oven approximately 20-25 minutes at 265 degrees.
Once ready remove the flans from the pan and set aside to cool.

Black Olive Froth

Ingredients
6 oz of finely chopped Ligurian black olives pitted
1½ qt of vegetable stock
Ground white pepper
8 grams of powder Lecithin
½ tsp of minced garlic
½ tbsp of olive oil
1 small shallot peeled and finely chopped
Salt
Ground white pepper

Directions
In a small pot sauté the garlic and the shallots with the olive oil, add the chopped olives and the stock, the white pepper and the salt.

Simmer until consumed to a qt of total liquid.
Taste and set aside to cool about 10 minutes.
Transfer to a high-speed blender till liquefied and smooth.
Set aside and cool completely to room temperature.
With a small handheld immersion blender combine the Lecithin with the liquid, filter through a fine mesh and set aside till serving time.

Farro and Roasted Garlic Crackers

Ingredients
½ lb of farro
1 cup of water
9 oz of canned coconut milk
1 tsp extra virgin olive oil
1 tsp salt
1 cup of milk
Pinch of crystallized salt
6 garlic cloves cleaned and peeled
1 tbsp olive oil

Directions
In a very small pan gently roast the garlic till golden with the olive oil.
Chop them and set aside.
In a wide sauté pan toast the farro a couple of minutes until golden brown with the extra virgin olive oil.
Add the water, the coconut milk, the milk, the salt and simmer about 10 minutes until the farro is fully cooked and soft and the liquids are almost gone.
Add the chopped roasted garlic to the mix and stir well.
Transfer to the food processor and run it long enough to purée the farro.
On half sheet pan over a silicone baking mat place a plastic template of tart bands of approximately 9 inches long and 1½ inch wide.
With the help of an offset spatula, spread a thin layer of the farro purée inside each template openings, creating a few long rectangular strips.
Remove the plastic template and bake in hot oven about 3½ hours at 215 degrees. When ready sprinkle a little crystallized salt on top of each strip.

Remove from sheet pan only once the crackers are completely cold and store in a wide airtight container and over parchment paper.

Soft Pecorino di Pienza Croquettes

Ingredients
2 oz of soft pecorino di Pienza 20 days old from salt brining process
Egg wash
1 tbsp of all purpose flour
2 tbsp of very fine sifted bread crumbs dust
Pinch of crystallized salt
Pinch of cracked black peppercorns

Directions
Cut the pecorino in cubes of about ½ inch each in size.
Dust them with flour, then pass them into the egg wash and lastly in the bread crumb dust to form a sealer through the frying process.
Fry the croquettes in abundant oil until golden and very crispy, remove and place apart on parchment paper; keep in a warm place until serving time.

Merlot Red Wine Caramel and Merlot Reduction
See the White Corn and Reggiano Custard recipe in the Appetite Openers (Page 44).

To Serve
On one side of a large and warm soup bowl, place an artichoke flan upside-down and out of its ramekin.
Spear in a few artichoke chips on top to give elevation.
Next to it on the same side of the bowl squirt a large coin-size Merlot caramel drop, creating the base for the pecorino croquettes.
Place 3 of them on the caramel and one more stacked on top of them.
Sprinkle with a little crystallized salt and cracked black peppercorns.
On the opposite side of the bowl lay across the rim the farro cracker and glue it on the plate on each end with a drop of the Merlot caramel if necessary in order to prevent it from sliding.
Warm up the soup and place in a serving carafe, whip the black olive froth firm, place in a small serving deep side plate and take to the table quickly.

Present the bowl to your guest, pour the soup in the bowl making sure not to cover entirely the cheese croquettes and the flan and place a generous spoon of black olive froth right on top between the cracker and the other garnishes.

Chapter Seven
The Pasta Chronicles

When I was a little kid on Sunday mornings I would wake up extra early, curious to learn the menu for the day. I could hear my mother working in the kitchen: the noise of the pots and pans, the electric pasta machine humming, but mostly I smelled the wonderful aromas that would slide under my bedroom door and drag me out of bed, kidnapping me for the rest of the day. In the early days she would make the pasta dough by hand and roll it just with a wooden pin, cut only with a knife or stuffed using only a spoon and a small glass as a cutter. She would knead the dough forever while singing or humming a song. She did not see it as a job or duty, rather as a personal and pleasurable time, an opportunity to reflect and let go, an escape from the everyday routine. No matter how hard she would knead the dough or for how long, she would always carry a perennial smile on her face throughout the whole process, with a constant motivation and rhythm, eager to see the final results of her hard work.

I was very impressed by all that as I could not understand at first how a person could put so much effort in flour and water alone. Then once I tried the first time I realized how hard it actually was to knead the dough by hand vigorously and uniformly, feeling my hands, arms and the whole upper body suddenly aching. I was in pain for days, sore and uncomfortable. What a workout! My mother had biceps the size of Lou Ferrigno and the strength of "The Terminator." However, despite my first physical experience with dough kneading, something clicked and made me crave for more. I started helping almost every Sunday and after a while I even experimented making different shapes of pasta or coloring the dough with natural products such as tomato paste or spinach purée, making a mess for my mom to clean afterward.

This indeed was something very unusual for an 11-year-old kid who took so much interest in cooking at such an early age. Most of my friends were into soccer, cartoons, playing sheriff and superhero. So was I, but my first priority and interest was the magical vision of making something from scratch in the kitchen, and transforming and combining many ingredients into something new, different and amazing. Mostly I recall the way I felt when I was finished with whatever culinary project I took on. I had this great feeling of accomplishment. I felt invincible and proud at the same time. I had experienced similar feelings whenever I was rewarded with an A at school or scored a goal playing soccer, or even when I cleaned my room and scrubbed every corner, making sure each detail of whatever task I took on was executed to near perfection. None of those experiences come close to the way I felt while I was in the kitchen. That was very unusual and I was determined to recreate it as often as possible.

Because of her heart condition, my mother finally gave in one day and got herself an electric pasta machine with cutter attachments in order to make her life in the kitchen a little easier, but I remember whenever I was helping her I would insist on doing everything by hand. It was like I made a bet with myself and wanted to make sure I could perform all the work she had done for years without the help of a machine. She had always cooked very simple food in a very simple way and for sure she was one of the reasons why I fell in love with cooking.

I have always tried to follow her example, combining just the right amount of spices and ingredients together in order to create something great. She has always encouraged me to follow my culinary dreams and supported me through the years, reminding me all the time that "more is not better" and that "if cooking really makes your eyes sparkle and it frees your imagination, then you should be a chef." After all these years, looking back I feel I have learned a valuable lesson I will never forget: Listen to your mother.

Once I learned the basic flavors and how to respect my ingredients, I took interest in the cooking process. I would say pasta was my first love regardless if it was freshly made or out of a box. It has always played an extremely important role in my everyday life. It brings out feelings of home, comfort and happiness. Pasta is one of the reasons for my everyday smiles. Italians eat pasta at least once a day or they genuinely feel "empty" and not fully satisfied with their meals. Do you know of any Italians who dislike rice, pasta, bread, focaccias or pizza? It's a cultural tradition that will never die.

Throughout my life I have always been very athletic and into sports, fit and very healthy. Between 1992 and 2006 I dedicated at least four days of the week to the gym and to bodybuilding. I am still very active and very fit, but unfortunately not anywhere near the shape I was. I am definitely not that cut anymore and my body fat is no longer at 8 percent. I guess I am enjoying too much of a good life and of course sometimes I forget I am not 25 anymore. A lot of people would not believe I was a professional chef. They would look at me and ask me if I was a personal trainer or a gymnast instead. I have always thought it was important to work out and to take care of my body, and I rarely found another professional chef so into it as much as I was.

The only one who was as obsessed as I is chef Robert Irvine from the popular TV shows *Dinner: Impossible* and *Restaurant: Impossible* on the Food Network. Back in the day, he and I would work out like crazy. Even during a chef trip to Alba, Italy, in 2002 while visiting vineries and Michelin-starred restaurants in Piedmont, we both brought all the necessaries to break a sweat at the hotel's fitness center. We would meet every day, mostly in the afternoon, and work out together on free weights for approximately two hours while other "full size" chefs such as Roberto Donna or Michel Richard would look at us and shout their discouraging and funny comments while passing by.

"Hey you two, are you done pumping each other?"

"If you guys need to make room for tonight's dinner, try the restroom instead. It's much quicker."

Of course Robert and I would reply something like, "Hey you slobs, why don't you get in here and try to break a sweat?"

"You guys should enter a wet T-shirt contest to see who wins the biggest belly prize."

How determined we were with such an audience and encouragements. Those were just a few days a year we would not care about what we ate and how much of it. But I would never pass on a good workout.

Any chef's trip is a fun event. You can imagine therefore how difficult it was for me to give up pasta for long periods when I was trying to make weight while lowering my body fat and creating more definition on my body. Imagine a professional Italian chef willingly giving up carbohydrates of any kind for periods of two to three months at a time. Unheard of! Nowadays I look back and admire such discipline, and I often ask myself how I could have possibly done that.

I cannot recall a single time when my mother made colored pasta. To her it was easier and more practical to make simple egg dough and create whatever pasta cut she had in mind without messing with looks or esthetics. I guess it was mostly because she was not trying to impress anyone. Her main concern was to feed a family and to prepare the most succulent meal possible. I was the exact opposite: I was always trying to be different and in constant search of diversity. I have always tried to create something new while using simple ingredients, but back then it almost never worked as I lacked discipline and understanding of the basics.

In recent years at my restaurants I was able to offer my guests the same original taste I grew up with in different forms, concepts and shapes. Making pasta is one of the most difficult and respected things. It is often considered an easy task by diners and not as important as preparing meats or fish or even desserts. Each and every area of cooking is to be taken extremely seriously and given the proper respect as in the end a great meal is made of many different components of people's work and put together at the last second while delivering excellence.

Pasta is the soul of Italy! Happiness on a plate! Love at first bite! A never-ending comfort! My best friend! If you look closely into an average Italian DNA you will find a pasta gene: not an ordinary one, but an extraordinary happy gene waving at you with a genuine, loving smile sharing its unconditional love and unmistakable pride.

It is amazing how a simple mixture of eggs and flour has changed the lives of millions and how it continues to satisfy the daily needs and the desires of those who have made pasta a routine in their daily diet.

Pasta is substance.

People credit the origins of pasta to the Far East, from the times when Marco Polo brought it back to Venice and introduced it to all Italians. However, back then it was a very different product made with very different ingredients and crafted in a very different manner. I would like to think Marco Polo brought back an idea, a revolutionary spark from China and the Italians have over the centuries perfected and customized it to their personal taste with local ingredients and developed that spark to an everlasting bonfire that has been burning ever since.

To me, pasta is mostly comfort, my best friend. It is an art that should be shown often and in various ways, in many forms and colors. It's a natural vehicle that brings many flavors to people's palates: an all-natural taxi that never makes a wrong turn and is always available each time you call it.

I was born in an environment where pasta was as essential as the water we drink or the air we breathe. Italians eat dry pasta from the box every single day of the week, for lunch or dinner, sometimes for both meals. However, fresh homemade pasta is a ritual for the weekend and a treat for the whole family. My wonderful grandmother, Corradina, who is now 95 years old, has created incredible memories I still carry in my heart: most of those are pasta-related. It is the enthusiasm of crafting something together, by giving me a little pasta dough to play with as if it was a toy, a very special partnership that was formed for a few hours at the time when my parents were not around.

I was just amazed by the way she worked the dough by hand, the way she was able to transform flour and eggs into a very thin sheet with a single rolling pin. I often asked questions as she worked and I often raised eyebrows by showing so much interest for something that at the time was mostly considered a woman's thing.

"Nonna, how do you make the dough so thin?".

"Nonna, why do you press it so hard with the rolling pin?"

"Nonna, why do you brush raw eggs on the pasta before you fold it?"

I was 4 years old! Watching her working to me was so much more exciting than watching the cartoons on TV on Saturday morning. She was wonderful: each and every time I asked a question she always answered in the best possible way, making it easy for me to understand and mostly to appreciate the work she was doing.

"These are questions your sister Daniela should ask, not you," was her most common initial reply to my gastronomic inquiries, followed by, "Where is your sister, by the way? Why isn't she here with us? Is she still in her room doing homework?"

My sister has always been strange in a way, a little different than the rest of the family, never showing interest in anything else beside studying, a little ice skating, a short stint at guitar lessons and an even shorter one at tennis. Her love has always been books and school. She has always been an incredibly dedicated woman—driven, very firm on ideas and beliefs. Today she is a successful professor with a PhD in American Literature teaching at the University of Torino, Italy. She has published two books and translated many from English to Italian, and she continues to excel in her field with great pride. The only interest she has in cooking is when she is absolutely starving and there are no snacks within reach. Then, cooking becomes a priority and a necessity. One of my most vivid pasta memories is when my mom was feeding me as a toddler in the high chair. She would cook pasta and cut it into small pieces while I would gladly get my whole face full of tomato sauce.

Pasta is probably the most difficult thing to make from scratch, if you want to make it right, of course. Pasta is not about mixing flour and eggs, but is about using the correct quality of flour in the right proportions. It is very easy to craft inconsistent dough: use one egg too many and we might end up having the consistency of plastic, use one less egg and the pasta could dry faster or it could crack in the cooking process. Use too much semolina flour and your pasta will be very grainy, too much oil and it turns very heavy, or if you use organic farm eggs the dough will absorb more color from the yolks and it will change in clarity.

Then we have variations for colored pasta: if we use black squid ink we will certainly have to reduce the amount of eggs. Same goes for red pepper, saffron or tomato pasta as we incorporate more liquid in the form of tomato paste and roasted red pepper purée while the saffron will have to be soaked in a small quantity of water to properly mix it with the flour and to color the pasta. For other types such as porcini mushrooms, spinach or red beet, I like to use powders.

Cooking pasta is another difficult task people take for granted. There is a very distinctive difference between dry, boxed pasta and fresh pasta: the first type is mostly made without eggs and, depending on the cut and thickness, it might take up to 16 minutes to cook in boiling water. Fresh pasta cooks in a matter of seconds, sometimes in under a minute if really thin, while stuffed pasta takes a little longer as it is thicker. No matter what type of pasta we cook, stuffed or freshly cut, it should ALWAYS be served al dente.

Independently if fresh, stuffed or dry, it is essential and vital to carefully time the cooking/serving/eating process: once pasta is taken out of the boiling water, it is then transferred to a sauté pan with its sauce about a minute, finally plated and then served to the guest, where it sits on a plate for at least six to eight more minutes before it is consumed. Throughout this process pasta keeps on cooking and often by the time the guest consumes the last two or three bites it is a completely different product and mostly overcooked. This is why it's a MUST to undercook pastas. The guest should be able to enjoy the first bite of a pasta dish with the same quality and consistency as the last.

There are so many variations and a million details in crafting fresh pasta, but my goal is to make this process interesting and exciting enough for everyone to follow general guidelines and be able to experience the making of a great product in the most simple way. For this reason I decided to list three distinctive pasta groups: risottos, stuffed pastas and freshly cut pastas.

Risottos are included in this chapter because they are part of the Italian first dishes group traditions and an essential and important part of basic Italian culinary routine. Stuffed pastas are my favorite as they host a second neutral component, or stuffing, between two sheets of pasta and are folded in various shapes and sizes highlighting their artistic visual importance, overshadowed only by the surprising explosion in taste they carry with each bite. Stuffed pastas store a lot more flavor than any others as their stuffing often steals the show. For this reason stuffed pastas are mostly accompanied by very light sauces such as butter and sage (very appropriate with meat stuffing) or with light tomato sauce, pesto or light cream as the idea is to complement their taste with a delicate flavor component and not to overpower its taste.

We have a completely different scenario with freshly cut pastas as the number of cuts and shapes are virtually endless throughout Italy, and their chosen sauces and ragùs are what give importance and identity to the dish. Throughout my professional career I have created many different kinds of pasta to complement any kind of sauce, and I have always taken pride in delivering a great colorful concept with extraordinary and surprising results.

Here are the basics for my pastas the way I see and interpret them today. Basic egg dough and colored ones, shapes, fillings, sauces and final unique visions that break away from traditional and regional Italian cuisine, but in their own ways they recreate and respect the original flavors, proposing a unique concept of diversity. Take an old movie from the '60s, add a contemporary director with an unusual vision, mix in a great new script and throw it all in a blender. 3-D goggles in this case are optional.

Risottos

Rice, like pasta, is an important and fundamental element of Italian culinary pride that stretches from the northern sides of the Piedmont and Lombardy regions (Po Valley) all the way down to the Roman areas and to Sardinia. Italy is the highest producer of rice in Europe and is the nation with the most types and varieties available to consumers. Although not all varieties are suitable for the preparation of risotto: only short, bold and chalky grain types are employed for this glorious dish.

Italians love risotto. Risotto is a treat, a luxurious diversity from the pasta course as it feeds the soul in the same exact way. The best quality risotto is made by using a small variety of short grain rice such as Arborio, carnaroli, vialone nano, baldo or padano. These have the ability to better absorb liquids and to release starch more than other kinds, being stickier than the longer grains. Overall for a good risotto I suggest using carnaroli or Arborio as they are less likely to overcook and they are most consistent in absorbing the liquid throughout the cooking process uniformly.

Risotto is made continuously, meaning the moment the grains get in contact with the liquid it should be cooked continuously to the proper temperature without stopping. Since risotto is not an easy dish to make and it requires 20 minutes of our undivided attention, many restaurants pre-cook risottos for the evening shift in order to shorten the cooking time. Unfortunately, all they are doing is cheating themselves and their guests by changing the quality and the properties of a dish that is supposed to be glorious and unique.

There are many tricks to shorten risotto cooking time. Many chefs make rice pilaf and set it aside, cooked and ready to be combined with liquid, butter and cheese and to be served in five or six minutes: A disaster as at this point the rice holds no starch whatsoever. Others toast the rice and add the wine, wait until it evaporates and then set the pan aside until the order is called. The cooking time from that point on is approximately 10 minutes. That is better than the pilaf approach, but the grains will not cook uniformly, often resulting in overcooked on the outside and way too al dente on the inside, basically a half cooked risotto or if we prefer, a double cooked one.

I have also witnessed chefs cooking risottos halfway for approximately eight minutes and then removing it from the stove and setting it aside until an order is called. Only then they resume the cooking process to completion. This is the worst kind of risotto you will ever taste. Risotto is so particular because it takes time to make it correctly. Mostly, what defines a delicate risotto is the amount of the starch the grains release during the cooking process, giving that pasty, thick consistency to the dish that identifies its uniqueness.

The best way to ensure a rich starchy risotto is to stir the pan only a few times while cooking, allowing the starch to be slowly released from its grains undisturbed. The more we stir the risotto, the more the chances of having it stick to the pan and minimizing the full release of the starch. The basic steps for cooking a risotto are toast the grains with the butter and the chopped onions, wet with wine, evaporate completely, and add the liquid and the chosen garnishes to cooking completion.

There is another fundamental step for a good risotto making. It is called "mantecare." This musical Italian word (unfortunately there is no translation for it in the English language) means to incorporate the butter and the grated Parmesan cheese by vigorously mixing in a circular motion with a spoon until its consistency turns pasty and creamy, releasing extra starch in the dish. This step is done once the risotto is fully cooked and right before serving.

Risotto Gorgonzola Sicilian Pistachio Candied Red Beets and Crunchy Yellow Chips

A marriage of cheese and beets is a marriage sure to last. The combination of these two ingredients is glorious in every way we serve it: from a crispy salad to a plain and simple cheese board to any kind of hot or cold terrine or appetizer. In Italy it is very popular to combine Gorgonzola cheese with celery for cold preparations or to a risotto, as well as to use red beets combined with nuts. I wanted to re-create the Gorgonzola risotto, similar to what people are used to and know, but different enough to be appreciated more for its uniqueness, concept and presentation.

I started by combining a variety of light creamy added Gorgonzola cheese (much lighter in taste and not as pungent) to the rice and then I roasted a small red beet, carved it into small spheres and caramelized them with white vinegar and sugar. This specific combination—beets and cheese—is absolutely fantastic as the cream from the cheese complements the sharp acidic-sweet taste of the beets into a very round and velvety balance. I thought I still needed an edge for color, taste and texture contrast to really make this complete. I found the answer in Sicilian pistachios and in golden beet chips.

Pistachios from Sicily are the best for taste and color: they are naturally bright green and their taste is so intense and round that they are mostly used for pastry preparations, making their natural sweet paste a unique item for export all over the world for those who can afford it. Indeed they are very expensive, but the results achieved in quality are outstanding and naturally flavorful. I slice the golden beets paper thin and I bake them at low temperature to crunchy chips in order to add color to the dish, diversity and taste.

The result is a very colorful risotto with different textures, a very delicate and elegant taste with visual alternatives to what we know and like.

Ingredients
½ lb carnaroli rice
¼ of white onion very finely chopped
2 leaves of fresh sage
¼ lb butter
½ cup grated Parmesan Reggiano cheese
½ cup Gorgonzola "cremificato" at room temperature (cream-added Gorgonzola cheese)
2 small red beets
½ tbsp of sugar
1 bay leaf
½ tbsp white wine vinegar
¼ cup Sicilian pistachios
1 garlic clove
Salt
Ground white pepper
1 glass of dry white wine
2 cups of chicken broth approximately
½ tbsp of extra virgin olive oil
½ small shallots
A few very small leaves of Italian parsley

Directions
Fry the parsley leaves in abundant oil till crunchy, but still bright green and set aside.
Boil the red beets in salted water till tender, but still al dente and peel them off.
With a melon baller tool, carve as many small balls as possible out of each red beet and set aside.
In a small pan melt a tablespoon of butter and the olive oil, add the peeled shallot and the garlic along with the sage leaves and let it cook at moderate fire for a minute.

Add the red beet balls, salt and pepper and sauté a few seconds, dust with the sugar and slowly caramelize.
Add the vinegar; reduce the liquid till it caramelizes again.
Set the pan aside.
Toast the Sicilian pistachio in oven a few minutes.
When cold chop only half of them and set aside.
In a medium-size pan or copper pan (best for risottos) cook the chopped onions with one tablespoon of butter and the chopped pistachios.
Add the rice, toast and wet with white wine, making sure to evaporate it entirely.
Now add the chicken broth only a cup at a time as needed, season with salt and pepper and stir occasionally, preferably with a wooden spoon.
Remove from stove when cooked (approximately 14-15 minutes) and still al dente.
Stir in the remaining butter, the grated Parmesan and the Gorgonzola cheese.
Mantecare (mix) with butter and Parmesan making sure the Gorgonzola cheese is well melted and blended to a creamy paste.

Crunchy Yellow Beet Chips

Ingredients
1 small yellow beet
½ tbsp of melted butter
Crystallized salt

Directions
Poach the beet in salted water until al dente.
With a small knife peel the yellow beet and slice paper thin with a mandolin.
Lay each slice on a silicone baking mat spaced apart from one another.
Gently brush each slice with a little melted butter and bake in oven at 220 degrees for approximately 2½ hours or until completely dry and crispy.
Remove the chips from the oven and slightly dust with crystallized salt.
Store them in airtight container over deli paper.

To Serve
Plate the risotto in a pasta bowl.
With the back of a spoon apply pressure on the very top of the risotto in a rotating motion, forming a small nest to place the candied beets in.
Put the beets in place without any of the leftover cooking liquid, sprinkle with some of the toasted whole pistachios and decorate the rest of the dish with crunchy yellow beet chips and the crunchy parsley leaves.

Risotto White Truffles Barolo Gel Reduction and Butter Braised Cardoons

I grew up in Torino, about 40 miles from the town of Alba, the world capital of white truffles, and I learned how to appreciate and to love them at a very young age. White truffles are considered the diamonds of cooking, a prestigious and incredible costly ingredient available only four months of the year. Over the past few decades people from all over the world have tried to grow white truffles in California, Oregon, Croatia, Serbia, France and in so many other areas with poor and often ridiculous results. The only place in the world for a healthy and respectable white truffle is the surrounding hilly areas of Alba in the Piedmont region, where they grow naturally thanks to its rich and unique geological conditions.

Occasionally you will find darker-colored white truffles from what once were the Yugoslavia regions: they might look good, they may be hard and crispy, but they do not carry the characteristics in taste or the aromas of an original white truffle from Alba. To simplify: an original Alba truffle can be compared to a one carat diamond, flawless with F color in clarity. Any other truffle not from the Alba region could be compared to an imperfect one-carat diamond with visible inclusions and poor color clarity. These last ones are often used for commercial jar preserves, canned sauces and mostly sliced and mixed with white truffle oil extracts and sold all over the world in supermarkets and gourmet stores.

White truffles are available from the end of September to generally the end of December depending on the given season and since the world demand is so high restaurateurs, chefs and aficionados pay insane prices for them. I remember one year the price tag reached $5000 per pound and thinking I could have bought myself a brand new car for the same as four pounds of them. Ordinarily the price varies depending on the season, ranging anywhere from $1200 to $2500 per pound, making it virtually impossible for restaurants to draw any profit at all. No wonder a simple risotto dish could reach up to $150 price tag at any local restaurant.

To me the prestige of cooking with white truffles and offering it to my guests is not only incredibly rewarding, but it helps to feed my culinary and professional soul, at least for a few weeks out of the year. In local Alba restaurants, white truffles are priced about half of what the rest of the world pays for them. Every time I find myself in Torino and in truffle season I usually take my family out to dinner to a great and unforgettable meal, creating new food memories for all of us.

To cook a traditional white truffle risotto it is suggested to use unsalted water instead of chicken broth as it could overpower the delicate taste of the tubers. I personally prefer to cook mine with chicken broth instead as I believe a good risotto needs a little substance. For this particular recipe I opted to use only salted water as I needed to create a higher contrast between the taste of the truffles and the Barolo gel. The crispy butter braised cardoons are a great addition to this dish, giving a surprise and delicate taste connecting the risotto to the wine gel.

Do not forget white truffles are best consumed and appreciated when sliced paper thin and always at the last second and right in front of your guests.

Ingredients
½ lb Arborio rice
¼ of white onion very finely chopped
¼ lb butter
2 tbsp of grated Parmesan Reggiano cheese
Salt
Ground white pepper
½ glass of dry white wine
2 cups of boiling salted water, approximately
Fresh Alba white truffles shaved at the moment
2 tsp of natural infused white truffle oil
A couple of fresh and crispy cardoon stalks
Crystallized salt

Directions
Peel and clean the cardoons and cut them in small thick sticks of approximately 3 inches long and ¼ inch wide.
Boil them in salted water till completely cooked and tender, but still al dente and retaining their bright green color. Set aside.
In a small sauté pan braise the cardoon sticks with a tablespoon of butter till it turns hazelnut color.

Remove from fire and season with salt and white pepper.
Remove the cardoons from the pan and set aside on a small warm plate.
In a medium-size pan cook the chopped onions with one tablespoon of butter only.
Add the rice, a few small slices and fragments of white truffle, toast and wet with white wine making sure it evaporates entirely.
Add the chicken broth, half cup at a time as needed, season with salt and stir occasionally, with a wooden spoon.
Remove from stove when cooked (approximately 15 to 16 minutes) and al dente.
Stir in the remaining butter, the grated Parmesan cheese and the truffle oil.
Stir vigorously with a spoon, combining all ingredients to a creamy and velvety paste.

Barolo Gel Reduction

Ingredients
2 cups and 1 tbsp of Barolo wine
Pinch of salt
Pinch of ground white pepper
A few pieces of chopped carrot
A few pieces of chopped celery
1 small shallot chopped
A couple of pieces of dry porcini mushroom
1 bay leaf
1 sage leaf
½ very small sprig of rosemary
½ very small sprig of thyme
A few cracked black peppercorns
Salt
¾ cup of veal stock reduction
1 gram of powdered agar

Directions
Combine all the ingredients in a small pot with the exception of the single half tablespoon of Barolo wine, the agar and the veal stock reduction.
Simmer till the wine is reduced to a single cup.
Now add the veal stock and reduce again down to half.

Remove from stove, taste for salt and pepper, filter the liquid and set aside to cool until it reaches room temperature.
Transfer the reduction to a new small pot and with the help of a small handheld mixer blend in the agar thoroughly.
Place this new mix on the stove and simmer till it reaches boiling temperature.
Remove from fire, filter one more time, add the half tablespoon of Barolo wine and set aside to cool.
Transfer to a refrigerator mixing the gel with a hand mixer every couple of hours till it reaches a fluid gelatin consistency.

To Serve
In the center of a pasta bowl place a tablespoon of the Barolo gel.
Cover the gel with the risotto and place four stalks of butter braised cardoons on it, fire-log style.
Sprinkle them lightly with crystallized salt and shave abundantly with white truffles.
Serve immediately.

Risotto with Edible Gold Asparagus Tips Black Truffles and Melting Saffron Leaf (Homage to Gualtiero Marchesi)

Gualtiero Marchesi is the founding father of modern Italian cooking and the first Italian chef ever to earn three stars from the prestigious Michelin guide. After working with influential chefs in Italy and in traditional strict French kitchens, he opened his first restaurant in Milan in 1977 where he was awarded his first Michelin star within the first year. Eight years later, in 1985, the third star arrived and consecrated him as a revolutionary of Italian cooking.

He was the very first chef able to express and implement a way of cooking that branched out of tradition, and the first chef who developed a style uniquely his own with dramatic presentations, surprising taste and very visual and colorful creations that have often left guests skeptical, confused and ultimately dazzled. A modernist of his time using exclusively the freshest and simplest ingredients and the continuous pursuit of new ideas, Gualtiero Marchesi has been for the past few decades one of the most famous and respected chefs in the world. At 87 years old and counting, his energy is as vivid and alive as it has ever been, hoping to leave behind his legacy as the chef who gave us the rebirth of Italian cuisine with elegance, sophistication and quality, but mostly a healthy-style cuisine.

Some of his creations are legendary, such as the famous "open raviolo" or the "poached lobster with roasted red pepper purée," "red beets pasta fettuccine with green asparagus, roasted goose liver and winter black truffles," and finally "saffron risotto with edible gold leaf." This last one along with the open raviolo is the dish that has been mostly imitated, reinvented and offered on restaurant menus worldwide for the past 30 years.

Myself, my mentor before me, and many of my peers have been influenced by Marchesi ideas and vision since my days in culinary school and he continues to inspire me for his excellence and innovation. Because of it I decided to include in this book a very personal take and recreation of the saffron risotto with the gold leaf dish.

This version is as tasty as colorful as it is complete in its concept with a few additions: the black truffles and the asparagus. The gold leaf is substituted by edible gold powder sprinkled on top of the dish at the last second and the saffron is present as an outside component placed on top of the risotto at the finish in a gelatin sheet form.

The saffron sheet is to substitute the traditional gold leaf with a twist: once the saffron leaf is laid, the heat melts down the gelatin into liquid, changing its appearance in color and flavor. The guest is then encouraged to mix the saffron into the risotto, recreating Marchesi's original version.

Thank you, "Knight of the Italian Republic"—a title given to him by the Italian president for his outstanding and continuous work and contribution to Italian excellence throughout the world. You will always be a source of inspiration, quality and elegance to me and to my work.

Ingredients
½ lb carnaroli rice
¼ white onion very finely chopped
¼ lb butter

2 tbsp of grated Parmesan Reggiano cheese
Salt
Ground white pepper
½ glass of dry white wine
2 cups of chicken broth approximately
½ cup of green asparagus tips
A few shaves of winter black truffles
2 tsp of powdered edible gold leaves
1 tsp of naturally infused black truffle oil

Directions

In a medium-size pan cook the chopped onions with one tablespoon of butter only.
Add the rice, a few small slices and fragments of black truffles, toast and wet with white wine making sure it evaporates entirely.
Add the chicken broth a half cup at a time as needed, season with salt and stir occasionally, with a wooden spoon.
When the risotto is about 3 minutes from completion add the asparagus tips and the black truffle shaves.
Bring to complete cooking and remove from stove al dente.
Stir in the remaining butter, the grated Parmesan cheese and the truffle oil.
Stir vigorously with a spoon combining all ingredients to a creamy and velvety paste.
Keep in mind this risotto will need to be cooked and served with a little less liquid than usual since at serving time the liquid provided by the melting saffron leaf should compensate for consistency.

Melting Saffron Leaf

Ingredients

½ cup of chicken broth
1 gram of powdered saffron
4 gelatin sheets soaked in cold water
2 tbsp of heavy cream

Directions

In a small pan combine the chicken stock, the cream and the saffron at medium to low fire.
Remove the pan from stove as soon as the stock reaches boiling temperature and let it cool about 10 minutes.

Stir in the gelatin sheets squeezed out of their soaking water and gently combine.
Filter the liquid into a half sheet pan covered with plastic film and deli paper previously chilled in the refrigerator for at least an hour. Make sure to level the liquid to a very thin and even layer.
Return the sheet pan to the refrigerator for one more hour until completely chilled and solid.
Remove the pan from the refrigerator, cover the gelatin top layer with plastic film, and with quick motion gently flip the pan upside down, transferring the whole sheet to a working table.
Remove the bottom layer of film, the deli paper and gently but quickly cut into 3½-inch squares.
Store each saffron leaf between two deli paper sheets of approximately 4 inches and wrap each package with film to prevent the leaf from drying.
Store it in cooler up to the last second before serving.

To Serve
Place the hot risotto into a pasta bowl and sprinkle with the gold powder.
Place the saffron sheet on top of the risotto flat and right in the middle and serve.
The saffron sheet will start melting almost immediately releasing its color and flavor in liquid form.
Instruct your guest to mix the melting saffron into the risotto thoroughly with a spoon and enjoy watching it change color, flavor and consistency.

Risotto with Fresh Tomatoes, Sicilian Frantoio and Stuffed Zucchini Blossoms with Burrata Cheese

In this recipe we are going to break all the rules in order to recreate a risotto that tastes like a raw tomato. Tomatoes, in my opinion, are best appreciated when raw and mostly when ripe and at room temperature. A bad tomato will only produce a bad dish, but a ripe, succulent and tasty one will enlighten my taste buds, put a smile on my face, and remind me why Italians (and those who know our secrets) excel in quality cooking whenever using this unique vegetable. It is a combination of things: Italy has one of the best geological conditions in the world for quality tomato production and

Italians have protected and embraced this jewel for centuries, making it a symbol of culinary pride and joy for everyone.

This risotto is a classic example of my never-ending quest to refine taste in the simplest dishes. For cooking I substitute the usual chicken stock with fresh-squeezed ripe tomato juice in order to have more of a unique taste sensation, reducing down with the rice it will deliver a fresh, distinct flavor that other liquids will not. I make a confit of extremely fresh cherry tomatoes cooked just a few minutes; barely warm inside, still crunchy, and I add some to the risotto while cooking, along with a very small quantity of tomato paste to reinforce the flavor. Cooking like a traditional risotto, you can imagine how the flavor of the tomato sets into the rice and how it gets absorbed and contained within the dish itself to create an exceptional tomato-lover wonderland.

When the risotto is ready I add fresh basil, Sicilian Frantoio oil, and cracked black peppercorns, whipping it to a paste the same way I would with a normal risotto with butter and Parmesan cheese. Its flavor is now highly elevated and concentrated within its liquid with accents of basil, olive oil, garlic and cracked peppercorns: all the basic ingredients of a simple tomato salad. I took it a step further as I felt the risotto needed a strong comfort component.

I love springtime because you can really take advantage of the season and its wonderful gifts: one of those is the zucchini blossoms I like to use in my cooking whenever possible. In Italy we mostly combine a good tomato salad with fresh mozzarella so I stuffed the blossoms with fresh burrata cheese instead because I needed a more delicate, milky and creamy component to connect to the dish. I made a tempura batter, fried them crispy and placed them on top of the risotto.

When breaking into the blossom, the inside melted cheese, liquid and flavor runs through the plate mixing with the rice, adding extra flavor for a fantastic and fresh risotto.

Ingredients
½ lb carnaroli rice
¼ white onion very finely chopped
Salt

Cracked black peppercorn
½ glass of dry white wine
2 cups, approximately of fresh squeezed tomato juice
4 leaves of fresh basil chopped
1 tbsp of tomato paste
1½ tbsp of excellent Sicilian Frantoio extra virgin olive oil
½ tbsp of butter
¾ cup of cherry tomato confit

Directions
Run a few ripe tomatoes through the juicer machine and measure about 2 cups of tomato water, set aside.
In a small pot cook the chopped onions with the butter till translucent and lightly golden.
Add the rice and toast lightly for a few seconds, add the wine and evaporate completely.
Pour the first cup of tomato juice into the pot, stir the rice, add salt and cook at moderate fire.
Add the tomato paste and the tomato juice as needed.
When the risotto is about 5 minutes to temperature, add the cherry tomato confit gradually as it holds a lot of liquid and finish cooking to completion to perfect consistency.
Taste for salt.
Remove the pot from the stove and whip in vigorously the Frantoio with the cracked black peppercorns and the chopped basil to a semi-soft paste.

Cherry Tomato Confit

Ingredients
4 whole garlic cloves, shaved or thinly sliced
¾ cup of extra virgin olive oil
1 lb of Italian San Marzano plum tomatoes, hand crushed
2½ lbs of cherry tomatoes halved
½ cup of chopped fresh basil
Salt
A tbsp of cracked black peppercorns
A couple of pinches of ground white pepper
A pinch of dry oregano

Directions
In a medium-size brazier pan pour the oil and the shaved garlic, turn the fire on and slowly cook to golden color.
Add the cherry tomatoes halved and the oregano, and cook about one minute only.
Add the crushed plum tomatoes, salt, white pepper and cook a few minutes under moderate flame, stirring delicately and occasionally with a rubber spatula.
Turn the fire off.
Taste for salt and pepper, add the basil and finish with the cracked black peppercorns and additional drizzle of extra virgin olive oil if needed.
Remove from the stove and chill the confit over ice bath.

Zucchini Blossoms Stuffed with Burrata

Ingredients
A few medium-size zucchini blossoms
1 small size of fresh burrata cheese cut in small strips
Tempura batter
2 cups of blended oil to fry
Crystallized salt

Directions
With a paper towel dry the extra milk of the Burrata strips and set aside.
Open each zucchini blossom's center and stuff them with the cheese.
Seal the top by twisting the hanging petals together and set aside in the refrigerator until ready to cook.

Tempura Batter
Please refer to the Fava Beans Stuffed Tempura Zucchini Blossoms recipe in Chapter 3 under "Appetite Openers." (Page 52)

To Serve
Set up the oil at 385 degrees.
Remove the zucchini blossoms and the tempura batter from the refrigerator and stir well before dipping the stuffed flowers in it.
Shake off the excess batter from each blossom and lay in hot oil one at a time.

Make sure to cook evenly on each side by flipping them over with the help of a large perforated spoon.
Cook till golden crisp.
Place on absorbing paper and sprinkle with crystallized salt.
Place the risotto in a pasta bowl and serve it with the crispy stuffed blossoms cut diagonally and stacked on top, showing the creamy filling inside.

The Marvelous World of Eggs and Flours

"If you have enough passion, you can stuff pasta with almost anything you want," my mother used to tell me. While that's true, it is important to understand stuffed pasta requires a certain kind of skill to be crafted. It takes practice, determination, understanding, time and patience, as well as freshly cut pasta. To do it consistently well you need to do it wrong a few times, but do not give up.

The combination of eggs, flour, salt, and oil has opened a window of culinary imagination far wider than anyone had ever expected, and created diversity and substance for the average everyday meal in so many different and comforting ways. You can stuff pasta with infinite fillings: from meat to fish, vegetables and cheese, even liquid stuffing for those who are open to try new concepts.

It all started in the Arabic world a few centuries back with what today could be compared to raviolis. Later this revolutionary idea was adopted in Italy in Medieval times at the beginning of the 14th century, available only to the rich and nobles, but Italians were not the first to combine flour and eggs. Marco Polo enlightened us with the findings of his many travels, and Italians took advantage, perfected it, and made it theirs.

Pasta was considered a luxury back then and not available to everyone. In that period many concepts of stuffed pasta were born, mostly because of the surplus of leftover ingredients that needed to be either used or thrown away if spoiled; there were no refrigerators and the cold days would preserve perishable items only a few months. When they started mixing chopped meats or vegetables they gave life to what today are known as tortelli miniature cakes or ravioli.

It is fascinating to me how the creativity of a few minds generated such curiosity and passion, and how it quickly expanded throughout Italy and generated in part a long string of traditions known today as Italian Regional Cooking. Each region, in time, adopted the concept of mixing flour and eggs to shape a thin, flat sheet of pasta and to stuff it with the local available ingredients, giving life to miniature culinary jewels.

Nowadays there are countless types of stuffed pastas, different shapes, colors, stuffing and concepts, more than any of the original artisan craftsmen would have ever dreamt of. The craft has truly evolved to culinary artistry, and it is appreciated and adopted all over the world in almost any type of cuisine. For us Italians pasta is practically as dear as a loving family member, something we truly adore, but when you talk about stuffed pasta a complete new window of pride is open and its importance is projected to higher levels. The best thing I could compare it to is the difference between silver and gold.

I grew up enjoying almost any type of pastas available thanks to my mother and grandmother. I got spoiled so much that I remember my happiness was often related to the quality of my daily meals. Spoiled eater? No! Young culinary nerd! Pasta is the essence of a sumptuous Italian meal: its driving force, its business card, the reason of many smiles around the table, the psychological satisfaction of the mind and belly, the creation of many afternoon naps and an immense source of comforting love.

To me, freshly cut pasta is like an adventure in the Amazon jungles: you think you know what you are getting into until you enter into marvelous revelations. When I craft pasta, my mind travels faster than my electric sheeter, always thinking of possible alterations to what I am making. How would my fettuccine taste and look if I had used spinach dough instead of white? And what if I had combined saffron in my gnocchi for color and taste? Well, if I did that I would have to find the right sauce to pair it with...another window opens and takes me deeper into a never ending excursion. The fascinating thing about stuffed pasta is you could choose almost any colored dough to wrap around the filling you most like, and by doing so give life to a colorful and creative dish that could be otherwise rated as common or at times boring. Many factors determine the good outcome of stuffed pasta crafting such as the humidity, the type of flour, type of eggs, their stuffing, time and personal skills.

I mentioned that to craft great quality pasta one has to do it wrong a few times. Making pasta is an indirect form of meditation. It is a solo performance between you and your mind in your comfort zone. It is very much like performing needlepoint work, reading, yoga, watch repairing, or even writing. You are driven to reflect and perform a task in your own world. Zen Pasta? Possibly, if you like, as we are not too far off from any realistic comparisons. There are infinite tools, forms, cutters and machines to help make the best-looking and most-delicious pasta; they all make our work easier and much more enticing while stretching our minds to new ideas and concepts.

What makes pasta wonderful? Its thickness, the quality of its filling, the sauces we combine with it. Any type of pasta, once cooked, should be light, inviting, appealing and thin to the eye. For stuffed pastas they should almost look like steamed Chinese wontons where you can barely see the stuffing through the dough, but it remains sealed and intact, ready to be tossed in the sauce without breaking, thus retaining its original shape.

There are many pasta machines available for home use—manual or electric—and they all come with specific attachments and cutters to facilitate an otherwise long and very difficult work. Unfortunately, when it comes to stuffed pasta, machines are basically useless as they are all manufactured and calibrated for faster commercial use and are not able to create thin layers in which to trap the stuffing. Stuffed pasta manufactured by a machine is almost always too thick and doughy, heavy and with very little flavor. Stuffing pasta is an art; a tradition that needs to be respected: pasta must be made by hand and with care. It is quite disappointing when pasta sticks on your teeth because it is too thick. There is no culinary pleasure or pride in crafting, consuming or serving any product that is way below quality expectations or altered and changed for faster consumption. All the basic elements have to come together as one. All ingredients must be carefully selected, starting with the eggs, the flour, the oil, and of course the stuffing: fresh, flavorful, delicious in taste and in consistency. Remember, any stuffing should be glorious in order to give life to little tasteful surprises that explode in your mouth, bite after bite, building the foundations of great savory and satisfying dishes.

Wrap the dough with plastic film once kneaded and let it rest in the refrigerator for at least one hour before using it. Pasta is very delicate and it gets dry very fast when exposed even for only a few minutes; therefore, cut only the needed quantities to avoid unnecessary drying or cracking. Keep the rest of the dough in the refrigerator or if you want to keep it on your working table for easier access make sure to cover it with a damp towel or plastic wrap. Time is of the essence: any type of dough tends to dry fast so you must work quickly to be able to successfully cut, fold and portion.

When it comes to freshly cut, it is a little easier as the most important thing is to be able to roll a sheet thin enough to cut the desired shape. For stuffed pastas it is a little more complicated as it takes longer and many more components are involved—therefore longer time, drier dough. Once the stuffing is placed on the first sheet of pasta, seal it properly without any air pockets and use your fingers to check thickness and consistency through them for quality control. All stuffed pastas, with the exception of lasagna and open raviolis are sealed by using a natural glue component: egg wash. Brush just enough to make the second sheet of pasta stick. Many people make the mistake of brushing way too much egg on the pastas. This creates a very wet and unstable base to build on as everything slides, making the good outcome of your work virtually impossible. Be conservative, as you can always brush more if needed. The aesthetics of stuffed pasta is also very important as it must look good as well as taste good. This is where personal skills come into play.

It takes time and a lot of practice to be able to produce a consistently good-looking product; therefore, do not get discouraged if at first your pasta will look like anything but what a picture in a cookbook shows or if it falls apart and breaks during the cooking process. Unfortunately, it is perfectly normal.

Familiarize yourself with what you are doing wrong. Fix your mistakes and implement what works best for you first. This means you have to get personal. If modifying techniques without compromising the end result makes your job easier or faster, please be my guest; however, be respectful and always follow guidance for any recipes.

There are infinite sauces to pair with any pasta: usually for stuffed ones it is more appropriate to prepare a lighter sauce such as a purée or an emulsion or a very light and simple condiment to complement the already rich taste of its stuffing. Avoid pairing stuffed pasta with heavy sauces such as ragù or thick reductions as the goal here is not to highlight an overpowering condiment, but to elevate the quality of its filling. We must create a balance of flavors within the dish's concept. The best way to appreciate any pasta is by consuming it within the first two days of production; however, feel free to bag and freeze any uncooked extras for as long as one month.

Since I have been often labeled as a revolutionary of the Italian culinary traditions (along with many other names from my guests and press and been compared professionally to Alfred Hitchcock...whatever that meant, and told I have the work intensity of Oliver Stone, which I must agree with) I figure it is only normal I have heavily added my personal input in all my pasta recipes. I get very personal and off track while respecting traditions. I changed a few things; I crafted new concepts, and provided new vehicles to transport the flavors to the guest's table: diversity in temperatures, progressive and visual concepts, combinations of textures—soft, crispy, powdery and liquid. Traveling through this pasta chapter, we will discover delicious ideas and surprising flavorful varieties combined with sauces, ragù and unusual ingredients to complement the final taste of our pasta and to complete them at best in their concepts.

I often ask my students attending culinary classes at my restaurant: Are you ready to get your hands dirty? When making pasta, remember to have a good time as you go: do not be afraid to get all dirty and dusted with flour. After all, crafting pasta is one of the most difficult tasks anyone could take on in any kitchen, but it is also one of the most fun and most rewarding. If the results are not exactly great at first do not despair, do not get frantic or discouraged, but mostly refrain from unleashing a deliberating scream like the one in the movie *Psycho* from the shower scene.

Pasta is first and foremost about happiness!

Pasta Dough Recipes:

Basic White
1 lb of AP flour
½ tbsp of salt
1 tbsp of olive oil
5 eggs

Saffron
1 lb of AP flour
½ tbsp of salt
4 eggs
1 tbsp of olive oil
1 tsp of powdered saffron dissolved in ½ oz of water

Tomato
1 lb of AP Flour
½ tbsp of salt
1 tbsp of olive oil
¾ cup of tomato paste
3 eggs

Black Squid Ink
1 lb of AP flour
½ tbsp of salt
1½ tbsp of black squid Ink
1 tbsp of olive oil
4-5 eggs

Porcini
1 lb of AP flour
½ tbsp of salt
1 tbsp of olive oil
Less than ½ cup of porcini mushrooms powder
5 eggs

Red Beet
1 lb of AP flour
½ tbsp of salt
1 tbsp of olive oil
½ cup red beet powder
5 eggs

Agnolotto
1 lb of AP flour
½ tbsp of salt
5 eggs
1½ oz of melted butter

Spinach
1 lb of AP flour
½ tbsp of salt
1 tbsp of olive oil
½ cup spinach powder
5 eggs

Whole Wheat
1 lb of whole wheat flour
1 lb of AP flour
½ tbsp of salt
½ tbsp of olive oil
10 eggs

Red Pepper
1 lb of AP flour
½ tbsp of salt
1 tbsp of olive oil
1 cup roasted red pepper puree
2-3 small eggs

Stuffed Pastas

Reginette Filled with Smoked Buffalo Mozzarella and Roasted Eggplants with San Marzano Caviar and Basil Froth

Reginette means small little queens. "Why would anyone want to cook a whole bunch of royals?" That is what one of my students bluntly asked me at one of my cooking classes. Funny, but also correct. In fact the name was given because of its shapes as they resemble small crowns and not majesties. Think of them as overly filled agnolotti of about two inches tall, round in shape and with six small doughy spikes pinched all around it to contain the filling between the two sheets of pasta. I love this type because it is so different and breaks the routine in expectations. Reginette are not very common. It is actually quite rare to find them on restaurant menus or for any housewife to make them at home. I like to stuff them with almost anything: ragù, meats, vegetables, cheese, lobster, you name it. The possibilities are endless, but what really makes reginette so unique are the accompanying sauces perfecting the dish.

I decided to combine some of the most common Italian ingredients and to recreate simplicity with a twist. I prepared a filling with smoked buffalo mozzarella and roasted eggplants. The tomato is present in the form of fine marinated chutney resting right on top of the just-cooked pasta. The frothed basil gives color, flavor and for sure a non-traditional and unusual texture.

Use Basic White Pasta Dough Recipe

Smoked Buffalo Mozzarella and Roasted Eggplants Filling

In order to simplify the process I decided to separate the eggplant and mozzarella filling procedures to facilitate the dynamics of it all. Once both fillings are ready we will combine them in a large bowl and create a unique single mix. The final product should have the consistency of a thick, solid purée. If it turns out a little too wet, return the filling to a colander again for a couple of hours in order to get rid of the excess and unwanted liquid.

For the Eggplant Filling Mix

Ingredients

½ lb of eggplants peeled and cubed small
2 garlic cloves peeled cleaned and hand crushed
½ medium-size onion finely diced
8 basil leaves chopped
Ground white pepper
Salt
1 tbsp of extra virgin olive oil
2 tbsp of grated Parmesan Reggiano cheese
½ cup of canned Italian peeled tomatoes hand-crushed

Directions

In a sauté pan golden the onions and the garlic with the oil.
When lightly colored, add the diced eggplants, the salt and the pepper.
Cook for 5 minutes, then add the hand-crushed tomatoes and continue cooking approximately 8-10 more minutes at moderate fire.
Taste for salt and pepper and cook until all the liquid will be reabsorbed by the eggplant mix.
Add the chopped basil and stir well.
Place the mix in a colander and let it strain all night in order to get rid of all the extra liquid.
The next day place the mix on a cutting board and with a knife chop the stuffing to a semi fine texture. Transfer to a small bowl and mix in the parmesan cheese.
Set aside.

For the Mozzarella Filling Mix

Ingredients

½ lb smoked mozzarella cut in small cubes
½ lb buffalo mozzarella pressed overnight with no water and cut in small cubes
2 tbsp of grated Parmesan Reggiano cheese
Salt and ground white pepper
¼ cup of ricotta cheese impastata

Directions
In a bowl mix the ricotta cheese, the salt, the pepper and the parmesan with a large spoon.
Mix in the two types of mozzarella finely diced.
Set aside.

To Combine the Fillings
Place both fillings in a large bowl and mix them together gently with a rubber spatula.
Set aside in refrigerator for at least 2 hours before using.

How to Make the Reginette
With the help of a pasta machine roll the dough until thin and elastic and form a long sheet. Using a round pasta cutter or approximately 3½-4 inches in diameter cut out a few pasta discs and set them aside.
Brush half of them with egg wash as they will serve as base to host the filling while the other half will top and seal the pasta.
Craft the reginette as quickly as possible as the dough dries out very fast.
Press the filling out from the bag and place in the center of each disc brushed with egg wash and form a small pile about 2 inches wide and 1 inch high.
Cover immediately with the second disc and seal the edges, getting rid of any air pockets.
Lightly brush the edges of the disc with more egg wash and by pinching with your fingers fold the dough together around the stuffing in a circular motion, creating a small crown. Model the reginette by pressing down its filling and by pushing up the side edges together toward the center until the pasta acquires the desired shape and form.
Dust with flour and store in refrigerator on a sheet pan over parchment paper and covered with a kitchen towel until cooking time.

San Marzano Caviar

Ingredients
1 lb of canned San Marzano plum tomatoes
2 pinches of cracked black peppercorns

½ clove of minced roasted garlic
1 tbsp of excellent extra virgin olive oil
2 fresh basil leaves
A pinch of dry oregano
A pinch of crystallized salt to use when plating

Directions
Strain the tomatoes about one hour, then with your fingers remove all the seeds and return the fillets to the strainer for another 30 minutes till all the extra water is completely washed out.
Dry the tomatoes on a large towel and transfer to a cutting board.
Chop the fillets by knife to a thick and fine paste and place in a small mixing bowl.
Add the minced roasted garlic, the oregano, the cracked peppercorns, the extra virgin olive oil, the salt and the chopped basil.
Mix delicately with a rubber spatula.
Set in refrigerator to marinate for a few hours.

Basil Froth

Ingredients
5 oz of fresh basil leaves
2 qt of water or chicken broth
12 grams of powder lecithin
½ tsp of minced garlic
½ tbsp of olive oil
A pinch of salt
A pinch of ground white pepper

Directions
In a small pot color the garlic with the olive oil, the white pepper and the salt.
Quickly add only ¾ of the basil leaves, stir into the hot mix for approximately 5 seconds and add the water or stock.
Simmer until consumed down to half of total liquid.
Add the remaining basil leaves, stir, and pass the mix immediately through a high-speed blender till velvety.
Filter the mix.

Once at room temperature, with a small handheld immersion blender combine the lecithin with the liquid and set aside till serving time.
Whip the mix right before serving to a solid and colorful airy froth.

To Serve
Cook the reginette in abundant salted water, once ready transfer them to a sauté pan with a drizzle of extra virgin olive oil and a drizzle of cooking water.
On an open fire move the pan in circular motion so the pasta does not stick and reduce the liquid down to a thick sauce.
Lay each reginetta one by one on a serving plate and cover them with a couple of tablespoons of sauce from the pan. Quickly, using 2 coffee spoons, craft a few small quenelles with the room temperature San Marzano caviar. Place a tomato quenelle on top of each reginetta, drizzle with more extra virgin olive oil and sprinkle the caviar with a few flakes of crystallized salt.
Finish with a spoonful of basil froth on top of each of them.
Serve immediately.

Saffron Triangles Filled with Burrata on Green Peas Emulsion with Morel Mushrooms/Parma Prosciutto Ragù Red Wine Caramel

To be honest I called this pasta Triangles because I felt way too embarrassed to call them for what they really look like: wontons. I just love the way wontons trap their filling by simultaneously sealing three sides of the dough from the top, creating a pouch that traps all the ingredients. It is quite different from the typical two pasta sheet layer principals of traditional pasta law. I love to fill them with fresh burrata cheese mixed with just a drop of Sicilian extra virgin Frantoio oil. While the pasta cooks the cheese melts, retaining its delicate milky taste, and the olive oil kicks in sending its flavor to a stratospheric quality level.

The fresh peas emulsion evaporates in your mouth when combined with the taste of the burrata while the morelles/prosciutto ragù add contrast and substance. Because of the mushroom's hearty taste I add sweetness and aroma to the dish by squirting just a touch of red wine caramel to balance it out at serving time. This dish is not only elegant, but also quite wonderful to eat. It is easy in its execution and without a doubt a crowd pleaser.

Use Saffron Pasta Dough Recipe

For the Burrata Filling
Place some fresh burrata cheese in a colander and press most of the water out for a few hours.
When ready chop with a knife in small chunks, drizzle with extra virgin olive oil and finely cracked black peppercorns.
Mix well and set aside in the refrigerator until ready to use.

How to Make the Triangles
With the help of a pasta machine, roll the dough until thin and elastic and form a long sheet. Using a round pasta cutter of approximately 3 inches in diameter cut out a few pasta discs and set them aside. Brush them with egg wash and fill each of them with about 1½ square inch of the burrata filling.
Craft the pasta by lifting up 3 edges of the dough around the filling and sealing it together with your fingers in the shape of a triangle or

a Chinese wonton, making sure to pinch firmly and to seal each one of them properly.
Dust with flour and store in refrigerator on a sheet pan over parchment paper, covered with a kitchen towel until cooking time.

Green Peas Emulsion

Ingredients
8 oz of fresh English peas
2 oz of sweet white onion thinly sliced
2 oz of shallots sliced
1 clove of garlic mashed
2 oz of butter
½ cup of chicken broth
Salt
Ground white pepper
4 large basil leaves
2 tbsp of excellent extra virgin olive oil
½ tsp of white truffle oil
Some assorted micro greens to decorate the dish (optional)

Directions
Blanch the fresh peas in salted water and set aside.
In a medium-size pan combine the onions with the butter cut in small cubes, the shallots, salt, pepper and the mashed garlic. Cook at moderate fire until the onions are translucent. Add the peas, the chicken broth and reduce approximately by half.
Remove from stove, add the truffle oil and the basil and transfer all to a high-speed blender about one minute until smooth.
Emulsify at high speed with the extra virgin olive oil until foamy.
Taste for salt and pepper and chill immediately in ice bath.

Morel Mushrooms/Parma Prosciutto Ragù

Ingredients
½ lb of fresh morel mushrooms coin sliced
2 oz of shallots minced
½ tsp minced garlic
4 oz of Parma prosciutto thin sliced in strips
2 oz of butter
3 sage leaves chopped

Salt
Ground white pepper
6 oz of chicken broth
2 basil leaves chopped

Directions
In a medium-size pan, cook the prosciutto with the butter till crispy. Add the sage, the shallots and the garlic and cook till translucent. Add the mushrooms and sauté just for a minute or so. Add the chicken broth, salt and pepper and reduce down to half.
Remove from stove.
Add the chopped basil and mix well.

Red Wine Caramel and Cabernet Reduction
See Appetite Openers chapter from White Corn and Reggiano Custard recipe (Page 44).

To Serve
Cook the pasta in salted water; once ready, transfer to a sauté pan with some butter and drizzle with cooking water.
On a round serving plate horizontally run a strip of green peas emulsion.
We will place all the components for our dish on top of the peas emulsion: on the right side place a few cooked triangles, in the middle a generous spoonful of the morel mushrooms ragù and on the left side some colorful micro greens.
To complete the dish squeeze the wine caramel out of a small plastic bottle in a circular motion from north to south of the peas strip, filling the empty part of the plate and giving balance to the entire dish flavorfully and visually.

Tomato Ravioloni Filled with Sweet Breads and Cotechino Sausage in Walnut/Ricotta Sauce and Roasted Pancetta with Sage Froth

A very particular and unusual dish: I craft larger-than-normal size ravioli using tomato dough to make a statement on the plate, giving color and flavor to an otherwise bland and boring presentation. Diversity comes in both its sauce and its filling. The first is a blend of excellent toasted walnuts, mixed with raw ricotta cheese impastata and broken down to a velvety paste, never cooked. The second is a combination of roasted veal sweetbreads and Italian country sausage cotechino, for an autumn/winter filling to give life to a perfect marriage that is savory yet delicate.

I have to admit, when I first experimented this combination I was pretty disappointed as the dish per se was not giving me back the vibes of a creation worthy to be listed on any of my menus. My rule is very strict and simple: If I first and foremost do not get excited about my work then I cannot possibly think anyone else would pay money for it. Every now and then great combinations of flavor take life when no one expects it and with very little effort: the combined sauce and pasta was good, but not great. Then I roasted some pancetta and added it to the dish: Wow! What a difference! That was the missing link I was looking for to elevate this dish to greatness.

It was crunchy, flavorful, dense in taste and yet so delicate when combined with all other elements. Now I was pleased and I suddenly found my culinary smile again. To decorate the dish I opted for a bright sage froth: when you serve it, dot a few small spoons of it across the dish and you will see how it will acquire elegance, visual interest as well as taste.

Use Tomato Pasta Dough Recipe

Sweet Breads and Cotechino Sausage Filling

Ingredients
8 oz of cotechino sausage thinly sliced
1 lb of lightly poached veal sweetbreads and chopped
4 shallots sliced
3 cloves of garlic sliced
1 tbsp of butter
3 tbsp of olive oil
5 sage leaves chopped
½ sprig of rosemary chopped
½ cup of chicken broth
½ cup of heavy cream
Salt
Ground white pepper
2 oz of grated Parmesan Reggiano cheese

Directions
In a medium-size pan sauté crispy the sweetbreads and the cotechino sausage with the sage, rosemary, sliced shallots and garlic in butter and olive oil.
Season with salt and pepper and add the heavy cream and the chicken broth and reduce until almost dry, set aside.
When cold, pass the mix through the meat grinder with the smallest possible plate, add the parmesan cheese and mix well. Transfer to a pastry bag.

How to Make the Ravioloni

With the help of a pasta machine, roll the dough until thin and elastic and form a long sheet. Brush it with egg wash and squeeze the filling out of the bag creating a strip of small little piles of about 1 inch square in size and distance each others about 3 inches. Lay a second pasta sheet on top of the fillings, very carefully stretching the dough around them flat and tapping gently on the filling in order to give more of a uniformed shape. With a ribbed pasta cutter wheel craft many ravioloni of 3 inches square.
Dust with flour and store in refrigerator on a sheet pan over parchment paper and covered with a kitchen towel until cooking time.

Ingredients
A few pancetta slices
A tbsp of excellent extra virgin olive oil
A pinch of cracked black peppercorns

Directions
Lay the thin slices of pancetta on a silicone baking mat and bake in oven at 200 for approximately 2 hours until very crispy. Store on various layers of parchment paper.

Walnut Ricotta Sauce

Ingredients
8 oz of toasted walnuts
3 oz white bread cut 2 inches square
2 oz of extra virgin olive oil
2 oz of grated Parmesan Reggiano cheese

½ tsp of minced garlic
Salt
Ground white pepper
½ cup of chicken broth (add a little more if needed)
½ tsp of ground nutmeg
8 oz of ricotta cheese impastata

Directions
Toast the walnuts in hot oven, set aside until room temperature, then place all the ingredients in a large bowl except the ricotta cheese and mix well.
Make sure to push the bread on the bottom of the mix in order for it to soak completely. Transfer the mix to a high-speed blender till velvety and pasty.
Taste for salt and pepper and add a little more oil or milk as needed.
Gradually add in the ricotta cheese to finish the sauce to a creamy consistency.

Sage Froth

Ingredients
4 oz of fresh sage leaves
2 qt of water or chicken broth
12 grams of powder lecithin
½ tsp of minced garlic
½ tbsp of olive oil
A pinch of salt
A pinch of ground white pepper

Directions
In a small pot color the garlic with the olive oil, the white pepper and the salt.
Quickly add the sage leaves, stir into the hot mix for approximately 5 seconds and add the water or broth.
Simmer until consumed down to half of total liquid.
Pass the mix through a high-speed blender till very fine.
Filter the mix.
Once at room temperature, with a small handheld immersion blender combine the lecithin with the liquid and set aside.
Whip the mix right before serving to a solid and colorful airy froth.

To Serve
Cook the pasta in salted water, once ready transfer to a sauté pan on open fire with some butter, a couple of sage leaves and a drizzle of the cooking water.
On a large warm plate, preferably square, spread a few spoonfuls of the walnut sauce around.
Plate the ravioloni, decorate with the crispy pancetta strips, drizzle with some excellent extra virgin olive oil and dot with a few small tablespoons of the sage froth across the plate.

Giant Agnolotto Filled with Sheep Ricotta/Spinach and Running Egg with White Truffle Shavings and Reggiano Snow with Crispy Sage

For those who love white truffles this dish is as sinful as it can be. It is quite rare to encounter pasta preparations this big to make a statement on a plate. This is a typical dish that "stinks" of home, or at least my home back in Torino. The "normal" version of this dish is called "agnolotti di magro" where many are crafted smaller and are filled with spinach and ricotta cheese only. They are usually served with farm fresh cream sauce and Parmesan cheese while the white truffles are shaved on top only for those gastronomic sinners who can afford it.

Very few traditional restaurants in the Piedmont region prepare this dish with an egg yolk in it. I am not a traditional chef, but I love the idea of continuously and pleasantly shocking my guests with progressive dishes where the element of surprise is constantly present. So I decided to craft a big giant agnolotto and to use sheep ricotta as more pungent in taste. I combined it with sauté spinach and Taleggio cheese and filled the pasta into one oversized pillow. The raw egg yolk is trapped between the filling and the pasta and it cooks just enough to produce an incredible running flavor to the dish once pierced with a fork. The white truffle shaves steal the show for their unique aroma and combine perfectly well with the Parmesan snow and the sage leaves.

Needless to say this is an incredibly filling dish, but one of those you will have a very hard time forgetting about once you try it.

Use Agnolotto Pasta Dough Recipe

Ingredients
A few crispy fried sage leaves to use when plating
1 tbsp of butter
Salt
Ground white pepper
2 oz chunk of Parmesan Reggiano cheese
Fresh Alba's white truffle shaves

Sheep Ricotta/Spinach Filling

Ingredients
1 lb of sheep ricotta cheese pressed out of its water
3½ oz of fresh sauté spinach
1½ oz of Taleggio cheese finely diced
¼ cup of grated Parmesan Reggiano cheese
Salt
Ground white pepper
1 tsp of white truffle oil
Pinch of nutmeg
1 small egg
1 small egg yolk to use when making the agnolotto
1 paper-thin slice of butter to use in the pasta-making process

Directions
Squeeze the water out of the spinach using a moist kitchen towel.
In a food processor combine the spinach, the parmesan, the egg yolk, the nutmeg, salt, pepper and the truffle oil.
Blend until smooth and transfer into a large bowl with the ricotta and the diced Taleggio cheese, mixing with a large spoon or a hard rubber spatula until perfectly mixed.
Transfer the mix to a pastry bag and refrigerate for a couple of hours before using.

How to Make the Agnolotto
With the help of a pasta machine roll the dough until thin and elastic and form a long sheet. Cut out various pasta circles of 4 inches diameter and brush half of them with egg wash.
Lay 2½-inch-wide round pasta cutter in the center of each disc to momentarily host the filling and, inside of it pipe in the

ricotta/spinach stuffing in circular motion from a pastry bag of 1-inch cutout opening.

Remove the pasta cutter vertically, leaving the filling tight and compact in the middle. With a tablespoon, press in the center of the filling in a circular motion creating a small nest to host the duck egg. Place a very small piece of butter, salt, pepper and finally the egg yolk on top of it. Be very careful as if the yolk breaks we will have to start all over again. Top the yolk with 1-inch square paper-thin slice of butter and lay a second pasta sheet on top of it.

Carefully stretch the dough around it sealing the two sheets by pressing firmly with your fingers. With a ribbed pasta cutter wheel cut all around the Agnolotto removing the excess trimmings.

Dust with flour and store in refrigerator on a sheet pan over parchment paper, covered with a kitchen towel until cooking time.

To Serve

Cook the agnolotto in abundant salted water. Make sure to give enough time to fully cook the filling and partially the egg yolk inside the pasta.

Transfer in a pan with butter, a little cooking water and a couple of fresh sage leaves and reduce the liquid on open fire rotating the pan in circular motion ticking it up to a whipped buttery sauce.

Place the agnolotto in the middle of a large plate and drizzle with a few tablespoons of the sauce.

Top the pasta with Parmesan Reggiano cheese freshly grated through a very fine micro plane, place 3 leaves of fried sage, vertically around the pasta and with the truffle mandolin shave enough fresh white truffles on top.

This dish has to be served immediately before the truffle shavings lose their crispiness or if preferred and I highly recommend this, shave right in front of your guests at the very last second.

Crunchy Squid Ink Cannelloni Filled with Broccoli in Spicy Cherry Tomato/Lobster Confit and Quick Chanterelles Mushrooms Ragù

I could not possibly write an Italian cookbook without including the famous and beloved cannelloni. In Italy, cannelloni are synonymous with comfort, family meal and happiness. They bring friends together and spread joy around the table. Traditionally they are usually filled with meats and fish, rarely with vegetables. There is a predominant element of surprise when eating any type of cannelloni. I do not know why. It might be the adventure in discovering what is beneath its wrappings even when you already know its shape. Maybe it is the way these small logs are stacked together, fooling the guest with the appearance of playing with a gastronomic toy. I wrap black squid ink rectangular shaped pasta sheets around a delicious purée of slightly spicy braised broccoli. I make a confit of tenderly cooked lobster meat and sweet cherry tomatoes and I create a third conductor in taste and texture with the quick chanterelles mushrooms ragù. The crunchiness of the pasta creates a wonderful balance for its soft broccoli filling, the lobster and the cherry tomatoes deliver taste and contrast in color and the mushrooms diversity in flavor. I like to stack them fire log style in order to give this dish its deserved importance in elevation for visual effect. However, you could also line them up on a rectangular plate one by one and delicately top them with the tomato/lobster confit and the mushrooms ragù. Either way this turns out to be a very colorful dish full of taste and flavors even for those traditionalists who insist cannelloni should only be stuffed with meat or fish.

Use Black Squid Ink Pasta Dough Recipe

Broccoli Filling

Ingredients
2½ lbs of broccoli thinly sliced
1 garlic clove peeled and sliced
1 large white onion thinly sliced
1 cup of basil leaves
1 cup of chicken broth
Ground white pepper
Salt
1 cup of extra virgin olive oil
1 small pinch of crushed hot red pepper
½ cup of grated Parmesan Reggiano cheese

Directions
In a medium-size pan sauté the onions and the garlic with only half the oil.

When lightly colored, add the sliced broccoli, salt, pepper and the spicy hot pepper.
Cook 4-5 minutes, add the chicken broth and back on the stove on open fire about 8 more minutes until all the liquid will be absorbed by the broccoli mix.
Turn off the fire and add the basil.
Taste for salt and pepper and run the mix through a food processor with the remaining extra virgin olive oil and the parmesan cheese.
When completely smooth and fine transfer the mix to the refrigerator for at least 4 hours before using.

How to make the cannelloni
With the help of a pasta machine, roll the dough until thin and elastic, and form a long sheet. With a ribbed pasta cutter wheel make various sheets of the dimensions of 5 inches long and 3½ inches wide.
Cook the pasta in salted water and chill them in ice bath immediately.
When time to make the cannelloni lay each pasta sheet on a kitchen towel and dry them on both sides. With a pastry bag with 1 inch cut out opening pipe in the broccoli filling horizontally, creating a log of 3½ inches in length. Roll the cannelloni tight and set aside in the refrigerator covered with a damp towel until serving time.

Quick Chanterelles Mushrooms Ragù

Ingredients
10 oz of fresh chanterelles mushrooms
½ tbsp of minced shallot
The tip of a teaspoon of minced garlic
Salt
Ground white pepper
1 tbsp of extra virgin olive oil
½ oz of butter
The leaves of one sprig of fresh thyme
2 tbsp of chicken broth
A few small fried basil leaves to use at serving time

Directions
Slice the mushrooms about 1½ inches and set aside.

In a hot pan combine the butter and the extra virgin olive oil, the shallots, the garlic and the mushrooms, cooking at very high flame. Dust with salt, pepper, and the fresh thyme.
Add the chicken broth, stir, and remove from the fire.

Cherry Tomato and Lobster Confit

Ingredients
1½ lbs of freshly shucked lobster meat cooked just enough to get it out of its shell and cut up in small chunks
4 garlic cloves sliced
1½ cups of extra virgin olive oil
1 lb of canned San Marzano plum tomatoes hand crushed
2½ lbs of cherry tomatoes halved
½ cup of chopped fresh basil
Salt
Ground white pepper
Cracked black peppercorns
2 pinches of dry oregano
1 pinch of crushed red hot pepper

Directions
In a large pan slice the garlic cloves into the cold oil, turn the fire on, and cook till golden.
Add the halved cherry tomatoes, oregano, hot pepper, and cook for a few minutes.
Add the crushed plum tomatoes, the salt and the pepper, and cook for a few more minutes only until all ingredients come together.
Stir in the lobster meat, taste for salt and pepper, and cook 1extra minute only, leaving the lobster meat tender and juicy. Do not overcook the lobster or it will turn very tough and inedible.
Finish by adding the fresh basil and a sprinkle of the cracked black peppercorns.
Remove from the stove and chill the sauce immediately over ice bath.

To Serve
On a small baking pan drizzled with olive oil, stack 6 cannelloni, lining up 3 of them horizontally and the other 3 on top of them vertically fire log style.

Bake in the oven at 350 for approximately 8 minutes until hot and crispy.

On a serving plate, preferably round, place a couple of tablespoons of the quick chanterelle mushroom ragù right in the center, rearranging them for visual display and to better balance the weight of the cannelloni.

Slide a wide spatula under the cannelloni stack and transfer it on top of the mushrooms.

Top the stack of pasta with 2-3 tablespoons of the spicy cherry tomato/lobster confit, drizzle the dish with excellent extra virgin olive oil, and decorate the dish with a few small fried basil leaves and some optional micro greens.

Porcini Tortelli Filled with Veal/Chicken/Cabbage in Taleggio Speck Cream and Crispy Vidalia Onions with Black Truffle Shavings

This is one of those pasta preparations that once you are finished eating you go back to the empty plate and keep looking for more, and you will find yourself dipping your fork in the leftover sauce or picking up a small piece of crunchy onion or the little slice of truffle left in the corner, using your fingers as instruments of satisfaction until your plate is finally cleared. I have seen guests do the famous "scarpetta," clearing the leftover sauce on the plate with bread and savoring every last bit of it, at times with visual embarrassment, indirectly facilitating the dishwasher's job.

You either love or hate Taleggio. It is one of those cheeses, like Gorgonzola or Roquefort, that are very pungent, direct and sharp, and my guests are usually divided between those who drool over them with a glass of wine and others who curl their noses and step back only by mentioning their names. If you belong to the first group of people, you are in pasta heaven.

The tortelli filling is a mix of Piedmont's traditions where a combination of cabbage, veal and chicken steal the show at each bite with intense flavor. The porcini mushrooms dough caresses the gentle filling with the robust sauce, and connect flavors and traditions on the plate.

Shavings of winter black truffles elevate this poor dish to luxury while the Vidalia onion crisps bring the dish back to its humble roots and create diversity in texture. As you can anticipate, this is indeed a very well-balanced dish. I find that nine pieces of the tortelli are more than enough for a single portion, but it has happened that some of my regular guests have asked me to increase it to 12. In the end your guilty pleasures are your own, so feel free to customize it any way you like and do not forget to arm yourself with fresh bread beforehand when it will be time to do the dishes.

Use Porcini Pasta Dough Recipe

Ingredients
A few paper thin sliced white onion rings to fry crispy
1 tbsp of corn starch
Freshly shaved winter black truffle

Directions
Dust the onion slices with the corn starch and fry them in abundant oil till golden crispy rings. Sprinkle with salt and white pepper and set them aside in warm place until plating.

Piedmont-Style Veal/Chicken/Cabbage Filling

Ingredients
2 lbs chicken breasts cut in cubes
2 lbs beef tenderloin trimmings cut in cubes
1 white onion sliced
6 oz of Savoy cabbage sliced thin
2 sprigs of rosemary chopped
2 sprigs of sage chopped
4 garlic cloves peeled and hand mashed
6 oz of pancetta diced
8 oz of mortadella cut in cubes
10 oz of fresh spinach
1½ medium-size carrots sliced
4 stalks of celery sliced
2 oz of Italian parsley
¾ cup of olive oil
3 eggs
1 tbsp of black truffle oil

1½ cups of grated Parmesan Reggiano cheese
A pinch of ground nutmeg

Directions

In a large pan cook the onions, garlic, carrots, celery, rosemary, sage and cabbage.

When lightly colored add the meats, salt, pepper, and parsley, and cook crispy for several minutes until all the meats and vegetables start to stick on the pan.

When the meat is ready and falls off by the touch, add the spinach, cook a couple more minutes, and remove from fire.

Transfer the mix to a bowl and let it rest till room temperature.

Pass the stuffing through the meat grinder twice, with the smallest hole plate attachment possible.

Adjust with salt and pepper and add the parmesan cheese, truffle oil, nutmeg, and eggs and mix it all very well till a solid, but moist paste.

How to make the tortelli

With the help of a pasta machine, roll the dough until thin and elastic and form a long sheet. Using a round pasta cutter or approximately 2½ inches in diameter cut out a few pasta discs and set them aside.

Brush them with egg wash and place about 1 inch cube in volume of the filling right in the middle of each disc. Gently fold each one to a half-moon shape, trapping the filling inside sealing the edges around it.

Get rid of any air pockets by pressing with your fingers.

Lightly brush the two corner tips of the half moons edges with the egg and while holding them with both hands, combine them with a single rotating motion pinching them together and giving life to a tortelli shape.

Dust with flour and store in refrigerator on a sheet pan over parchment paper, covered with a kitchen towel until cooking time.

Taleggio Speck Truffle Cream Sauce

Ingredients

1 qt of heavy cream
12 oz of Taleggio cheese diced
3 oz of speck sliced and cut in fine strips

2 tbsp of olive oil infused and preserved sliced winter black truffles
½ shallot finely minced
2 oz of butter
Ground white pepper
Salt
½ cup of grated Parmesan Reggiano cheese
2 leaves of sage finely chopped

Directions

In a small pot melt the butter with the shallots, and cook till translucent.
Add the speck and the sage, and cook till crispy.
Add the heavy cream and the diced Taleggio cheese, the salt, the pepper, and bring to boil at moderate-low flame.
As the cream boils, remove from the stove and gradually add the Parmesan cheese, whisking until completely melted.
Add the sliced truffle and oil mix, and delicately stir.

To Serve

Cook the tortelli in salted water, and transfer them to a pan with butter and a couple of sage leaves about a minute on open fire.
On a large serving plate spread a few tablespoons of the Taleggio sauce, enough to cover the entire surface of the plate.
Place the tortelli symmetrically on top of the sauce, creating a clean and well-lined-up presentation.
Place a few onions crisps on top of the pasta randomly, and finish by shaving fresh black truffles on top.

Red Beet Fagotti Filled with Fonduta and Running Quail Egg in Green Asparagus Broth and Parmesan Crisps

These fagotti are comparable to the Triangles recipe because they share the same shape; however, their use for this dish is completely different. It is a winner for concept, colorful presentation, and addictive for those who love pasta in their soup. In Italy there is a very inexpensive and comforting dish for the cold rainy days considered of low culinary importance because of its simplicity: "tortellini in brodo" or tortellini pasta in chicken broth.

I wanted to elevate the simplicity of this dish and to change it to a glamorous one. I made a very delicate green asparagus broth/sauce to host all the components and I crafted the fagotti using bright-red beet pasta dough filled with fontina cheese fondue and quail eggs. I followed the same principles of the agnolotto recipe by spreading flavor and substance using the running quail yolk and the cheese fonduta as gastronomic vehicles. The white asparagus tips enhance the taste of the broth with crunchiness, while the Parmesan cheese crisps provides sharp taste and texture. This is a great dish to shave winter black truffles on if you wish, or for those who want to take a step further and indulge use white ones from Alba when in season.

Use Red Beet Pasta Dough Recipe

Fonduta Cheese Filling

Ingredients
1 lb of fontina Valle D'Aosta cheese DOP
1 cup of milk
1/3 cup of AP flour sifted
5 egg yolks
A few fresh quail eggs to be used when crafting the fagotti

Directions
Cut the fontina cheese in small cubes and place them in a bowl, add the milk and place in refrigerator overnight.
The next day wait until the cheese and milk come to room temperature, and then stir in the flour, mixing delicately with your hands or by using a rubber spatula.

Place the bowl on very delicate hot bath at moderate temperature about 30 minutes, stirring occasionally till the cheese is completely melted, incorporating the milk with the cheese into one thick paste. Remove from the bath and gradually stir in the egg yolks, mixing rapidly with a whisk until golden and smooth in texture.
Refrigerate overnight.

How to make the fagotti
With the help of a pasta machine roll the dough until thin and elastic and form a long sheet. Using a round pasta cutter, approximately 3 inches in diameter, cut out a few pasta discs and set them aside. Brush them with egg wash and fill each of them with about 1 inch of the cheese filling. Create a small pocket to host the quail yolk pressing gently on each of the fonduta piles.
Lay one egg for each fagotti and seal them close by lifting up 3 edges of the dough around the filling and sealing it together with your fingers in the shape of a Chinese wonton.
Pinch firmly and properly.
Dust with flour and store in refrigerator on a sheet pan over parchment paper, covered with a kitchen towel until cooking time.

Green Asparagus Broth

Ingredients
8 oz of fresh green asparagus sliced
2 small shallots sliced
1 tbsp of butter
14 oz of chicken broth
10 each basil leaves
Salt
Ground white pepper
2 tbsp of extra virgin olive oil
A few blanched white asparagus tips to use when plating

Directions
In a sauté pan golden the shallots with the butter, add the asparagus, and cook with salt and pepper a couple of minutes. Add the chicken broth and simmer about 3-4 minutes until the asparagus will be cooked, but still crunchy and very green. Remove from the pan and transfer into a high-speed blender.

Mix with the basil leaves and the extra virgin olive oil until bright green and very velvety.
Taste for salt and pepper.
Chill right away on ice bath.

Parmesan Crisps

Preset the oven at 325 degrees.
On a silicone baking mat form 1-1½ inches flat circles of grated Parmesan Reggiano cheese, making sure they are proportionally distant from each another by at least 3 inches.
Press delicately on each circle with your fingers and bake a few minutes until golden.
Let the crisps cool completely before transferring them to deli paper.
Do not refrigerate.

To Serve
Cook the fagotti in salted water and transfer them to a pan with butter and a couple of sage leaves about a minute on open fire.
In a warm pasta bowl place 2-3 tablespoons of the green asparagus broth right in the center and delicately place the fagotti on top of the broth. Continue with the white asparagus tips and place 3 or 4 of the parmesan crisps upright possibly leaning on the fagotti for elevation. Finish with a light drizzle of excellent extra virgin olive oil.

Whole Wheat Pansotti Filled with Liquid Black Truffle over Artichoke Fondue and Pancetta/Porcini Mushrooms/Sweet Water Shrimp Ragù

It would be easy for me to write an introduction for the pansotti dish, taking full credit for this genius, and I repeat genius, idea of stuffed pasta making, but I learned lies have very short legs, so here goes the real story behind the pansotti with the liquid black truffle filling.

A couple of years ago I took a trip to Rome and had a fantastic meal at the Michelin's Guide 3 stars La Pergola where chef Heinz Beck (a transplanted German in Italy) adopts centuries old Roman traditions and transforms them in avant-garde modern preparations. One of those is a recreation of the classic Roman spaghetti alla carbonara where the combination of excellent products such as local pecorino, farmed eggs and traditional cured pork cheek steal the show on a plate. What he did, however, captured my attention: he whipped a robust zabaglione with the yolks and the grated pecorino and once cold he folded into whipped cream. He then created the "fagottelli" by folding rectangular pasta sheets stuffed with the cold zabaglione. The fagotelli are then cooked and tossed with local crispy pancetta and melted butter. The revelation is inside the pasta as while the fagottelli cook the filling melts and creates a liquid stuffing with a pungent and authentic flavor of the traditional carbonara sauce. It was an incredible dish to sample and for sure it created an unprecedented all new sensation in savoring homemade pasta filled with liquid.

When I came back to the States I could not wait to recreate it in my kitchen, but after a few unsuccessful tries I realized a wonderful combination in flavor and concept can only be achieved in its birthplace because of the pureness of its local ingredients. I went to work and I came up with a liquid filling that follows the same concept and principals of the Roman fagottelli: by making a black truffle reduction I was able to add incredible flavor to the yolks, zabaglione and stuffed the pansotti with it, creating a brand new and equally excellent liquid filling. By using the whole wheat pasta dough I was able to simplify the dish without overwhelming it with too many additional ingredients stressing down its concept.

I like to use a hint of squid ink to highlight the color of the filling and wanted to pair it with robust ingredients to accompany the intense flavor of the truffles. I made an artichoke fondue and a ragù of fresh diced porcini mushrooms, pancetta cubes and roasted fresh water shrimp.

When you bite into the pansotti, the truffle liquid unleashes an incredible aroma preparing the palate to host all the surrounding ingredients, the pancetta gives flavor and crispiness, the mushrooms and shrimp substance and the artichoke fondue a wonderful blanket of creative diversity.

Use Whole Wheat Pasta Dough Recipe

For the Liquid Black Truffle Filling

Black Truffle Reduction

Ingredients
1 can of black truffle juice
3 oz of olive oil infused and preserved sliced winter black truffles
2 sage leaves chopped
½ shallot chopped
½ tbsp of butter
Salt
Ground white pepper
1 tbsp of frozen black squid ink

Directions
In a small pot cook the shallot with the sage and butter.
Add the truffle juice and the sliced winter black truffle mix, salt, pepper and cook at low/moderate fire till it reduces down to a quarter of its original amount.
Add the squid ink and simmer for 3 more minutes.
Remove from the stove and while still warm, liquefy in a high-speed blender till perfectly smooth.

Black Truffle Zabaglione

Ingredients
5 egg yolks
1 oz of grated Parmesan Reggiano cheese
1 tbsp of black truffle oil
1 tbsp of black truffle reduction
3 oz of whipped heavy cream
2 gelatin sheets

Directions
Soak the gelatin sheets in cold water and set aside.
Make a warm zabaglione over hot bath by whipping the egg yolk.
Gradually sprinkle with the grated Parmesan cheese a little at a time until whipped and foamy.

Remove from heat and transfer to a new bowl with the help of a rubber spatula.
Chill the mix over ice bath till completely cold and set aside.
Whisk in the truffle oil and the truffle reduction, mix well and transfer to the refrigerator for a couple of hours until firm.
Now fold in the stiffed peaks whipped cream to the cold zabaglione very delicately.
Melt the gelatin sheets in a very small pan at very low heat without any of the soaking water and fold it in rapidly with the help of a whisk.
Transfer the filling into a disposable pastry bag and place in the refrigerator again for at least 2 hours before using to craft the pansotti.

How to make the pansotti
With the help of a pasta machine roll the dough until thin and elastic, and form a long sheet.
Brush with egg wash and pipe in the filling spaced one inch apart from left to right across the entire length of the pasta sheet.
Craft the pansotti by rolling the dough on the miniature filling logs, pinching them sealed one by one. Using a ribbed pasta cutter wheel, cut across to form numerous stuffed pocket jewels. Remove the excess pasta trimmings, dust with flour and store them in refrigerator on a sheet pan over parchment paper, covered with a kitchen towel until cooking time.

Artichoke Fondue

Ingredients
3 artichoke hearts cleaned and thinly sliced
½ small onion sliced
2 garlic cloves sliced
1 tbsp of extra virgin olive oil
Salt
Ground white pepper
1½ cups of chicken broth
8 basil leaves
½ tbsp of excellent Sicilian extra virgin olive oil
½ tbsp of heavy cream

Directions

In a small pan sauté the sliced artichokes with the salt and pepper until crispy.

Add the onions and the sliced garlic and cook for a few minutes till translucent.

Add in the chicken broth and cook at low flame till the liquid is reduced almost entirely and the artichokes are tender.

Stir in the heavy cream and cook for a few more minutes.

Transfer the mix to high-speed blender with the extra virgin olive oil and the basil leaves to a bright green color and a velvety silky paste.

Chill the sauce on ice bath.

Pancetta/Porcini Mushrooms/Seared Sweet Water Shrimp Ragù

Ingredients

3 oz of fresh porcini mushrooms diced fine
½ sprig of thyme
1 oz of pancetta diced the same size of the porcini
½ shallot finely chopped
3 oz of shelled fresh water shrimp diced twice the size of the mushrooms
2 tbsp of vegetable stock or lobster broth
½ tsp of minced garlic
Salt
Ground white pepper
A small pinch of dry oregano
A very small pinch of crushed hot red pepper
1 tbsp of extra virgin olive oil
2 fresh basil leaves chopped
½ tbsp of butter
A drizzle of excellent extra virgin olive oil for serving time

Directions

In a hot pan crispy the pancetta cubes, then add the garlic and the shallots with the olive oil, and sauté until translucent.

Add the porcini, thyme, salt, pepper and oregano and cook for a minute only on very high flame.

Add the diced shrimp and immediately follow with the broth or stock of your choice and the butter.

Cook until the liquid reduces almost completely and add the crushed hot red pepper with the basil.
Remove from stove and keep warm until serving time.

To Serve
Cook the pansotti in salted water and transfer them to a pan with butter about 30 seconds on open fire.
In a warm plate place a couple of tablespoons of the artichoke fondue in the middle and in circular motion create a large disc.
In the middle of the artichoke purée, place a tablespoon or two of the porcini ragù and distribute the langoustines symmetrically in well balanced order.
Lay the pansotti on top of the ragù and finish with a drizzle of excellent extra virgin olive oil

Freshly Cut Pasta

Cavatelli with Smoked Lobster and Porcini with Green Peas in Sweet Garlic/Mascarpone/Thyme Cream

Cavatelli is one of those freshly-made Italian regional pastas that need the help of a particular machine/cutter to be crafted. This is indeed one of my favorites to eat: I could have a bowl full of it and still be tempted to have seconds. I love how the combination of the ricotta, flour and Parmesan cheese creates dense, moist dough that hardly dries out even while kneading it. In the past, before the creation of the cavatelli machine, housewives used to line up thin rolls of dough, dime-size in diameter, and cut small morsels of it, applying pressure with two fingertips and rolling them in a quick motion. Today, there is a wonderful machine that even though it crafts one piece at a time makes our job much easier and more precise. The machine can be conveniently purchased online for home use through various culinary sites and is pretty affordable. The one I use for the restaurant comes from Sicily from a small store in a town called Modica near Ragusa that only makes cavatelli machines and sells them all over Italy. They are made of plastic and are practically unbreakable.

Think of the cavatelli dough as the consistency of potato gnocchi, just a little denser, but still very delicate and extremely flavorful. The dough marries very well with a variety of meat ragù and vegetable purées, and even though it is made of ricotta cheese it combines beautifully with fish and shellfish.

After I barely cook the lobsters and shell them out, I smoke them for 24 hours in applewood chips. I combine fresh sauté porcini mushrooms, peas, and a very delicate sweet garlic/mascarpone cheese and thyme cream: the result is very addictive and absolutely glamorous.

Cavatelli Dough
1 lb of AP flour
4 oz of finely grated Parmesan Reggiano cheese
1 egg
1 lb of ricotta cheese impastata
½ tbsp of salt

How to make the cavatelli
Work the dough by hand into long rolls about the size of a penny in diameter and pass them one by one through the cavatelli machine maker.
Flour the pasta and store in refrigerator on a sheet pan over parchment paper and covered with a kitchen towel.

Ingredients
1 slightly poached Maine lobster tail
1-2 oz of porcini mushrooms sliced
1 very full tbsp of blanched English peas
1 tbsp of extra virgin olive oil
The tip of a teaspoon of minced garlic
4-5 tbsp of sweet garlic/mascarpone/thyme cream
Salt
Ground white pepper
Cracked black peppercorns
Fresh basil leaves chopped
A drizzle of Sicilian Frantoio extra virgin olive oil
A few small fried basil leaves
Smoking applewood chips

Directions
Smoke the lobster tails for at least 24 hours using the applewood chips.

When ready, chop it in about half-inch chunks and set aside.
In a sauté pan sauté the porcini mushrooms with the extra virgin olive oil, very little garlic, salt and pepper.
Add the peas and 4-5 tablespoons of the sweet garlic cream and cook about 30 seconds.
Add the smoked lobster, the chopped basil and turn the fire off.
Set aside.

Sweet Garlic/Mascarpone/Thyme Cream

Ingredients
2 cups of heavy cream
8 oz of mascarpone cheese
4 sprigs of fresh thyme
1 tbsp of extra virgin olive oil
5 whole garlic cloves mashed
Salt
Ground white pepper

Directions
In a small pan roast the garlic with the extra virgin till golden.
Add in only the florets of the fresh thyme without the stems, the heavy cream, the salt and the pepper, and bring to boil.
Remove from stove and whisk in the mascarpone cheese gently.
Bring the sauce to boil again and transfer to high-speed blender till smooth.

To Serve
Cook the cavatelli in salted water and sauté a few minutes with the sauce on open flame.
On a flat plate, serve the cavatelli finishing with a drizzle of the Sicilian Frantoio extra virgin olive oil, a sprinkle of the cracked black peppercorns, and decorate the dish with a few small fried basil leaves.

Red Peppers Bowties over Sicilian Sword Fish Ragù with Crunchy Wild Fennel Flowers and Smoked Tuna Prosciutto

What do you get when one combines traditions with innovation? In this case, a fantastic result for those who love rustic and homemade cuisine.

When I was a little kid I used to spend three months in Sicily vacationing over the summer. I know, poor me! I remember my relatives from a little town called Pachino; we used to visit very often. They cooked the simplest things at home combining only products of their land, being proud and excellent growers. It was then I started appreciating simple ingredients such as tomatoes, olives, spices, freshly slaughtered pork, lamb and anything else the land would have to offer. Simple and at its best.

One day my cousin got a huge piece of fresh swordfish loin from a relative who was a fisherman. She cut a big chuck out of it and she smoked it in the brick oven all day long. The next day she ran some salt around it and let it sit under the Sicilian sun a few hours. That evening she cut the fresh swordfish into small pieces and cooked it with green olives and capers and garlic. She drizzled some extra virgin olive oil and sautéed freshly made taccuna (thick tagliatelle) in it. Right before serving, she sliced some of the now cured and smoked swordfish and tossed it with the rest of the pasta.

Almost 30 years later I still remember it all: the combination of flavors and its procedures were, to say the least, impressive even for a 12-year-old who at the time had more soccer in him than cooking. I changed a few things: I made tomato-based pasta dough and crafted beautiful gigantic bowties to rest on top of the swordfish ragù. I was able to find a few wild fennel blossoms and decided to add the element of crispiness by frying them with a light tempura batter and to complete the dish with them right before serving. The ragù-making process has been changed based on the quality of the local ingredients. I smoke the tuna with applewood chips whenever I can or I buy the smoked Sicilian's if available on the market.

This remains an incredibly rich dish, but at the same time very delicate and elegant and full of memories.

Use Red Pepper Pasta Dough Recipe

How to make the bowties

With the help of a pasta machine roll the dough until thin and elastic and with the help of a ribbed pasta cutter wheel form small rectangles of 4 inches long and 2 inches wide.

any colorful bowties by folding each ribbon of pasta
n style, and right in the center of each one pinch them very

Dust with flour and store in refrigerator on a sheet pan over parchment paper and covered with a kitchen towel until cooking time.

Ingredients
A few slices of Sicilian smoked tuna prosciutto
A few fresh wild fennel flowers
1 tbsp of corn starch
Salt
Ground white pepper
A pinch of cracked black peppercorns

Directions
This procedure has to be done at the very last second before plating the pasta as we want to create a very crunchy contrast for the whole dish.
Dust the fresh fennel flowers with the corn starch, shake off the excess, and deep fry them in abundant oil till crispy and lightly golden.
Dust with salt and pepper, and set aside.

Sicilian Sword Fish Ragù

Ingredients
1 lb of swordfish loin cut in small cubes
2 oz of small capers
1½ oz of shaved garlic
3 cups of chicken broth
½ cup of extra virgin olive oil
8 fresh basil leaves chopped
4 oz of Castelvetrano Sicilian green olives pitted and sliced
A pinch of crushed hot red pepper
A pinch of dry oregano
Salt
Ground white pepper

Directions

Heat a large sauté pan on live flame till very hot.

Pour only half the olive oil in the pan, followed immediately by the cubed swordfish. Make sure not to stir the fish or shake the pan as we want a nice and crispy sear on the fish. With the help of a wide spatula, flip the swordfish cubes once crispy, add the remaining oil, the salt, pepper, the capers, the garlic slices, the oregano and the hot pepper, and cook about a minute more or until the garlic is nice and golden.

Add the chicken broth and reduce till half of the original amount. Taste for salt and turn the fire off, add the basil and set aside.

To Serve

Cook the pasta in salted water.

On a large round or square plate, spread a few tablespoons of the swordfish ragù and with the help of culinary tweezers place each butterfly on top of the sauce, well lined up.

Delicately place the crunchy flowers on top of the pasta, giving balance in presentation and repeat with the smoked tuna slices.

Finish with a sprinkle of cracked black peppercorns before serving.

Potato Gnocchi in Artichoke Ragù and Port Braised Veal Cheeks with Shaves of Fresh Castelmagno Cheese

There are countless versions of gnocchi around the world: The Germans like to make their nocken with potato and semolina, the French use the mix for their éclairs and pastry choux boiled in water and tossed with cream sauce, the Croatians have a version of it called njoki served usually with their traditional beef and vinegar stew Dalmatinska pasticada. The Chinese have an old version of it in their culinary traditions as well as the Middle Eastern. The concept of gnocchi is everywhere, and it is as comforting and satisfying as it is poor and simple. In Italy alone there are countless types of gnocchi: I cannot say I have tried them all, as much as I would like to. Gnocchi is a combination of traditions, needs and personal taste typical of Italian regional cooking.

There are numerous new versions and adaptations of it that come about on a daily basis from restaurants and chefs who want to break out from culinary parameters. My favorite, however, is the potato gnocchi. Ever since I was a toddler I had three food items that would tattoo an incredible smile on my face: pasta, potato gnocchi and patatine fritte (roasted potatoes or French fries). I love how the potatoes and the flour combine together in perfect marriage, giving life to an incredible delicate and fluffy texture. It is very easy to make gnocchi, but very difficult to make them light. Gnocchi should be little light pillows that disappear in your mouth, delicate and cloudy puffs performing the task of transporting the sauce they are tossed with. Nothing more and nothing less: simple and delicate pleasure, hard to pass on. I like to cook them in various versions, but I composed this dish pairing it with thin slices of braised veal cheeks for hearty flavor and a delicate ragù of artichoke hearts as delicate counterpart. The unmistakable taste of the creamy Castelmagno cheese produces a very insisting, but delicate, edge to the dish.

The most difficult part is to find the right balance and ratio between potatoes and flour: since the amount of the potato starch varies depending on quality and age, even if you follow a recipe and scale to perfection each ingredient, there are always adjustments to be made when kneading the dough into a fluffy and delicate mix. Resist the temptation of adding more flour when forming the rolls: you will notice the difference only once the gnocchi are cooked. You will realize how easy it is to eat them, but how challenging it can be at times to craft them correctly and well.

Potato Gnocchi Dough

Ingredients
2 lbs of cooked Yukon potatoes
10 oz of AP flour
A pinch of freshly grated nutmeg
1 egg
A pinch of salt
A pinch of ground white pepper

Directions
Wrap the potatoes in aluminum foil one by one and bake them in hot oven at 375 until they are completely cooked through.
Peel the skin off and while still warm, press them through the potato ricer a couple of times.

Place the flour on the worktable with the riced potatoes, salt, pepper, nutmeg and egg, and combine all ingredients with your hands working the mix to semi-soft dough.
Sprinkle with flour and set aside covered with a kitchen towel about 10 minutes.

How to make the potato gnocchi
Work the dough by hand into long rolls about the size of a penny in diameter and with a dough cutter cut each roll into morsels of half-inch size. If you rather, cut them bigger; I suggest then to roll them on a cheese grater or on the back of a fork applying a little pressure to smooth out the density of their texture.
Dust with flour and store in refrigerator on a sheet pan over parchment paper and covered with a kitchen towel until cooking time.

Ingredients
A small chunk of fresh Castelmagno cheese from Piedmont, and a tablespoon of finely grated Castelmagno cheese.

Braised Veal Cheeks with Port Wine

Ingredients
2½ lbs of meaty veal cheeks
1 carrot sliced thick and lengthwise
1 stalk of celery
½ white onion sliced in thick coins
1 shallot sliced
4 sage leaves
1 rosemary sprig
2 garlic cloves hand mashed
1 oz of dry porcini mushrooms
1 cup of veal stock
1 cup of cooking Port wine
2 tbsp of olive oil
Salt
Ground white pepper

Directions
Sear the cheeks on open fire with the olive oil and abundant salt and pepper, and place them in a small baking pan.

Lay the herbs and the vegetables on top of the cheeks, and add the veal stock and Port wine in it.
Seal the hotel pan with two layers of aluminum foil, making sure it is firmly sealed on the edges.
Bake in hot convection oven at 300 degrees about 2 hours.
When cooked through remove the foil and set aside about an hour.
Remove the cheeks from the pan and filter the cooking juice in a small pot reducing it down to almost half.
Taste for salt and pepper, return the cheeks to their liquid and refrigerate.
When cold cut the cheeks with a knife to medium/thin slices and preserve them in their own cooking juice until serving time.

Artichoke ragù

Ingredients
4 whole fresh artichokes
The tip of a teaspoon of minced garlic
3 tbsp of dry white wine
2 fillets of anchovy
½ tbsp of small capers
¾ cup of chicken broth or vegetable stock
1 tbsp of extra virgin olive oil
1 tsp of butter
Ground white pepper
Salt
½ lemon

Directions
Clean the artichokes, completely removing the leaves and the core to bare artichoke hearts. Run the lemon on them to prevent oxidation and set them aside.
In a very small baking pan combine the wine and the broth, salt and pepper, spread the minced garlic and drop the anchovies.
Stir well so all the ingredients are well-mixed and place the artichoke hearts in the baking pan with their stems upward.
Seal the pan with aluminum foil and make sure to pinch the edges sealed.
Bake in hot oven at 375 for approximately 20-25 minutes until the artichokes are completely cooked, but still al dente.

Remove the aluminum foil, cool and filter the juice into a small container.
Slice the artichokes with a very sharp knife when at room temperature and store them in their own cooking juice.

To Serve
Warm up the veal cheeks with some of their own juice and reduce to a dense ragù, without stirring, to avoid breaking the veal slices.
In a different sauté pan, heat up the artichoke hearts with a little juice and the butter to a dense sauce.
Cook the gnocchi in lightly salted water and transfer them into the pan with the artichoke ragù.
Sauté the pasta and sprinkle with very little grated Castelmagno cheese and transfer to a large flat plate.
Place a couple of tablespoons of the braised veal cheeks right on top of the gnocchi in the center and finish by shaving thin slivers of Castelmagno cheese all over the gnocchi just like we would do with fresh truffles using the mandolin.

Modern Spaghetti Chitarra Style with Instant Carbonara Sauce and Poached Duck Egg with Soft Roman Pecorino Fondue

Change it, switch it, diversify it or rearrange it: bottom line, the taste concept is the same. There is an osteria in Trastevere, Rome, called Checco er Carrettiere where in my opinion they make the best spaghetti alla carbonara I have ever tasted. Insanely good, well-balanced, delicate, each ingredient pops in your mouth leaving you wanting more with a frown on your face, but happily satisfied and dazzled like the very first time you were kissed. Every time I travel to Rome my face gets covered with kisses like a silly cartoon character over and over. As much as I wanted to recreate that same original and sublime flavor in my restaurant, I knew I was going to fail if I only tried: the lack of the local pecorino cheese, the farmed eggs, the traditional Roman cured pork cheek, the Roman pride, all hard to find in Washington, D.C.

I decided to make a different version of carbonara by making chitarra style spaghetti with the chitarra tool. Imagine a rectangular open wooden box with aluminum strings tied very tight on both sides just like a guitar. The pasta sheet is forced through them by rolling a kitchen pin on it, giving life to fresh, handmade spaghetti. I created a soft Roman pecorino cheese fondue as the base of my sauce and tossed the cooked pasta in it. I barely poached a duck egg and placed it on top of the pasta and finished with a sprinkle of the crispy pork jaw, cracked black peppercorns and fried parsley leaves.

The concept involves recreating the carbonara sauce in your own pasta bowl by piercing the poached duck egg and tossing all ingredients together to a silky and uniform amber sauce. Indeed the taste concept remains the same in an excellent and modern savory version, but I must confess I often dream of my very first dazzling Roman kiss, the one you never forget.

Use Basic White Pasta Dough Recipe

How to make the chitarra spaghetti
With the help of a pasta machine, roll the dough until thin and elastic.
With the help of the chitarra, place the sheet of pasta on top of the wires and with a small rolling pin apply as much pressure as possible in order to cut the spaghetti through it. Dust with flour and store in refrigerator on a sheet pan over parchment paper and cover with a kitchen towel until cooking time.

Ingredients
1 poached duck egg *(See Hot Starters chapter for Winter Poached Duck Egg (Page 126)*
A few slices of cured pork jaw cut in small cubes
Cracked black peppercorns
2 tbsp of chicken broth
A few leaves of fried parsley for decoration

Soft Roman Pecorino Fondue Sauce

Ingredients
1 lb of young soft Roman pecorino cheese
1½ cups of milk

Directions
Cut the pecorino cheese in small cubes and put them in a bowl, add the milk, and place in refrigerator overnight.

The next day, wait until the cheese and milk come to room temperature, then place the bowl on very delicate hot bath at moderate temperature about 30 minutes, stirring occasionally till the cheese is completely melted into one thick paste.
Remove from the bath, transfer in a different container, and set aside.

To Serve
In a small sauté pan, crisp the pork jaw in its own fat.
Reduce the flame to low and add the chicken broth and about 3 tablespoons of the pecorino fondue.
Stir well and set aside.
Cook the pasta in salted water and transfer to the pan with the sauce. Sauté quickly a few seconds only as the sauce will thicken up very quickly.
Transfer to a serving bowl, sprinkle some cracked black peppercorns, and place the just-poached duck egg right on top of the spaghetti.
Decorate the dish with a few leaves of fried parsley and a drizzle of extra virgin olive oil.
With the help of a tablespoon and a fork, break into the poached egg and toss the pasta repeatedly in order to form an instant carbonara combining the yolk and all other ingredients into one pasty sauce.

Tomato Ricotta Gnocchi Whipped in a Pecorino Cheese Wheel and Braised Lamb Ragù

A wonderful way to diversify from the well-known and common potato gnocchi is the ricotta cheese-based gnocchi. I love to mix fresh ricotta with the flour and a hint of tomato paste for color and flavor. The lamb ragù idea came about when one day I mistakenly overcooked a leg of lamb: my sous chef and I were having a late lunch feasting on double-cooked pork from a nearby Chinese restaurant and completely forgot about the leg cooking in the oven.

I had no idea what to do with an almost-well-done leg of lamb other than possibly make a filling for stuffed pasta, when it suddenly hit me: why not double-cook the lamb in a similar way of the Chinese pork I just ate? I experimented by combining pancetta, sweet onions, rosemary and garlic in a slow cooking process to achieve a flavorful, rich yet delicate braised lamb ragù.

The result was so positively surprising that from that day on I have adapted and perfected the recipe into one of my trademark pasta sauces. However, what makes this dish different is that I whip the gnocchi into a carved hollow pecorino cheese wheel where the heat of the pasta slowly melts the cheese, creating the basic pasty condiment for the gnocchi. Once plated, I complete the dish with the lamb ragù, the artichoke chips, and the fried parsley florets.

I like to toss the gnocchi tableside while explaining the necessary procedures to my guests. They have a full visual of the ongoing process and the opportunity to savor its aroma and its fragrance while the pasta is being tossed. Needless to say the shock and visual values are very dramatic and, most importantly, quite delicious.

Tomato Ricotta Gnocchi

Ingredients
1 lb of ricotta cheese impastata
8 oz of AP flour
1 egg
½ cup tomato paste
A pinch of freshly grated nutmeg
½ tbsp of salt
2 tbsp of grated Parmesan Reggiano cheese

Directions
Press the ricotta cheese through a fine sifter.
Place the flour on the worktable with the ricotta, salt, pepper, nutmeg, egg and tomato paste, and combine all ingredients with your hands working the mix to semi-soft dough.
Sprinkle with flour and set aside covered with a kitchen towel about 10 minutes.

How to make the Tomato Ricotta Gnocchi
Work the dough by hand into long rolls about the size of a penny in diameter and with a dough cutter, cut each logs into morsels of half-inch size.

Dust with flour and store in refrigerator on a sheet pan over parchment paper and covered with a kitchen towel until cooking time.

Ingredients
A few artichoke chips
A few fried parsley florets

Braised Lamb Ragù

Leg of lamb

Ingredients
3 lbs of lamb leg boneless
1 small white onion halved
4 garlic cloves
2 sprigs of rosemary
1 tbsp of olive oil
Salt
Ground white pepper

Ragù

Ingredients
½ lb of pancetta
1½ large onion thinly sliced
2 cups of dry red wine
1 qt of chicken broth
½ tbsp of garlic minced
1½ sprigs of fresh chopped rosemary
½ cup of extra virgin olive oil
Salt
Ground white pepper
8 leaves of fresh basil chopped

Directions
With a small knife make 4 incisions in the lamb leg and stuff with a whole garlic clove and a folded sprig of rosemary in each hole. Sear the meat on open fire with salt, pepper and the halved onion in olive oil and transfer in hot oven at 375 until medium well. Once ready set aside and refrigerate overnight.

With the help of a slicer machine carve thin slices of the leg and pancetta in equal thickness. With a knife cut both meats in thin strips and set aside.

In a large pan, crisp the pancetta in its own fat, add the onions, the minced garlic and the chopped rosemary and cook until translucent. Add the lamb and cook on high flame until the mix begins to stick to the bottom of the pan. Add the red wine, reduce by half and follow with the chicken broth.

Simmer the ragù at very low heat about 45 minutes until all the ingredients come together and the meats are totally braised. Remove from the stove, taste for salt and pepper, and add the chopped basil.

To Serve

Cook the gnocchi in salted water, and then transfer them inside the empty pecorino wheel and a couple of tablespoons of the hot cooking water.

Stir the pasta in a circular motion, sprinkle with a pinch of cracked black peppercorns and drizzle with extra virgin olive oil.

Now that the gnocchi are tossed with the cheese, plate in a warm pasta bowl.

Top the gnocchi with a couple of tablespoons of the lamb ragù and decorate with a few artichoke chips and fried parsley florets.

Lithograph-Style Pasta with Shellfish Stew and Spicy Broccoli Rabé and San Marzano Tomato Emulsions

This is one of those dishes where one person's creativity comes alive the same way a talented painter would deliver his personal message on a canvas. The idea is to send a message you can read along with your meal for diversity in concept. What if you could actually read today's paper printed on your pasta sheet before you eat it? Or what about the fortune cookies we eagerly open at the end of each meal to read the random proverbs on a small piece of paper? I went to a local printing shop, and I commissioned a hard plastic stamp of the logo of Elisir, my tasting-menu restaurant. I wanted to explore the idea of stamping the restaurant logo on a pasta sheet using natural and edible ink.

Printed pasta is available for purchase in a few decent gourmet stores. The ink does not change its taste, and its novelty is limited in its visual presentation and quickly forgotten at the end of your meal. If I were to produce an inked sheet of pasta that is very visual and very delicious I could send a message of quality and creativity my guests would remember. I decided to personalize my work with fresh squid ink; once applied, I dried the ink with rice flour as it better absorbs humidity and created the basic canvas for my project.

Since I imprinted fresh squid ink on the pasta, the choice to use fresh shellfish for my dish was quite logical. I quickly stewed a few shrimp, scallops, mussels and clams, and I adorned the cooked pasta on a long rectangular serving plate almost like a mosaic in harmony and with balance. The mollusks and the pasta are combined by two emulsions that accompany the dish: fresh San Marzano tomato and spicy broccoli rabé for taste and contrast. The fresh oregano leaves give flavor and the micro basil the expected aroma in a fish preparation.

Use Saffron Pasta Dough Recipe

Lithograph Pasta/Ink Print

Ingredients
1 tbsp of black squid ink tempered with a little water
½ cup of rice flour

Directions
With the help of a pasta machine roll the dough until thin and elastic, and form a flat ribbon about 10 inches long and 6 inches wide.
Pour the tempered squid ink in a rectangular plate and adjust for thickness adding some more water if needed. Press the logo stamp in the ink and apply it onto the pasta sheet, pressing firmly for a few seconds. Repeat the process a few times for the entire size of the pasta sheet.
Dust with rice flour to absorb the excess ink and let it dry for a few minutes.
Place in refrigerator until cooking time.

Ingredients
Fresh micro basil leaves and a few fresh oregano leaves

Shellfish Stew

Ingredients
5 large mussels
8 littleneck clams
5 small size shrimp head on
8 bay scallops
1 tbsp of extra virgin olive oil
A pinch of dry oregano
Salt
Cracked black peppercorns
A pinch of Sicilian spicy pepperoncino ground
½ tsp minced garlic
½ cup of water
A few micro basil leaves

Directions
In a small pan sear all the shellfish with the olive oil, the garlic, the pepperoncino, the oregano, the salt and the cracked peppercorns. Add the water, cover the pan with a lid and let it simmer for a couple of minutes.
Remove from the pan, filter the cooking liquid, remove each mollusk from its shell and place them inside the liquid.
Drizzle with extra virgin olive oil and set aside.

San Marzano Tomato Emulsion

Ingredients
8 oz of canned San Marzano tomatoes drained from their water and seeds completely
The tip of a teaspoon of minced garlic
2-3 tbsp of extra virgin olive oil
Salt
Ground white pepper
2 leaves of fresh basil
Pinch of dry oregano
Pinch of Sicilian spicy pepperoncino ground

Directions
Combine all ingredients in a high-speed blender and mix, drizzling in the extra virgin olive oil a little at a time until the purée whips into an emulsion.

Spicy Broccoli Rabé (or Rapini) Emulsion

Ingredients
4 oz of fresh rapini
½ tsp of minced garlic
1 anchovy fillet
Ground white pepper
Salt
1 big pinch of hot spicy pepper
1 tbsp of extra virgin olive oil
2 tbsp of Sicilian Frantoio extra virgin olive oil
1 cup of chicken broth or lobster broth
5 large basil leaves

Directions
Blanch the broccoli rabé in salted water for a few seconds and set aside.
Chop the rapini and sauté in hot pan with the garlic, the hot spicy pepper, the anchovy fillet, salt and pepper.
Add the chicken broth or lobster broth and simmer about one minute, add the basil and transfer to a high-speed blender.
Combine all ingredients and emulsion by drizzling in the Frantoio extra virgin olive oil a little at a time until the purée foams into a bright green sauce.
Chill on ice bath immediately.

To Serve
Cook the pasta al dente in salted water and transfer it into a pan with the mollusks and some of their hot cooking liquid.
Sauté the pasta ribbon and place it on a hot rectangular plate face up showing the lithograph work. With the help of cooking tweezers position each piece of the shellfish on top of the pasta sheet symmetrically. With a teaspoon adorn the dish alternating dots of the tomato and dots of the broccoli rabé emulsions.
Decorate the dish with a few leaves of micro basil and fresh oregano leaves.

Make sure to work quickly when decorating the pasta as the pasta sheet is openly exposed and tends to cool quite rapidly; it definitely helps if the serving plate is overheated in order to extend the life of its warmth.

Spinach Pappardelle in Duck Ragù with Duck Livers and Liquid Toma Cheese Croquettes

I love duck. It is definitely one of my favorite meats to cook and to eat. I like to use as much as possible when cooking as, aside from its breasts and thighs, there is not much left in this bird that can be used in the kitchen. However, I like to cook its livers, heart, head, neck and carcass, of which I often make savory stock and broth.

If you are able to collect a few fresh duck carcasses, I suggest to roast them first and to make a duck broth following the guidelines for the chicken broth recipe. I love to pair this ragù with fresh pappardelle pasta. The spinach, in this case, contributes to the dish with vivid color and delicate taste, once mixed with the duck ragù the combination is absolutely hearty and delightful. I am not a fan of livers and I like few chicken and goose livers, but to my surprise I realized that by adding fresh chopped livers at the end of the cooking process the ragù enriches in flavor and benefits in substance.

In the old days I completed the dish with slivers of aged toma cheese, but later I realized that by using the same cheese in different form and texture I can add quality with small flavorful surprises. I make a light fondue of fresh toma cheese and craft a few small marbles. I deep-fry them Milanese style and add them to the dish right before serving. I like the way they pop in your mouth and spread their taste. While cooking the cheese melts, creating a crispy/liquid sensation when bitten into.

Use Spinach Pasta Dough Recipe

Pappardelle Pasta
With the help of a pasta machine, roll the dough until thin and elastic and with the help of a ribbed pasta cutter wheel form ribbons of pasta of 6 inches long and 2 inches wide.

Dust with flour and store in refrigerator on a sheet pan over parchment paper and covered with a kitchen towel until cooking time.

Ingredients
Some optional fresh micro yellow pea tendrils

Duck Ragù with Duck Livers

Ingredients
2½ lbs of ground duck meat
1 white onion diced
1 medium-size carrot diced
1 stalk of celery diced
2 cups of dry red wine
1 qt of chicken broth or duck broth
½ tbsp of minced garlic
1 rosemary sprig chopped
3 leaves of sage chopped
½ cup of extra virgin olive oil
Salt
Ground white pepper
1½ oz of dry porcini mushrooms
¼ cup of heavy cream
8 oz of chopped duck livers
½ cup extra virgin olive oil
2 oz of butter
1 bay leaf

Directions
In a large pan cook the celery, the carrots, the onions, the garlic, the herbs and the bay leaf with the butter and oil until translucent.
Add the duck meat, stirring often with a big spoon and cooking on high flame until the meat begins to stick to the bottom of the pan.
Add salt and pepper and the wine.
Reduce by half, and then follow with the broth.
Simmer at low heat about 25 minutes until all the ingredients come together and the ragù is totally braised.
Add the chopped duck livers and cook 15 more minutes, stir in the heavy cream and finish cooking for 5 more minutes at moderate flame.

Liquid Toma Cheese Croquettes

Ingredients
5 oz of fresh toma cheese diced
2 egg yolks
¼ cup of heavy cream
A few tablespoons of bread crumbs
2 eggs for egg wash
1 tbsp of flour
Salt
Ground white pepper

Directions
Combine the heavy cream and the cheese in a small mixing bowl and melt over hot bath.
Once the toma is completely melted add the egg yolks and mix thoroughly with a rubber spatula to a thick and dense paste.
Transfer to a small container, cover with plastic film and set in the refrigerator for a couple of hours until it solidifies.
Form a few small marbles with the palms of your hands and dip them in flour, the egg wash, and finally the fine-sifted bread crumbs.
Deep fry at 350 a couple of minutes until golden.
Salt, pepper, and serve immediately while hot and liquid in the center.

To Serve
Cook the pappardelle in salted water and sauté in a pan with the duck ragù.
Sprinkle the pasta with some grated Parmesan Reggiano cheese and serve in a bistro bowl.
Place a few of the toma cheese croquettes on the pasta, giving an appealing visual balance.
Finish with optional micro yellow pea tendrils.

Deconstructed Fresh Spaghetti "Aglio e Olio" with Solidified Olive Oil and Roasted Garlic Powder and Raw Parsley/Parmesan Cheese Foam

Gimmicky tradition = explosive taste.

Growing up in Italy I was lucky to live and experience even the most bizarre traditions of my homeland. One of these is stretching your fun evening into one last meal before calling it a night. This usually takes place on weekends when friends get together for an evening at a local disco, a movie, or a friendly poker night. In small villages, once the decision to have a "spaghettata" is made, it is tradition to collect the basic ingredients from those friends who were absent that very evening. It is a sort of punishment for not being able to be with the rest of the group, therefore subject to a penalty. We used to knock on friends' doors at 2, 3, 4 o'clock in the morning, shouting their names, demanding olive oil, parsley, garlic, spaghetti, you name it, and once they paid their dues we would give life to a late feast in one of our homes. Once again, the food brought people together, an excuse to enjoy each other's company just a little longer while creating memories.

I remember the numerous spaghettatas we had at Galileo restaurant with friends after returning from a club late at night. Chef Roberto would shave the garlic in hot oil like the scene in the *Goodfellas* movie, proudly and carefully like a science project. He would toss the pasta with a sprinkle of cheese and parsley, and we would all enjoy each other's company a little longer with a glass of wine. How could I possibly serve something so basic and so simple at my restaurant? Most of my clientele expects the "wow factor" in taste, concept and presentation. Even though there is absolutely nothing wrong in serving a perfectly well-executed dish of plain spaghetti I took all the fun memories of this dish I stored from past years and created a new version of it, very respectful to its original taste, but absolutely unrecognizable for its traditional process.

I found the way to solidify a "stew" of extra virgin olive oil and roasted garlic with Tapioca maltodextrin powder. I made fresh spaghetti and created a foam of Parmesan Reggiano cheese mixed with raw parsley. The beauty of this dish is the combination of its original ingredients in different forms, texture and temperature: they all come alive when some of the pasta's cooking water hits all the ingredients set in the serving bowl in front of the guest, giving life to the traditional taste of the spaghetti aglio e olio.

This is definitely a wonderful way to surprise your guests visually, but especially for its taste.

Use Basic White Pasta Dough Recipe

Fresh Spaghetti Pasta
With the help of a pasta machine, roll the dough until thin and elastic.
Form several pasta sheets of 12 inches long by 6 inches wide and pass them through the spaghetti cutter attachment, dust with flour and portion in 4 oz bundles.
Store in refrigerator on a sheet pan over parchment paper and covered with a kitchen towel until cooking time.

Solidified Olive Oil and Roasted Garlic Powder

Ingredients
¾ cup of extra virgin olive oil
5 garlic cloves shaved with the truffle slicer
½ fillet of anchovy
1 small pinch of Sicilian spicy red pepper dust
2 cups of maltodextrin
1 pinch of salt
1 pinch white pepper

Directions
In a small pan at extremely low fire cook the shaved garlic and the anchovy fillet in the oil till the garlic turns gold.
Remove from fire and set aside to cool about 20 minutes.
Transfer the oil mix into a high-speed blender and liquefy.
Pass the mix through a strainer into a big mixing bowl, add the hot pepper, the salt and the ground white pepper, and let it cool completely to room temperature.
Put latex gloves on and add one cup of maltodextrin, mixing well with your hands till it turns into a crumbled powder.
Refrigerate in an air- tight container.

Raw Parsley/Parmesan Cheese Foam

Ingredients
1 qt of heavy cream high fat 40 percent
½ qt of milk
5 oz of parsley leaves chopped
2½ cups grated Parmesan Reggiano cheese

1 pinch of salt
1 pinch of ground white pepper

Directions
In a small pot boil the milk and the cream to 150 degrees with the salt and pepper.
Whisk in the Reggiano cheese till completely melted.
Add the chopped parsley in the milk/cream mix while still hot and transfer to a high-speed blender till completely liquefied and bright green in color.
Filter the sauce through a fine mesh cone and chill immediately on ice bath.
Transfer to a siphon and add approximately 2 CO_2 tanks.
Keep refrigerated.

To Serve
In a hot bowl place 3 tablespoons of the solidified olive oil powder.
Cook the pasta in salted water and place it sitting on top of the olive oil powder.
Top the spaghettini with the equivalent of 3 tablespoons of the raw parsley/parmesan foam and serve immediately as the foam has only 30 seconds of life before it melts down.
Once the dish is served in front of your guests pour enough hot pasta water in it to be able to toss it, mixing all ingredients into one creative and glorious dish melting the solidified olive oil and the foam all together.

Chapter Eight
Tales of Culinary Road Trips

After a restaurant has reached a decent popularity level it is usually approached by numerous charity organizations and institutions soliciting it to participate in various programs to raise money for their causes. I always enjoy giving; I have given a lot all my life to different people and for no specific reasons or personal interests. I love to make people happy as it really takes so little doing so and it makes people feel appreciated and loved even just for a moment. However, to me the real giving is when you are able to give up something dear to you, willingly and with no regrets, and have someone else enjoy it.

It is very hard to experience the feeling of true giving, but I strive to be a better person whenever my ego does not interfere. In my opinion the real charity is done when we are all alone and we do not have to show off our good deeds to anyone else. It is more meaningful when we are not seeking public appreciation or recognition. Everyone gives in different ways: some more, some less. There are those who give without even realizing it and others who think they give, but take instead.

In the restaurant industry the words benefit and charity are always associated with marketing and public exposure for our own gain. There is no pure charity or complete giving, rather a trade for goods in exchange for publicity. Some charity requests are sent in the form of generic letters simply stating, "Can you please donate?" Others play the guilt trip on you by trying to make you feel bad for your success, touching your conscience in the hope you give in. I have come across dubious requests throughout the years ...and I still do.

I am extremely careful who I donate my time and money to as there are many dishonest organizations out there pocketing most of the money to justify in-house processing fees, personal expenses and salaries and in the end less than 20 percent goes to the real charity. I always meet with my publicist, managers and partners at the beginning of the year to determine a charity budget for the following 12 months, what culinary trips I will take, what events the restaurant will participate in, and what kind of chef appearances I will make.

It is virtually impossible to satisfy each and every request as we receive an average of 200 on a yearly basis, so we pick and choose. The ones that are poorly written or that seem suspicious usually find their way to the trash bin almost immediately; others I might send gift certificates for their raffle or silent auctions. There are bigger organizations that lure chefs into traveling programs with luxurious accommodations—fishing trips, ski resorts, Caribbean islands, guest appearances, bike trips, etc. It is indeed incredibly hard to turn down such appealing invitations and I personally never do unless there is a scheduling conflict. These events fetch incredibly high figures. The organization allocates higher budgets for chef expenses as the bigger the name the bigger the attendance, and the bigger the profit.

But not all chef trips are for charity purposes. Some, such as culinary trips, are for professional intent, and others are for pure personal pleasure. In the restaurant industry coworkers spend so much time together on daily basis it is inevitable friendships flourish and endure.

In the Washington metropolitan area we all have known each other for decades. Even if we do not work together we make a point to learn about one another. We meet at local events, and some of us are selected to participate in specific travels or charity events. We share personal time with those we like the most, our families know each other, we get together on Sundays and we attend family functions, picnics, barbeques, dinners, etc.

Even if we are rivals or competitors, the industry leaves a mark of respect and the doors open welcoming new restaurant owners, their chefs, and their employees in the community. We all visit each other's restaurant sooner or later. We have dinners and lunches, and we experience our competition as guests and as paying customers. We form an opinion and we compare their concept, their cooking and their level of professionalism to ours. We learn, and almost always we criticize.

I have made great friends through the industry and met incredible and remarkable people throughout the years. Most of them are still in the business and others had enough of the crazy everyday routine and decided to ease their lives with better schedules fit for the needs of their families. It is very hard to completely detox from this business as its roots stay with you forever. After a while it becomes part of who you are. It is a daily fix of adrenaline throughout a busy dinner shift that shoots into your veins. You want more of it the next day. You need more of it the next day. Doing something else other than this becomes unimaginable. It is a very dangerous addiction.

For those who quit, it makes sense to seek similar job substitutes in the form of sales representatives for wine and food companies. It does not require working crazy hours, and it is definitely an easier way to stay involved in the industry on a daily basis. For many that is an intelligent, suitable and healthier substitution. Not for me. I think I will die cooking. Some of us are doomed and cannot simply escape from our pre-determined destiny. This industry is our life.

Over the past 15 years I have taken part in numerous trips for professional, educational and personal reasons. I was lucky to travel to places I have never visited before with friends and colleagues and to explore different local lifestyles, and of course sample products and ingredients. I ate in some of the best restaurants in the world. I have met and worked with some of the most charismatic food and wine icons of our times. I have been able to experience and learn very personal inside views on who we really are whenever we all travel together freed from the professional shell we live behind day after day. There is an ethical code we all respect because people know who we are, they recognize our names, they know what we look like, they eat at our restaurants and they have seen our faces on papers and magazines. Washington is a very diplomatic and conservative town where one has to be careful when speaking, especially to the press, as interviews and statements can be misinterpreted or misquoted altogether. This can be detrimental to our reputation and image. Chefs and restaurateurs must fit into the benevolent consensus of those who constantly watch us and judge us. If a popular chef is spotted partying, drinking heavily or acting improperly in a bar or a club, chances are people will learn about it and it could eventually affect business.

During my travels I have noticed many chefs changing into different personas: the real personality comes out and we are suddenly free to do and say whatever we want. The well-respected ethical code we all live by is thrown out the window and an immediate feeling of freedom kicks in right after crossing the city limits. What happens in Vegas stays in Vegas? Just about.

Because of the friendship I share with many chefs and colleagues I will limit myself by telling my stories without associating names to specific situations out of respect for those who are more visible to the public eye or currently involved in TV programming. Others, I am sure, will share my enthusiasm remembering some of those fantastic and memorable moments we all lived together over the past 20 years, situations that made us laugh till we cried, practical jokes we played on each other, personal and culinary trips we took together and spicy occurrences that left a momentary grin on a selected few while in wicked mode.

In the past 27 years I have had the opportunity to share very private moments with fellow chefs, lived incredible and very often comical situations during our travels. I have categorized my stories by destinations and specific trips as each tale is incredibly unique to me, and no matter how many times I tell the same story it always make me break out in a healthy and genuine laugh.

Enzo and Roberto's Big Jamaican Adventure

Chef Roberto Donna was the winner of the 1996 James Beard Award for best chef Mid-Atlantic. In the '80s and '90s he was a true and genuine genius I often labeled with pride as being "from a different culinary planet." His vision, his dynamic drive and execution was so impressive, constant, powerful and precise it made him one of the top 10 chefs in the country.

His restaurant, Galileo, was considered the best in Washington, D.C., and Roberto was an incredibly popular chef who marketed himself 24 hours a day, nationwide. A real celebrity and very influential for so many young, aspiring chefs. He was a real and unique friend to me for more than two decades, someone who helped me and defined the person I am today. He gave me the opportunity to dive into co-ownership in many of the restaurants we opened without any personal financial investment.

Roberto will always have a special place in my heart, but unfortunately sometimes people change due to the negative experiences we endure, leaving a deep scar in all of us. Roberto has experienced great troubles in the past few years: Many things went wrong because of his poor choices. As he said himself a few times, "I went through a meat grinder." But I choose to remember him for the genuine good-hearted person he is, and for all the amazing things he has done for so many people, along with all the happy moments we have spent together.

Roberto Donna, through good and bad, is essentially a very kind man, defined by many as a teddy bear. Roberto and I became close only after I departed from his employment. A few years on my own were enough to shake off the "employee status" and to begin a closer personal friendship based on professional respect. We opened a total of five restaurants together, along with other partners.

In the mid-late 1990s Roberto's empire stretched across the Washington metropolitan area with a total of 12 restaurants, all operating following his vision of traditional Italian cooking. Indeed, he was the well-respected king of the castle in Washington.

He was mostly cooking at Galileo Restaurant, but his chain consisted of five locations of Il Radicchio Restaurant in partnership with me and some other employees turned partners: Pesce Restaurant, in partnership with the late chef Jean Louis Palladin; Dolcetto Restaurant; Cesco Restaurant in partnership with chef Francesco Ricchi; and Barolo Restaurant on Capitol Hill, where I was mostly cooking. There was also Il Laboratorio, a very elite glass-enclosed restaurant within a restaurant inside Galileo, where Roberto would cook a different 10 course tasting menu three or four nights a week for a few guests only, and Arucola Restaurant, co-owned with a common long-time friend of ours, George Bogdanovich. Nowadays I still enjoy George's company through poker games while smoking a good Cuban cigar. Last but not least was I Matti Restaurant, his solo venture that lasted more than 15 years in the Adams Morgan area of D.C., offering the traditional fares of an authentic Italian trattoria.

Aside from operating restaurants, Roberto was involved with everyone and everything. He co-owned a bread making company, a fresh mozzarella making operation, and had interests in an Italian wine import company named Il Cuoco in partnership with one of his then best friends, Mr. Corrado Bonino.

In short, he was a very busy man and a self-made millionaire. Every time we would have dinner at a restaurant there were always people approaching our table paying their respects just like in the *Godfather* movies. I was very proud to be his friend, not for what he had, but for who he was.

As our friendship strengthened we occasionally met with our respective significant others on our days off for dinner or a casual day grilling out on the patio with other friends and family members. Other times we planned personal mini-trips to various destinations to break up our working routine and relax.

One day Roberto called me and asked if I had any interest in going away for a few days to the tropics. The timing was perfect as Il Radicchio on Capitol Hill had been open for eight months and it was practically operating on its own, and the soon-to-open Barolo restaurant had a small delay.

"Where did you want to go and what did you have in mind?" I asked.

There was a pause for a second and then he started laughing satanically. I knew exactly what that evil laugh meant: trouble.

Then he laid it out flat: Hedonism II in Jamaica. I checked the website and learned it was a luxury swinger/nudist retreat near Negril so I kind of wondered why he wanted to go there with me and not with a beautiful woman. That was Roberto: he always wanted to push his limits of excitement. I loved the idea of getting away and to relax, but I also knew Roberto has always had the evil eye for excitement. I sure thought we were going to be involved in some kind of sinful vacation pushing our limits by disobeying all ethical and moral rules. This time he really meant what he said and we actually and innocently relaxed for most of our trip, with a few exceptions. I have always been very adventurous and a little wicked myself so I accepted right away. We enrolled in the new corporate business American Express gold card and I bought tickets for a four-night five-day getaway.

Despite our physical differences Roberto and I have always gotten along very well and participated in sports and activities we both loved and enjoyed, shared everything equally with no reservations for one another and without any jealousy. He has always been borderline obese throughout his life and has never been a sex symbol or a chick magnet. But Roberto always had plenty of women and got into strange and awkward long-term loving relationships, a few hit and runs and a number of occasional month long fun experiences. Roberto was a giver and back then many people loved to take from him. Even if shy at times, he was quite the charmer and the social butterfly. Five minutes into a conversation with a beautifully fit and quite stunning woman who would appear completely out of his league and you would be surprised to see how much she would appreciate a genuine and charming man like Roberto.

He was mostly confident and comfortable with who he was and with what he could bring to the table no matter who he was talking to. Back then he was also a very respectful man and therefore a polite charmer.

I have always been a very polite and respectful person myself, but in a different way. I used to work out a lot and I was extremely fit, full of muscles, a young professional with an incredible smile who would model on occasion. But I was mostly quiet, shy by nature, in my private life very happy and content, determined and driven in business. I cannot recall a single time I approached a woman at a bar and initiated a conversation. I always thought the act of bothering someone you do not know, trying to force them into a conversation only I wanted, was quite disrespectful and inappropriate. I think I used to lack self-confidence.

By the third week of March in the early spring of 1997 we were scheduled to depart to Jamaica. I was very excited and sure this was going to be a fun and relaxing vacation. Little did I know it was going to be one for the books, and memorable. A week later the tickets finally arrived at the restaurant via courier, compliments of a common friend of ours who back then owned a travel agency. The day before our departure Roberto suggested I should hold onto his ticket as well and decided for us to meet the very next morning at what was then called Washington National Airport. The next day I woke up bright and early. I was excited and eager to get on the flight to Jamaica. On my way through the walkway from the parking garage into the terminal I saw an express check-in stand for US Airways. I remember being paranoid I was going to miss our flight, so I checked my bag quickly and walked directly to our gate, hoping to meet Roberto there, holding both our tickets in my hand.

I waited at the gate for a good hour, but no sign of Roberto. I tried to call his cell phone, but it was off. The plane was now boarding: where the hell was Roberto? Did he fall asleep? Did he forget? No clue. Now frantic, I rushed to explain the situation to one of the nearby representatives. He tried to page him: no answer. He paged him again and again. Roberto was nowhere to be found. I really did not know what to do. I even called him at home and at the restaurant, hoping he was there. I figured maybe he had a flat tire or he got stuck somewhere so in a fit of panic I boarded the plane and left his ticket with a US Airways representative and instructed her to give it to him should he show up to board a later flight.

I was quite worried.

I finally got to Montego Bay on my nonstop flight and boarded a very small six-passenger charter to Negril, and in a matter of 15 minutes fly time I got to the destination. Soon after I was welcomed with floral bouquets, a tour of the facilities, and a nice and rejuvenating bubble bath massage. Soon I was sipping a cold drink with my feet up overlooking the gorgeous view of the bay, the beautiful girls in bikinis playing volleyball, and the occasional topless hard-bodied women walking by with wicked smiles. Laughter and giggles accompanied the background music in a paradise-like scenario. All I could say was, "Wow, this is fantastic!"

And Roberto?

Well, he had quite a different travel experience down to Negril, very comical and definitely not as smooth as mine.

The morning of our scheduled flight he woke up nice and early, drove down to the airport and arrived before I did. He parked his car and went directly to the International Flight Departures upper level area and set up camp, first in line at the US Airways stand. He was way too early to check in his luggage so he stood in line protecting his pole position, waiting for the green light, for me and for his ticket. Unfortunately, Roberto left his cell phone in the car; therefore there was no possible way to contact each other.

Our flight was scheduled to depart at 9:05 a.m. By 7:45 the check-in process started, so he moved aside and let other passengers in line pass by in front of him, one by one, waiting for me to arrive. By 8:15 he started to worry, by 8:30 the boarding process started and panic took over. He got so agitated that by 8:45 he was approached by security as he was visibly upset, sweating, and his hands and arms started to move up and down as they were coordinating each thought in his head while I am sure I was called every possible name in his book. Indeed, while I was seated in the cabin my ears were bright red and needless to say burning hot, but who cared? I was happy as I had an extra empty seat next to me (Roberto's) so I was able to stretch to a more comfortable flight and truly relax. He quickly explained the situation and they invited him to go by the gate area to the lower level. They radioed a representative and a few minutes later she showed up with his ticket in hand.

Roberto is known to be a very impulsive person. It does not matter where he is or who he is with. When the light bulb goes off in his head you could expect anything to come out of his mouth. He was a human volcano. I have seen him yelling at the top of his lungs to a police officer with his finger pointed, picking a verbal fight with an FBI agent over a parking space. I saw him throwing spoons and sauté pans at employees, and I saw him turning as red as a tomato, his veins popping out from his forehead and neck, accompanied by a repertoire of insults just to make a point. The funny thing is that five minutes later he would relax and would go back to his same normal being, loving and funny. He would approach you in a gesture as he was apologizing for letting himself go that far, and he would put his arm around you and sweet talk you, explaining his reasons for losing it completely. He would make jokes until you finally cracked a smile, winning you back, knowing you understood his point and his reasons. He would do this out of guilt once he realized his was not the proper respectful behavior. The next day, however, he would do it all over again. Go figure.

When the US Airways representative showed him his ticket and explained what happened, Roberto asked if it was too late for him to board the plane. The response was prompt and silent: the representative simply pointed his finger to the window behind him overlooking the tarmac and showed flight 1028 to Montego Bay taking off. The volcano erupted, but what did I know? I was comfortably stretched over two seats and heading to paradise with a big smile on my face. Lucky me.

Roberto quickly had a triple chamomile tea, got on the phone and called his travel agent friend who miraculously was able to book him a Band-aid itinerary from D.C. to Charlotte, N.C., to Miami, Fla., to Montego Bay, Jamaica, scheduled to arrive in Negril at 10:30 p.m. that same day: an express 12 extra hours' journey. After a three-hour wait at Washington National Airport and $1,000 later he finally boarded a plane and was on his way to North Carolina flying coach in the middle seat between two other oversized passengers, with no arm rest support or additional extra seat belt extension. Squeezed like a sandwich, sweating and claustrophobic, my dear friend landed two hours later and sat on the plane an extra hour on the tarmac before he was able to get up for his connecting flight.

He made his first connection to Miami, where his next flight to Jamaica would not depart for at least six more hours. Not sure what he did for all that time in an airport, but I for sure was having fun by the pool, sipping on all-you-can-drink margaritas, having snacks and sampling local gastronomic preparations, walking on the white sand beach and, finally, meeting fellow guests and making new friends. The resort is divided into two sections: nudist and non-nudist. We booked our rooms in the non-nudist section, but any guest could cross into the nudist area and experience a completely different way of excitement. So I did.

Driven by wicked curiosity I crossed, wearing nothing but a European-like Speedo, heading directly to the gigantic rounded-shaped hot tub hosting more than 30 people. I felt very much out of place since everyone around me was buck naked. People of all sizes, races and age were mingling together recreating one of the rounds of Dante's Inferno in the *Divine Comedy*: body parts hanging around, so close as to occasionally bump into each other, while wicked laughs and malicious smiles accompanied almost every conversation in that pool. I was amazed, however, how well-behaved and respectful each guest was with the others. There were obviously rules and regulations to be followed and to be obeyed in order to enjoy personal time in the nudist area. One of those, of course, was to be naked or security would invite you to leave the premises at once. I felt a tap on my shoulder and an irritated, "Hey man, get naked please." So I did. As shy as I was I lost my bathing suit and entered the pool as paranoid and uncomfortable as I could be.

After five minutes I was just fine. It felt very much natural, my shyness had gone away and a sense of confidence replaced my paranoia. It was actually quite nice. I loved it! While relaxing with my eyes closed and my head tilted back I felt the evil wheels moving real fast, thinking of Roberto, almost 350 pounds, naked and shy in that same pool. I grinned. I was sure I could convince him to jump in just to mess with him as I knew he must have been fuming all day long thinking of the best way to slowly and painfully kill me. But Roberto's real journey was just about to start.

Apparently Saturday and Sunday mornings were open market days in Montego Bay. Many vendors travel from Miami to Jamaica for a profitable two-day trip, taking their goods on the plane as carry-on: some in open boxes, others in oversized plastic trash bags, and a few more even hiding live animals such as rabbits and chickens in their own tunics, tied up to their belts in order to pass security undisturbed and undetected.

Roberto finally called from a pay phone and was able to reach my cell. I will spare you the conversation details as I was mostly listening. Bottom line, after he vented he calmed down as usual and gave me an update on his arrival time, reassuring me he was looking forward to our vacation and to relax, finally. Seated by the gate he was surrounded by departing vendors and passengers and their goods, and the aroma and the stench of the live animals that up to that moment he had not been able to locate.

I was told people start their trading process at the gate as well as on the plane, comparing goods, making deals, yelling at each other in such unordinary ways that gate 84 suddenly turned into an instant bazaar. Roberto was one of the only six non-Jamaican passengers on that very full flight. As he was trying to work on his laptop he was constantly bumped and poked by his surrounding traveling companions and started to get very irritated and stressed. Was he ready to explode again? Not until a large lady pulled up her tunic to show someone her live sleeping inventory and a chicken suddenly woke up. It started jumping and flying everywhere, across the room, on top of the check-in counter and Roberto's laptop, leaving a trail of droppings right on his pants. That was it! He stood up, walked to the counter and demanded to purchase a first-class ticket.

He finally arrived in Jamaica, tired, hungry, stressed and upset. It was hard to blame him, really, but now he had to board the small charter plane to get to the resort. He asked around, but no one was helpful. He went back to the counter and showed his ticket, so they sent him to a different terminal about half mile away next to the cargo area. There were no shuttle buses or other transportation available at that time of day.

So he walked through the people, the unpaved dusty streets, barking dogs, jerk chicken vendors and the heat of Montego Bay carrying his luggage all the way. When he finally arrived at the terminal he was told he missed the last flight of the day by 10 minutes, and they invited him to return the next day after 3 p.m. for the first resuming flight. Fortunately, the resort had a list of daily incoming guests and their itineraries, monitoring arrivals and departures. They sent a van ahead of time to pick up the last arriving passengers, and the driver was able to locate Roberto and provide what should have been a relaxing one-hour transfer to Negril.

He sat all the way in the back of the beat-up van. Being the only passenger aboard, he finally stretched across three seats and closed his eyes.

"Ready man?" the driver asked with a big smile on his face.

"Yes, yes, sure, go," he replied with a dismissal tone in his voice while keeping his eyes closed.

"Oh yes, man," the local driver said. "We'll do fast, yes? I know a shortcut. This is my last run for today."

He pulled a huge joint out of his pocket and started puffing away, singing out loud to Bob Marley tunes while shaking his head and speeding away through narrow and secondary streets, cutting through villages, unpaved roads and hitting each and every pothole on the way. Time was indeed of the essence, and the van had exhausted every little bit of its shock absorbers, making the ride a little more adventurous.

Roberto was suddenly awake, up and alert: his eyes wide open, bouncing off to the left and right at each bump while inhaling puffs of the marijuana cloud that took over the van in a matter of minutes. The driver at one point turned around and offered him some. Roberto, who has never done drugs in his life, politely declined, being already dizzy from the fumes, trying to hold on tight with both hands and not pass out.

When he finally arrived at his destination I was there to welcome him with a heavy guilty feeling on my shoulders. We went to our room and quickly I convinced him to put his bathing suit on and follow me to the hot tub for some relaxing time.

"They're all naked here," he said when we entered the nudist side of the resort.

"Well, you're the one who wanted to come here, now get rid of your shorts and get in the pool," I replied and made my way in.

Roberto needed to break the ice, but he was obviously very uncomfortable with the whole scenario. He took a deep breath, got rid of his bathing suit and slowly sat in bubble land on my right side.

It took him a few minutes as well to feel at ease among 30 naked strangers, but then he finally opened his arms and leaned back in total peace. We finally had time to catch up and started making plans for the next few days. I was listening to his detailed story of his very unorthodox and amazing trip down. We were laughing like crazy, joking and finally doing what two friends were supposed to do when vacationing together when he noticed an older gentleman seated across from us with a steady smile on his face, mumbling something while staring right above him, looking at the stars.

Roberto asked, "Did you see that one there? What the hell is he doing? Is he talking to himself?"

There were about 15 people around him, watching. They looked like they were all waiting for something about to happen. The situation made us a little nervous. Then, suddenly, an older woman emerged from the water from between his legs. She was obviously short of breath but smiling while everyone around her started clapping and cheering with great appreciation. We looked at each other in disbelief.

"God! We are sharing the same water," I said.

Roberto, with a more impulsive and direct reaction, said, "I'm out! Let's go!"

Often, the most amazing and unbelievable day in someone's life happens when everything goes wrong, surprise after surprise, unexpectedly. Almost like if the gods up there decided to pick one person to play with for one day as a personal puppet or doll. It reminded me of the movie *Planes, Trains and Automobiles* with Steve Martin and John Candy who, while traveling home together for Thanksgiving, lost their flight, burned their rental car and got robbed, but in the end made it home to a happy ending.

But our story has a funny cherry that needs to be placed on top of the cake to conclude a less-than-perfect day. When Roberto decided to get out of the hot tub, he quickly turned his body to his right side, stepping out of the water. A tall Jamaican man was leaving almost simultaneously in the opposite direction. In a split second and of course involuntarily the man's huge penis slapped Roberto on his forehead wet and loud, filling the silence. The man apologized immediately like nothing had happened, but Roberto turned slowly toward me almost in shock, undecided about breaking into a polite laugh or a liberating emotional cry. I, for sure, was laughing like crazy with tears running down my face until my abs hurt so much I could not take it any longer.

What a day!

An incredible, true story we often told friends whenever we had the opportunity while traveling together; we always had an audience eager to listen and to share genuine laughs, amused by the unique and the very personal way Roberto told his unfortunate experience.

One day we watched a spectacular sunset overlooking the bay from the patio of a popular bar, and right after we followed some of our new friends to a Ziggy Marley concert at a nearby arena, led by Belinda, a resort employee. This was one of those situations where cultural differences clashed. As we made our way onto the field, the stage was blocked by a cloud of smoke. We could hear the music, but we could not see the show except for the flashing lights. Security personnel and police officers on duty and in uniforms were chilling by smoking weed with their eyes closed, waving their hands above their heads in slow-motion following the rhythm of the music.

So much for security.

We started to feel dizzy, my eyes were watering and Roberto was coughing. Any teenagers at this point would have loved to be in our shoes, but I guess we felt very much like two fish out of water. Roberto was trying to make a point of the situation, explaining his short experience thus far in the manner of a typical Italian, screaming five feet away from me, moving his hands as if he was directing traffic. He suddenly stopped, turned his head and looked down. Someone slapped a joint in his hand.

"Ten dollars, man," a very tall and built Jamaican guy said.

"No thanks, I don't smoke," Roberto replied.

"Ten dollars, man," he insisted with aggressive attitude.

Roberto reached in his pocket and handed him $20 dollars. The man took off while Roberto shouted, "What about my change?"

A nearby police officer, who witnessed the exchange, stepped over immediately as if he was to make a bust. He looked at Roberto, looked around in a very suspicious way, then cracked the biggest smile and finally said, "If you don't smoke it I will, man."

He took the weed cigarette from Roberto's hand, lit it up and went back to his post puffing away.

We were not the least stunned.

The rest of our vacation was absolutely fantastic. We spent the next few days in the non-nudist area making friends, playing volleyball, sipping on margaritas and sunbathing while enjoying great cigars and conversations. We had everything we needed. No one knew us in Jamaica and we were able to truly enjoy ourselves.

Even the food was delicious and worth remembering.

Washington's Inner Circle of Friends

It is very unusual to create genuine and long-lasting friendships with business rivals. The fashion industry, for instance, is a very cutthroat environment where everyone tries to edge the competition in order to prevail with very little respect or fairness; so are many other industries where jealousies develop, gossips arise and critics abound. The restaurant industry is no different: to stay competitive and to win the favors of your customers you must outwork the competition at all times, stay current with the latest trend and understand the market in order to make it work in your favor even if that means not respecting ethical or professional rules.

But in Washington, D.C., it is a different story.

When I came to town in 1986, I remember there were only a few chefs who personally knew each other and who would willingly socialize with rival restaurateurs. Back then the town was not populated by too many establishments and the number of quality chefs who made D.C. their home could be counted on a single hand.

Roberto Donna was one of those social butterflies who would engage conversations with anyone and everyone, likeable, ever-smiling. His teddy-bear behavior has always won many hearts, especially in the early years of his career: a secret weapon that made him rise to success and catapulted him to national acclaim. He made a friend and a supporter out of everyone he met.

As a novice chef, he met Jean Louis Palladin, who liked him from the start, took him under his wing and introduced him to each and every national journalist and predominant culinary figure in the U.S. He introduced him to the James Beard Foundation and taught him standards for quality and details. Jean Louis had also taught him how to be snobbish whenever the need arose, and believe me when I say Roberto made use of his teachings his entire career, and indirectly so did I.

There was also a different angle about him and a personal need to bond with perfect strangers who brought him to the idea, some 18 years ago, to create a once-a-month meeting with fellow coworkers, chefs and local restaurateurs on Friday nights after dinner service. There were no agendas, no specific needs, no political angles or suspicious professional insights. There was just the passionate will to bond and to get to know one another, to support each other.

When Roberto first told me his idea I immediately asked, "Friday night after service? Too late!"

He replied, "Too late? What are you, 80 years old? We make some pasta, serve some cold cuts. I'll ask everyone to bring a bottle of wine. We play cards. We tell jokes. It will be fun. No one works on Saturday morning so we can stay up late and sleep in the next day."

This is how the Chef Club About Nothing was born.

This idea immediately reminded me of the Italian social clubs on Mulberry Street in Little Italy, N.Y., where old timers gather, socialize, play cards and tell each other stories from the old country, driven by the need to create a new circle of friends just like it was their own family, sipping wine and anisette, bonding. We created an email list and contacted everyone two weeks in advance, inviting them to come spend some quality time with us. The first three or four times it was just me, Roberto, Francesco Ricchi, at times a common friend of ours, a sushi chef named Kaz Okochi, a few people here and there and that was it.

A few meetings later we had more newcomers: Jose Andres, after exchanging kisses and hugs as the good European he is, would share a bite to eat and play poker for a couple of hours, laughing, cracking jokes, betting on anything no matter what he had in hand, making plans already for the next meeting, promising to cook paella for all of us at his house one day...Jose my friend, I am still waiting, chico.

So did many others: Jeff Buben, Jeff Tunks, Robert Wiedmaier, Todd Gray, Chris Willis, Enzo Febbraro, George Bogdanovic, and our unofficial professional photographer Len De Pas, who often shared his passion for food and wine with us. Our idea worked and for the following couple of years our club grew, gathering up to 30 people at a time. To better spread awareness and to offset the cost of food we decided to rotate the hosting site among us restaurateurs: the host would provide the space and service, along with the food. Any attendees would provide two bottles of wine and gratuities for those off-service servers who would tend to our needs throughout the evening.

Many new friendships and acquaintances were born; surprisingly, we really enjoyed spending time together. We ended up being very close and supportive to one another professionally, but even more on a personal level. We would organize benefit auctions to raise money for good, genuine causes, we would discuss our possible participation for future charity events, we would always help those who knocked at our door in need of assistance, and thanks to the connections we had with the press we were always able to promote a just cause and to spread the word, creating awareness and curiosity across town and beyond.

We did this for years with genuine smiles on our faces, never pocketing a single dime for our time, efforts or labor. We created so much interest and helped so many people representing local and national worthy causes *The Washington Post* in 2005 wrote a huge article about us on the front page of the food section about how the Chef Club About Nothing had done so well for the community over the years and how the name of our club turned out to be so inaccurate.

When a cook got hit by a car and ended up being out of work for three months we all voluntarily collected personal funds and made sure his bills were paid in a timely fashion. When a veteran server suffered a heart attack we all chipped in to assure his family the needed support and the financial peace of mind throughout his lengthy recovery. When the Riverview special school for kids with Down syndrome in Cape Cod asked the proud parent, chef Francesco Ricchi, to help his son and other students to create a charity dinner to raise money to build better facilities, we did not hesitate and committed year after year, raising as much as half a million dollars in a single night along with many other celebrity chefs from all over America.

We have always been there for each other with care, compassion and commitment. We took many trips together for noble causes, but it was also fun to travel together and enjoy our time away from home while creating memories, unplugging from our routine, and benefiting from press recognition whenever possible.

Today it is a completely different club. None of the old guard attends the meetings anymore. The club is pretty much dead. It is inconsistent with no continuity, occasionally we receive emails from young chefs who have momentarily taken charge, trying to revive its purpose with secondary hidden agendas to shine some light upon them with the hope to get noticed. Nowadays new and upcoming inspiring chefs have different goals: they watch *Top Chef* and try to emulate TV personalities with big dreams and hopes for a lottery call. Why not? The industry has changed so much, so radically no one should let any opportunity pass by. We have all grown and taken different directions, driven by our businesses and career needs, busy battling our demons while searching for a healthy balance between work and that place we once all stayed away from, called home.

I feel I am always in good company whenever a memory or two arises and makes me smile with nostalgic melancholy. In the mid '90s, Roberto and I received an invitation to a social political gathering to welcome the newly appointed Italian ambassador to Washington at his residence, Villa Firenze. We dressed up like a couple of penguins wearing old brushed-off tuxedos, got in the car, and arrived at the destination soon after. Roberto was in a semi-frustrated mood that day, complaining about taking the time off to attend the event, about his tux being way too tight and riding on his butt, about the fact it was raining and we had no umbrellas—about not wanting to be there, basically.

We got screened and patted down by security and quickly entered the majestic foyer set for the occasion with an incredible buffet table stretching 20 feet across the room and adorned with any imaginable sort of Italian food preparations. A few handshakes and fake smiles later we decided to grab a bite to eat before fleeing the scene from the back door, like good Italians.

Walking together down the buffet table, side by side, Roberto started, "God, I hate these functions. They are a total waste of time. Look at that idiot with the plate full of food. I guarantee you he has not eaten in a week in anticipation of today's feast. By the way, did you try the salmon?"

And he finally turned and faced me only to find he had been flanked by a distinct gentleman of my same height staring at him with a somewhat surprised look on his face and who had in the meantime taken my place and walked next to Roberto for the past 10 feet. I had stopped to grab a roll of bread and was unaware of the ongoing situation until I looked up and witnessed the following:

"Oops, I am sorry. You are not Enzo. Who're you?" Roberto asked, totally surprised, while paranoia set in quite quickly.

"I'm the new Italian ambassador. Welcome. Tell me, how are you enjoying your time so far?"

Rarely I have seen Roberto blushing, but that was one of those times where he turned as red as a tomato. Visibly embarrassed, he excused himself and marched toward me holding his plate, smiling like a five-year-old boy who got caught with his hands in the cookie jar.

"Let's go, let's go! Where the hell did you go? I thought you were next to me...that was the new ambassador. Do you think he heard?"

I could not control my laughing while tears ran down my face. I wiped them off with my sleeve. "Are you kidding? I heard you from here!"

We rushed to our car and left at once. From that moment on we have never received any invitations from the Italian Embassy again. I wonder why...

In the spring of 1995 I was asked to lend a hand for a dinner Galileo restaurant was scheduled to cook at the James Beard House in New York City.

Roberto left a message on my voicemail saying, "Come to the restaurant tomorrow morning at 8 a.m.; make sure to bring cash and change of clothes. We'll stop by in Atlantic City on our way back to rest a little. We'll depart at 9 a.m. sharp. If you're late we'll leave without you."

That was my very first trip to the James Beard House. I arrived punctual at 8 and of course no one was there, but I noticed a 15-passenger van parked right in front of the restaurant, dismissing the option of being the victim of a practical joke. Fifteen minutes later, one by one the crew arrived and I suddenly realized this was going to be a very fun trip: my friends Francesco Ricchi, Enzo Febbraro, two other Italian cooks and a couple of longtime Latino friends showed up.

Roberto arrived 20 minutes later screaming sarcastically, "Damn! You guys are late!"

We loaded the coolers, got in the van and left. We lit cigars and puffed the morning away going through checklists, menus, schedules, funny stories and bizarre tales of recent happenings.

Enzo Febbraro is a dear friend: a very talented chef with an incredible sense of humor who shines in home-style cooking better than anyone I know. Originally from Naples, he worked in his early years with internationally popular rock star chefs Gualtiero Marchesi and Gianfranco Vissani before going to London and Los Angeles to work for chef Mauro Vincenti at Rex Restaurant. He also worked with Guy Fieri before he moved to D.C., and nowadays he is the executive chef at Allegro Restaurant by Wynn Corporation in Las Vegas. Over the years our friendship grew stronger sharing trips and culinary journeys together along with our families. Our memorable times together are always highlighted by wine, laughs, and the amazing Neapolitan-style food he cooks whenever we meet at his house for the day.

It is inevitable that whenever a few male friends get together hilarious situations happen: from the crude jokes played on each other to the comical scenarios that paint the entire trip when we are unsheltered and unprotected by that political and diplomatic code full of morality and rightfulness we abide so well. That code went out the van's window past the first exit leading to Interstate 95 North to New York.

In our three-and–a-half-hour record time trip we stopped only once, at the Maryland House for coffee, snacks and gas. The rest was a race against time through the New Jersey Turnpike only to exit in Secaucus overlooking the amazing and inspiring Manhattan skyline that always sends chills down my spine each time I visit this amazing city. While driving through the Lincoln Tunnel onto 42nd Street, overlooking restaurants and deli shops, the most important question of the day was asked by the always tempted Roberto.

"What are we going to eat for lunch? OK, OK, I got it. Let me make a few fast calls."

We ended up picking up pizzas, pastrami sandwiches, and some Mexican treats at various pit stops, then, armed with lunch, we rushed straight to the James Beard House. We unloaded our gear, coolers, and uniforms and marched down into the kitchen for the ritual check-in, where we were welcomed with open arms by the house's staff. We devoured our lunch in a matter of minutes and finally got to work.

Enzo was in charge of the pasta course, Francesco the meat course, I the fish, and everyone else was taking care of the rest. We had to portion 85 servings with such detailed precision and accuracy enough to make a brain surgeon jealous, while Roberto was yelling left and right as usual, sandwich in hand, to a crew of friends constantly cracking jokes and truly having fun despite the pressure of manufacturing what was intended to be a memorable and unique dinner.

No matter how detailed or organized the event was someone would always forget something crucial: tools, a particular sauce, pastry garnishes, even basic elements such as proteins or stuffed pasta made especially for that evening. This time was no different. Right around the time when the first guests arrived, passing through the kitchen, tasting small bites on their way to the dining room, Enzo realized the much needed Arborio rice for the evening—Piedmont's black truffle risotto with goose liver stuffed quail and quail jus—was missing and nowhere to be found in any coolers or bags. After a quick but intense display of rage with veins popping out of his neck, Roberto stormed out of the kitchen and ventured out in the streets with the quest to find rice in time for our dinner.

We were all so mortified that none of us realized in time the rice was missing. This really put us in hot water: just the thought of being unable to deliver an important preplanned meal, especially in one of the most prestigious international venues, was professionally and morally devastating to all of us. Mostly we cracked comments like, "I wouldn't want to be in the shoes of who packed that cooler," or, "Do you think the guy will survive once Roberto is done with him?" and, "I would start looking for a job in the Alaska's classifieds if I were him." We had no word from Roberto, his cell was off and we were about to serve the first course of the evening. The second course was the risotto. We were pressed for time.

Roberto is usually a very resourceful man. I remember when a few summers ago I was visiting Roberto's restaurant for dinner. We grabbed a bite together; we played poker with friends while his wife Nancy was working in the upstairs office throughout the evening. Later on it was time to leave, but Roberto came to work that day with his Harley-Davidson motorcycle while Nancy was dropped off by a friend. He quickly realized their only way home was to ride the bike together, but he only had one helmet. Since there was a police sobriety check road block down the street, he felt fearful to have anyone ride with him without a helmet, risking almost sure and expensive fines.

"No problem, wait here," he said and then he went into the kitchen. He reappeared five minutes later with a medium-size aluminum salad bowl and some duct tape. He placed the metallic salad bowl on Nancy's head and secured it with the tape strapped around her head, under her chin. They went through the security check and sped home safely. Hilarious, but quite effective. (However, I do not recommend trying this at home.)

Finally, Roberto reappeared, red in face, out of breath and armed with a shopping bag.

"This is the best I could find. We need to make this work somehow."

I emptied the bag, looked at its content and cracked a smile in disbelief. All four boxes were generic long grain rice Roberto had purchased at the local convenience store.

"I looked everywhere and this is the best I could find," Roberto said in his defense with a daring challenging tone. I for sure was not going to pick a fight, so we got cooking.

Needless to say, the end result was an absolute disaster. The rice had no starch, it would not cook to temperature and even when trying to whip it with Parmesan cheese and butter in the traditional mantecato method, the grains would separate without holding the desired texture like any common risotto does. But it got served along with all the other ingredients that complemented the dish and we saved face.

It is tradition at the James Beard House for the kitchen staff to walk to the various dining rooms of the house, meet the diners, and answer any questions once the entire dinner is served. After the host introduced the whole culinary team, Roberto was handed a microphone.

"Roberto, wonderful dinner, I especially enjoyed the risotto. There was something different about its texture, what was it? Can you explain?"

We all looked at each other with a smirk on our faces accompanied by a soft exclamation of a common four letter word. Roberto, after a few seconds of hesitation, grabbed the mike with confidence and just like if his karaoke song was queued up, he started his performance.

"Good evening, hee hee hee. Thank you, thank you. So, first of all I wanted to be precise that there was a mistake printed on your menu. It says risotto to make sure you understood the concept of this dish, but it is not a classic risotto. This particular rice was sent to me by my mother, and it's a very rare and unique grain that grows only in a football field size about six miles away from my house in Italy. It's an almost 300-year-old traditional Piedmontese recipe. I hope you liked it as I am sure you will never get the chance to taste it again."

There was an unusual silence in the dining room a few seconds. Then a very excited guest commented, "Yes! My wife and I went to Torino last year and visited the wineries. We had something similar at a local trattoria. It was wonderful, but I can't remember what the name was..."

"Wow, you had it? How unusual. Lucky you! It's very hard to find. Its name is...is...Zioben," Roberto replied. "All organic."

Zio in Italian means uncle. In a fit of panic, he translated the name on the package and gave it a Piedmontese dialect sound to it for credibility. After a few more questions we returned to the kitchen, laughing, in awe and disbelief about how the entire evening unfolded, how we were able to pull it off and made believers out of everyone. We picked up the empty rice boxes from the trash and packed them in the coolers, hiding the evidence. We loaded the van and left in a hurry: our next stop was a two-hour drive to Atlantic City where Roberto had reserved a few rooms to spend the night and to finally rest a little, as he had mentioned before we left.

Once on the Atlantic City Expressway it was a smooth ride all the way. We checked in, showered and met downstairs on the casino floor for the well-deserved and anticipated rest until 6 a.m., gambling the morning away, smoking cigars, laughing like crazy and why not? Even winning some cash. We slept about three hours, had breakfast, gambled for one more hour, then got in the van and drove back home to Washington, D.C. This schedule became a ritual for all future journeys whenever Roberto or I cooked at the James Beard House for the next 18 years.

Many trips to New York have always been instructional, motivating and fun. I remember when my friend chef Jeff Buben of the acclaimed Vidalia Restaurant in D.C. hired a stretch limousine in May 1999, and we all drove up to the James Beard Award ceremony, where the next day he won the Best Chef Mid-Atlantic prize. We stopped for whiskey shots at 11:30 a.m. at Jameson's bar on 2nd Avenue, then to Lombardi pizzeria, savoring various pies cooked in their coal oven at 800 degrees, along with wine of any sort. Because of my low alcohol tolerance, after lunch I took a two-hour nap in my room: I felt drunk and quite dizzy. What a wimp.

The next day we all met at Daniel Restaurant, had a fantastic lunch, and spent one hour in the kitchen where I met for the first time Daniel Boulud, joking and laughing like old friends only to see him again a few months later in Washington where I was asked to cook a dinner in his honor at the Watergate Hotel for his new cookbook presentation. That very same night we went to my first awards gala, mingling and chatting with Mario Batali and Lidia Bastianich, conversing with winner chefs like Charlie Trotter and Marc Samuelsson, a young Tom Colicchio and the not-quite-yet-gray-haired Eric Ripert. I met many influential people, TV personalities and fantastic passionate professionals who created so much energy in the room, enough to inspire me for the next few years.

This was an unforgettable first time experience I will always cherish with pride.

The Cape Cod Travels

When Danny Ricchi entered the Riverview School for kids with Down syndrome in East Sandwich, Massachusetts, more than 18 years ago he had no idea how important he was going to be for the future of his school.

His parents, Christianne and chef Francesco Ricchi, wanted to ensure a healthy and fair future for their son, who needed special direction and attention on a daily basis. The school, like any other, always looked to improve its programs, facilities, and structures; therefore, school officials host an annual charity dinner with the hope of raising enough money to drastically improve their programs.

In his very first academic year, Danny's school hosted a dinner performed by local chefs and restaurateurs raising well over $27,000, but Francesco was not impressed and with his always-driving gentle spirit asked to help organize the following year's event by flying in big name chefs from Washington, D.C., to create an over-the-top menu and dinner event along with sponsors, live auction, donations and an all-around majestic event in an attempt to raise enough money to change the school forever.

At the very next Chefs Club About Nothing meeting, Francesco asked us to help. "Anything for Danny and for the kids" was our unanimous response. The very first year me, Roberto Donna, Jean Louis Palladin, Michel Richard, Enzo Febbraro, Kaz Okochi and a couple more met at the airport on a Tuesday morning, tickets in hand, to fly over to Boston where a rental car took us to the school in a short one-hour ride.

The school compound was breathtaking to look at: dorms and recreational fields sat in the middle of the woods, and just a mile away from the ocean fresh, crispy air blew in while the sun colored it all with gentle shades of hope, birds singing in flocks while the occasional pelicans would fly over and sit on the walkway wooden benches, making their presence known. I felt at peace thinking they could have not created a better setting for any kids to live in, normal or special.

When we got out of the car, organizers, teachers and kids came to greet us so warmly we immediately knew we made the right decision by coming to help. We noticed a huge white tent set in the open field ready to accommodate 300 people. This event was usually a four-day trip: we would fly in a couple of days prior for orientation, the next day we would start prep in the kitchen and we would attend entertaining dinners and lunches, half-day fishing trips, and the day of the event we would work 14 hours together producing a multi-course meal for the evening guests.

Our very first year was such a success that over the next eight years Francesco invited Boston local star chefs Todd English and Lydia Shire, chef and Food Network personality and TV host Ming Tsai, and Robert Irvine, who at that time had not experienced the taste of TV fame. More chefs included Kirk Avondoglio from the beautiful Perona Farms in New Jersey, D.C. locals Jeff Tunks, Jeff Buben, Robert Wiedmaier, the onetime French pastry chef at the D.C. Lespinasse restaurant Monsieur Didier, local TV anchors, personalities and many more.

The event grew larger than we expected year after year. Sponsors like Coca-Cola and American Express started to flock in, and one year we even got a framed poster from the band Matchbox Twenty, personally autographed by all members, especially customized for this event. A different year a car dealership donated a brand-new Mercedes for the $100 per ticket raffle, where nearly all 600 attendees tried their luck for the evening.

At the end of each dinner all the chefs would gather on the podium, cheered in appreciation by 600 people for their work and valuable contribution. Chef Michel Richard has always had a way of making people smile, and one time he drew a sketch on his own chef coat with color pastels. We all signed it. He took it off and while standing shirtless in front of everybody, waved it above his head like in the movie *The Full Monty*. He auctioned it off for $1,000. What a nice and humanitarian gesture that was.

The extraordinary amount of more than $4.5 million was collected during the nine years of our participation. School officials built a gym, a pool, a brand-new wing for academic needs, and a laboratory, and enhanced the lives of those who struggle to live among us every day. Everyone was very nice to us; we always loved our time there as it was always filled with many funny situations over the years.

I recall one time when Jean Louis Palladin was set with the appetizer course, Todd English with a chilled green pea soup served in a martini glass that tasted more like mowed grass, Roberto Donna and I cooked the risotto, Ming Tsai and Kirk Avondoglio the fish, Lydia Shire with the very adventurous and nerve-wracking 17-step meat course adorned with a plastic cowboy hat. The hat was the last straw for Jean Louis, who abandoned the line that evening refusing to complete his duties as improvised assembler for what he later declared the most ridiculous and insulting culinary disaster ever experienced. Michel Richard made his famous Kit-Kat chocolate bar and Robert Irvine was everywhere around us, helping everybody and always in good spirit.

In order to involve everyone and to stimulate participation, the organizers decided to have the students act as servers by bringing the finished plates from the satellite kitchen to their respective tables as instructed. Everyone knew Jean Louis was a perfectionist and difficult to work with at times. He had no limits when it came down to the execution or the serving of any meals, anywhere and at any levels. This time was no different. We had approximately 600 plates laid out on various tables and Jean Louis insisted on inspecting each one of them before serving. His country plate with warm brioche was ready to be sent out and a brigade of 30 disoriented students patiently waited for a "go" in order to begin their very first experience as servers.

"OK, let's go! Pick up," Jean Louis shouted. "Pick up the plates, c'mon, the brioche is getting cold." He began shouting even louder as the only response from those kids was a blank stare, lost, their mouths opened and so intimidated a couple of them started crying. Jean Louis at this point lost it completely and shouted even louder.

"What's the matter with you? Why aren't you moving? Don't you know how to do anything?" There was a silence in the tent a few seconds then Francesco stepped in, realizing Jean Louis had forgotten where we were.

"Jean Louis, calm down. They are not professional servers; they're just trying to help."

It was a very awkward moment for Jean Louis, who at once collected himself and insisted in an almost apologetic tone in order to defend his point, "OK, but the brioche is getting cold."

At the end of each dinner we would usually relax a long while before called on stage for the ritual grand finale. Some of us would enjoy a good cigar and a chat, others would sip wine and drink beer, and there was always one or two who would hide in a car, sitting back and relaxing while creating clouds of smoke, trying to reach the next level in a momentary and surreal fake reality.

Our culinary trips are always highlighted by comical situations, pranks played on each other and real life, odd happenings that create memories I proudly store in my happy vault. Pastry chef Didier has always been one of our favorite victims during the Cape Cod travels: we have played pranks on him for years. I never got to know him very well, but he has always been very nice to me. One morning for our ritual get together at BWI Airport he showed up carrying only a medium-size business travel suitcase he just purchased the day before. He was obviously very proud of it as he was carrying it around the airport with a big smile on his face, initiating conversation about it with anyone he met.

"Hello, Enzo. How are you? Long time no see. Is that your luggage? I decided to bring this instead. I just bought it yesterday. Beautiful isn't it?"

And so the same broken record went on about an hour with each chef and member of that trip. Some of Didier's close friends decided to hide his suitcase in one of their coolers with the hope he would quiet down. They checked the cooler and left him looking for it right up until we boarded. He was visibly worried and upset; he sat next to us mumbling the whole trip while the responsible ones were cracking jokes about it and teasing him for a good laugh. Needless to say, he did not think it was funny.

Once arriving at the house that had been rented for us for the occasion, we quickly unpacked the coolers only to realize Didier's brand-new suitcase had slipped all the way to the bottom of it, completely submerged in water. The organizers were waiting to take us to lunch and later on to the scheduled afternoon orientation at the school. We were obviously pressed for time so a very inventive chef, for lack of a better idea, decided to place the small suitcase holding Didier's clothes and toiletries in the freezer for the reminder of the day.

When we came back late that afternoon, Didier made his presence felt for a joke that in his opinion had gone on too long. The suitcase was returned to its rightful owner in one piece, completely frozen solid, and of course among the laughs of everyone who was there. It took 12 hours before he could even open it. Reciting unpleasant words in French, he walked to the nearest store and purchased a toothbrush, soap and a T-shirt. The rest of the trip was not so bad at all for Didier: a few eggs hidden in his shoes, the occasional garden rocks placed inside his pillowcase and a bucket of sand in his bed, spread out between his sheets for a crunchy night's sleep.

The funniest part of it is he would only get upset for a couple of minutes before cracking a smile and laughing along with us about it. It felt like he was expecting the joke to come and when it finally arrived he was pretending to get mad. It seemed like in the end he really loved the attention.

Chefs Jeff Buben and Roberto Donna started the ritual of playing pranks on each other a couple of years before the Cape Cod trips began, and on each trip they made sure to keep the tradition interesting and alive. I cannot quite remember how it started, but since Roberto and I were always together I naturally sided with him and helped him to execute and master any evil plans we would think of.

It was quite funny because we would meet to review our duties, make a schedule for the next few days such as gathering ingredients, set time to prep a certain dish, coordinate the cooking event with other chefs, as well as finding the best way to sneak into Jeff's bedroom to mess up his bed or suitcase on a precise day and time in order to carry out our plan successfully and without any suspicions.

I recall a specific time when Roberto and I felt extremely proud of a job well-done. One year after concluding our charity dinner at the school we all decided to take a day trip to Boston to try out a few restaurants. We all drove in separate cars and once at our destination we booked a few hotel rooms for the very same night. It is, of course, a ritual among us to acknowledge each other's room number in order to better communicate and coordinate scheduled activities.

"OK, Jeff, we'll call your room five minutes before we come down tonight. Our reservation is at 7 so we should really meet around 6:30," Roberto said.

"OK, no problem. Just give me a ring. I'll be ready by then," Jeff replied.

We had it all figured out. We called Jeff from our room at 6:15 and five minutes later he was on his way down. In the meantime Roberto ran downstairs to the lobby and was able to convince the very young receptionist to open Jeff's room for us to gain access to his suite. Roberto fabricated a story saying we needed to leave a crucial folder and a package containing vital info needed for that same evening's "national executive board meeting" where Jeff, according to us, was scheduled to give a nationally televised speech and presentation.

"My associate is already waiting at Mr. Buben suite's door," Roberto lied.

"Please hold. I am not sure this is possible. Let me make sure he's not in his room," she said.

Roberto, in order to motivate the young lady, asked for her first and last name and wrote it down in his fake executive pad, leading her to believe her unhelpful behavior would have certainly faced unpleasant consequences. Jeff, who of course could not answer the phone, was on his way down to get the car from the valet. He walked right past the front desk and out to the parking lot unnoticed. I was standing in front of Jeff's room holding a bag full of eggs, flour, pancake syrup, potato chips, salt and my personal travel bag. I was wearing a black suit and an executive tie, dark sunglasses and the most serious face I could improvise, just like in the movie *Michael Clayton* with George Clooney. The elevator doors opened suddenly. The young lady and Roberto marched toward me, key card in hand.

"Do you have the package?" Roberto asked.

"Yes sir, affirmative" I replied without moving an inch of my body.

The young lady, Stacey, was obviously uncomfortable. She opened the door and said, "You have three minutes. You shouldn't even be here," and motioned to come in with us.

I turned my body toward her, blocked her entrance with my right hand, read her name tag and said, "Please wait here, Stacey. This is classified information."

She nodded at me with a worrisome but obedient smile, and insisted, "Just three minutes. OK?"

We closed the door behind us and went to work trying not to laugh too loud to blow our cover while Stacey was standing outside. Roberto took the bedroom and I the bathroom. In matter of seconds the bed sheets were filled with mixed foods, syrup, broken eggs, flour and more: a real mess. I untwisted the shower nozzle and placed a diabetic glucagon tab inside. I used to carry all sorts of supplies in my toiletry bag as my daughter, being diabetic, traveled with me often in her younger days. The idea was to have the hot water force its way out through the glucagon tab, melting its sugar down through the shower and onto Jeff's body. Basically he would have showered with simple syrup, remaining sticky for the rest of the day. Stacey came in right as we accomplished our mission.

"We need to leave now. This is unacceptable."

We went down to the lobby and met Jeff and other friends who were waiting for us. We had a wonderful evening and visited five different restaurants for a hop-on, hop-off five-course dinner that consisted of sampling a single course at each restaurant. That was a really fun experience organized by a reporter of a local Boston magazine who was at the time writing a piece about our chef club and covering the event dinner we cooked the night before at the Riverview School.

We do not know exactly what happened when Jeff returned to his room that night, but we assumed we succeeded in our intent to surprise him beyond his expectations. The very next morning we got his response confirming our plan worked: our rental car parked in the open lot of the hotel was covered entirely with flour, eggs, sugar, and God knows what else that had been thrown on top of it. There was so much stuff on it we could have literally baked the whole thing and made a cake out of it. It took us an hour to clean it up.

As usual no one ever gets upset. It is expected and we all laugh about it at the next chef's club meeting. It is part of a game that has gone on for almost two decades and created wonderful memories for each and everyone involved. Sadly, our touring days are not as common as they used to be. Nowadays we mostly cross each other's paths at local culinary events, for the occasional quick TV gig, or if any of us has dinner at any of our restaurants.

When Danny Ricchi finally graduated from Riverview School a few years later he moved to the West Coast, settled into his community, and obtained a job he really enjoys. Mostly he now benefits from a better quality life that he could not have had without the help of the school. I feel extremely proud, and satisfied knowing that even though most of our charity culinary trips are offset by the luxuries and the enticements of an all-expense-paid mini vacation in exchange of one day of work. The Cape Cod trips have significantly improved and forever changed the lives of so many children who desperately needed help.

All the culinary trips I have taken over the years are memorable for many different reasons. There is a constant need to escape the chef's routine and branch out to new places, see new concepts, meet new people, and taste new food whenever possible, and of course it is so much better when doing it in great company.

In 2002, I and 25 other chefs, restaurant owners, and passionate professionals met in Alba, Italy, in November (white truffles season). We visited incredible wineries such as Gaja, Ceretto and

Braida, and met wine makers and enologists, toured the facilities and ate at six different Michelin-starred restaurants in four days. It was worse than force feeding ducks, but we had so much fun and laughed so hard while truly enjoying ourselves. And of course I collected tales, stories, and hush-hush situations that for the record have never occurred.

Many of us have participated in the yearly Disney's Food & Wine Festivals, where the chefs are as important as rock stars. They fly you down to Florida for five days, free hotel accommodations, free meals, free tickets and a private tour guide for one day to visit all the parks and go on all the rides we desired: no lines, no wait, no fuss.

When we are down there we are as important as Johnny Depp, who one year was standing next to me with his private guide and his family, going in front of everyone in order to get on his ride that had three hours' wait time.

The Disney trips are indeed my favorite: I have been invited and have participated for 10 years. I truly hope no one figures it out and decides to stop this trend. Everyone is extremely nice and polite and it is a true joy to help in any possible way I can whenever called to "duty." Can you really blame me?

Another great trip I have taken regularly the past few years is a bicycle tour, where for a whole week you ride a few miles a day with the paying guests through the countryside of Tuscany, Sicily or Apulia, and experience wine tastings, olive oil classes, mozzarella-making courses and, naturally, dining at the best restaurants in the area while making new friends. Sometimes I feel guilty as I basically get paid to go on vacation to do exactly what I love to do: passionately cooking.

I am a very fortunate cook. The most important advice of my life came from an older man back in Italy when I was barely a teenager. He came out of nowhere while my friend Giorgio and I were lingering with others from the church community. He asked me what I wanted to do when I grew up. Not sure why, but I felt very comfortable talking to him even though he was a complete stranger. I simply replied I wanted to cook as it was a great hobby of mine.

The man wisely put his hand on my left shoulder, smiled and said, "If you're able to convert your hobby into a profession, you'll love your job forever."

That was the only time I saw that man. I never saw him again. That man was my guardian angel.

Chapter Nine
Ever Felt Like a Fish Out of Water?

Sometimes I do, especially when I experiment and try new fish preparations and techniques, and I get carried away with culinary projects and ideas. It is very easy to combine odd ingredients with procedures that hardly work, and it is extremely easy to disrespect the simple gifts Mother Nature has given us. One of those is the incredible variety of fish and shellfish that has been hidden underwater: the most ancient and reliable source of food.

I have never been a fan of seafood. As matter of fact I have always preferred meat and pasta to fish. I used to observe my parents feasting on intimidating octopus and squid with ferocious tentacles, grilled or roasted whole fish were looking at me with inquisitive eyes, and some of the fish stew preparations I could hardly bear the smell of. As a little boy I often remember holding my nose throughout lunch or dinner: I clearly did not want to have anything to do with fish back then. I created an imaginary safety barrier for a few years until one day my mother prepared (among many other dishes) platters of fried shrimp adorned with lemon slices. My cousins, Massimo and Luisella, were spending the day with us and strangely enough they ate any kind of seafood at a speed way too complex for me to understand: how could they eat that smelly food and enjoy it so much? I thought that food was made for adults only, not for kids.

I did not want to be left out from the circle of cool things to do while in good company so I reached out to the plate with stunning confidence and served myself a few shrimp like the big boy I always thought I was. The whole gimmick of squeezing the lemon juice on top of the shrimp made the process of eating much easier for me as suddenly I found the procedure to be fun and entertaining and, you know what? The shrimp did not taste bad at all. I actually liked them a lot.

Over the following months I repeated this process when introduced to fried calamari rings, miniature fried whole fish, and to my surprise I got tempted many times to taste different kinds of seafood pastas my mom would make. She loved to go on a Saturday morning to a specific open seafood market called Porta Palazzo in Torino about 15 miles from where we lived.

My mother never liked to drive, so she used to drag my dad out of the house early in the morning for a quick lift. They had it all figured it out: since it was very hard to find parking, my father would double-park right at the entrance and wait in the car, reading the newspaper and avoiding parking tickets, while my mom would venture into the always over-crowded market to buy some of the freshest fish I can remember. It was like Bonnie and Clyde robbing a bank: my dad with the getaway car, engine running and my mom inside hitting different stands in record time with the hope of still finding my dad in the same spot for a quick escape.

One time I remember her rushing out of the market with heavy bags. She paused a second; she visually located my father's car and sprinted to it. She opened the door, quickly sat, situated all the shopping bags inside, slammed the door shut and shouted "OK! Let's go!" A bearded man in the driver seat, who apparently owned the same make and color car as ours, looked at my mom, stunned, and asked "Where?" She looked at him, and said, "You're not my husband!" The man replied "Yes, I know." "I'm sorry," she said and got out. My father was parked a couple of cars behind and witnessed the whole scene, amazed. His jaw dropped and he started laughing hysterically while waving his position to my mom, who in the meantime was walking toward him holding the bags while cracking an embarrassed smile.

But it was not until I entered culinary school that I really started to familiarize and appreciate numerous varieties of fish and shellfish. In the classroom we would study all aspects of seafood: shapes, textures, cooking methods and of course taste. In the school's kitchen we would attempt to prepare, clean, cook and portion. Seafood was not so bad at that point, and I started to enjoy it more and more as I got exposed to it on a daily basis.

I experienced my very first working summer in Sicily at the age of 14. While the rest of my family was vacationing I decided to get a job in the kitchen six days a week and to learn as much as I could for a couple of months. The restaurant I was working at was very traditional and seasonal: Sicilian dishes and fish preparations populated the menu with very little interest by yours truly. However, I have always been thankful for that time as back then I at least learned how to handle any sort of seafood.

I remember it was the freshest quality I have ever worked with: live branzinos still jumping on the table while head-on shrimp would still kick back to the touch. I got sprayed several times by aggressive squids, and I remember littleneck clams to be delivered in a bucket filled with seawater. I used to find it incredibly hilarious when fresh mussels were singing on the counter: they were clearly gasping in and out of the water, and I found myself imitating their sound precisely. At times I engaged in wrestling matches with live octopus and got temporary dotted tattoos from their ventosas all over my arms until I got the best of them. I cannot remember any other times in my professional career to have encountered fresher seafood quality, and for someone like me who only a few years back disliked fish it was an immense pleasure to work with such glorious ingredients.

My perspective of things has of course changed over the years. I can still be a little reserved when it comes to seafood, but for the majority I eat, enjoy, appreciate, cook and love all of it. I always keep alive the memories I gathered while working in Sicily: standards for freshness and quality, and respect for prime ingredients guide me all the time when selecting and cooking seafood as in my opinion fish and shellfish is one of the most delicate and difficult foods to cook.

It's hard to encounter the same high quality of freshness anywhere in the world. Almost 30 years later I only find it occasionally in Europe and in parts of the U.S. It seems like the days when you can pick and choose among fresh varieties are more and more scarce. The memories I treasure about chasing my mother's escaped live eels from the kitchen sink in my younger days is becoming an isolated bedtime story to eventually tell my grandkids. I am genuinely concerned about sourcing from our oceans, lakes and rivers, and I worry about the rapid decline of quality and availability I have witnessed from the past 30 years. It is not too hard to imagine what may be ahead of us in the next few decades unless we start protecting and preserving our natural resources with a little more love and a lot more care. I feel we are slowly slipping away to an inevitable ecological crisis.

On the other end, the farm-raised seafood business has been blooming at an incredible rate, saturating the market with the "just add water" products. Fish and shellfish are abundant in every grocery store; they populate large frozen food coolers and the "Fresh Catch" seafood counters now often smell of ammonia instead of the seashore. I always find it extremely awkward to be standing in front of a wall of frozen seafood in the aisle of any supermarket. Flashbacks of that small, humble Sicilian kitchen are still so vivid and realistic: every kind of live seafood had walked down an imaginary runway modeling for me one by one, showing off the true meaning of freshness with arrogance and snobby attitude.

At times I love to work outside the parameters of culinary realism, but when it comes to seafood I consider myself a moderate traditionalist. If you are lucky enough to work with incredibly fresh product, half the work is done: Boiled, sauté grilled, baked, roasted or stewed, it is difficult to screw up unless proper cooking times or temperatures are ignored. Sometimes cooking is not needed at all. The Latinos are masters of marinating raw fish with lemon and lime juices, red onions, and cilantro and in a day's time you can have an incredible tasty ceviche.

I occasionally read seafood descriptions on restaurant menus that involve four or five different types such as "river trout stuffed with crab meat over a sauce of clams and shrimp." I ask myself why? What's the purpose of mixing and matching so many varieties unless you are making a gumbo, a cioppino or a French bouillabaisse? And even then, there are rigid guidelines any cook at any level should respect when venturing in such complicated and delicate dishes. As I mentioned earlier it is very easy to disrespect the simple gifts from our waters, each fish or shellfish has a particular taste, a different cooking time and different texture. I store many memories in my happy box. The one of a trip to Havana, Cuba, with my then partners in crime chef Francesco Ricchi and chef Roberto Donna in February 1999 is a sure classic.

We were sunbathing on the beach of Villas Los Pinos in Playa Santa Maria just a few miles outside Havana, smoking Cuban cigars, away from everything and everybody. Pure relaxing paradise! At noon we were making plans for lunch; undecided we asked a local employee for suggestions. He pointed out a local diver who emerged from the ocean like in a James Bond movie holding his spear gun in one hand and a couple of live red snappers in the other.

Roberto sprinted toward him, handed him a $20 bill, and walked to the open kitchen in the restaurant section of the Cabana bar and asked the chef in charge to cook the fillets for us on a flat top right before our eyes. A little salt, some pepper and a drizzle of olive oil. After lunch we all agreed it was possibly the best and freshest fish we had ever had. A similar situation occurred when the very next evening we ventured out to a nearby restaurant and personally fished three spiny lobsters out of a natural stone seawater tank. A single 3-pound lobster for each of us at the mere price of $15 each, simply grilled, absolutely amazing with just a drizzle of lime juice on it. A $120 value at pocket change price: nowadays $15 barely covers the price of gas needed for a local seafood company to deliver its products from Baltimore to Washington, D.C.

It is stunning to me how one can find such comfort and happiness in simple things: good company, good food, and good health. I have always been very thankful in my life, especially for my always-positive attitude even when drastic moments strike and the whole world seems suddenly to not like you very much. I experienced a great deal of good and bad seafood dishes in my past, and I tried to learn the very basics for proper execution when cooking.

Because I have been exposed to so many techniques, I wanted to offer different takes on fish preparations: you will notice how in this chapter I do not employ any foams, froths or gelatins with the exception of only one recipe because I felt it was a necessity in neutralizing the dense taste of the braised pig's ears in the soft-shell crab dish. I did stick to simplicity as much as possible, but then of course I had to twist things my way for my chef's ego. My goal is to respect seafood for what it is and to combine it with ingredients, sauces, and progressive executions to complement and elevate its natural taste without modifying it. In the end, after tasting, experimenting, and tweaking recipes, I always ask myself, "Am I completely satisfied with it?"

I will always feel like a fish out of the water each time I am about to taste any kind of seafood preparations as I am one of the toughest judges there is on the subject. I think it is because I came to love seafood later in life, therefore I feel I appreciate it more. The following dishes deliver a message of simplicity for their cooking methods and a more complex one about their whole concept. They all aim to please even the toughest judges, especially me.

Baked Chilean Sea Bass, Study of 3 Fennels Saffron Broth and Smoked Purple Potatoes

About 23 years ago when I was working in the old Galileo restaurant on P Street, on a Saturday morning we had the pleasure of hosting a culinary event featuring renowned cookbook author Giuliano Bugialli, who at the time was extremely popular in the U.S. He made an entrance worthy of a Hollywood star: constantly running his hand through his hair, the other hand in his pocket, walking like Ace Ventura, snapping his fingers to his assistant and rolling his eyes at any questions Roberto Donna was asking him in preparation for his presentation. To say he seemed bothered to be there and that he was wasting his valuable time is an absolute understatement. I disliked him the moment he opened his mouth. He showed arrogance, cockiness and disrespect, but I have to say he had a way to attract attention from the press and everyone else in that room. He was an excellent speaker.

He showed us how to make three recipes from his new book, followed by a sample tasting. One of those recipes involved a baked whole red snapper filled with dry fennel sticks and garlic cloves placed in the belly's opening for flavoring. Ironically for most of the audience this was a real shocker as no one would have thought about using wild fennel sticks that grow naturally all over Sicily and in the California side roads, but for me it was a welcome return to my youth. Having spent many summers in Sicily, I thought the author's intent was just genius to say the least.

In fact, while the snapper slowly roasted in the oven, the fennel stick released an incredible delicate scent throughout the whole fish and into its flesh. When I finally tasted it, I quickly determined it was among the best I ever had. Giuliano Bugialli was indeed full of himself. Back then he even refused to shake my hand and dismissed me because I was asking technical questions about his book and recipes with vivid interest, but he did teach me something very valuable about baking with fennel and about people: you must respect them both.

With this in mind, many years later I decided to rediscover fennel with white meat fish. After many attempts and retouching, I came about this recipe that highlights the true taste of anise from three different sources, and the marriage of smoky, starchy purple potatoes for color and contrast within its saffron broth to an incredible marriage of flavors, colors and substance. Fennel is so delicate when baked that if used in larger quantities it can overwhelm with its distinct flavor, so make sure to dose conservatively.

And what to make about the bad manners of a disrespectful popular cookbook writer who does not want to be bothered by questions of aspiring cooks like me at the beginning of their career? Karma works in mysterious ways: be polite and always dedicate time to answer the questions of your fans that idolize and support you. Do not turn off their hopes or dreams: embrace them and encourage them respectfully because you never know that 25 years later someone somewhere could write a book about his most vivid memories and you could be in it.

Ingredients
7 oz of Chilean sea bass
1 small fennel bulb cut into thin slices
The tip of a teaspoon of minced garlic
1 tbsp of extra virgin olive oil
1 star anise
1 cup of water, chicken broth or vegetable stock
1 small pinch of saffron treads
1 purple potato
A couple of Sicilian (or Californian) dry wild fennel sticks cut 4 inches long

Salt
Cracked black peppercorns
A couple leaves of fresh basil
A few apple wood chips for smoking

Directions
With a medium-size melon baller carve 5 spheres out of the purple potato of about ¾ inch each.
Boil them in salted water and set aside to be smoked.
Sprinkle the wood chips with a little water and place them on the bottom of a deep hotel pan.
Light the chips with a torch until they smoke and place a perforated, small hotel pan on top of it with the potatoes.
Cover very well with aluminum foil and smoke about 4 hours.
Drizzle some extra virgin olive oil in a small baking pan, sprinkle with salt and spread the minced garlic.
Fan out 3 thin slices of fennel on the bottom of the pan and place the bass right on top of it.
Add the anise star, the wild fennel sticks, and the broth.
Bake at 400 degrees for approximately 6-8 minutes.

To Serve
With the help of a perforated spatula transfer the fish to a hot pasta bowl, making sure to collect the fennel slices and the fish in one motion without moving them out of place.
Add the saffron in the baking pan with the liquid, and over high flame reduce the broth about 30 seconds until it colors the broth.
Add the purple potato rounds and the basil.
Place the potatoes around the fish, and generously add the hot saffron broth into bowl.
Drizzle with the remaining extra virgin olive oil and finish decorating by grouping the fennel sticks on top of the fish and by dusting the cracked black peppercorns in the liquid.

Roasted Norwegian Salmon Green/White Asparagus, Yellow/Red Beets Pearls Black Truffles, Piedmonte Hazelnuts and Progressive Sweet Garlic Broth

Sharing my life with a native Norwegian has surely helped me to better appreciate salmon over the years. Of course my life partner claims Norwegian salmon is the best for quality and taste, and since we have already fought many domestic battles about this topic I would limit myself by saying Norwegian salmon is indeed one of the best qualities available on the market. I will spare you the details of occasional sit-com scenarios of an Italian chef with Sicilian blood going head to head in a discussion with a finance executive Viking who desperately wants to make her point.

I appreciate all kinds of salmon: the Scottish is drier, the Alaskan types more vivid in color and taste, the Norwegian fatter and thicker. After licking my wounds I put together a wonderful and tasty recipe that combines Italian traditions with Norwegian flavors. I pan sear a fillet of Norwegian salmon cooked medium/medium-rare crispy, and place it on top of a crunchy and barely blanched ragù of white and green asparagus.

I roast red and yellow beets, and I pearl them with a very small melon baller and alternate them around the salmon. I crush imported Piedmonte hazelnuts, drizzle some hazelnut oil, and generously shave black truffles on it. My dish is halfway finished. I now needed a third component to combine all the flavors together into one explosive taste, so I made a reduction of sweet garlic and saffron that once poured on top of the fish warms all other ingredients. Combine them all in one super aromatic dish and it brings the flavor of the black truffles alive, bite after bite. Every time I feel I am on the ropes I throw in my domestic towel and I prepare this dish. It works every time, better and far less expensive than marriage counseling, and enriches my romantic life with the person I love.

Ingredients

7 oz of Norwegian salmon fillet
2 green asparagus
2 white asparagus
1 medium-size red beet

1 medium-size yellow beet
1 tbsp of Piedmonte hazelnuts
Salt
Ground white pepper
2 tsp of hazelnut oil
Assorted micro greens
Winter black truffles shaves
1 tsp of Frantoio extra virgin olive oil
1 tsp of infused black truffle oil
Crystallized salt
Cracked black peppercorns
1 tbsp of olive oil
1 rosemary sprig

Directions

In separate pots boil the yellow and red beets in salted water till al dente.

Peel them and carve small about 4 balls of each of approximately half-inch diameter and set aside.

Cube in ¼-inch size the white and green asparagus, keeping the tips intact, and set aside.

Toast the Piedmonte hazelnuts, crush them, and set aside.

In a small pan sear the salmon on both sides with the olive oil and the rosemary sprig, add salt and white pepper, and finish the cooking process in the hot oven a few minutes to medium/ medium rare.

Keep warm.

Sweet Garlic Broth

Ingredients

4 oz of fresh garlic cloves
7 oz of vegetable stock
1 pinch of saffron
Salt
1 small pinch of ground white pepper

Directions

Combine the garlic cloves with the vegetable stock in a small pan and cook at very low fire until the garlic is completely cooked and breaking to the touch.

Turn the fire off, and add the saffron.
Let the liquid infuse about 15 minutes, and then blend the mix in a high-speed blender.
Pass the mix through a fine strainer and preserve the liquid.
Remove the excess foam from the top and set aside.

To Serve

In a hot pasta bowl place the mixed cubed white and green asparagus, sprinkle the crushed hazelnut over them, and drizzle with some hazelnut oil.
Place the cooked salmon fillet on the asparagus in the middle of the plate, and alternate the red and yellow beets around it in circular motion.
Drizzle the salmon with black truffle oil and the Frantoio extra virgin olive oil, the crushed black peppercorns, and some crystallized salt.
Place some assorted seasonal micro greens on top of the salmon and shave abundant black truffles all over the dish.
Serve immediately to your guests and finish by pouring at least 1½ oz of the hot sweet garlic broth on top of the salmon and on the other ingredients.

Baked Black Cod with Spicy Yellow Curry Rub, Pickled Purple Potatoes, Celery, Sun Chokes, Charcoal Oil and Celery Juice Sauce

A couple of years ago I was having dinner with my family in Torino at one of my sister's favorite Indian restaurants. She loves ethnic food and since she also is celiac she follows a gluten-free diet. Aside from their baked breads, it made perfect sense to dine on fish, meats and vegetable preparations over steamed rice. That evening my father ordered one of his favorite fish. His black cod was strangely baked with an incredible amount of spices: way too many for my taste. What I was impressed with was how a transplanted Indian restaurant had successfully combined local and imported flavors, simple ingredients and elevated the importance of this fish to an Italian/Indian marriage on a single plate. I started exploring a way to create an Italian-type curry dish using only fresh Italian ingredients, adopting Indian-based culinary traditions, converting my idea into a surreal, but delicious reality. It was a hell of a challenge! I gathered local sun chokes, celery and purple potatoes. I made a celery sauce and created a combination of salt/curry to rub on top of the cod for color and taste. The biggest challenge was to create a shocking component that would elevate the interest in the dish for flavor and novelty. I came up with edible charcoal oil, black and thick, but light and very flavorful that offsets the taste of the pickled purple potatoes and combines perfectly to the taste of the curry.

Odd combination, but it worked so well that for a while it was the most sold fish preparation at my tasting-menu restaurant Elisir.

Ingredients
7 oz of black cod fish fillet
1 cup of chicken broth
Salt
Ground white pepper
1 medium-size purple potato
1 small stalk of celery
2 small sun chokes
1 tsp of spicy yellow curry rub
A few eggplant chips to use at serving time

Directions
Peel and cut the celery and purple potatoes in 8-10 pieces in the shape of matchsticks.
Blanch the celery and boil the potatoes in salted water al dente, and place in a small container. Set the celery sticks aside until serving time.
Warm up the pickling white vinegar marinate and pour enough liquid on top of the purple potato sticks to cover them entirely. Marinate a couple of days before using.
Peel the sun chokes and cut in medium-size slices, poach in salted water and set aside.
Sprinkle the bottom of a small baking pan with a little salt, white pepper, and the chicken broth.
With your thumb apply a strip of the spicy yellow curry rub right on top of the cod fillet from side to side and place it face up in the baking pan with the liquid.
Bake in hot oven at 375 degrees for approximately 6-7 minutes.
Remove the fish from the liquid with a perforated spatula, set aside and keep warm.

Place the sun chokes and the celery sticks in the hot cod fish's cooking liquid and keep them warm until serving time.

Pickling White Vinegar Marinate

Ingredients
1 cup of white wine vinegar
½ cup of water
1 garlic cloves mashed
½ stalk of celery diced
1 shallot diced
1 small carrot diced
½ sprig of fresh thyme
3 sage leaves
1 bay leaf
1 tsp of whole black peppercorns
Salt
½ tsp of mustard seeds
1 clove

Directions
Place all the ingredients in a medium-size pot and bring to boil at moderate fire about 5 minutes.
Taste for salt and pepper, remove from the stove, and rest about one hour.
Filter the liquid, discard the herbs and vegetables, and while still hot pour the marinate on top of the food you want to pickle.
Pickle in a glass jar, air-tight and sealed.

Spicy Yellow Curry Rub

Ingredients
½ cup of fine sea salt
2 tbsp of excellent curry powder
½ tbsp of ground turmeric

Directions
Mix all ingredients together in a medium-size bowl and store in an air-tight container.

Eggplant Chips

Ingredients

1 small Chinese eggplant
1 tbsp of olive oil
Salt

Directions

Preheat the oven to 225.
Cut the eggplant into paper-thin slices and place on a silicone baking mat on a sheet pan.
Brush them with the olive oil and sprinkle with salt.
Cook about 2½ hours till crispy.
Once cooled, stock them between deli paper and store in an air-tight container.

Celery Juice Sauce

Ingredients

2½ cups of fresh celery juice
1 shallot thinly sliced
½ small sweet onion, thinly sliced
1½ oz of butter
1 tbsp of minced garlic
½ stalk of celery finely chopped
5 large basil leaves
Salt
Ground white pepper

Directions

In a medium-size pan braise the garlic, the onion, and the shallot with the butter till translucent.
Add the chopped celery, salt, pepper and cook a couple of minutes until it combines with the other ingredients.
Add the celery juice and cook at moderate fire and reduce by half.
Remove the pan from the stove and let the sauce cool a few minutes.
Stir in the basil leaves and immediately blend in a high-speed blender till perfectly smooth with a velvety consistency.
Chill the sauce in ice bath.

Charcoal Oil

Ingredients
1 medium-size white onion
1½ cups of extra virgin olive oil
1 pinch of salt
1 pinch of ground white pepper

Directions
Peel the onion and cut it in half.
On an open flame gas burner or on a hot grill cook it to complete charcoal on all sides.
Once ready and black chop the onion in small pieces and transfer it to a high-speed blender with the salt, the pepper, and the extra virgin olive oil.
Blend till very fine and velvety to a semi-liquid paste.
Store in a plastic squeeze bottle in the refrigerator.

To Serve
On a flat, round hot plate, place a couple of tablespoons of the celery juice sauce in the center and delicately spread it in a circular motion.
Using kitchen tweezers place the room-temperature pickled purple potatoes, the sun chokes, and the celery sticks symmetrically on top of the sauce, creating a bed for the fish.
Place the black cod on top of the veggies and top with a few eggplant chips, leaving the bright yellow color of the crystallized curry visible to the eye.
Shake the charcoal oil bottle, and right before serving drizzle some in a circular motion right around the fish.

Pan-Seared Striped Bass on Fennel Emulsion, Candied Lemon Rings and Milanese Style Oyster Mushrooms

This is one of those rare dishes where each component pops in your mouth and explodes in taste, blending with delightful balance and harmony. I have seen guests devour this entrée in less than five minutes, wiping the plate clean, and others ordering seconds, but the most unusual thing I have witnessed was a large gentleman from Texas who dined with us. He had two portions back-to-back at the dinner table and later on, when his guests had moved to the bar area, he ordered a third one as dessert. Guilty pleasures, I guess.

This is a quick dish, a spring/summer dish, one that brings comfort, substance, and a very delicate sense of lightness with so many flavors. I love the way it presents: it has elevation, stacked up between layers of candied lemons and crispy mushrooms sandwiched within the seared bass fillets. I shave garlic slivers and apply them on the fillets before I sear them: the garlic roasts, sticking to the fish, the bass acquires taste and it opens a virtual welcoming door to the candied lemon slices offsetting its acidity with their gentle sweetness.

Be quick when cooking the bass as you do not want to burn the garlic slices, but give it a quick sear at high temperature, and if needed finish it in the oven a few minutes to make sure it is properly cooked, but still moist.

Ingredients
7 oz of striped bass fillet skin on
1 garlic clove
1 tbsp of olive oil
Salt
Cracked black peppercorns
Ground white pepper
1 sprig of thyme

Directions
Cut the stripe bass fillet in half, producing two pieces of equal size.
With the truffle slicer shave a few slivers of garlic, and apply them only on the white part of the fish, not on the skin sides.
Sear the bass in a hot pan with the olive oil, the remaining unshaved garlic clove, and the sprig of thyme.
Dust with salt and white pepper on both sides.
Once cooked, remove from the pan and keep warm till serving time.

Fennel Emulsion

Ingredients
½ small bulb of fresh fennel, shaved
½ lb of sweet white onion thinly sliced

1 clove of garlic mashed
1 shot of sambuca liquor
4 oz of butter diced
1 cup of fresh fennel juice
2 whole anise stars
Salt
Ground white pepper
3 medium-size basil leaves
¼ cup of excellent extra virgin olive oil

Directions
Juice a few fennels to gain 1 full cup of pure juice and set aside.
In a medium-size pot combine the onions with the shaved fennel, the butter, the fennel juice, salt, pepper, the anise stars, the sambuca, and the mashed garlic.
Cook at medium/low fire, stirring occasionally until the liquid reduces by half and the fennel and onions are translucent.
Remove from fire, add the garlic chips, and transfer all to a high-speed blender about one minute until paste.
Add the basil leaves and emulsion at high-speed incorporating the extra virgin olive oil a little at a time until foamy.
Taste for salt and pepper, and chill immediately on ice bath.

Candied Lemon Rings

Ingredients
1 Meyer lemon
1 cup of sugar
2 cups of water

Directions
Cut the lemon in very thin slices, remove all the seeds, and place in a small metallic container.
Combine the sugar and the water in a small pot and bring to boil, reduce to a light syrupy consistence and pour on top of the lemons, covering them completely with the liquid while still hot.
Cool the mix naturally, once at room temperature transfer to an air-tight container and keep in refrigerator.

Milanese-Style Oyster Mushrooms

Ingredients
2 oz of oyster mushrooms
1 tbsp of bread crumbs, sifted
1 egg for egg wash mix
Salt
Ground white pepper

Directions
Clean the mushrooms from impurities with a damp towel, and with a small knife trim the stems.
Dip in egg wash, then in bread crumbs, and deep fry a few minutes till golden crispy.
Sprinkle with salt, pepper, and set aside in warm place until serving time.

To Serve
On a round, hot plate, scoop a couple of tablespoons of fennel emulsion in the center, and in a circular motion, spread out the sauce, creating a circle.
In the middle place a few Milanese-style mushrooms, followed by the first slice of candied lemon.
With a spatula lay the bass fillet on top of the lemon slice and the mushrooms, and repeat this process one more time. Be careful stacking as at times if not well set the bass fillets tend to fall if uneven or unbalanced.
To finish top the last fillet with more mushrooms, one more lemon slice, and a few mixed seasonal micro-greens.
Sprinkle the fish lightly with excellent extra virgin olive oil and a few cracked black peppercorns.

Crunchy Semolina-Encrusted Soft-Shell Crabs over Braised Pig's Ear, Tuscan-Style Cannellini Beans Stew, and Spicy Raw Tomato Froth

Every time I prepare this dish I hear: "Chef Enzo Fargione paging Chef Jean Louis Palladin." Jean Louis was as good as unpredictable when it came to mixing flavors. I remember he used to make a dish with overcooked pig's ears toasted in semolina flour and meat juice. At times he would add in roasted lobster and goose liver just for the hell of it. He was famous for his odd combinations in flavors and ingredients. I saw him stuffing a venison heart with goose liver and slowly cooking it for hours. After dinner he would smoke cigarettes with his friends and drink either Port or Armagnac just to cut all the fat he had just eaten. Good old, but not so healthy, days.

The first time I tried to combine such drastic flavors and ingredients I was afraid of breaking imaginary cooking laws. I started experimenting and over the past few the years I applied some exceptions to the rules. I love this recipe as it could be my unofficial version of surf and turf. The soft-shell crabs are plump and crispy, and keep a constant crunchiness texture thanks to the semolina, while the braised pig's ears and the cannellini deliver substance, taste and density. I created a light and natural connection between meat and fish with a froth of spicy raw tomato that cuts through the taste of the soft shells and picks up the tomato flavor in the baked beans.

Ingredients

2 large soft-shell crabs
2 small tbsp of semolina flour
1 garlic clove mashed
1 rosemary sprig
1 thyme sprig
2 eggs for egg wash
2 tbsp of olive oil
1 tbsp of extra virgin olive oil
A few fresh thyme florets to use at serving time
Salt
Ground white pepper

Directions
Remove the face and lungs of the soft-shell crabs, and dip them in the egg wash.
Sprinkle them with some semolina flour and set aside.
In a sauté pan, sear the crabs on both sides with the olive oil, the salt and pepper, the rosemary, thyme sprig, and the mashed garlic, and transfer in the oven about 5 minutes till cooked. Set aside.

Braised Pig's Ears

Ingredients
5 medium-size pig's ears
2 tbsp of olive oil
Salt
Ground white pepper
1 sprig of rosemary
1 sprig of thyme
4 medium-size sage leaves
1 medium-size shallot cut in half
2 garlic cloves mashed
3 cups of veal stock reduction
½ cup of red wine
½ cup of Port wine
1 stalk of celery cut in 3 pieces
1 small carrot cut in 3 pieces
½ cup of white wine vinegar
¼ cup of San Marzano canned tomatoes purée

Directions
Boil the pig's ears at low flame approximately 45 minutes in salted water and white vinegar, and place them on parchment paper.
In a large skillet sear both sides of the pig's ears with olive oil, abundant salt and pepper, the herbs, the shallots, and the garlic cloves.
Add the red wine and the Port, reduce about 30 seconds, add the tomato purée, and remove from the fire.
Transfer the entire contents of the skillet into a small baking pan, add the veal stock reduction, mix, and add the carrot and celery pieces.
Seal the top with two layers of aluminum foil and bake in hot oven about 1½ hours at 300 degrees.

When ready remove the pig's ears from the liquid and set aside to cool at room temperature.
From the baking pan discard the herbs, the shallots, the garlic cloves, the carrots, and the celery pieces. Transfer the cooking liquid to a high-speed blender till smooth and filter through a fine mesh, taste for salt and pepper.
Collect the filtered liquid in a small pot, slice the pig's ears in matchstick strips, and place them in the pot with their cooking liquid.

Tuscan-Style Oven-Baked Cannellini Beans Stew

Ingredients

1 lb cannellini beans soaked in water for one day
8 oz of crushed plum tomatoes
2 garlic cloves hand crushed
½ sprigs of fresh rosemary chopped
3 leaves of fresh sage chopped
1 tbsp of extra virgin olive oil
1 oz of prosciutto slab
1 oz of pancetta slab
1 bay leaf
1 tsp cracked black peppercorns
½ stalk of celery uncut
½ medium-size carrots uncut
½ Vidalia onion secured with tooth picks
2 cups of chicken broth
Salt
Ground white pepper

Directions

In a terra cotta pot (preferably) or in a small, deep baking pan, combine and mix in all the ingredients.
Stir well and make sure to keep the beans under the liquid.
Double seal the baking pan with aluminum foil and bake in hot oven at 275 about 3 ½ hours.
When ready lift the aluminum foil on one side only letting most of the heat escape and let it cool down to room temperature.
Remove the pancetta and the prosciutto slabs, and store the cooked beans with the remaining liquid.

Spicy Raw Tomato Froth

Ingredients

1 qt of juice of fresh raw tomato
1 tsp of spicy Sicilian pepperoncino powder
8 grams of powdered lecithin
6 basil leaves
1 tbsp of tomato paste
3 garlic cloves shaved
1 tbsp of olive oil
Salt
Cracked black peppercorns

Directions

In a small pot golden the garlic shaves with the olive oil.
When crispy add the Sicilian pepperoncino for a few seconds without burning it, and add the tomato juice at once, the tomato paste and the cracked black peppercorns.
Bring to boil at high flame and remove from stove.
Add salt, the basil, and transfer to a high-speed blender till liquefied.
Filter the tomato juice, add the lecithin, and with the help of a hand-held immersion blender whip to create the desired froth.

To Serve

In an oversized hot pasta bowl place a couple of spoons of the oven-baked cannellini beans right in the middle of the plate.
Repeat with the braised pig's ears, and place the soft-shell crabs on top of each other.
Drizzle some extra virgin olive oil and sprinkle some of the fresh thyme florets.
Whip the spicy tomato froth, and top the crabs with 3 or 4 tablespoons of it.

Seared Ahi Tuna in Lardo di Colonnata, Bagna Cauda Sauce and Sicilian Caponata

Having spent many summers in Sicily, it is only natural to absorb Sicilian traditions and customs with much appreciation. Sicilian cuisine is one of those rustic ones you never forget. It is so fresh and humble, rich and at times aggressive in flavors, and extremely satisfying. This recipe is a combination of Sicilian folklore and Piedmontese influences, two places so far apart from each other, but so very close in my heart. They both helped me form professionally while understanding that North and South culinary barriers can be broken by combining suitable ingredients into one innovative dish. This is definitely one of those that witnesses odd but traditional marriages of flavors such as the Piedmontese bagna cauda and the Sicilian caponata: vehicles to better appreciate the seared tuna.

I like to use very lean tuna to build a lean/fat contrast, in my opinion there is no better quality than the Hawaiian ahi. It flakes almost by the touch; it is very flavorful and elegant in its presentation, showing layers of lean flesh, graciously and elegantly, both on the plate and while you eat it. It is very important to create a respectful balance when cooking, as in this case it is best to only sear the fish, leaving it moist and rare on the inside. To add flavor, I combined two elements.

First is a paste of dry porcini mushrooms mixed with a purée of black olives. I stuff the loin with it to enrich in flavor. Second is the lardo di Colonnata that I wrap the tuna with before cooking.

Lardo is a type of Italian charcuterie made by curing strips of fat with herbs and spices. The most prestigious one is from a small little town called Colonnata in Tuscany where the locals have made it since the Roman times. It is extremely delicate and flavorful, and it tastes glorious and delicate, just like the best pancetta you could find on the market. By wrapping thin layers around it, the tuna acquires unique flavor and crispiness when seared.

I like to decorate the halved tuna logs with the assorted dry vegetable chips before serving. They give elevation and diversity in texture as well as taste and spark my creativity while arranging them on the loins in the same way when I was a kid playing with the Legos.

This is a very simple dish: three elements and without a doubt the most intense fish preparation in flavor combination you will find in this book.

Very addictive for those who love strong flavors.

Ingredients
7 oz of ahi tuna loin cut in a log of about 5 inches long and 1½ inches square
4-5 paper thin slices of lardo di Colonnata
1 tbsp of olive oil
Salt
Cracked black peppercorns
2 tsp of black olives/porcini stuffing purée
1 shallot halved
1 garlic clove mashed
1 rosemary sprig
Crystallized salt
A few drops of balsamic vinegar glaze
Assorted dry vegetable chips

Directions
Lay the tuna flat on a working table, and with the tip of a small knife make 4 holes into its flesh distanced about one inch from one another across the log.
Fill each hole by squeezing in the black olives/porcini stuffing purée using the plastic squeeze bottle.
Lightly salt, pepper, and wrap the loin with the lardo slices very tightly.
In a hot sauté pan sear the tuna on each side with the olive oil, the shallot, the rosemary, and the mashed garlic till the lardo turns crispy on the outside, but make sure to leave the tuna at rare temperature.
Remove from the pan, and set aside until serving time.

Black Olives/Porcini Stuffing Purée

Ingredients
1 tbsp of black olive paste
½ tbsp of porcini powder
The tip of a teaspoon of minced garlic
½ sprig of chopped rosemary
1 tsp of extra virgin olive oil
Salt
Ground white pepper

Directions
In a small bowl mix all ingredients till pasty.
Transfer in a small plastic squeeze bottle with a fine tip and refrigerate.

Sicilian Caponata

Ingredients
¼ cup of pitted Ligurian black olives
¼ cup of Sicilian pitted green olives
3½ oz of diced celery in ½ inch cubes
3½ oz of diced carrots in ½ inch cubes
2½ oz of diced white onions in ½ inch cubes
¼ cup of small capers
6 oz of diced eggplants in ½ inch cubes
¼ cup of extra virgin olive oil
2 tbsp of honey
2 tbsp of white wine vinegar
½ tbsp of minced garlic
½ cup of halved cherry tomatoes
½ cup of hand crushed San Marzano plum tomatoes canned
4 basil leaves chopped
¼ cup of Italian parsley leaves
Salt
Ground white pepper

Directions
In a large pan sauté the eggplants with the garlic, the celery, the carrots, and the onions in olive oil at high flame a few minutes till all ingredients are well-seared.
Add salt and pepper.
Add the honey and caramelize a few minutes, splash with the white wine vinegar, and stir well a couple more minutes.
Add the capers, the plum tomatoes, and the olives, and cook till all ingredients are well combined about 3 minutes, leaving a little liquid on the bottom of the pan.
Taste for salt and pepper, adjust if necessary, remove from the stove, and add the cherry tomatoes, the basil and the fresh parsley.
Set aside till room temperature.

Store the caponata in glass jars and pour the remaining cooking liquid on top. Screw on the top and let it rest upside-down at room temperature until completely cold. Keep refrigerated.

Bagna Cauda Sauce

See Appetite Openers chapter from "Anise Dusted Tuna Lollipops" recipe (Page 46).

Assorted Dry Vegetable Chips
Artichoke Chips

See Hot Starters chapter from "Crunchy Monkfish Liver Custard with lemon-honey preserve" recipe (Page 139).

Eggplant Chips

See Fish chapter from "Baked Black Cod with spicy yellow curry rub, pickled purple potatoes, celery, sun chokes, charcoal oil and celery juice sauce" recipe *(Page 370)*.

Fried Basil Leaves

See Hot Starters chapter from "Butter Roasted Baby Octopus in spicy orange caramel" recipe *(Page 144)*.

Tomato Chips

Cut a small, hard, red tomato in paper-thin slices, and lay the slices on deli paper well distanced from one another.
With a dry towel gently press on them, absorbing all the extra water.
Transfer the slices on a silicone baking mat flat, sprinkle with a little salt, and bake in hot oven approximately 2½-3 hours at 225 degrees until totally dry and crispy.

Fried Parsley

Pick a few large Italian parsley leaves, and deep fry them at 375 a few seconds till they curl and are completely crispy, bright green. Set on deli paper.

Balsamic Vinegar Glaze

See Cold Starters chapter from "Cold Stone Veal Carpaccio" recipe *(Page 102)*.

To Serve
On warm, round plate spread the hot bagna cauda sauce with a spoon from one end to the other in the middle of the plate, forming two parallel lines distanced about 4 inches apart to look like train tracks.
Slice the seared tuna log lengthwise, and place both logs on top of the sauce parallel as well, forming a double cross showing the uncooked tuna facing up.
Decorate each tuna log with a sprinkle of crystallized salt, cracked black peppercorns, a drizzle of extra virgin olive oil, and the assorted dry vegetable chips lined up in symmetry, giving elevation with visual variety in colors and assortment. This bonsai-like process shall result in a stunning visual art on top of each tuna log.
With the balsamic vinegar glaze, out of a small plastic squeeze bottle dot the very center of the plate in-between the tuna loins and the bagna cauda sauce. Repeat this 4 more times for each of the cardinal points around the dish.
Place a single fried parsley leaf on top of each of the five balsamic dots and serve while still hot.

Sweet Water Shrimp and Spicy Salame Stuffed Calamari over Braised Leeks/Potato/Green Olives Ragù and Riesling/Carrot/Thyme Sauce

The problem with stuffing calamari is they usually burst open during the cooking process. This happens when they are too stuffed, when they cook longer than they are supposed to, or at very high temperatures. Many years ago I loved the stuffed squids a chef friend of mine cooked at a local restaurant. I have to be honest. I loved the stuffing more than I loved the dish per se: the squids would always be presented burst open, showing the filling like it exploded minutes earlier. Not a beautiful sight for any diner.

Since the calamari tubes are very thin, they should be stuffed with delicate fillings and only at ¾ of the tube's capacity. For my preparations I usually choose ingredients that cook in minutes and do not necessarily expand or shrink during the cooking process. I realized sweetwater shrimp work very well for this recipe.

This filling has substance, flavor, kick and aftertaste, the Riesling and carrot sauce combines all flavors together with taste and balance. I add spicy salame to the shrimp stuffing for flavor and prepare a ragù of leeks, Castelvetrano green olives, and pearled Yukon potatoes that marries perfectly with the sauce. I love its presentation and the different colors beautifully show on the plate, highlighting very simple ingredients to higher levels of appreciation.

Ingredients
10 fresh, large, whole squid tubes
Enough sweet-water shrimp and spicy salame stuffing for 10 squids
¾ cup of white wine
¼ tsp of garlic minced
Salt
Ground white pepper
A few toothpicks
¾ cup of chicken broth

Directions
In a small baking pan combine salt, pepper, the garlic, the chicken broth, and the white wine.
Fill the squid with shrimp and spicy salame stuffing using a pastry bag for easy access into the squid tubes.
Seal each end with a toothpick and lay them in the pan with the liquid mix and bake approximately 15-20 minutes at 350 covered with aluminum foil.

Sweet Water Shrimp and Spicy Salame Stuffing

Ingredients
1 lb of fresh sweet water shrimp
4 oz of spicy Italian salame thinly diced
½ tsp of minced garlic
1 pinch of dry oregano
¼ tsp of powdered Sicilian spicy hot pepper
5 medium-size basil leaves sliced in very thin strips
¼ cup of extra virgin olive oil
Salt

Crushed black peppercorns
A few fried parsley leaves to decorate the plate

Directions
In a food processor crush the shrimp to a semi-fine, coarse texture for a few seconds only.
Transfer into a bowl and add all the other ingredients, mixing well with a rubber spatula until the oil is completely absorbed in the mix.
Store in a plastic pastry bag and refrigerate an hour before stuffing the calamari.

Braised Leeks/Potato/Green Olives Ragù

Ingredients
2½ oz of leeks cut in matchstick strips and double-washed
4 Sicilian green olives removed from the pits and sliced
The tip of a teaspoon of minced garlic
1 tbsp of olive oil
2 oz of chicken broth
6 small potato balls carved with a melon baller approximately ½-inch in diameter and poached in salted water
Salt
Ground white pepper
2 medium-size basil leaves chopped
A drizzle of Frantoio extra virgin olive oil

Directions
In a medium-size pan sauté the poached potato balls with the olive oil until golden crispy.
Add the onions, the garlic, the leeks, and sauté for a few minutes.
Add the green olives, salt, pepper, and the chicken broth; braise at medium-low flame until the liquid is totally reduced and add the basil.
Set aside until serving time.

Riesling/Carrot/Thyme Sauce

Riesling Reduction

Ingredients
½ bottle 750ml of Riesling
2 shallots peeled and sliced
½ sprig of rosemary
4 sage leaves
1 sprig of thyme
1 tbsp of butter
1 bay leaf
1 garlic clove mashed
Salt
1 tsp of whole black peppercorns

Carrot Sauce

Ingredients
2 cups of carrot juice (through the juicer)
4 oz of carrots peeled and sliced paper thin.
1 tbsp of excellent extra virgin olive oil
1 tbsp of heavy cream
2 garlic chips

Directions
For the Riesling reduction combine herbs, garlic, shallots, and butter in a small pot and roast till golden.
Add the black peppercorns and the Riesling, and reduce at moderate fire till down to ¼ of total liquid.
Filter through a fine mesh and transfer to a new small pot.
Add the sliced carrots, the 2 cups of carrot juice, and cook at moderate fire until reduced to half its original volume, making sure the carrots are almost dissolved.
Transfer the mix to a high-speed blender; add the roasted garlic chips, the extra virgin olive oil, and the heavy cream.
Liquefy to a smooth and velvety sauce.
Taste for salt and pepper and chill immediately on ice bath.

To Serve

On a large plate set a medium-size rectangular metallic mold lengthwise to be filled with the warm leeks ragù at the 12 o'clock mark.

Make sure to push the ragù down and to press hard in order to be able to lift the mold, leaving the leeks in a solid rectangular shape. Cut the end of one of the stuffed squid and place it on top the leek ragù pile. Cut a second squid in five slices, coin size, and place them on the plate one-by-one creating a long vertical line all the way down to the six o'clock mark. Decorate the plate with some extra virgin olive oil, cracked black peppercorns, fried parsley leaves, and serve to your guests placing the plate in front of them showing a T shape.

Delicately, pour some of the hot Riesling/carrot/thyme sauce on top of the sliced calamari and on the whole one set on top of the leeks ragù.

Pastrami-Style Butter-Poached Maine Lobster, Roasted Beets, Mosaic Petrossian Caviar, Creme Fraiche, Blood Orange Dressing, and Red Ribbon Sorrel

Who says pastrami is only for beef?

I love this dish: I serve it as an appetizer as well as a light summer entrée. It is a stunner to look at and quite marvelous to eat. I first had the idea of combining pastrami spices and lobster a couple of years ago when Julia and I went to Philadelphia for our yearly spooky tour at Eastern State Penitentiary for Halloween and we stopped by for dinner at chef Marc Vetri's restaurant. We sat down for a tasting menu meal, Marc came out to say hello, we chatted for a while, and then we went on with the first course: pastrami goose liver.

I love good pastrami, but I am not a fan of it. I have enjoyed Marc's version so much that the following spring I decided to revisit the possibility of converting his idea into a light seafood dish.

After a few tries I customized a delicate version of the pastrami mix. I combined all ingredients in a high-speed blender and reduced them to powder. I boiled a lobster tail a couple of minutes only, just enough to be able to take it out of its shell in one piece while still raw, and I butter-poached it with the pastrami mix. The tail absorbs the flavor of the pastrami dust and the taste of the poaching butter while leaving the lobster meat very moist and tender.

I thought about creating a very visual dish to look like a mosaic. Using different varieties of sliced beets, I made a dressing with blood oranges and added diversity in taste by adding Petrossian caviar and crème fraiche. Right before serving I place a few leaves of red ribbon sorrel to help neutralize the spiciness of the pastrami. At times I like to add a small Italian version of crab cake to it when I serve it as a main course, barely warm: I like my crab cakes to be moist and soft with lots of flavor. I add diced pancetta, braised leeks, and diced starchy potatoes as well as sour cream and stone mustard.

For a wonderful mini-feast on crab cakes alone, I included with the recipe one of my favorite sauces I use for seafood preparations: Warm broccoli emulsion.

Ingredients
1 uncooked Maine lobster tail
8 oz of high-fat butter
2 tbsp of pastrami dust
2 small size, poached candy-striped beets
1 medium-size poached golden beet
1 tsp of Petrossian caviar
1 tsp of crème fraiche
Crystallized salt
Ground white pepper
1 tbsp of chopped chives
5 leaves of red ribbon sorrel
4 segments of blood orange and cut in half to gain 8 pieces

Directions
In a small pot combine the butter with the pastrami powder and melt on very low flame.
Add the raw lobster tail and poach it a few minutes only. Remove from the butter and set aside to cool at room temperature.
Filter the butter and preserve in refrigerator.

Slice the golden beets and the candy-striped ones very thin and of the same thickness, lay them on deli paper and set aside at room temperature until serving.

Pastrami Spice Dust

Ingredients
¼ cup of kosher salt
½ tsp of ground sweet paprika
3 tbsp of coriander seeds
3 tbsp of brown sugar
2 tbsp of black peppercorns
2 tbsp of mustard seeds
1 tbsp of white peppercorns
½ tbsp of fennel seeds
8 garlic cloves thinly sliced and fried into dry chips

Directions
Combine all ingredients in a high-speed blender until powder.
Preserve in an air-tight container.

Blood Orange Dressing

Ingredients
½ cup of blood orange juice
½ cup of blended oil
½ cup of extra virgin olive oil
1 pinch of each salt and white pepper
The juice of 2 lemons
1 orange zest, grated

Directions
Combine all ingredients in a high-speed blender to a creamy and thick consistency.
Taste for salt and pepper, and store in a plastic squeeze bottle and in the refrigerator.

To Serve
On a round plate place the golden beet slices in a circular motion covering its entire surface. Symmetrically lay 8 slices of the candy-

striped beets on top of the golden ones to create a mosaic of circle inside a circle design.
Dust with salt and pepper, and squeeze some of the blood orange dressing, covering the whole beet surface. Sprinkle the chopped chives evenly all over and place the half blood orange segments on top of each candy-striped slice.
Cut the poached lobster in 8 thin medallions and rest each piece on top of the blood orange segment.
Place a teaspoon of Petrossian caviar on one side of the plate and one of crème fraiche on the opposite side, delivering visual balance. Finish decorating the dish with 5 small leaves of red ribbon sorrel and serve at room temperature.

Italian-Style Crab Cakes

Ingredients

8 oz of jumbo lump crab meat
8 oz of back fin crab meat
1½ oz of scallions thinly chopped
1 oz of ground stone mustard
4 oz of sour cream
3½ oz of diced pancetta
3 eggs
2 tsp of minced garlic
8 oz of sauté leeks
12 oz of cubed Yukon potatoes
Salt
Ground white pepper
1 big pinch of dry oregano
1 small pinch of crushed hot red pepper
2 cups of heavy cream
2 tbsp of olive oil to roast the diced potatoes

Equipment Needed

1 silicone flexi mold for baking with 2½ oz form compartments

Directions

In a medium-size pan roast the cubed potatoes crispy with a little salt and pepper. Remove from the oil and set aside until cool.
In a salad bowl mix the two kinds of crab meat gently with your hands without breaking the lumps.

Add the chopped scallions, the stone mustard, the sour cream, the pancetta, the sauté leeks, salt, pepper, and the roasted potatoes along with the oregano and the crushed hot red pepper.
In a separate bowl beat the eggs with salt and pepper, whisk in the heavy cream, marry it with the crab mix, and with the help of a rubber spatula mix well.
Fill each compartment of the silicone mold with the mix and bake in hot oven at 325 degrees approximately 15-20 minutes.

Warm Broccoli Emulsion

Ingredients
8 oz of small broccoli florets
1 cup of extra virgin olive oil
4 fillets of anchovies
2 oz of warm chicken broth
½ tbsp of small nonpareilles capers
Ground white pepper
Salt
½ tsp of minced garlic
3 medium-size basil leaves

Directions
Blanch the broccoli florets with salted water and purée as much as possible in the food processor with no added liquids.
Transfer the chopped up broccoli to a high-speed blender, add salt, pepper, garlic, warm chicken broth, capers, basil and anchovies.
Blend till a smooth paste, and then drizzle in the extra virgin olive oil a little at a time to a foamy and dense emulsion.

Chapter Ten
The Simple Pleasures of the Flesh

Meat is meat.

Independently of what type of meat we choose, like or consume, meat is synonymous of gastronomic luxury, the king of proteins, a satisfying and compelling substance. Almost everyone enjoys a perfectly cooked juicy steak or a perfectly roasted chicken, but not everyone is comfortable venturing into game meat, fowl or more exotic selections.

Meat is tricky. It is all about cultural comfort and every day routine. In the U.S. we consume enormous amounts of beef, chicken, pork and veal. We also consume good amounts of turkey, lamb and fowl, but not much game such as venison, pigeons, boar or rabbit. Only a small percentage of the courageous and brave venture off their daily routine of comfort. Beef and chicken are the basic, most-consumed choices for our everyday meal. Pork has become the "other white meat," while turkey is more and more appreciated throughout the whole year, not only at Thanksgiving.

Of course I am speaking in general context: in the Southern states of Louisiana, Tennessee, Mississippi, Alabama and Georgia (just to name a few) pork is the number one choice of meat. For example, their wonderful barbeque preparations are pure gastronomic dreams. From their ribs to the whole slowly spit-roasted hog, there is absolutely nothing about it I do not love. I adore Southern pork preparations; it makes me weak at the knees and turns me back into a little kid with a permanent smile tattooed on my face. A few years back I was invited to judge the world-famous international barbeque contest, "Memphis in May," where the best pit masters and BBQ gods gather in Tom Lee Park to smoke for three days, fighting for the top prize and dreaming of being crowned king smoker.

I had the honor to be a guest judge on two different occasions and both times the experience opened my eyes in appreciation for the quality of the food, the hard work of everyone involved, and the thick sense of pride among the participants. The same sense of love and pride I encountered in Texas, where they master the art of barbequing beef, ribs, briskets and more: insanely good and amazingly tender. But if we move to North America, game becomes more and more available and routinely consumed and appreciated by many: venison, deer, rabbit and fowl meat is an everyday treat.

The European market is vaster and more open than any others I have encountered. I grew up in Italy where at a very young age I was introduced to extensive different types of meats. My mom, like any other mothers in Italy, would cook a vast variety in different ways. She would bring home whole rabbits and make fantastic stews, horse meat (which I hated) innards, game and whole pheasants, pigeons and quail with feathers still on them, and whole freshly butchered baby lamb that looked like aliens from another planet. I did not always like or enjoy the daily selection on our dinner table, but there were many options available for us to choose from; availability to the consumer was always high, fresh and affordable.

In Scandinavia, people consume seal meat; in Asia, dog and cat meat consumption is absolutely normal and considered a delicacy, as well as raw chicken breasts. It is indeed hard to imagine such a selection at our local grocery stores or supermarkets, but we are all raised with gastronomic and cultural differences.

Throughout the Tuscan and Umbrian regions two of the most popular meats are wild boar and rabbit; not very popular in the U.S., but those wild animals populate their woods and meadows and are considered regional treasures. Their meats appear on almost every restaurant menu, prepared traditionally, and are a common choice for the average everyday meal as well.

In my native region of Piedmont, the famous breed Fassone is a type of veal renowned for its tenderness, milky taste and very light color. For my mother's 72nd birthday, a couple of years ago I made an unexpected visit to Torino and took the whole family out to a typical Piedmontese restaurant that specialized in local and traditional preparation. When the first course arrived I was presented with a volcano-shaped off-white, pinkish ground raw meat. The server shaved fresh white truffles on it, sprinkled crystallized salt and added a drizzle of olive oil. The meat literally evaporated in my mouth; never in my life had I experienced anything like it. It was light, tasty and absolutely phenomenal in every possible way. Another delicate and famous veal breed also from Piedmonte is the Sanato. The veal is fed only with milk and egg whites to preserve the white color of its flesh; it is extremely tender and considered a rare delicacy.

There are countless types of meats everywhere in the world: each country has traditions and each province has local breeds. At times people go too far and out of their way to create a market available only for a few: in Japan the traditional Wagyu is the most famous type of beef. It is genetically predisposed to produce the most intense marbling and commands a very high price. It is also known as Kobe or Mishima. In smaller farms the animal is hand-massaged for hours in order to soften its flesh. Believe it or not they also add sake to their daily diet to enhance (so they say) meat flavoring, but that result is so far unproven. I have great respect for the Japanese Kobe breed and I am a huge fan of it, but it becomes an almost comical situation when I envision a couple of bulls getting an hour-session massage right after they meet at a local bar for happy hours downing shots of sake. What a life!

Nowadays, we have our own American-style Kobe beef in Colorado, which is fantastic and at a more reasonable and affordable price. Japanese Wagyu cattle were bred with Angus cattle, creating a crossbreed named U.S. Wagyu, delicious, expensive, but extremely flavorful, and they are fed exclusively with corn, barley and wheat straw.

It is amazing how meat quality has changed over the past 40 years. One thing I always remember from my young kitchen days is how long it took my grandmother to cook a simple chicken. I remember her quartering and cooking it almost an hour before it would finally get juicy and tender. Back then, the market was almost entirely free-range and therefore the meat was much tougher, containing a lot more fibers. It is becoming harder to find free-range chicken plants where chickens are fed only with organic feed. Nowadays steroid hormones are often added to some chicken feeds and especially to those that need to grow faster in order to develop more muscle content before butchering. This process allows some farmers to raise and to sell chickens faster for slaughtering and with less cost on their part. Their meat is much more tender, and cooks faster even when those gigantic chickens look like they belong in a gym rather than on somebody's dinner plate. The bad part is those steroid hormones are still present even after cooking, and therefore ingested by consumers on a daily basis. Not exactly the healthiest thing for any human.

Duck is another type of meat I really love and enjoy. I am a sucker for Chinese food, and I have to admit no one cooks duck like they do. I love the way we Italians cook it, I adore many versions of the French ones, and I am a big fan of the local duck preparations in upstate New York, but my preference goes out to the Chinese. They have a way to cook it (whenever it is done correctly as at times it is way overcooked and dry) by slowly melting all the fat, leaving its flesh tender and juicy and bright pink. Its flavor is intense yet delicate, silky and lingering.

I also love goose and particularly goose liver. I like it roasted or seared, but I often cook it as an appetizer in the form of custard torched like a crème brûlée and accompanied with crunchy pears poached in Port wine. It is so light and delicate that one evening at the restaurant we were serving it as the first course to a private dinner party. The servers informed the kitchen there was one vegetarian restriction and to therefore apply a suitable substitute for the goose liver course. I have no idea how it happened, but the custard got served to the vegetarian guest anyway and no substitution was made. I got very worried and felt guilty, responsible, and compelled to inform him I decided to personally go to the table to apologize.

I marched to the private room rehearsing my speech in my head. When I approached the guest I noticed his custard was gone and before I could say anything he stood up, laid a hand on my shoulder, and said, "I am so thankful for accommodating my vegetarian request: I must tell you, the eggplant custard you served was the best I ever had." Funny, true story.

It is wonderful how different cultures envision and make use of meat products. Take for instance the Asians: they eat the whole animal. There is absolutely nothing they discard. They cook and eat intestines, feet, heads, nerves and tendons, eyes, gizzards and snouts.

Italians and French tone it down a little, but not by much as they cook an incredible variety of odd or "not so common meat parts" for better words: sweetbreads, brains, pig's ears, tripe, hearts, tongue and livers.

It seems to me the further West we travel the less variety of choice we use. Americans are not very adventurous when it comes to breaking out of their comfortable eating habits and routines. The typical daily choice is mostly limited to beef and chicken cooked and prepared in very basic ways such as grilled or roasted. Then of course there are those who appreciate and value delicacies such as offal, even though only a small percentage become fans of it. In the past few years Americans have re-discovered buffalo meat, and it is becoming more and more available and in demand across the country, as well as ostrich meat.

This last one is considered a direct competitor to our everyday beef; its meat has the lowest fat and cholesterol content, is incredibly high in protein, and tastes very similar to veal and beef. It's kind of hard, however (or at least for me), to imagine taking a bite of the biggest bird in existence. Every time I hear the word ostrich I have visions of the Sesame Street character Big Bird, my daughter loved so much when she was a toddler.

My personal memories are so various and vivid I can still smell, 30 years later, the incredible fumes of a slowly roasted spit baby lamb with garlic and rosemary on a summer day or the traditional Sicilian link sausages made by my uncle roasting on wooden coals. I remember glorious Sundays spent around the table among 20 family members feasting on cold cuts, pasta dressed with various meat ragùs and infinite amounts of veal, beef, lamb, chicken, game, and so much more for many unforgettable feasts.

Funny fact is when we are children we all take moments like that for granted as we do not know any better and cannot realize or comprehend how lucky we all have been growing up in a society where everything is available just for the asking.

I could not possibly imagine a way of life without meat consumption. Our resources and availabilities are so great meat has become a way of our everyday life on multiple levels, from the unhealthy fast food category featuring surrogates such as hamburgers, hot dogs, sausage patties and chicken nuggets to luxurious preparations of famous chefs at their four-star restaurants, to simple home-cooked meals.

Meat has been, and it will always be, synonymous of compelling substance, luxury and comfort.

Salt Cured Duck Breast, Black Olives Sauce, Artichoke Hearts, Gruviere Cheese/Thyme Turnip Cake

This could be labeled a lazy way of cooking recipe. In fact, there is really not much cooking for this fantastic breast of duck; a couple of minutes in a hot pan at the most and we are ready to go.

Having worked side by side, even if only occasionally, with great and famous chefs, I picked up a few things here and there observing how secret techniques were applied and I have appreciated a different way of cooking. Of course, in the end I twisted things my own way. During one of our many culinary trips together I saw Jean Louis Palladin salting a few breasts of duck with pepper and powdered cloves. He was having a very bad day, one of those where you just had to keep away from him.

He had been pressed for time, with very little help, and of course he was not a happy camper or patient with the interns and young volunteers who dedicated their time to help put together the charity dinner we were cooking that very evening. The kitchen was separated by a wall dividing the cooking line and the prep area. At one point we heard, "Get the hell out of here! All of you! You're lucky you don't work for me!" And so a string of young kids in culinary uniforms, visibly blushing and embarrassed, rushed out of the prep room as if they were chased by hungry wolves. They never came back.

We all looked at each other unsure about breaking into a laugh or keeping quiet. Then one of us, concerned, asked our steaming chef friend, "Jean Louis, do you need any help? It's only 3:30, but service is at 7 and the number of guests for tonight just went up to 550." So some of us lent a hand to prep his dish of roasted salt-cured duck breast and saved the day.

The way the duck was prepared is very similar to the one for this recipe. I like to mix the salt with curry, coriander and cumin, and I salt the raw breasts of duck just like they do in Parma when they salt the prosciutto. I pat both sides with the salt and place in the refrigerator for 24 hours. I love this technique as the salt slowly cooks the meat and penetrates deep, delivering flavor.

As a matter of fact I only sear the breast on both sides a few seconds, and I finish in the oven if needed a couple of minutes only. When you slice through it the meat appears to be raw, but I assure you it is perfectly cooked and intensely flavorful. I decide to offset its taste with a light black olive sauce and to pair it with roasted artichoke hearts and simple shaved turnips cooked with creamy Greyere cheese and fresh thyme.

This is one of my favorite recipes in this book, one of those I would rarely get tired of eating. You could also make a nice duck prosciutto if aged longer and air-dried under optimal temperature and conditions.

Ingredients

1 breast of Muscovy or Mallard duck of about 7-8 oz
1 artichoke heart cleaned and poached al dente in salted water
1 dash of chopped chives
1 tbsp of olive oil
The tip of a teaspoon of minced garlic
Salt
Ground white pepper
2 tbsp of curing seasoned salt
1 sprig of rosemary
1 sprig of thyme
2 leaves of sage
1 garlic clove mashed
Cracked black peppercorns
Assorted seasonal micro greens
Red wine caramel for plate decorating

Directions

Cure the breast of duck with the seasoned salt by repeatedly patting both sides, and place in the refrigerator for 24 hours.

Quarter the artichoke heart and sear all 4 pieces in a small sauté pan with a little olive oil, garlic, salt, and pepper. Right before serving, add a dash of chopped chives and set aside.
In a larger sauté pan, bring the oil to temperature, scrape off the excess salt still on the duck breast, dry it, and sear it well on both sides with the mashed garlic and the herbs till well colored and crispy.
Transfer to a baking pan and finish the cooking process by baking it about 3 extra minutes at 450 degrees. The breast of duck should be cooked rare.
Set aside to rest in a warm place till serving time.

Curing Seasoned Salt

Ingredients
12 oz of sea salt
1½ tbsp ground cumin
1½ tbsp ground coriander
1 tsp of ground white pepper
1 tsp curry powder

Directions
Place all ingredients in a medium-size bowl and mix well.
Store it in a dry place in an air-tight container.

Black Olive Sauce

Ingredients
1 cup of pitted Ligurian black olives
½ small carrots diced finely
½ small stalk of celery diced finely
¼ small white onions diced finely
The needles of ½ sprig of rosemary
The florets of 1 sprig of thyme
2 sage leaves
½ oz of dry porcini mushrooms
1 small shallot diced finely
Salt
Ground white pepper
1 garlic clove hand mashed
1 oz of pancetta slab

1 cup of chicken broth
2 cups of veal stock reduction
1 oz of butter

Directions
In a small size pot sear the pancetta crispy, then combine all ingredients except the veal stock, the chicken broth, and the olives, and cook at medium heat until translucent.
Add the black olives, the chicken broth, and the veal stock, reduce by half, remove the pancetta slab, and then transfer to a high-speed blender until smooth and in velvety texture.
Taste for salt and pepper and set aside.

Gruviere Cheese/Thyme Turnip Cakes

Ingredients
2 medium-size white turnip
4 oz of Gruviere cheese grated
Salt
Ground white pepper
Pinch of ground nutmeg
1 cup of heavy cream
2 tbsp of thyme florets
4 oz of grated Parmesan Reggiano cheese
Butter at room temperature

Directions
Slice the turnip very thin and blanch in salted water a few seconds only.
In a small mixing bowl combine the thyme florets with the heavy cream, the salt and the pepper, the nutmeg and mix well.
On a small sheet baking pan, spread the butter at the bottom of it and make the first layer by overlapping the turnip slices. Sprinkle with grated Gruviere cheese and a little Parmesan Reggiano cheese. Repeat this step two more times to build a multi-layered moist cake.
Before baking sprinkle the top with more Parmesan cheese and transfer into a hot oven at 400 degrees for approximately 15 minutes or until the turnips color to a nice golden/brown crust.
Let the pan cool at room temperature and with the help of a square cookie cutter of about 3 inches cut out the turnip cakes.

Set aside on parchment paper.

To Serve
Run a strip of the black olive sauce vertically on the very left side of a large warm square plate of about two inches wide.
Overlap the artichoke hearts on it, creating a chain-like effect.
On the bottom-left side of the plate fan the duck breast sliced very thin and in a circular motion inside a round mold of about 4 inches in diameter.
Remove the mold and on the top-left side of the plate place the gratinee-square turnip cake.
Decorate the duck with assorted micro greens, drizzle some olive around all the components and dot with cracked black peppercorns.
Repeat with the red wine caramel.

Roasted Veal Fillet and Sweetbreads, Blood Orange/Mascarpone Sauce Black Trumpets Mushroom Ragù, Sour Cipollini Onions, and Rosemary Froth

I am not a huge fan of the sous vide technique, but it makes cooking so much easier and much more precise in terms of temperature control, consistency and execution. Most food cooked for long periods of time at low temperature benefits in taste and flavor. The explosion of the sous vide phenomenon in the past eight years has brought even the least knowledgeable or savvy cook to, in part, adopt this technique for his daily work.

Its preparation is quite laborious: each food category in question would need to be portioned, bagged and prepped—some combined with additional ingredients like butter and herbs, others with different components—then sealed by a vacuum-sealing machine and finally cooked by a water-temperature-controlled circulator in a warm bath. The results in quality are fantastic, the shelf-life prolonged, and the timing for cooking and serving are definitely shorter once the orders are called. Because of its increasing popularity, I forecast the next generation of restaurants will include sous vide built-in tanks in their kitchen construction layouts for cooking, re-heating, and water circulator fixtures right beside their serving lines.

This recipe adopts the sous vide technique, but the fillet of veal can definitely be prepared in the old-fashioned way by searing it first and roasting it a few minutes in the oven, and it is equally fantastic. The only difference lies in the gradual and even cooking process of the meat and, slightly, in its final taste. Sous vide is a cooking technique that makes sense when a large amount of preparation takes place. Restaurants and home cooks who have a vacuum-sealing machine have the advantage of preparing ready-made dinners for the entire family or customers ahead of time and to benefit from it for the following several weeks. I love how the creamy mascarpone cheese cuts into the acidity of the blood orange, and how the rosemary froth and the cipollini onions combine all other ingredients together in a unique salty-savory combination.

The roasted sweetbreads bring substance and diversity in texture, and the black trumpet mushrooms bring color and unmistakable hearty taste. The whole dish is extremely well-balanced; complete and extremely satisfying even for those who are still hesitant in breaking away from old or traditional veal preparations.

Ingredients

Veal fillet of about 6 oz cleaned and peeled
2 oz of blanched veal sweetbreads lightly poached in salted water
4 oz of butter
Salt
Ground white pepper
1 shallot halved
1 rosemary sprig
1 thyme sprig
2 sage leaves
The peel of ½ orange
Cracked black peppercorns
Excellent extra virgin olive oil
Crystallized salt

Special Equipment Needed

Sous vide heating immersion circulator unit
Sous vide cooking plastic bag
Vacuum-sealing machine

Directions

In preparation to cook the veal fillet in sous vide style, wrap one leaf of sage and half sprig of rosemary in plastic film, creating a small roll about 2 inches long, and cut both ends open so the flavor of the herbs can easily escape during the cooking process. By doing this we avoid direct contact with the meat; when this happens the flavor of the herbs are concentrated only to that specific area of the veal, overpowering it and creating bitterness.

Place the roll in the bag along with 1 oz of butter and the veal fillet seasoned with white pepper only. Vacuum-sealing the bag sealed and immerge it in the already hot water tub with the thermo-circulator and cook approximately one hour at 46 degrees Celsius. If your intent is to serve it right away and complete a meal, then open the bag and sear to completion. However, if your intent is to

cook and preserve for later use we will need to stop and reverse the cooking process by dropping the bag in ice bath till completely cold. We will use this reverse step each time we cook any sous vide protein: immerge the already cooked bag into the already hot water tub with the thermo-circulator and bring it back up to 46 degrees Celsius before searing it.
Prepare 3 small pots with boiling water on the stove. Quickly immerge the orange peel in the first one for 20 seconds and transfer it to the second pot for 20 more seconds. Repeat this process a third time with the last water pot and finally set the orange peel aside. When cold, slice the peel into extremely thin matchstick slivers and set aside till serving time.
In a medium-size pan melt 2 oz of the butter with the shallot and the herbs and at high flame. We will reuse this pan to cook the veal fillet crispy and sauté the sweetbreads: then dust with salt and pepper. Remove both meats and set aside ready to serve.

Blood Orange Mascarpone Cheese Sauce

Ingredients

8 oz of mascarpone cheese
The juice of 7 medium-size blood oranges
1 cup of veal stock reduction
½ shallot diced finely
2 oz of butter
Ground white pepper
Salt
½ sprig of rosemary

Directions

Reduce the orange juice to only ¼ of its original volume and set aside.
In a different small-size pot, sauté the diced shallot and the rosemary sprig with the butter, add the veal stock, and the reduced blood orange juice.
Remove the rosemary sprig and simmer till reduced by half.
Turn the fire off and whisk in the **mascarpone** cheese till completely melted in the mix.
Adjust salt and pepper, and transfer to a high-speed blender till of smooth consistency.

Black Trumpets Mushroom Ragù

Ingredients
2 oz of black trumpets mushrooms
1 tsp of shallots finely chopped
1 tbsp of butter
1 tbsp of olive oil
The tip of a teaspoon of minced garlic
2 sage leaves finely chopped
Salt
Ground white pepper
2 basil leaves chopped
1 tbsp of chicken broth

Directions
Clean the mushrooms of impurities with a damp towel and slice them into pieces of about 2-3 inches.
In a medium-size sauté pan and at high flame, color the chopped shallot with the sage and the garlic in olive oil and butter. Add the mushrooms and sauté about 30 seconds, adding salt and pepper and the chicken broth.
Remove the pan from the fire and mix in the basil.
Set aside until serving time.

Sour Cipollini Onions

Salads chapter from "Sweet Sour Pearled Onions" *(Page 179)*.

Make sure to choose cipollini onions of one-inch size. Follow directions accurately, extending the cooking time from 18 to 25 minutes.

Rosemary Froth

Ingredients
2 oz of fresh rosemary
1 qt of chicken broth
6 grams of powder Lecithin
½ tsp of minced garlic
½ tbsp of olive oil
A pinch of salt

A pinch of ground white pepper

Directions
In a small pot cover the garlic with the olive oil, the white pepper, and the salt.
Quickly stir in the chopped rosemary approximately 5 seconds, and add the chicken broth.
Simmer until evaporated to half of total liquid.
Pass the mix through a high-speed blender till very fine, filter through a fine mash and into a metal container. Set aside to cool.
Once at room temperature, with a small hand-held immersion blender, combine the lecithin with the liquid and whip the mix to a solid and flavorful airy froth right before serving.

To Serve
On an oval or long hot plate place a couple of spoons of the blood orange sauce across it, creating a long thick strip.
Place one sweet and sour cipollini onion right in the center of the plate on the sauce and two more on each ends of the strip. Place a tablespoon of the black trumpets mushrooms ragù between the onions, creating two individual piles.
Slice the ends of the seared veal fillet and cut it in half into two short logs, place them both on the mushrooms, and place the two slices of the seared sweetbreads between the veal and the onions.
Finish the dish by sprinkling a few slivers of the orange peel right across the dish as well as a few rosemary needles; place a pinch of crystallized salt on the veal fillets, a dash of the cracked black peppercorns and a drizzle of the extra virgin olive oil across the whole dish.
Whip the rosemary base to a frothy consistency and place it on top of each veal log.
Serve immediately.

Barolo Marinated Squab in Speck Cage with Chestnut Mashed Purée, Caramelized Quince Ragù, Barolo Glaze, and Crunchy Spinach Leaves

The most vivid memories about squab come from my childhood when I was just 10 years old and my family and I were visiting Venice. Strolling around for hours on an incredibly hot summer day, I barely cared for the beauties or history of my surroundings. As a hyper kid on vacation my interest was captured by the side-street artists' drawings, details of the gondolas, and by the every corner-present gelato stores. I had no interest for the natural beauties of the city, its churches, canals, or its architecture. I remember feeling negative energy for some reason instead of appreciation for such an incredible and spectacular place. I am sure a lot had to do with the fact I was just a child and in any case I just did not care much for the trip. I was tired of walking, and I could not wait to leave until we reached San Marco's Square. It was an amazing sight: thousands and thousands of pigeons flying around, landing gracefully by my feet looking for leftover crumbs, unafraid and territorial as if they were saying, "Hello, would you like to play with us?" People would feed them crumbs out of paper bags, crackers and any other sort of leftovers in order to attract their attention for a quick photo op. I tried to give them some of my gelato, with no luck, until my mom threw a handful of cracker chips at my feet, and in a split second I got attacked like in the 1963 Hitchcock movie *The Birds*.

A few years later in my second year of culinary school my professor, Mario Sobbia, composed a menu that included roasted squab for one of the weekly scheduled kitchen services. I immediately had flashbacks. With much needed guidance I learned how to clean them, prep them, marinate them, cook and mostly appreciate them. But it was not until I started working as an extra at local restaurants on Saturdays and Sundays that I would truly understand how a farm raised pigeon should be properly elevated to wild game glory.

Squab is not for everyone, I realize, but it is for many who love game just like quail or partridge. I chose to include this recipe for many reasons, but mostly because it is a very tasty and complete dish I am sure many will love. I like how the wine marinates the meat, turning the whole bird into a deep and thick purple color, and how through the cooking process it retains most of its wine flavor with insistent notes of the marinating spices and herbs.

I created a round cage for it made out of dehydrated speck prosciutto to present the whole dish in it, setting an elegant and humorous message for the diners while hosting the chestnut purée, the caramelized quince ragù, its sauce, and the crunchy spinach leaves.

It is very visual, different, and presents beautifully. I hope you will enjoy it as much as I do.

Ingredients

1 fresh whole squab of about 6-8 oz cleaned and washed
2 cups of Barolo wine
½ carrot chopped
½ stalk of celery chopped
½ white onion chopped
1 bay leaf
1 cinnamon stick
2 juniper berries cracked
1 sprig of rosemary
3 sage leaves
1 sprig of thyme
2 garlic cloves hand mashed
2 tbsp of olive oil
5-6 thin slices of speck
A few large spinach leaves
Salt
Ground white pepper

Equipment Needed

Small, round, metallic cake mold 3½ inches wide and 2 inches tall.

Directions

In a very small tub create the marinate, combining the wine with half the herbs, one garlic clove, the carrot, celery, onion, bay leaf, juniper berries and the cinnamon stick.

Stuff the squab with the remaining herbs and the garlic clove and place in the wine marinate, making sure it stays completely submerged under the wine at least 4 days in the refrigerator.

Apply a very thin film of olive oil on the small cake mold with your fingers and delicately wrap the speck slices around it, covering the whole surface. Place in hot oven at 225 degrees for approximately 2½ hours or until the speck is totally dry and crispy.

Set it aside at room temperature and only when completely cold carefully and in circular motion untwist it from its mold, creating a free-standing, crispy, round cage.
Deep-fry the spinach leaves in hot oil at 375 till completely crispy, but still bright green. Set them aside on parchment paper and sprinkle with salt and white pepper.
When the squab is fully marinated, remove it from the liquid and pat it dry with a towel. You will notice the bird is now totally red in color and you will notice how the wine has penetrated through the flesh entirely.
In a small hot sauté pan sear the squab breast first in the remaining olive oil and on the sides; keep on cooking a few more seconds until it creates a nice brown crispy layer all around it. Salt and pepper and transfer to hot oven at 400 degrees for approximately 3-4 minutes to medium rare temperature.
Set aside in warm place until serving time.

Chestnuts Mashed Purée

Ingredients
8 oz of chestnuts peeled and cleaned (frozen are just as good)
1 small shallot diced finely
2 small sage leaves chopped
½ sprig of chopped rosemary
¾ cups of veal stock reduction
1 oz of chicken broth
4 slices of speck sliced paper thin and finely chopped
1 small thinly sliced potato
2 oz of butter
½ garlic cloves sliced
Salt
Ground white pepper

Directions
In a large pan sauté the speck with the herbs, garlic and shallots in the butter till crispy.
Add the chestnuts and the sliced potatoes salt and pepper, and cook a few minutes.

Add the veal stock and the chicken broth, and cook at moderate-low fire till 80 percent of the liquid is reduced, and the potatoes and chestnuts start to break apart and overcook.
Blend in a food processor, warm and refrigerate.

Caramelized Quince Ragù

Ingredients
2 medium-size quince peeled and diced in ¼-inch size
1 small shallot finely chopped
2 oz of hand crushed canned plum tomatoes
2 cloves mashed with a blade of a knife and powdered
1 tbsp of butter
2 sage leaves chopped
¼ cup of balsamic vinegar
¼ cup of honey
Salt
Ground white pepper
1 oz of chopped fresh basil
The tip of a teaspoon of minced garlic

Directions
In a medium-size pan cook the shallots with the sage, the garlic, and the butter until colored.
Add the diced quince, salt, pepper, and the cloves powder for a few minutes.
Stir in the honey and caramelize.
Add the balsamic, stir well, and reduce it by more than half.
Now add in the crushed tomatoes and cook a couple of minutes longer until to paste.
Remove from the heat, mix the basil in, and set aside.

Barolo Glaze

Ingredients
1 qt of Barolo red wine
½ carrot finely diced
½ stalk of celery finely diced
2 small shallots finely diced
1 oz of dry porcini mushrooms

1 tsp of whole black peppercorns
1 sprig of rosemary
2 sage leaves
2 sprigs of thyme
2 bay leaves
2 cups of veal stock reduction
Salt

Directions
Combine all ingredients in a small pot, except the veal stock, and reduce the liquid by half at moderate fire.
Now add the veal stock, bring to boil again and simmer down to more than half its original volume again to a thick glaze.
Filter through a fine mash and set aside.

To Serve
On a hot square plate place the dehydrated round speck cage right in the center.
Very carefully place the first layer of chestnut mashed purée inside and spread it all the way through the sides, creating a base for our dish.
The second layer of the caramelized quince ragù is applied in the same way, pressing down firmly with a spoon and in circular motion. It is very important not to break the speck cage or the whole dish will need to be re-plated.
On a cutting board slice the breasts of squab out of its carcass and repeat with the legs. Set aside on a towel in order to soak the excess juices and to dry it out a little.
Place the portioned squab on top of the quince inside the cage with the legs up, leaning on the breasts, apply a thin film of the Barolo glaze, and finish decorating with the crunchy spinach leaves right on top of it, creating a little elevation.
Drizzle more Barolo glaze around the dish in a circular motion and finish by dotting with extra virgin olive oil.

Rabbit Crépinette with Parma/Artichokes, Black Truffles, Creamy Sage Sauce, Port Wine Reduction, and Savory Ramps

I am aware that in America rabbit meat is not very popular and definitely not a first choice for any average dinner table across the country. Every time I get in a conversation about rabbit preparations, recipes, or traditional dishes there is always one person who gets horrified by the thought of eating the poor, loved and defenseless Easter bunny.

Jaw dropping, head-shaking and wide-open eyes often accompany comments such as, "Oh noooo! Dear Lord, how could you? Poor baby! That's terrible!" I could write an entire chapter about comments I have heard over the past 27 years.

Unfortunately for those who never tried rabbit meat or for those who have preconceived ideas about diversifying, rabbit is an incredibly delicate, tasty and intelligent alternative to chicken or pork for white meat. Cultural differences divide masses about gastronomic preferences on comfort food, on what is considered a delicacy, and on what is ordinary.

In most of Europe rabbit meat is as ordinary as chicken, beef or pork, and it is widely available and appreciated in all markets and butcher stores. Rabbit is considered a backyard animal where up until 50 years ago most of the countryside families would raise them along with chickens and ducks. Times change and with it the way people eat: rabbit is becoming more popular in America, and people tend to appreciate it now more than ever. It makes its appearances on Italian and French restaurant menus, but also on new American bistros and in some Asian eateries. This recipe is quite different from any of the commonly known traditional preparations as I marinate its boneless meat and mix it with prosciutto, black truffles and artichoke hearts, and wrap it in caul fat (the thin membrane which surrounds the stomach) in a thick-shaped log. I roast it crispy on the outside, but extremely moist and juicy on the inside, and I portion it over silky sage sauce, Port wine reduction, and savory ramps.

If this is your first time experimenting with rabbit meat I would definitely suggest you try this recipe in order to fully understand and appreciate how delicate and tender it really is.

Ingredient

2 lbs of boneless rabbit meat from thighs and loins cut in small strips
6 slices of Parma prosciutto cut in small strips
4 roasted artichoke hearts cubed in half inch size
½ sprig of rosemary chopped
2 sage leaves chopped
4-6 oz of caul fat
½ oz of black truffle shaves
Salt
Ground white pepper
1 tbsp of black truffle oil
The tip of a teaspoon of minced garlic
2 tbsp of olive oil for cooking
1 shallot halved
2 garlic cloves mashed
1 tbsp of butter
1 sprig of thyme
Seasonal micro greens

Directions

Marinate the meat by combining it with the herbs, the minced garlic, the Parma, the diced artichoke hearts, salt, pepper, the sliced truffles, and the black truffle oil.
Mix well and set in the refrigerator about a day.
Roll out the caul fat and on a working table create a layer, keeping it moist with water in order to prevent from drying it out.
Form a small log with the marinated meat right in the center of it.
Wrap the caul fat around it just like a burrito: on the sides and by rolling it forward, keeping it very tight and firm into a log approximately 2 inches in diameter.
With a butcher string tie the log across it to prevent it coming undone during the cooking process.

Creamy Sage Sauce

Ingredients
2 oz of fresh sage leaves
¾ cup of veal stock reduction
1 cup of heavy cream
4 slices of paper thin cut potatoes
1 small shallot finely chopped
1 tbsp of butter
Salt
Ground white pepper

Directions
Blanch the sage leaves in boiling water a few seconds and set aside.
In a small pan cook the shallots and the potatoes with the butter and only half the sage leaves till translucent. Add the veal stock, salt and pepper and reduce by half at moderate fire.
Now stir in the heavy cream, the rest of the sage leaves, and reduce to half.
Transfer the sauce to a high-speed blender to create a fine, smooth, bright-colored sauce.
Chill over ice bath immediately.

Port Wine Reduction

See Hot Starters chapter from "Winter Poached Duck Egg and Crunchy Stuffed Sage Leaves" recipe *(Page 126)*.

Savory Ramps

Ingredients
2 oz of small young ramps
1 thin slice of pancetta chopped
½ tbsp of butter
½ tbsp of olive oil
The tip of a teaspoon of minced garlic
½ tbsp of honey
1 tbsp of white wine vinegar
Salt
Cracked black peppercorns

2 basil leaves chopped
2 tbsp of chicken broth

Directions

Wash the ramps and blanch them in salted water. Cut them in half lengthwise once cold and set aside.

In a small pan roast the pancetta with the oil, the butter and the garlic, add the ramps, salt and pepper. Drop the honey, let it caramelize a little and add the vinegar, reduce almost entirely and add the chicken broth and simmer a couple of minutes.

Remove from the stove, add the basil and set aside till serving time.

To Serve

In a hot medium-size pan sear the rabbit crépinette with the olive oil and the butter, the mashed garlic cloves, the thyme sprig, and the halved shallot. Color well on all sides, dust with pepper and salt, and transfer to a hot oven at 400 degrees about 8-10 minutes.

Once ready, set the crépinette aside on a warm place.

On a round hot plate place a couple of spoons of the creamy sage sauce right in the center and in a circular motion spread it evenly with a spoon.

Cut 8 oz piece of crépinette from the roasted log and lace it in half, creating two thick discs of 4 oz each.

Place the first one flat off-center on the sage sauce and the second one upright resting on a side right next to it, looking like a wheel showing its stuffing.

Carefully place the roasted ramps one by one on top of the flat crépinette piece, creating elevation, and finish decorating with seasonal micro greens.

Drizzle some of the Port wine sauce with a spoon in a circular motion around the dish.

Serve immediately.

Slow Roast Porchetta with Cracked Fennel Seeds and Piadina Bread

If I wrote a cookbook just about comfort food I would insist on a picture of this recipe for the front cover. It does not come any simpler than this: pork stuffed with pork. What's the catch and who's the genius who elevated poor, simple street food to a salivating joyful culinary party each time the name of porchetta is mentioned out loud? Its simplicity is basic; the cooking process elementary. The ingredients used are ordinary and the concept of this dish is so mediocre and plain the only other similar preparation that comes to mind is bread.

Bread is even simpler, but even more important on the table of each and every diner: when there is abundance no one pays attention to it, but when there is none, it is like missing oxygen, gasping for much needed air. No one really knows the origins of this dish or how it came about other than it is from the Umbria region, but many swear the Romans were the ones who started cooking it on underground spits for hours, stuffing it with innards instead of the traditional pork loin. Porchetta in central Italy is so common and ordinary that you can find food trucks in the streets selling the whole stuffed animal, carving it into sandwiches and selling it by weighted portions. The most difficult task is the boning part that usually takes time, skill and undivided attention. It is very important not to cut through the skin as it serves as a protective blanket throughout the cooking process and keeps the inside meat moist.

Nowadays, using young pigs is preferred over other larger animals (in Roman and Medieval times they roasted 100 pound pigs on a spit in the town square for many hours). The meat is much more tender, and the whole dish cooks much faster, under three hours. I like to add cracked fennel seeds from Sicily that my mother provides me from time to time: they are so full of flavor, spreading an incredible and unmistakable aroma through the meat while cooking. They blend perfectly with the garlic, the herbs, and the cracked black peppercorns. During the cooking process the fat melts and the skin turns crispy, creating an incredible combination of flavors and comfort even when the meat is reheated a few days later.

If you are a fan of pork, you will find your Mecca in this preparation: it is very easy to let yourself fill with excitement for something so simple and comforting, especially if paired with compatible food such as rustic homemade piadina.

This is a skillet or oven-cooked thin bread made only with warm water, flour and lard. Originally from the Emilia Romagna region, piadina is round-shaped, thin, and consumed on a daily basis, warmed, with cheese, prosciutto, in sandwiches, and for quick snacks. There are stands that make piadina bread on a skillet right in front of you. I remember I was in Riccione with my sister many years ago and the smell of freshly cooked piadina captured me to a nearby roadside stand. I ended up having three orders of it filled with sliced Parma prosciutto and scamorza cheese. I felt like I was in paradise.

I love to serve my version of porchetta with freshly made hot piadinas as I feel it completes this dish and elevates it to higher level of appreciation.

Ingredients
1 whole baby pig of about 15-18 lbs
1 whole pork loin boneless of about 6-8 lbs
The full amount of one porchetta spice marinate recipe from below
Salt
2 qts of chicken broth

Directions
Remove the head from the body and with a boning knife carefully bone out the entire baby pig without piercing its skin.
Spread some of the marinate spice all over the pork loin and set aside.
Salt the inside of the boneless pig and evenly spread the marinade thoroughly.
Lay the pork loin in the middle of the pig and roll the skin over it, closing any openings by rolling it a few times so the loin can properly set tight.
Tie the porchetta very tight with a butcher string, dust with salt and transfer to a large baking pan.
Cook in hot oven at 325 degrees approximately 2½-3 hours.
When done, cool at room temperature, and then cut the whole porchetta into 4 large logs for easier handling and storing.
Place the baking pan on the stove and add the chicken broth in with the cooking liquid and roasting juices. Scrape the bottom and the sides of the pan until all comes off and reduce on medium heat about 10 minutes.
Filter through fine mesh and set aside until serving time.

Porchetta Spice Marinade

Ingredients
½ cup fennel seeds cracked
½ cup olive oil
1½ cups chopped rosemary
5 tbsp minced garlic
½ cup cracked black peppercorns

Directions
In a mixing bowl combine all ingredients together and store in refrigerator.

Piadina Bread

Ingredients
2 lbs of unbleached flour
1 tbsp of salt
7 oz of lard
Less than a cup of hot water

Directions
In a small mixer with the hook attachment, combine the flour and the lard with the salt at low speed, adding the hot water gradually until the dough turns smooth and elastic.
Remove the dough from the mixer and cover it with plastic film for approximately 45 minutes at room temperature.
Roll the dough in a long log, divide it in 10 portions, and roll them into small balls.
With the help of a rolling pin flatten each ball into a thin disc of about 10 inches in diameter; heat a skillet pan on a stove at moderate flame, and cook the piadina on both sides about 3 minutes total, pressing occasionally with a spatula on the bubbles that will rise out of the dough.
Best if served immediately.

To Serve
It is kind of hard to set rules for how the porchetta should be served or consumed. I like mine thin-sliced and crispy with very little sauce. Others would rather have very thick slices served on their plates like a steak. Fast pacers would fold a hot piadina around warm or

cold slices of porchetta and enjoy it as a sandwich with a simple glass of wine, standing up at lunch time on their break at a local taverna or at a roadside vending stand shooting the breeze.
For culinary correctness I would slice some in thin/medium thickness and warm it with a little of the stock made from the baking pan's leftover juices.
Additionally, I would serve some crunchy fingerling potatoes and/or sautéed broccolini and of course a warm piadina.

Grappa Marinated Venison Saddle with Balsamic Chocolate Sauce, Mashed Cauliflower Purée, Crunchy Porcini/Potato Mat, and Sour Huckleberries Jam

Deer meat is one of those foods either consumed a lot or not at all. Take such places as the northern and midwest states of America: venison, elk and deer meat is fresh and abundant and a natural part of daily family meals. Other parts of America have never tasted deer meat and are not very familiar with it. I had numerous conversations with people whose understanding or notion of deer and venison was strictly limited to Disney's animated feature cartoon *Bambi*. I had the privilege of spending a whole fantastic year in Cooperstown, home of the Baseball Hall of Fame, in upstate New York consulting for a bed and breakfast scheduled to open at the end of summer 2006. A beautiful property located by the spectacular and breathtaking Otsego Lake, a trap for quality tourists. When I started interviewing and hiring employees I wanted to build a team I could really rely on with continuity, hard work and professionalism, but when hunting season opened the majority of them disappeared for days at a time. I was aiming high!

They would not even call to notify us. When a few days later they reported back to work the most common excuse was: "I went hunting for a few days. Sorry, I could not call. There was no cell service in the woods." Hunters load on venison meat like I have never seen before: they butcher the whole animal, portion and freeze mostly the loins and occasionally a few legs for the next several months.

I personally love venison. I enjoy it all: the loins and the legs. I enjoy making sausages and stews; I love to braise the shoulders and to make osso buco out of their shanks. I shape its ground meat into hamburgers and make meatballs. In Cooperstown, once I even salted the whole leg and made a fantastic prosciutto out of it. The possibilities in preparations are infinite, just like this recipe that highlights the natural ingredients commonly found in a deer's natural habitat.

The real surprise, however, is in the sauce. By making a balsamic vinegar sauce and melting in a few dark chocolate chips I create a very unusual sweet and sour aroma dense with silky heartiness. It is a perfect match for the grappa-marinated loin. The porcini mushrooms deliver comforting taste in a crunchy tablecloth-like concept for the whole dish to sit on. The mashed cauliflower is a wonderful alternative for the too often present on every menu potato purée. The sour huckleberry jam is very well balanced between its own sugar and the added vinegar/lemon juices serving as an unusual, but intelligent palate cleanser.

Ingredients
7 oz of venison loin cleaned and peeled
2 oz of unflavored grappa
1 sprig of thyme
1 sprig of rosemary
1 sage leaf
1 juniper berry crushed with the knife
1 bay leaf
1 oz of red wine
1 garlic clove mashed
Crushed black peppercorns
1 tbsp of olive oil
Salt
Ground white pepper
A few midnight spice micro greens
A few burgundy amaranth micro greens

Equipment Needed

One rectangular metallic mold approximately 5 inches long x 1½ inches wide x 1 inch tall.

Directions
Combine and mix all the ingredients together in a small deep pan, and marinate the venison loin in it for at least a couple of days, making sure the liquid covers the meat entirely.
At serving time dry the loin with a towel and sear both sides in a small pan with the mashed garlic and the herbs taken from the marinating liquid and olive oil.
Dust with salt and pepper and finish in the oven a couple minutes at 400 degrees till medium rare.
Set aside and keep warm.

Mashed Cauliflower Purée

Ingredients
1 lb of cauliflowers thinly sliced
3 garlic cloves mashed
1 very small white onion thinly sliced
2 small fillets of anchovies
3 oz of chicken broth
1 oz of excellent extra virgin olive oil
2 oz of butter
1½ oz of heavy cream
Salt
Ground white pepper

Directions
In a medium-size pan heat the oil and the butter, and golden the mashed garlic.
Add the anchovies and the onions, and cook a few minutes till the onions are translucent.
Now add the cauliflowers, salt and pepper, and cook till soft.
Pour in the chicken broth and reduce by half, finish by adding the heavy cream and reduce by half under moderate fire.
Transfer the mix to a high-speed blender till extremely fine.
Taste for salt and pepper and chill immediately on ice bath.

Balsamic Chocolate Sauce

Ingredients
3 cups of balsamic vinegar
1 sprig of rosemary

2 sage leaves
1 sprig of thyme
1 garlic clove mashed
1 very small shallot sliced
1½ cups of veal stock reduction
Salt
Ground white pepper
½ oz of dry porcini mushrooms
A few slices of carrots chopped
½ stalk of celery chopped
2 tbsp of honey at room temperature
8 pieces of dark chocolate chips
1 tbsp of olive oil

Directions
In a medium-size pan cook the rosemary, sage, celery, carrots thyme, garlic, and shallot with the olive oil until translucent.
Add the honey and caramelize golden, now add the balsamic vinegar, the dry porcini mushrooms, salt, pepper, and reduce the liquid by half.
Add the veal stock reduction and reduce the liquid by half again.
Remove from the stove, add in the chocolate chips and stir well until completely melted.
Filter the sauce through a fine mesh and set aside.

Crunchy Porcini Potato Mat

Ingredients
1 medium-size fresh porcini mushroom, thinly sliced
1 small Yukon potato paper, thin sliced
A dash of chopped rosemary
A dash of chopped sage
The tip of a teaspoon of minced garlic
1 tbsp of grated Parmesan Reggiano cheese
½ tbsp of melted butter
Salt
Ground white pepper

Directions
With a hand mandolin slice the potato and the mushroom paper-thin and set aside separately.

Create a rectangular strip of approximately 3 x 8 inches by overlapping and alternating slices of potatoes with the mushrooms on a silicone baking mat.
Brush the top with melted butter, sprinkle with salt, white pepper, the herbs and the grated Parmesan cheese.
Bake in hot oven at 375 degrees approximately 15 minutes.
Remove from the oven when crispy and colored, and set aside to cool.

Sour Huckleberries Jam

Ingredients
2 cups of fresh or frozen huckleberries
1 cup of sugar
¾ oz of fruit pectin
1 lemon juice each
The grated peel of ¼ lemon
Salt
Ground white pepper
1 tbsp of white wine vinegar
1 bay leaf
Less than half tsp of butter

Equipment Needed

Small glass jars with metallic cap.

Directions
In a small pot combine the huckleberries, the lemon juice, the vinegar, and the lemon peel.
With a spoon lightly crush the berries, add the pectin, the bay leaf, and bring to boil over high flame.
Stirring constantly add the sugar, salt, pepper and the butter, and keep cooking about one minute more.
Remove from the stove and skim the foam from the top.
Discard the bay leaf.
Fill a glass jar, cap it, and process in hot bath boiling water about 3 minutes.
When ready, place upside-down on a working table till at room temperature.

To Serve

Place the warm, crunchy porcini potato mat in the middle of a hot rectangular plate.

Right on top of it place the metallic mold perfectly centered.

Fill its base by half with the mashed cauliflower purée.

Thinly slice the venison loin and set on a towel to absorb all the excess juices.

Place on top of the mashed cauliflower purée fan-style, covering its entire surface lengthwise.

Press down gently to set firm and remove the mold.

Coat the fanned venison with a couple of spoons of the balsamic chocolate sauce and decorate the top with some of the midnight spice micro greens.

On the plate, alongside the venison bar, pipe a very small strip of the sour huckleberry jam and top with a few of the burgundy amaranth micro leaves.

Finish by dotting some more of the balsamic chocolate sauce in various areas of the plate.

Bento Box: Marinated Pork Ribs, Italian Sausage, Meatballs "Al Sugo," Oven-Cooked Veal Stew

I love Japanese culture, its food, and its traditions with great admiration.

When I originally had the idea to combine very simple Italian home food into a Japanese bento box I think I broke every culture barrier there was. Sometimes I come across culinary ideas that make perfect sense in my head and work well when I combine it with opposite lifestyles, even if different or traditionally apart from each other.

I remember a few years back I used to serve spaghetti in a traditional Chinese to-go container with chopsticks for visual shock and playfulness. Guests would open and find homemade spaghettini tossed with mixed shellfish: an Italian trademark hosted in a symbolic Asian vehicle. It worked great as it gave the appearance and the idea of eating Chinese lo mein in an Italian restaurant. The goal was to shock my guests at first, then to acknowledge the mismatch, and finally to appreciate both food and concept. The bento box delivers the exact same message.

This is a dish I exclusively serve for lunch as in my past restaurants I have always created a sort of "deal meal" for my regular customers, especially those who were on a short timeframe or wanted a variety pack in terms of diversion and value. I have always been somehow against multi-compartment accessories evoking fast food or cafeteria-like trays made of Styrofoam or plastic. I just hate to serve the food I love so much in an inadequate vehicle. If I were given a choice I would rather eat it with my hands directly out of the pan it cooked in.

But Japanese culture is fantastic in dedicating time even to the smallest details, and so I purchased various beautifully designed 4-compartment ceramic bento boxes to elevate this poor and simple food court-like concept to one of high quality.

All four sections of the box are filled with comfort food: Pork ribs are marinated and slowly cooked in a spice mix I personally love and combined myself. The grilled pork sausage is made in the same fashion my late uncle Peppino made in his glorious days when I was just a little kid and was fascinated by the way he would manually fill the casings, pushing the ground meat through an old meat grinder. The meatballs are cooked the same way my Nonna Corradina used to make, slowly braising in the oven with its sugo tomato sauce. Finally, the veal stew brings comfort to the cold and chilly days, potatoes and peas marry perfectly with the veal cubes.

In few words, this is a quality variety pack for home-food meat lovers.

Marinated Pork Ribs

Ingredients

2 slabs of baby pork back ribs
1 cup of ribs marinating wet dust
Salt
4 oz of butter slices

Directions

Spread the marinating wet dust abundantly on the rib slabs with your hands and transfer to the refrigerator, marinating a couple of days covered with plastic.

Take the slabs out of the refrigerator and set them out till at room temperature.
Color the slabs on a very hot grill on both sides a few minutes, dust with abundant salt and sit them on a perforated double pan.
Pour the leftover marinating juice on top of the meat, and place the butter slices across and double-cover with aluminum foil.
Bake in hot oven at 325 for approximately 2½ -3 hours.

Rib's Marinating Wet Dust

Ingredients
5 garlic cloves
2 shallots chopped
1½ sprigs of rosemary chopped
1½ tablespoon cracked black peppercorns
2½ sprigs of thyme chopped
1½ tablespoon of paprika
½ tablespoon red-hot crushed chili pepper
1 cup honey
¾ cup red vinegar
1 tablespoon cumin ground
1 tablespoon coriander ground
1 teaspoon Tabasco® sauce
1 tablespoon salt

Directions
Blend all ingredients and generously brush the ribs and marinate for a day in the refrigerator.

To Serve
Slice the hot ribs, sprinkle with a little crystallized salt as needed, and place them in their bento box compartment.

The Italian Sausage

Ingredients
2½ lbs of pork butts
1 tsp of sugar
½ tbsp of cracked black peppercorns
1 tsp of cracked fennel seeds
½ cup of iced water

1 tbsp of salt
1 tsp of ground cumin
1 tsp of cracked caraway seeds
1 tsp of minced garlic
½ lb of excellent lard cut in thick slices
Pork casings

Tools and Equipment Needed
A small sausage stuffer

Directions
Clean the pork butt, removing all the cartilages and excess fat.
Cut the pork and the lard in medium/small size cubes, and transfer to the refrigerator about 3 hours.
When chilled pass it all through a meat grinder with large-hole blade.
In a small bowl combine all other spices and ingredients mixing into the marinade base for the sausage.
Combine the ground meat with the marinate mix, transfer to the refrigerator, and marinate one day.
Load the sausage stuffer and fill in the casings to approximately 4-5 inch-long sausages.

Pistou Green Sauce

Ingredients
½ cup of basil leaves
1 cup of Italian parsley leaves
1 large garlic clove
½ oz of white bread
1½ tbsp of white wine vinegar
½ cup of extra virgin olive oil
Salt
Ground white pepper
½ tbsp of small capers
1 fillet of anchovy in oil

Directions
Soak the white bread with the vinegar and combine all ingredients in a high-speed blender, drizzle the oil in a little at a time to form a smooth paste.

Taste for salt and pepper.

To Serve
Place a tablespoon of the room-temperature pistou green sauce in the bento box compartment.
Grill the link to medium and place the sausage on top of the sauce.

Meatballs "Al Sugo"

Ingredients
1 lb of ground beef
1½ lbs of ground pork
¼ cup of toasted pine nuts
½ cup of raisins soaked in water
¼ cup of chopped parsley
1 tsp of minced garlic
½ cup of grated Parmesan Reggiano cheese
½ tbsp of salt
½ tbsp of ground white pepper
Enough vegetable or blended oil to fry the meatballs

Directions
In a bowl combine all the ingredients and mix them together to form 2 oz meatballs.
Fry them in hot oil until golden and set them aside on parchment paper.
Place all the cooked meatballs in a deep baking pan and add the sugo tomato sauce, covering them completely.
Double-seal the pan with foil and bake in hot oven at 250 degrees about 2 hours.

Sugo tomato sauce
¾ cup of extra virgin olive oil
5 lbs of canned San Marzano tomatoes puréed
2 onions thinly sliced
8 garlic cloves hand mashed
2 tbsp of salt
1 tbsp of ground white pepper
2 cups of chicken broth
3 leaves of basil

Directions
In a pan sauté the sliced onions and the mashed garlic with the olive oil.
When translucent add the tomato purée, the salt, the pepper, the basil leaves and the chicken broth and cook about 8-10 minutes.
Set aside to cool.
Transfer the sauce to a high-speed blender till velvety.
Add salt and pepper if necessary.

Soft Black Pepper Polenta

Ingredients
7 oz of freshly ground organic yellow polenta
3 cups of water
2 oz butter
½ tbsp of cracked black peppercorns
½ cup of grated Parmesan Reggiano cheese
Salt

Directions
In a small pan bring the water to boil with the butter and the salt.
Whisk in the polenta slowly, drizzling and combining into a soft paste cooking for a few minutes only under low fire until it thickens.
Remove from the fire, add the pepper, the remaining butter, the cheese, and stir until all ingredients are mixed together into a smooth soft paste.

Sauté Broccoli Rabé

Ingredients
Broccoli rabé florets
Extra virgin olive oil
A few garlic shaves
Salt
Crushed black peppercorns
Spicy hot red pepper
Freshly grated pecorino cheese snow
½ fillet of anchovy

Directions
Blanch the broccoli rabé florets in salted water a few seconds only.
In a small pan golden the garlic slices with the extra virgin olive oil and the anchovy fillet.
Add the broccoli rabé in and dust with the hot pepper, salt, black pepper.
Toss for a few seconds and remove from the fire.
Transfer the broccoli to a plate.

To Serve
Place a couple of tablespoons of soft polenta on one of the bento box compartment, add one meatball and cover with one spoonful of tomato sauce and a few florets of the sauté broccoli rabé.
Finish with a sprinkle of the grated pecorino cheese.

Oven-Cooked Veal Stew

Ingredients
2½ lbs of veal shoulder cubed in one inch
2 medium-size carrots diced
1 small onion diced
3 garlic cloves shaved
2 medium-size Yukon potatoes cubed in one inch
½ cup of dry porcini mushrooms soaked in one cup of water and finely chopped
¼ cup of extra virgin olive oil
5 leaves of sage chopped
2 sprigs of rosemary chopped
1½ cups of hand crushed Italian plum canned tomatoes
1¼ cups of red wine
10 oz of English peas
1½ cups of chicken broth
Salt
Ground white pepper
A few assorted micro green leaves

Directions
Sauté the veal cubes in olive oil at high flame till brown.
Place a large baking pan on the stove and at high flame sauté the onions, the carrots, the garlic, and the herbs with the extra virgin olive oil till translucent.

Add in the sautéed veal cubes, salt, pepper, and cook about 10 minutes, stirring occasionally.
Add the red wine and evaporate almost entirely, now add the tomatoes, the potatoes, and the chopped porcini and its soaking water.
Simmer 10 more minutes and then add the chicken broth.
Bring the stew to boil, taste for salt and pepper, double-cover the pan with aluminum foil and bake in hot oven at 365 degrees approximately 2 hours.
Take the stew out of the oven and remove the foil, stir in the raw peas and mix well, but delicately in order not to break the veal cubes.

To Serve
Place a couple of tablespoons of the hot veal stew in the bento box compartment and top with a few micro green leaves.

Roasted Beef Tenderloin with Gorgonzola Pistachio Sauce and Morelles /Prosciutto Ragù with Black Truffle Stuffed Zucchini Blossoms, Balsamic Spray Scent

No! That is not an error. It really says "roasted beef tenderloin with Gorgonzola pistachio sauce." It may sound vulgar, inappropriate and unappealing, yet it made a believer and a fan of me. I chose to include this recipe because I was introduced to it by Roberto Donna over 27 years ago. On November 17, 1986, I landed at Washington National Airport directly from San Diego, California. A very skinny, young and energetic Roberto was at the domestic arrivals area wearing a red sweater, holding his car keys, fidgeting, and looking at his watch every few seconds.

"Are you Enzo? Hee hee hee. Roberto. Nice to meet you. C'mon, let's go! I need to get back to the restaurant. We're very busy tonight."

Before I could open my mouth or formulate an answer he had already grabbed my suitcase, turned his back, and sprinted toward the exit doors into the parking lot. I guess it did not really matter at that point if I had answered, "No, sir, my name is Roger." I must have looked like the usual and average Enzo.

He opened the back door of his green Jeep Cherokee.

"Oh no!" he said, pausing a second. He looked over both his shoulders and then asked me, "Do you see anyone around? Well, it does not matter. It's dark, no one will see us. Give me a hand."

Roberto apparently had cleaned his yard that very morning, filling nine 50-gallon trash bags of leaves, and forgot to dispose of them before he came to the airport. So now we are unloading the bags from his Jeep to the nearby sidewalk to make room for my suitcase like a couple of outlaws pressured for time during a heist. Once finished, he asked me to hurry. I got in the car, and we sprinted like mad men. As he drove away, I saw the bags all lined up in my side-view mirror. I turned toward him with inquisitive eyes and before I could say a word he spoke.

"Don't worry! They got people to clean stuff like that. It's normal," he reassured me, and off we went.

We entered the legendary Galileo restaurant's kitchen from the back door facing the alley. The very first dish I saw coming out from the hot line was a grilled fillet of beef entirely covered with a thick cheesy sauce, looking like a mediocre cafeteria item. "Where the hell am I?" I started wondering. As the evening progressed I was explained the concept of the restaurant, studied a few dishes and met everyone, but what really intrigued me was the dish I first saw, so I asked about it.

"It's a very simple and basic steakhouse-like dish," he said. "I had dinner with my girlfriend last year at a local restaurant and my rib eye was covered with creamy blue cheese sauce, so I changed it and now I use Gorgonzola and pistachio to make it Italian. It's actually quite good. Here, taste."

Very hesitantly I did. He was right. It was not good: It was excellent. What a surprise. Not in 100 years would I have imagined such a spot-on marriage of textures and flavors, yet so comforting and basic. Over the past three decades I have only cooked this dish on occasion, but in the past five years I decided to reinvent, finesse and flirt with it to elevate it to a higher level of appreciation and give it the proper attention it deserves. As usual I implemented changes and made it mine.

I chose to sous vide the beef tenderloin for a better and a more uniform cooking process. Then I seared it instead of grilling it and made a much lighter version of the Gorgonzola sauce. I made a ragù of fresh morelles mushrooms and Parma prosciutto to better connect the sauce to the meat and to give more substance to the dish. What I really love, however, are the tempura-style zucchini blossoms filled with black truffles. They are miniature explosions of flavor: it is like eating a hamburger and a side of fries.

When I bite into the blossoms I feel like my palate is traveling to an unexplored crunchy and luxurious dimension. The balsamic vinegar adds diversity and the right tones of acidity connecting sauce and mushrooms just like a microscopic stinging rain falling down on a cloudy day: tolerable, pleasant and definitely different sprayed out like a perfume bottle in front of your guests.

Ingredients
7 oz of cleaned peeled and portioned beef tenderloin
3 oz of butter
Salt
Ground white pepper
1 shallot halved
1 rosemary sprig
1 thyme sprig
2 sage leaves
Assorted micro greens

Special Equipment Needed
Sous vide heating immersion circulator unit
Sous vide cooking plastic bag
Vacuum-sealing machine
A small decorative spray perfume bottle

Directions
We are following the same directions as for the Roasted Veal Fillet recipe on page 405 in preparation to cook the beef tenderloin sous vide style: wrap one leaf of sage and half sprig of rosemary in plastic film creating a small roll of about 2 inches long, cut both

ends open so the flavor of the herbs can easily escape during the cooking process.
Place the roll in the bag along with 1 oz of butter and the beef tenderloin seasoned with white pepper only.
Vacuum seal the bag and immerge it in the already hot water tub with the thermo-circulator and cook approximately 1 hour at 46 degrees Celsius. If your intent is to serve it right away and complete a meal, then open the bag once cooked and sear to completion. However if your intent is to cook and preserve for later use we will need to stop and reverse the cooking process by dropping the bag in ice bath till completely cold. We will use this reverse step each time we cook sous vide: immerge the already cooked bag into the already hot water tub with the thermo-circulator and bring it back up to 46 degrees Celsius before searing it.
In a medium-size pan melt 2 oz of the butter with the shallot and the herbs and at high flame, dust with salt and pepper and sear all sides crispy. The beef tenderloin should be at rare-medium rare temperature at this point, however if it needs to cook longer transfer the fillet to a hot oven for a few extra minutes.
Set aside ready to serve in warm place.

Gorgonzola Pistachio Sauce

Ingredients
1 oz of Gorgonzola cheese cubed and at room temperature
1 oz of pistachios chopped
2 sage leaves chopped
Less then ½ oz of shallot finely chopped
1 oz of butter
3 oz of heavy cream
2 oz of veal juice reduction
Ground white pepper

Directions
In a small pan cook the chopped shallots with the butter, the sage, and half the pistachios, and then add the cubed Gorgonzola cheese.
On low flame stir with a spoon a few seconds, making sure the cheese melts without burning or cooking excessively.
Add the veal juice reduction, the pepper and blend in.
Reduce to half the amount and pour in the heavy cream.

Cook one more minute or so until the sauce turns velvety and smooth.
Sprinkle in the rest or the chopped pistachio, mix and set aside.

Morelles Mushrooms and Parma Prosciutto Ragù

Ingredients
4 oz of fresh morelles mushrooms coin sliced
2 medium-size shallots thinly sliced
The tip of a teaspoon of minced garlic
2 oz of Parma prosciutto thinly sliced in wide strips
1 oz of butter
2 sage leaves chopped
Salt
Ground white pepper
3 oz of chicken broth
2 basil leaves chopped

Directions
In a medium-size pan cook the prosciutto with the butter, add the sage, the shallots, and the garlic and cook till translucent.
Add the mushrooms and sauté about a minute.
Pour in the chicken broth, add the salt and pepper, and reduce the liquid down to half.
Remove from stove, add the chopped basil, mix, and set aside.

Stuffed Zucchini Blossoms with Ricotta and Black Truffles Tempura-Style

Ingredients
3-4 fresh large zucchini blossoms
4 oz of ricotta cheese impastata
1½ tbsp of grated Parmesan Reggiano cheese
1 oz of fontina cheese Aosta diced in small cubes
Salt
Ground white pepper
½ tsp of black truffle oil
¼ oz of finely chopped fresh black truffle

Directions
Mix the ricotta cheese with the salt, the pepper, the truffles, the truffle oil, the Parmesan, and the finely diced Fontina cheese to a very thick paste
Taste for salt and pepper, and transfer to a disposable pastry bag.
Stuff the zucchini blossoms, seal by twisting the tops, and set aside till serving time.

Tempura Batter

See Appetite Openers chapter from "Fava Beans Stuffed Tempura Zucchini Blossoms" recipe *(Page 52)*.

Balsamic Spray Scent

Place some aged balsamic vinegar into a decorative empty perfume bottle, test for the amount of liquid released at each pump in order to better dose the needed amount, and set aside.

To Serve
Preferably on a square hot plate lay a couple of tablespoons of Gorgonzola sauce across the plate. In the center of the dish place the seared fillet of beef and top it with a couple of tablespoons of the morelles mushrooms ragù.
Place the crispy zucchini blossoms firelog-style on one side of the dish, preferably not on top of the sauce in order to preserve their crispiness, and fill the empty middle space of it with a few micro greens.
Delicately place additional micro greens on top of the mushrooms for elevation and serve immediately.
Hold the perfume bottle towards the beef and delicately spray a couple of pumps of balsamic vinegar to aromatize the dish.

Boneless Braised Lamb Shank in Gremolata Sauce, Roasted Bell Peppers in Polenta Cage, and Savory Caramelized Bruxelles Sprouts

Everyone knows and loves traditional Italian veal osso buco. In the past decade there has been a nationwide explosion in popularity for lamb osso buco: same concept, different kind of meat. Nowadays it is not unusual to find variations of this great dish made out of venison, pork, boar, and even out of horse meat. Braising our daily choice of shank for hours has become a way of cooking emulated and implemented by many chefs. The word osso in Italian means bone, and buco means hole. This dish is not just about a hole in the bone, it is about the ability and the mastery to cook it correctly, with grace, passion and infinite love. Too many versions are disappointing, a few satisfying, and only some are truly outstanding. During the cooking process most of its fat melts and the meat turns so soft one could literally break it apart using a single breadstick. Many people are under the impression timing is everything: you could bake my shoes in the oven for hours and I can assure you that eventually they will be tender enough to be sliced with a knife.

To correctly braise any shank, one has to understand the basic cooking process and the proper pairing of the ingredients that accompany the overall procedure, while braising each added ingredient is intensified in flavor and smell. Therefore it is extremely important to measure the ingredients accurately in order to create the correct balance for a successful dish. It is not as easy as it seems, and very often simple tasks turn out to be very difficult to achieve. Only after a successful combination/ratio of ingredients and cooking procedure is achieved do I focus on variations for presentation, concept and pairings.

Every time I order a lamb shank at any given restaurant I get surprised by its size: the bone itself reminds me of the *Flintstones* cartoon characters, and the amount of the inedible extra fat wrapped around the meat is so great that at the end of my meal I usually discard more than what I actually eat. Lamb shank is not a fine dish, one of those you will remember for its finesse or for its delicate presentation, but one of the most informal that shares the same group category with meatballs, ribs or meatloaf.

I did not want to reinvent the lamb shank; I just wanted to explore the possibilities to create an elegant and more presentable option without sacrificing the taste or its concept. I cook the shank and I discard its bone and extra fat. I select only the braised meats, along with part of the cooked diced vegetables, and I roll it in a tight, solid logs. I basically serve a thick osso buco patty without the osso and without the buco: an elegant and flavorful dish without any extra added work for the diner. I make a sauce with its cooking juices and vegetables and I create a bright and aromatic gremolata. I love the idea of roasted bell peppers caged within fried polenta logs representing traditional comfort, and the barely poached Bruxelles sprouts sitting on its savory caramelized sauce.

Even after all the changes I applied to it, this is still considered humble comfort food. Sometimes great concepts are achieved by simply moving a few things around without sacrificing the basic elements. Every time I return to the basics it is always a humbling experience: I remember my mom cooking veal osso buco, one of her most exquisite and successful dishes for our enjoyment. A real treat. A real feast. I hope this lamb shank version will give you the same great feelings of love and comfort I experienced while growing up under the mastery of a real wizard who was able to transform a third-rate cut of meat into a delightful delicacy worthy to be craved 35 years later by yours truly.

Braised Lamb Shank

Ingredients

4 medium-size lamb shanks
1 medium-size carrot diced in large cubes
2 stalks of celery diced in large cubes
1 medium-size white onion diced in large cubes
1 rosemary sprig chopped
4 sage leaves chopped
1 small tbsp of minced garlic
1 lb of Italian plum canned tomatoes hand crushed
Salt
Cracked black peppercorns
1 qt of dry red wine
2 cups of chicken broth
2 bay leaves
½ cup of olive oil

Directions

Sear the lamb shanks with salt pepper in olive oil, and set aside. In a bowl prepare the cooking marinate mix combining the diced vegetables, the chopped herbs, the garlic, the hand crushed tomato, salt, pepper, and the red wine, and mix well.

In a baking pan place the seared shanks with the chicken broth and gently cover them with the cooking marinate mix. Dust again with salt and pepper.
Double-seal the pan with aluminum foil and bake in hot oven at 325° about 3 hours. When the meat is tender and falls off its bones, remove it from the oven, uncover the pan, and set aside at room temperature.
Separate the bones and excess fat from the braised meat.
Skim the cooking fat from the liquid, discard the fat, and preserve the remaining cooking liquid with the diced vegetables in a smaller pot for later use.
Lay a sheet of plastic film on a working table and horizontally place some of the braised lamb shank meat mixed with some of the cooking diced vegetables.
Delicately roll the plastic over the meat and by holding the sides roll into a firm and hard log of approximately 2½ inches in diameter and about 8-10 inches long.
Prick the log through the plastic just enough to release the excess air pockets, and place in refrigerator for one day to firm up.

Gremolata Base Sauce

Ingredients
8 oz of Italian parsley
2 basil leaves
1 cup of extra virgin olive oil
2 lemon peels grated
6 garlic cloves
8 oz of chicken broth
Ground white pepper
Salt

Directions
On a cutting board, using a large blade knife roughly chop the parsley, the garlic, and basil.
Transfer to a high-speed blender; add the grated lemon peel, salt, pepper, the extra virgin olive oil, and the chicken broth.
Blend all till a smooth paste of bright-green color.
Taste for salt and pepper.

Roasted Bell Peppers

Ingredients

1 yellow pepper
1 red pepper
1 tbsp of extra virgin olive oil
Pinch of dry oregano
The tip of a teaspoon of minced garlic
Salt
Ground white pepper
½ fillet of anchovy
2 basil leaves chopped
1 tbsp of chicken broth

Directions

Place both peppers in hot oven at 375 degrees about 15 minutes until completely cooked, but still bright in color.

Place them in a small bowl and cover with plastic film, set aside about 30 minutes, then peel them clean.

Quickly wash out the seeds and place them in a strainer about 15 minutes and get rid of the extra water, cut them in strips of about 2 inches wide, and set aside.

In a small hot pan melt the anchovy fillet with the oil; add the garlic and the peppers, salt, white pepper, and the oregano.

Sauté a few seconds only, and add the chicken broth and the basil.

Wait till the liquid is consumed and remove from the stove.

Polenta Cage

See Meat chapter from "Soft Black Pepper Polenta" recipe under "Bento Box: Meatballs Al Sugo." *(Page 431)*

Directions

Make the soft polenta as directed (without the black pepper).

Once cold, cut 6 logs to the dimensions of 4 inches long and ½-inch-thick square.

Dust them very lightly with flour and deep-fry them till crispy at 375 degrees.

Transfer to warm place on deli paper till serving time.

Savory Caramel Sauce

Ingredients
1 shallot chopped
3 oz of pancetta cut in small strips
1 garlic clove shaved
2 tbsp of balsamic vinegar
1½ tbsp of honey
1½ cups of veal stock reduction
2½ oz of Yukon potatoes thinly sliced
3 sage leaves chopped
1 cup of heavy cream
Salt
Ground white pepper

Directions
Roast the pancetta in a medium-size pan in its own fat till crispy and set aside on deli paper.
Preserve the melting fat of the pancetta and with it cook the potatoes, the shallots, the garlic shaves, and the sage till colored.
Add salt and pepper and the honey, caramelize a little, add the balsamic, and reduce by half before adding the veal stock reduction.
Simmer till the sauce is reduced by half and add the heavy cream, simmering 5 more minutes.
Remove from the stove and transfer to a high-speed blender till velvety.
Cool the sauce over ice bath and add the crispy pancetta strips into it while chilling.
At serving time peel, wash and halve the sprouts coin-size.
Blanch them in salted boiling water with a little butter for less than a minute, preserving their bright, natural green color.

To Serve
With a sharp knife slice a portion of the lamb shank roll of approximately 2 inches thick.
Leave the plastic around it and heat it up in warm oven with a couple of spoons of chicken broth until ready to be served.
On a warm square plate place the lamb shank slice on the top left side, delicately remove the plastic around the meat, and dress it with a couple of spoons of the hot gremolata sauce right on it.

On the bottom-left of the plate place one strip of the red and yellow sauté peppers twisted together for visual effect.
Cage them with the fried polenta sticks firelog-style creating elevation.
Finish by decorating the top with a few leaves of micro greens.
On the right side of the plate run a strip of the savory caramel sauce vertically and in symmetry with the rest of the ingredients already plated in order to create a good visual balance.
Place five halves of the Bruxelles sprouts on the sauce, facing up.
Decorate the whole dish by drizzling extra virgin olive oil and cracked black peppercorns.

Chapter Eleven
Delicious Desserts

Albert Einstein once said, "Imagination is more important than knowledge." To my friends, it is no secret I am a huge admirer of Albert Einstein and Leonardo da Vinci, two people who have changed the world forever by simply pursuing their visions and passions with their incredible strengths and beliefs. Wisdom is partially achieved in life only if there is the will to learn from our own mistakes and mentored by wise and superior minds with caring and gentle hearts. At times I think there must be a wisdom gene in our DNA where some are blessed with extras and others have none at all. Wisdom is the missing fifth element of the human nature: only a few individuals are granted the gift of handling life wisely.

It is like being a restaurant manager in so many ways. We must be able to make a decision in situations when professionalism and personal feelings come in conflict. I have learned over the years to choose my battles: fight only the ones worth fighting as I cannot win them all.

Pastry is where the imagination and the full artistry of the mind are put on display for everyone to admire and savor: there must be a little bit of wisdom and a lot of genius in order to shine and to deliver beauty, joy, taste and innovation in a unique and glorious blend. It would be very easy for me to write that I know all the known culinary techniques and procedures and that I excel in anything I do in the kitchen. But the truth is I do not: I excel in some areas and not so much in others. To learn everything there is to learn is one of my personal and professional tasks I am sure I will carry with me forever. Imagination is a different thing, or at least for me. I truly believe I have the gift to foresee the final results of an idea when it first comes to mind: the look of a final progressive dish, the concept of a multi-layered cake, the various ingredients and colorful sauces that pair a culinary assembly or a plated architectural presentation. Some label this as a "vision" or "artistic gift". I label it pure and simple imagination. This is why I agree with Einstein's statement that imagination is more important than knowledge: we must possess a great amount of imagination in order to excel in anything we do because at first there is a lack of knowledge.

I love to dive into pastry work, and when I do I feel like I have been kidnapped in my own isolated cove for hours at a time. Pastry is an art only for those who are predisposed to it. Only those who are patient and fully committed, driven by the desire to see visual results by putting together ingredients can master the craft of pastry in all its glory. Many tasks in pastry work are amazingly discouraging, lengthy and frustrating, but they are all part of the basics. Just imagine how long it takes to temper chocolate, cooking through the different temperature stages when doing sugar work, to bake, to mix, to rise and to assemble. Persistence and patience play major roles for those who are keen to start a career in a pastry workshop before it turns into a daily routine.

Over the years I have noticed many diners lose interest in having dessert at the end of their meals, therefore they waive the option to end their supper with a sweet taste in their mouths. A quick explanation of this is because they are full, but that is not always the case: our brain works in such bizarre ways that our body responds to it consequently.

Just ask yourself why we have cravings when we enter a pastry shop or a candy store even if we are not hungry. What causes temptation? If we ate a sponge we would fill our stomachs, sending signals to our brains we are full. Everything we experience starts from our head. Many times I have read those unappealing menus or heard servers reciting dessert descriptions while dragging their words with notes of discouragement in order to wrap up their evening faster: there is no excitement for the diner to look forward to a great finale. "No, thank you, we will pass on dessert this evening. We're full." But I guarantee there is always room for dessert if the choices are visual and glorious enough to tickle our interest and to trick our brains.

I have formed my personal theory in regards: when a guest starts the meal there is excitement about it as bread and oil are on the table, wine is poured and the food arrives, but throughout the dinner the level of excitement and interest diminishes to a point of steadiness and filling satisfaction. So how can we revive the sparkling enthusiasm that brought my guests to sit at our table in the first place? How can we jump-start their interests again at the end of a meal? That is indeed a very difficult task as only a bolt of lightning would shake them from their seats, unless the dessert options are so tempting and masterfully prepared and absolutely stunning in colorful visual concepts. That is where imagination comes in. That is when I have most of my fun.

Especially in pastry I love to craft preparations that resemble something they are not: see my take on the traditional Sicilian cannolo shaped as a lit cigar with spun sugar smoke and ashes, served in an ashtray, or the vanilla panna cotta crafted as sunny-side up eggs with fake bacon and served in a ceramic sauté pan. Visuals are extremely important at the end of a meal as they are the last thing customers taste, see and remember.

I also like to play with ingredients that are not gastronomically or politically correct for pastry. Take fresh basil for instance: it is used in the kitchen virtually everywhere, but not in desserts. If you find the right way to blend delicate aromas into valid culinary concepts, things might just work well. After playing long enough with it I was able to create a basil sorbet so silky, so aromatic, and so well-balanced it made the talk of the town.

Desserts are often labeled as the best part of a meal and not just by kids. The anticipation of sampling desserts must be rewarded with full satisfaction: proudly, the cannolo cigar attracts so much interest when presented that most of my guests take pictures of it right at the table. To me, that is the greatest compliment I can possibly receive.

I am not a pastry chef by any means, but I have the passion and the will to learn and to experiment with simple ingredients such as sugar, flour, eggs or chocolate that have the power to change my daily mood for the better, to restore a smile on my face, and to make me feel like a kid all over again.

When I was staging food back in Italy as a teenager I loved to visit the pastry room. I always had an interest in watching master pastry chefs at work while tempering chocolate, crafting and decorating multi-layered cakes, combining different textures together, and finally shaping small little jewels way too beautiful to eat. I could watch them for hours absolutely fascinated, taken from reality.

Nowadays I can still spend hours watching and learning, just like a little kid stuck in front of a window looking at desserts and cakes on display in a pastry shop with both hands on the glass, my eyes wide open while my imagination runs wild.

Cannolo Cigar in an Ashtray with Spun Sugar Smoke and Mascarpone Cheese Mousse Ashes

Throughout my childhood I spent long summers in Sicily with my family. Being the son of a very traditional Sicilian man I tend to basically learn and appreciate everything about this glorious island, its history, its people, its dialect, and its culinary traditions. One of the many trademarks of Sicilian cuisine is the worldwide famous cannolo filled with ricotta cheese that populates the tables of most Italian restaurants and pastry shop display cases across the globe. I remember as a kid enjoying cannolos filled with same-day-made fresh ricotta cheese, mixed with bits of chocolate, candied lemon and orange peels. Pastry shops would make the shells right in front of you, and they would fill them at the order to preserve crunchiness. They would dust them with powdered sugar and you were on your way to sweet Heaven.

When I first arrived in America, I remember noticing empty cannolo shell packages at the local grocery store: the shells were laid in a plastic tray over clear wrappings displaying the colors of the Italian flag, advertising "imported handmade Sicilian shells." As any naïve 17-year-old boy who had just landed in a new country and who was about to dive into a different lifestyle, I got so excited about sampling the authentic flavors I grew up with again. With an incredible sense of pride and joy I purchased those shells and went home in such excitement I tore the plastic tray and I shoved a cannolo shell in my mouth the second I crossed the front door. It took me five seconds into chewing to spit it out in absolute disgust: it tasted like plastic, it was stale, and I could still taste the rancid oil it was fried in. "Imported handmade Sicilian shells?" Who are you kidding?

However, I learned not to believe everything you read.

Throughout the years I kept telling that funny story until one day a dear friend of mine who travels for business all over the U.S. and eats at some of the best restaurants in America told me, "I have yet to find a great quality cannolo worthy to be served in any Italian restaurant. Why don't you come up with a spectacular one to blow all the bad ones away?"

Blow away? Sometimes even a simple word can trig and inspire.

It is no secret I love cigars. What if I could create a very delicate version of a Sicilian cannolo looking like a smoking cigar resting in an ashtray? I made a very thin and delicate shell and filled it with impastata ricotta mixed with Sicilian candied orange and lemons, bits of milk chocolate and Sicilian pistachios. I placed a real cigar band on it, and I spun enough sugar to create a lit smoking effect coming out of one end of the cigar. This version of cannolo is incredibly delicate and tasty, and extremely respectful of its origins for taste, but it is also a showcase piece for its inventiveness and a shocking crowd pleaser: almost every time a single order is delivered to the table someone takes pictures of it in appreciation and awe.

It is indeed a very dramatic dish and a very elegant one: I serve it on a cigar ashtray creating a very visual and credible illusion.

Equipment Needed
Large cigar ashtray
Cylindrical metallic cannolo form, ¾-inch diameter
Metallic wand to spin sugar
Large cigar label band
Rectangular plastic template cut out in dimensions of 5 inches long x 4 wide to create the cannolo shell

Ricotta Cheese Filling Cream

Ingredients
1 oz egg yolk
1½ oz sugar
12 oz of ricotta cheese impastata
½ oz of Grand Marnier
2 tbsp of chopped pistachio
2 tbsp of milk chocolate coins quartered
1 oz of Sicilian candied orange peel chopped

1 oz Sicilian candied lemon peel chopped
½ tsp of vanilla beans

Directions
In a table top mixer combine the yolks with the vanilla beans and the sugar till white and foamy.
Gradually add the Grand Marnier and fold in the ricotta cheese.
Add the chopped candied orange, the candied lemon, the chopped milk chocolate, and the pistachio and place in a disposable pastry bag.
Fold in a smooth paste and refrigerate.

Cigar Tuile Shell

Ingredients
4 oz of butter at room temperature
4 oz of honey
¾ cup of AP flour sifted
1½ cups of sugar powder
¼ cup of egg whites whipped stiff peaks

Directions
Whip the egg whites to stiff peaks and set aside.
In a small mixing bowl combine the soft butter with honey and the sugar.
Add the sifted flour and delicately fold in the whipped egg whites to a smooth paste.
Refrigerate 30 minutes.
Lay the plastic stencil for the cannolo on a silicone baking mat and fill in with the mix with the help of an offset spatula.
Remove the stencil and bake at 325 about 6 minutes till golden in color.
Remove from the oven and carefully roll the tulle on the round metallic cannolo shell till hard and perfectly shaped to a cannolo shell.
Twist off the shell from the mold and set aside.

Spun Sugar Smoke

Ingredients
3 oz of decomalt isomalt
1 oz of water

Directions
Combine decomalt and water in a small pot and cook at low flame to hard-crack stage: about 155-165 F.
Set aside.
Dip the wand in the sugar mix and lift it to a steady thick drip before spinning to solid wires.
Shape into a string of smoke and set aside on deli paper.

Mascarpone Cheese Mousse

Ingredients
1 oz of egg yolk
1 oz of sugar
The tip of a teaspoon of vanilla beans
8 oz of mascarpone cheese
½ cup of heavy cream

Directions
Whip the heavy cream till stiff and set aside in the refrigerator.
In a small mixing bowl combine the yolks, the vanilla beans, and sugar till white and foamy.
Delicately, with a spatula, fold in the mascarpone cheese and then add the whipped cream to a smooth consistency.

Cigar Ashes

Ingredients
1 oz of amaretto cookie
1 oz of toasted pistachios
Powdered sugar

Directions
Blend the amaretto and the pistachios together to fine powder.

To Serve
Fill the two ends of the shell with the ricotta mix filling.
Dust the cigar with powdered sugar and place a cigar label on one end.
Lightly wet the opposite end of the shell with Grand Marnier and roll it into the ashes mix to give the visual illusion of a burning cigar.
Place a tablespoon of the mascarpone cheese mousse on one end of the ashtray and sprinkle it abundantly with the cigar ashes.
Place the spun sugar smoke inside the cigar by the burning side and place it facing the mascarpone mousse.
Serve immediately as the sugar smoke will only stay stiff about 45 seconds.

Dark, Milk and White Chocolate

Unlike any other ingredient, chocolate is often associated with happiness, sinful treats, forbidden passions, rich indulgences. Amazing how a single bean produces so much joy: there are infinite types of chocolate available—bitter, milk, dark, even white, which is actually made without the cocoa beans. Originally from Central America, chocolate has been around forever, and it has evolved so much throughout the centuries: these fermented, roasted and ground beans were at first employed as beverages by the Mayans, who would also use them to cook such dishes as the famous Mexican Mole sauce.

Christopher Columbus brought chocolate beans back to Europe, and a century later the first recorded public chocolate house opened in London in the mid 1600s. However it was not until late 19th century that John Cadbury, English craftsman, found a way to emulsify the beans into solids, giving birth to the now commonly known chocolate bar. Mills were built across Europe to extract the butter and an incredible new commercial product was born, one of today's highest in demand.

The taste of chocolate is so good, so intense, and so sensual that inevitable jokes associated with sex are so abundant and common they are often put on the same level of importance. I do not just love chocolate. I really love chocolate with infinite passion.

Pastry chefs who have worked with me in the past often had to hide their work from me as they would always fall short on their daily portions whenever I lurked around their station, just like a shark in search of its prey.

I wanted to compose the ultimate chocolate tribute for those who, like me, are weak and defenseless whenever in presence of such temptation. I often resist temptations of many sorts, but I rarely resist evil chocolate calls. I often go back in time and act like a little a kid, and I never repent. Is that wrong?

It was just a matter of time until I decided to put together different kinds of chocolates in forms, shapes, textures and temperatures in an ensemble that would highlight what the cocoa bean means to me. By combining dark, white and milk I figured I would cover the entire basis for basic indulgences. A mousse, sauces, crumbled cookies, flan, cigarettes, and even a playful take in texture of flexible lookalike "play dough."

This dish is as sinful as it can be: it has layers of evil diversity and delightful temptations that will leave you so satisfied and with an everlasting passionate grin on your face, big enough to make friends out of your worst enemies.

Equipment Needed
A few 2½-inch square metallic molds for the flan
Nonstick flexi-mold with multi-cube cavities of one-inch square for the mousse
A round metallic mold of approximately one-inch diameter for the cookie crumbs
An infrared thermometer to test chocolate temperatures
Acetate sheets for chocolate work

White Chocolate Flan

Ingredients
8 oz of milk
4 tbsp of sugar
½ vanilla bean
3 eggs
4 oz of white chocolate coins

Directions
Lightly whip the eggs in a bowl and set aside.
Boil the milk with the sugar and the vanilla bean, remove from the stove, and with a whisk delicately temper in the whipped eggs to a smooth mix.
While still hot, pour the liquid mix directly on the white chocolate coins in a mixing bowl, and whisk until completely melted to smooth consistency.
Filter through a fine mesh and fill a few square 2½-inch metallic molds sitting on a silicone baking mat over a half sheet pan.
Bake in hot oven approximately 20 minutes at 200 degrees.

White Chocolate Mousse

Ingredients

5¼ oz of white chocolate coins
1½ oz of heavy cream
4 gelatin sheets
1 tbsp of sugar powder
1 egg yolk
8¼ oz of softly whipped heavy cream

Directions

In a small pot bring the heavy cream to boil and temper in the white chocolate coins till completely melted, and then set aside a few minutes.
Bloom the gelatin sheets in water and add to the warm white chocolate mix
Stir well and once at room temperature, fold in only 1/3 of the softly whipped heavy cream and set aside.
In a small mixing bowl and over hot water bath, make a zabaglione with the sugar powder and the egg yolk.
Whip with a soft whisk till nice and fluffy, and chill over ice bath, then fold in the remaining 2/3 of the softly whipped heavy cream and combine it to the white chocolate mix to complete the mousse.
Transfer the mousse into the cubed, nonstick, flexi-mold cavities.
Cover with a deli paper sheet and freeze till hard.
Once frozen, remove from the molds, store in the refrigerator till soft and ready to be combined with the other components at serving time.

White Chocolate Sauce

Ingredients

9 oz of white chocolate coins
8¾ oz of cold water
4½ oz of heavy cream
2½ oz of sugar

Directions

Place all ingredients in a small sauce pan, and under low flame combine to a smooth and velvety sauce stirring constantly about 4-5 minutes.

Strain the sauce through a fine mesh and refrigerate.

Milk Chocolate Sauce

Ingredients
4½ oz of milk chocolate coins
8½ oz of water
4½ oz of heavy cream
2¼ oz of sugar

Directions
Place all ingredients in a small sauce pan and under low flame combine to a smooth and velvety sauce, stirring constantly about 4-5 minutes.
Strain the sauce through a fine mesh and refrigerate.

Flexible Chocolate

Ingredients
9 oz of heavy cream
1¼ oz of corn syrup
6 oz of sugar
2 pinches of salt
7½ oz of dark chocolate coins
3 oz of soft butter
1 tsp of vanilla extract
6 gelatin sheets

Directions
Place the chocolate coins in a mixing bowl and set aside.
Bloom the gelatin sheets in water and set aside.
In a small sauce pan combine the heavy cream with the corn syrup, the sugar, and the salt.
Bring to a boil.
While still hot pour the entire contents over the chocolate coins and with a spatula stir well till completely melted.
Using a handheld immersion blender, whip the chocolate sauce till perfectly combined while adding the vanilla extract and the soft butter gradually.
Melt the gelatin sheets in it while still warm and continue mixing to a ganache-type consistency.

Pour the mix into a half sheet pan covered with plastic film.
Place in the refrigerator to solidify about 30 minutes.
Cut the flexi-chocolate into strips of about ½-inch wide and 8 inches long.
Set aside till serving time.

Chocolate Crumb

Ingredients
5 oz of soft butter
5 oz of sugar
1 egg
10½ oz of AP flour sifted
2 oz of cocoa powder
1 tsp of baking powder

Directions
In a mixing bowl combine the baking powder, the flour, and the cocoa powder.
In a small mixer whip the soft butter with the sugar until white and fluffy, and then add the egg and combine.
Gradually fold in the cocoa powder, the flour, and the baking powder while mixing at low speed.
Place the dough on plastic film and form various rolls.
Place in the refrigerator until firm.
Set the oven at 325, roll out the dough at room temperature into a thin sheet, and form various cookies with a cutter of approximately 2½ inches in diameter.
Cook over silicone baking mat about 5 minutes.
Grate the desired amount of crumbs over a micro-plane grater and set aside till serving time.

Milk Chocolate Mousse

Ingredients
5¼ oz of milk chocolate coins
1½ oz of heavy cream
4 gelatin sheets
1 tbsp of sugar powder
1 egg yolk
8¼ oz of softly whipped heavy cream

Directions
In a small pot bring the heavy cream to boil and temper in the milk chocolate coins till completely melted.
Set aside a few minutes.
Bloom the gelatin sheets in water and add to the warm milk chocolate mix.
Stir well and once at room temperature, fold in only ⅓ of the softly whipped heavy cream and set aside.
In a small mixing bowl and over hot water bath make a zabaglione with the sugar powder and the egg yolk. Whip with a soft whisk till nice and fluffy and chill over ice bath, then fold in the remaining ⅔ of the softly whipped heavy cream and combine it with the milk chocolate mix to complete the mousse.
Store in refrigerator in a small container covered with plastic film until serving time.

White and Dark Chocolate Cigarettes

Directions
In a bowl using the hot bath method, melt the desired chocolate coins or shavings, stirring occasionally until the chocolate reaches the melting temperature of approximately:

DARK CHOCOLATE: 120F/49C
MILK CHOCOLATE: 116F/47C
WHITE CHOCOLATE: 114F/45C

While stirring continuously with a wooden spoon, gently add additional chocolate coins or shavings into the melted batch (seeding technique). Carefully monitor the temperature as the new added chocolate will slowly lower its temperature. Our goal during the tempering process, depending on the type of chocolate we are working with, is to reach the following approximate temperatures:

DARK CHOCOLATE: 84F/29C
MILK CHOCOLATE: 81F/27C
WHITE CHOCOLATE: 79F/26C

In order to work with tempered chocolate we must raise its temperature by using either a microwave in intervals of 10 seconds each, stirring between each interval, or by placing the chocolate over a warm bath, monitoring its temperature to rise to but not exceed:

DARK CHOCOLATE: 89F-90F/32C
MILK CHOCOLATE: 86F-87F/30C
WHITE CHOCOLATE: 82F-83F/28C

With the help of an offset spatula, spread some chocolate on a marble work table or on an acetate sheet to form a strip of about 5-6 inches wide by approximately one-foot long.
With a wide spatula or a pastry dough cutter clean the chocolate strip edges to a clean and smooth strip.
Starting at one end of the strip, scrape one cigarette at a time with the dough cutter in one fast and sharp movement, having the still-soft chocolate roll on its own, forming the desired cigarette.
Set aside until serving time.

To Serve
There is not a specific way to present or to properly put this composition together. It can be changed in so many ways depending on a personal state of mind. What's important is to respect the textures and shapes when assembling. Here is my recommendation:
On a rectangular plate horizontally run a string of milk chocolate sauce with a spoon.
Place a rectangular slice of the white chocolate flan in the center and top it with the cubed white chocolate mousse.
On the right side of the flan, with the help of a round metallic mold of approximately one-inch in diameter, form a perfect circle with the chocolate crumbs.
Place a quenelle of the milk chocolate mousse right on top of it with a few cocoa nibs.
Wind the flexible chocolate strip in a small spiral, place it on top of the cubed mousse, and run the leftover string down on the side, slightly twisted.
Horizontally run a string of white chocolate sauce with a spoon at 1 o'clock of the flan on the right side.
Dot the plate with white and milk chocolate sauce and sprinkle a few leftover crumbs around them for visual balance.

Decorate the dish with a dark chocolate cigarette above the flan and a few shaves of the white chocolate cigarette on top of the mousse.

Vanilla Panna Cotta Sunny Side Up with Orange Yolks, Gelatin, and Virtual Bacon

A pleasant illusion usually creates a genuine smile. During my early years in culinary school the very first dessert I learned to make was a very simple vanilla panna cotta.

This dessert is very popular in Northern Italy—mix boiled heavy cream with sugar and vanilla, gelatin sheets and flavored with grappa, and set in refrigerator to jelly-custard consistency. Everyone can make it at home as it does not require much time or great culinary skills. It is a crowd pleaser and always welcomed on any dining table. Panna cotta is just as popular in Italy as crème caramel is in France. Everyone loves it—kids, adults and even those who do not like sweets. This is considered a soft dessert and enjoyable in all its simplicity with a spoon. Nowadays its variations are endless: chefs have created all kind of sweet and salty panna cottas, stretching their imagination in search of taste and innovative concepts.

A few years ago when I was visiting my family in Italy I had lunch at a very small osteria with my sister and my niece, and I noticed on the menu a whole page dedicated to different kinds of panna cottas: salty, sweets, cheese, fruit-and-vegetable-based, and paired with infinite selections of breads, crackers, cookies- or muffins. What an intelligent alternative to the usual sandwiches or paninos, I thought.

Taken by curiosity and excitement I ordered a few, but once my order arrived, neither its presentation nor its taste was appealing enough for me to keep my excitement alive. Quite the opposite. The panna cottas I tried were really tough with not much flavor. It seemed to me as if the chef had tripled the amount of gelatin from a basic recipe, and turned what was supposed to be creamy and soft treats into hard plastic dog toys. I could have literally thrown them against the wall and played fetch with my dog Max. I left disappointed and hungry, but the whole experience taught me a very valuable lesson: the simplest dishes have the highest expectations.

From that moment on I radically changed my understanding of how panna cotta is supposed to be prepared, consumed and presented. Even simple boiled cream should be glorious.

I set myself with the task to elevate this simple dish to a delicious and elegant concept. I started by making a softer texture; I cut down the amount of gelatin and folded in fresh sour cream for a more acidic taste.

Instead of pouring the bright white panna cotta base into traditional cups I decided to try a new presentation and poured the base mix into small ceramic ramekins shaped like mini oval sauté pans with handles. I reduced freshly squeezed orange juice and boiled it with a dash of turmeric, enhancing its yellow color. I mixed it with gelatin and formed half spheres resembling bright yolks.
But no breakfast in America is complete without bacon, so I cooked crunchy tuiles and shaped them in wavy strips. I sprinkled them with cocoa nibs and served them with the look-alike eggs dish.

This indeed is quite a pleasant gastronomic illusion for anyone who cherishes traditions served with a splash of humor.

Equipment Needed
Multi half-sphere, nonstick flexi-mold, half-inch size
Plastic template with rectangular cutout strip cavities in dimensions of 8 inch long x 1 inch wide
Sauce gun
Oval ceramic ramekins for the panna cotta, approximately 5 inches long, 4 diameter and about 1 inch high

Vanilla Panna Cotta

Ingredients
1 qt of high fat heavy cream 40 percent
¾ cup of sugar
12 oz of sour cream
A pinch of salt
½ tsp of vanilla beans
1 tbsp of granulated and unflavored gelatin

Directions
Bloom the gelatin in 4 tablespoons of water about 5 minutes.
In a small pot boil the heavy cream with the sugar, the salt, and the vanilla beans.
Set aside to cool a few minutes and then stir in the gelatin with a whisk.
Filter the mix through a fine mesh and set aside until cooled to room temperature.
In a medium-size metallic mixing bowl place the sour cream and gradually add the boiled cream, constantly mixing with a whisk to a thick, but smooth consistency liquid paste.
Fill the ceramic ramekins and transfer into the refrigerator for at least 2 hours.

Simple Syrup

Ingredients
1 qt of water
6 oz of sugar
The peel of half lemon
The peel of half orange
¼ stick of vanilla bean

Directions
Combine all ingredients in a small pot and boil down to more than half.
Filter through a fine mesh and set aside till at room temperature.
Keep refrigerated.

Orange Yolk Gelatin Spheres

Ingredients
1cup of fresh squeezed orange juice, filtered
¼ cup of corn syrup
½ tbsp of gelatin granulated and unflavored
½ tsp of agar
½ tbsp of ground turmeric
¼ cup of sugar
3 oz of frozen concentrated orange juice

Directions

Bloom the gelatin with two tablespoons of water.

In a small pot combine the fresh-squeezed orange juice, the frozen concentrate orange juice, the simple syrup, the sugar, the turmeric, and the agar.

With a handheld immersion blender mix it all before bringing it to boil about 3 minutes.

Set aside and cool a few minutes only before adding the bloomed gelatin in it.

Whisk in till dissolved.

Filter the mix through a very fine mesh and wait till completely cold.

With the help of the sauce gun pour the liquid in the silicone mold cavities, cover with deli paper, and freeze till totally hard.

About 4 hours before serving transfer the desire amounts of orange yolks to the refrigerator and wait until completely thawed out to gelatin consistency.

Virtual Bacon

Ingredients

4 oz of egg whites whipped stiff peaks
5 oz of powder sugar
2¼ oz of AP flour sifted
2½ oz of melted butter
A few cracked cocoa nibs (optional)

Directions

In a small tabletop mixer bowl combine the stiff peak egg whites with the sifted flour, the sugar, and the melted butter to a thick, but smooth paste.

Refrigerate about half hour before using.

On a silicone baking mat over a half sheet pan lay the plastic template with rectangular cut-out strips and fill them in with the tulip mix.

Remove the plastic template, sprinkle a few cracked cocoa nibs (optional), and bake till golden at 325 approximately 5-6 minutes.

As soon as the tulips come out of the oven shape them into short wavy bacon look-alike strips and set them aside till serving time.

To Serve

Remove the panna cotta from the refrigerator.

With a small off-set spatula place both egg yolks on the custard distanced about two inches apart.
Decorate only the white part with a few cocoa nibs and a few pieces of Sicilian pistachios.
Dust the bacon with a little powder sugar and place it right across the custard giving the illusion of a very common breakfast dish.

Hazelnuts and Lemons

What an odd combination. I do not really have a name for this dessert. I basically discovered lemons and hazelnuts work well together when paired correctly. There is always a way to blend ingredients by elevating their flavors, by toning them down, or by incorporating a third component to work as a bridge to transport a needed essence, making everything sparkle in a gastronomically perfect world.

As mentioned, the best hazelnuts come from Piedmont, but the best lemons are from the south of Italy, ending up with a traditional marriage between North and South. If you taste both individually, it is apparent the nutty taste does not combine with the acidity of the lemon. However, if we add just a little texture and a light gianduja ganache everything starts to make sense as the saltiness in the hazelnuts comes out once a sweet counterpart such as chocolate is paired with it. At this point an aggressive cleanser component such as lemon is welcome in the mix of flavors.

I made a linzer dough cookie stuffed with hazelnut cream, very light, but very sharp in taste. I created a lemon curd cream and a gianduja ganache as a base for this canvas and spackled it on tulip petals as well to intensify the chocolate depth in the dish. What really surprised me was how the input of the hazelnut brittle made a huge difference when sprinkled around: crushed in coarse powder it is a joy for the palate in saltiness, crunchiness and sweetness. The lemon sorbet is a neutral component: its job is to involuntarily clean the palate and to transport the floral essence of the fruit throughout the dish.

Equipment Needed
A round cookie cutter of 2 inches diameter for the Linzer dough discs

Tulip Petals

Ingredients
4 oz of egg whites whipped stiff peaks
5 oz of powder sugar
2¼ oz of AP flour sifted
2½ oz of melted butter

Directions
In a small table top mixing bowl combine the stiff peak egg whites with the sifted flour, the sugar, and the melted butter to a thick, but smooth paste.
Refrigerate about a half hour before using.
On a silicone baking mat over a half sheet pan and with the help of a small offset spatula form a few petals 2 inches wide in size, and bake till golden at 325 approximately 4 minutes.
Set them aside, once cold, until serving time.

Linzer Dough

Ingredients
⅔ cup of almond flour
1⅔ cups of AP flour
4 oz of butter cut into small cubes at room temperature
3/4 cup of powdered sugar
1/2 tsp of salt
1 egg
The tip of a teaspoon of vanilla beans

Directions
In a small mixer whip the butter with the sugar and the salt.
Add the egg, the almond and AP flour, and mix with the hook attachment until all ingredients come together as thick dough.
Place the dough on plastic film, form a couple of rolls, and transfer to the refrigerator a couple of hours before using.
Roll the dough into a thin sheet and with the round cookie cutter cut out a few discs, transfer them on a silicone baking mat over a baking pan, and cook them in a hot oven at 325 approximately 7 minutes.

Hazelnut Cream

Ingredients
2 cups of milk
4½ oz of sugar
4 egg yolks
1½ oz of corn starch
1¾ oz of butter
4 gelatin sheets
1 vanilla bean
5¼ oz of Piedmonte hazelnut paste

Directions
Bloom the gelatin sheets in water and set aside
In a small pot bring to boil only half the milk with the sugar and the vanilla bean.
In a small mixer whip up the other half of the milk with the cornstarch and add it to the boiled mix, stirring constantly under low flame along with the yolks about 4 minutes until the mix thickens up to a cream.
Remove from fire.
Whisk in the bloomed gelatin to the warm cream, stir in the Piedmonte hazelnut paste and the butter to a velvety and smooth custard-like consistency.
Transfer into a disposable pastry bag and set in the refrigerator.

Hazelnut Brittle

Ingredients
2 cups of sugar
9 oz of water
⅓ cup of glucose
1½ tbsp of salt
12 oz of Piedmonte hazelnuts
4 oz of butter

Directions
In a small pan caramelize the glucose, the salt, the water and the sugar till golden.
Remove from fire and gradually add the hazelnuts and the butter, stirring constantly to a thick paste.

Pour over a silicone baking mat and with the help of an offset spatula spread the mix evenly.
Wait until completely cold and crumb into small bits.
Set aside.

Lemon Curd

Ingredients
10½ oz of butter at room temperature
9 oz of sugar
9½ oz of freshly squeezed lemon juice and filtered
½ oz of freshly grated lemon zest, very finely
9 oz of egg yolks

Directions
Applying the zabaglione technique method, whip over hot bath the sugar, the egg yolks, the lemon juice, and the lemon zest to a thick paste.
Transfer to a new mixing bowl and cool to room temperature.
Fold in the butter at room temperature and mix well to a velvety mix.
Refrigerate.

Lemon Sorbet

Ingredients
9¼ oz of sugar
8½ oz of water
2 oz of glucose
1 tbsp of sorbet stabilizer
1 cup of freshly squeeze lemon juice, filtered

Directions
In a small pan bring to boil the water with the glucose and the sugar.
Remove from the stove and cool a few minutes, add the stabilizer, mixing well with a whisk. Add the lemon juice last.
Filter through a fine mesh and once completely cold spin in the gelato machine.

Lemon Chips

Ingredients
A few paper-thin seedless lemon slices
2 tbsp of simple syrup

Directions
Immerse the lemon slices in the syrup a day or two.
Place the slices on a silicone baking mat over a baking pan and dry in oven at 200 degrees about 2½ hours until completely caramelized, dry and crispy just like a potato chip.
Once cold set them aside over deli paper until serving time.

Gianduja Ganache

Ingredients
5.3 oz of heavy cream
½ oz of glucose
2 oz of Piedmonte hazelnut paste
5.3 oz of dark shaved chocolate or in small thin coins

Directions
In a small pot combine the glucose and the heavy cream and bring to boil.
Place the hazelnut paste into a mixing bowl and pour the hot glucose-cream mix on top of it at once whisking until completely smooth.
Pour the still-hot hazelnut mix onto the dark chocolate in a different mixing bowl.
Stir and rapidly transfer to a high-speed blender and process while still hot until completely smooth.
Refrigerate.

To Serve
On a medium-size rectangular plate run across one curved strip of lemon curd and one of Gianduja ganache parallel to each other.
On one of the linzer dough cookies pipe in a generous amount of the hazelnut cream, place a second disc on top of it, gently press down and sprinkle the top with powdered sugar.
Set it at 9 o'clock on the plate.

Spread a teaspoon of gianduja ganache on 6 tulip petals and stack them together vertically, forming a small, irregular multi-layers tower and place it right in the center of the plate.
Scoop the lemon sorbet and place it on the right side at 3 o'clock, top it with a lemon chip vertically and sprinkle the dish with the crushed hazelnuts brittle and a pinch of Maldon salt.

Barolo Crème Brulé Saffron Poached Pear Gelato, Caramel Sauce and Warm Vin Brulé (Mulled Red Wine) Shot Glass

I always loved saffron, and I always loved good Barolo wine (who doesn't?) A few years back when I was opening my Italian tapas restaurant concept, Atrium, in Palm Beach, Florida, I suddenly felt very nostalgic. As much as I loved Florida and the whole Treasure Coast, it was kind of hard to get professionally inspired since there are only two seasons to live through the whole year: summer and a very mild winter where the lowest temperatures reach a very comfortable 50 degrees.

In early February 2006 I remember watching the opening ceremony for the XX Olympic Winter Games hosted in my hometown of Torino during dinner service on a busy weekend. An incredible sense of pride set in while watching places I knew so well and where I grew up and lived my entire childhood with my family, featuring local food and folkloristic traditions.

I watched the snow falling on the parade, the white-colored mountains around the stadium hugging the whole city while the Alps army, Alpini, marched on while sipping vin brulé. I walked outside the restaurant a few seconds while flashbacks exploded in my head like popcorn: Memories of mountain weekends spent with my parents, snow fights with my sister, and ski trips with my best friend Giorgio on the chilly slopes of the nearby Bardonecchia Mountain. I sat at one of the patio's tables and suddenly woke up to reality in warm 60 degrees weather. Bummer!

I decided to create a dessert based on traditions of my hometown that everyone would understand and enjoy. After much soul searching I twisted one of the most common French/American desserts into a flavorful postcard from Torino: Barolo crème brulé with a refreshing gelato made of pears poached in Prosecco and saffron. The combination is just astonishing for so many reasons: the granular pear purée matches perfectly with the delicate taste of the reduced wine while all the bright natural colors display harmony and logical match choice on a serving plate.

But I just could not put aside those Alpini on TV sipping vin brulé: This is a traditional beverage made of red wine and spices on the side of small mountain city streets where the Alpini used to mull in cold days to keep warm during war times.

So I mulled my own and served a warm shot glass of it as homage to those who used to keep us safe in freezing temperatures...while intoxicated.

Equipment Needed
1 crème brulé torch
A few oval ceramic ramekins for the crème brulé, approximately 5 inches long, 4 inch in diameter and about 1 inch high
1 small shot glass

Barolo Reduction

Ingredients
2 qts of Barolo wine
1 clove
1 cinnamon stick
½ cup of sugar
½ orange peel
½ lemon peel
½ vanilla bean stick

Directions
Place all ingredients in a small pot, and under moderate flame reduce the wine to 2 cups only.
Filter and set aside.

Barolo Crème Brulé

Ingredients
1 qt of heavy cream
2 cups of Barolo reduction

8 oz of sugar
½ vanilla bean stick
A pinch of salt
15 oz of egg yolks
Sugar to dust and burn at serving time

Directions
In a small mixing bowl mix 4 oz of the sugar and the egg yolks, and whisk till combined.
In a small pot place the Barolo reduction with the heavy cream, the vanilla beans and the remaining 4 oz of sugar.
Bring to boil and remove from stove, cool aside a couple of minutes, then add the yolks mixed with the sugar, tempering with a whisk.
Filter through a fine mesh, with a spoon remove any extra foam from the cream and fill in the ramekins.
Bake in water bath at 275 degrees with low fan approximately 30 minutes.
When ready remove from the water and set aside to cool.
Refrigerate.

Caramel Sauce

Ingredients
7 oz of sugar
2 tbsp of corn syrup
The tip of a teaspoon of vanilla beans
½ cup of heavy cream
½ oz of water
1½ oz of butter

Directions
In a small pan caramelize the sugar with the corn syrup and the vanilla beans.
Gradually add the heavy cream and the water, and cook a few minutes under low flame.
Remove from stove and whisk in the butter to a smooth and dense sauce.
Filter through a fine mesh and set aside.

Saffron Poached Pear Purée

Ingredients

4 Bartlett pears peeled quartered and cored
1 liter of Prosecco
2 pinches of saffron finely crushed
Pinch of salt
The tip of a teaspoon of vanilla beans
3 tbsp of sugar

Directions

In a medium size pan combine the Prosecco, the salt, the sugar and the vanilla and reduce it by half over moderate fire.
Add the saffron, the quartered pears and simmer about 10-15 minutes till completely cooked.
Set the pan aside and cool to room temperature, then combine the poached pears with some of the cooking liquid.
Purée finely in a high-speed blender.
Filter the remaining liquid through a fine mesh and bring back to fire reducing down to a thick and syrupy sauce.
Use the sauce for plating and decoration at serving time.

Saffron Poached Pear Gelato

Ingredients

2 cups of milk
1 cup of heavy cream
8 egg yolks
10 oz of sugar
½ tbsp of salt
1 lb of saffron poached pear purée
A few crumbled pistachios
A few threads of saffron for decoration

Directions

In a medium size pan combine the milk, the cream, and the sugar and bring to boil.
Add salt and temper in the egg yolks previously whipped.
Filter through a fine mesh and set aside till at room temperature.
Fold in the pear purée, mix well, and spin in gelato machine.

Vin Brulé (Mulled Red Wine)

Ingredients
½ orange sliced
3 cloves
¼ nutmeg
½ cinnamon stick
2 cups of Barolo wine
3 cracked seeds of cardamom
½ tbsp of chestnut honey
2 tbsp of sugar

Directions
Mix all the ingredients into a small pot.
Cook at low flame.
As soon as it comes to a boil fire the evaporating alcohol with a match and remove from the stove.
Patiently wait till all the fire is consumed, filter the liquid through a fine mesh, and consume immediately.

To Serve
Dust a teaspoon of sugar on the crème brulé and torch it to golden brown.
Set in the refrigerator 2 minutes until the burnt sugar hardens and set aside.
On a long and narrow rectangular plate run a string of the caramel sauce from side to side horizontally.
On one end place the brulé ramekin, next to it in the center sprinkle a few crumbled pistachios and set a spoon of the pear gelato on it, drizzle the top with some of the syrupy reduced cooking liquid and decorate with a few saffron threads.
On the opposite side of the plate place the shot glass filled with the vin brulé and finish decorating the custard by dusting some powdered sugar on it.

Warm Zuccottino Cake, Gianduja Sauce, Crunchy Quince/Vin Santo Gel, White Truffle Gelato, and Tulip Cigarette

In the early spring of 1999, I was invited to cook at the prestigious James Beard House in New York again. The kitchen at the Beard House is very small, equipped with almost anything a chef needs to produce a great meal, but very limited for mass production. So I usually do most of the preparation in my kitchen a couple of days in advance before my crew and I pack everything in large coolers. Proteins and pasta are cooked at the moment, but sauces, decorations and all components for desserts are usually prepared ahead of time and put together at the moment, on-site at dinnertime. I remember we prepared mini, individual soft-cream chocolate custards for the dessert course. The pastry chef packed them beautifully in one of the coolers along with the sauce, the tulips and the spun sugar.

Driving to New York in a large and comfortable 15 passenger van, we encountered an early morning snowstorm north of Philadelphia. Suddenly a car in front of us slammed on the breaks and so did I to avoid the impact. Unfortunately, the cooler with the pastries flew across the van, hit the back door, and rolled a couple of times, destroying all the work for that evening's final course. Panic and desperation set in.

We rushed to New York at such speed our white van could have been mistaken for an ambulance carrying a sick patient in need of immediate care: flying through the New Jersey Turnpike and into the Lincoln Tunnel to 42ndStreet and down through 9th Avenue. Indeed it was a fight against time.

Once in the kitchen we assessed the damage and took vitals: Custards were destroyed, the sauces painted the inside of the cooler as an abstract Jackson Pollock painting and the tulips were reduced to mere crumbs. What to do? I could have bought Twinkies, dipped them in espresso, dusted them with cocoa powder, and told everyone they were a futuristic version of tiramisu. Not really! So I improvised.

I started my frantic search around the pantry and found some flour, ground espresso, butter, and an open bag of hazelnut flour. I sent someone to buy eggs and sugar, and went to work. I needed to create something fast, delicious and visual, and the best I could come up with was a bandage muffin to be produced in two hours' time.

Once I took the first batch out of the oven we could not help but pay attention to its wonderful aroma: Wow! This is actually great. It turned out to be a very fragrant, tasty, and delicate treat all the guests really enjoyed. The producers at *Top Chef* would have been very proud of me. When we returned to Washington the next day I perfected it. I ordered hazelnuts and hazelnut flour from Piedmont, I made a classic gianduja sauce, and decided to create a gel made of a reduction of Vin Santo and quince purée.

To this day, zuccottino is one of the most appreciated desserts and one I love most because it is so simple and so humble. I serve it warm with a tulip cigarette for much-needed crunchiness. It delivers a sense of comfort and it balances off very well with the white truffle gelato and the gianduja sauce.

In the autumn months when white truffles are available I love to offer the option to indulge into a realistic and ultimate Piedmontese treat by shaving a few slices of white truffles right on it and to give those guests who love to splurge the illusion of being in rural Alba even if only for a few minutes.

Equipment Needed
A few ramekins or a few round metallic ring molds of the dimensions of approximately 3 inches high and 1½ inches in diameter for the zuccottino
1 rectangular plastic template cut out in dimensions of 5 inches long x 2 wide to create the tulip cigarette
A round metallic mold of approximately one-inch diameter for the crumbed pistachios

Zuccottino

Ingredients
12 oz of sugar
11 oz of high-fat soft butter at room temperature
6 egg yolks
4 egg whites
10 oz of AP flour
5 oz of Piedmonte hazelnut flour
1 tbsp of baking powder
1 vanilla beans stick

1tbsp of powdered espresso beans coffee
¾ cup of milk
1cup of toasted and crushed Piedmonte hazelnuts
Zest of ¼ orange
2 oz of melted butter to brush the molds with
Some powdered sugar to dust the zuccottino and cigarette at serving time
A few crumbled pistachios
A tsp of powdered pistachios

Directions
In a small mixing bowl combine 6 oz of sugar, the soft butter, and mix at medium speed.
Once combined add the 6 yolks one at a time, the hazelnut flour, the AP flour, the salt, the baking powder, the espresso powder the vanilla beans, the milk and the orange zest gradually.
Separately whip 4 egg whites to stiff peaks with the remaining 6 oz of sugar and fold in with the flour and butter mix with a rubber spatula till perfectly combined.
Brush the molds with the melted butter, dust them with the crushed toasted hazelnuts, and place them on a small sheet pan over deli paper.
Using a disposable pastry bag, fill the molds only up to ¾ of their capacity and bake in a hot oven at 375 degrees about 25 minutes.
Remove when ready and let them cool completely before shelling them out of their molds.
Set them aside.

Gianduja Sauce

Ingredients
8 oz of heavy cream
½ oz of glucose
2 oz of Piedmonte hazelnut paste
5.3 oz of dark shaved chocolate or in small thin coins

Directions
In a small pot combine the glucose and the heavy cream, and bring to boil.

Place the hazelnut paste into a mixing bowl and pour the hot glucose-cream mix on top of it at once, whisking until completely smooth.
Now pour the still-hot hazelnut mix onto the dark chocolate in a different mixing bowl.
Mix very well till the sauce is smooth and well combined.
Transfer to a plastic squeeze bottle and set aside until serving time. Refrigerate after use.

Tulip Cigarette

See "Virtual Bacon" ingredients (Page 468). From "Vanilla Panna Cotta Sunny Side Up" recipe (Page 468) without the cocoa nibs.

Directions
In a small table top mixing bowl combine the stiff peak egg whites with the sifted flour, the sugar and the melted butter to a thick, but smooth paste.
Refrigerate about a half hour before using.
Lay the plastic cigarette template on a silicone baking mat and fill it with the mix using an offset spatula.
Remove the template and bake at 325 about 5 minutes till golden.
Carefully roll the tuile as soon as ready under the palm of your hand, forming a perfectly rolled cigarette. Be careful however that the tuile is very hot when removed from the oven; therefore follow the above procedure wearing protective gloves.
Set aside till serving time.

Quince Vin Santo Gel

Ingredients
10 oz of quince peeled cored and cubed
1 cinnamon stick
1 anise star
½ cup of Vin Santo wine
½ cup of Prosecco
1 oz of sugar
Tip of a teaspoon of vanilla beans

Directions
Combine all the ingredients in a small pan and cook at moderate fire until the liquid is reduced to half and the quinces are cooked through.
Remove the cinnamon stick and the star anise.
Transfer to a high-speed blender and purée the mix very fine to smooth consistency.
Refrigerate.

White Truffle Gelato

Ingredients
2 cups of heavy cream
2 cups of milk
1 cup of sugar
1 vanilla bean
10 egg yolks
2 oz of white truffle oil
A few shavings of fresh white truffles whenever available and possible

Directions
Combine the cream and the milk in a small pot with the vanilla and bring to a boil.
In a small mixing bowl whip the egg yolks with the sugar and fold in delicately to the boiled milk and cream.
Remove the vanilla stick and whisk in the truffle oil.
Filter the mix through a fine mesh, and then add the fresh white truffle shavings.
Spin in the gelato machine.

To Serve
On a large square or round plate divide this dish symmetrically as follows: at 10 o'clock, off-centered, place the warm zuccottino dusted with powdered sugar.
On its right side with the help of a round metallic mold of approximately one-inch diameter, form a perfect circle with the crumbed pistachios and place a perfectly molded spoon of the white truffle gelato right on top of it.
At the feet of the zuccottino, from left to right, horizontally run a string of the quince Vin Santo gel.

Decorate the dish by dotting with various sizes of gianduja sauce, creating a visual balance, and finish by delicately placing the tulip cigarette dusted with sugar powder, working as a bridge from the gelato to the top of the zuccottino.
Dust with powdered pistachio and serve.

Deconstructed Caramelized Apple Pie with Cinnamon Fumes

I have stressed many times throughout this book the importance of using the right vehicle to deliver a food concept to the table. This is a classic example of how I came up with the idea of using a round-shaped hollow multi-compartments glass tea light holder for a tasting menu's pre-dessert course. As stated, we eat and dine using all our senses even if we do not always realize it.

One day I was shopping at Crate & Barrel when I saw a five-compartment tea light holder on one of the shelves. Sometimes good ideas come unexpectedly: I immediately thought how neat it would be to serve a miniature pre-dessert course using something so visual and so clear you could actually see through it, almost as a tease.

When I took my daughter, Chiara, to amusement parks in her very young years I always loved the smell of the nearby side cart vendors roasting apples, caramel, popping corn, mixing it with chocolate and cinnamon and of course all types of freshly baked pies. A real tease for us both: I still clearly remember how that incredible fragrance and aroma stayed with me for the rest of the day. I decided to use the multi-compartment tea candle holder to deliver the same fragrance, or at least in part. I roasted an apple, and created a sour gel to balance the sweet taste of the caramel. I re-created the pie crust in the form of cookie crumbs and refreshed the whole dish with green apple sorbet. I produced all the basic elements for a deconstructed caramelized apple pie.

I assembled the pie by placing each component inside each cavity of the tea candle holder. However, I needed a better way to transport its fragrance to my guests. I armed myself with a very long cinnamon stick, and I torched both its ends and slipped it in the underneath hollow cylindrical compartment. This trick really works and not only as visual statement, mostly as an aromatic one as while the holder is placed in front of the guest the fumes of the roasting cinnamon delicately escape, delivering a sense of sweetness, evoking sweet childhood memories.

Equipment Needed
One 5 cavity cylindrical glass tea candle holder about 12 inches long
One long decorative cinnamon stick
One metallic round cookie cutter of one inch diameter

Roasted Apple

Ingredients
1 Granny Smith apple
2 tbsp of sugar
Tip of a teaspoon of vanilla beans
Juice of one lemon
1 tbsp of butter
Tip of a teaspoon of powdered cinnamon

Directions
In a small bowl mix the sugar with the cinnamon and the vanilla beans.
Transfer the mix to a large plate and set aside.
Peel the apple, core it thoroughly and baste it with the lemon juice entirely.
Roll the apple on the sugar/vanilla/cinnamon mix on all sides and place it in a small deep dish ramekin with a couple of tablespoons of water.
Place the butter on top of the apple and bake in a hot oven approximately 35 minutes at 325 degrees until soft.
Transfer the apple to a high-speed blender till smooth and place in refrigerator a few hours.
When completely cold and solid, roll a few one inch balls with your hands and set aside until serving time.

Orange Caramel

Ingredients
1½ cup sugar
1 cup fresh-squeezed orange juice and filtered

Directions
In a small pot golden the sugar.
Add the orange juice and cook down about 10 minutes.
Remove from fire and set aside a few minutes.
Pass the mix through a fine mesh cone.
Set aside to cool and keep in refrigerator in a plastic squirting bottle.

Green Apple Sorbet

Ingredients
9¼ oz of sugar
8½ oz of water
2 oz of glucose
1 tbsp of sorbet stabilizer
1 cup of fresh green apple purée
2 tbsp of freshly squeezed lemon juice, filtered

Directions
In a small pan bring to boil the water with the glucose and the sugar.
Remove from the stove and cool a few minutes, add the stabilizer, mixing well with a whisk, and add the fresh green apple purée and the lemon juice.
Once completely cold, spin in the gelato machine.

Lemon Sour Gelatin

Ingredients
½ cup of simple syrup
¼ cup of lemon juice filtered
The tip of a teaspoon of vanilla beans
1 tbsp of glucose
2 tbsp of excellent limoncello liquor
½ tbsp of powder gelatin granular unflavored

Directions
Bloom the gelatin with 2 tablespoons of water.
In a small pan warm the lemon juice with the simple syrup, the vanilla and the glucose for few minutes.
Remove from stove and add the limoncello liquor.

Stir in the gelatin and filter through a fine mesh.
Ice bath the liquid, and then transfer it into in a square plate or container with high borders.
Cover with plastic film and refrigerate at least 4 hours.
When firm, cut out small circles of the same size of the candle tea cavity diameter (approximately one inch) and set back in refrigerator till serving time.

Simple Syrup

See "Vanilla Panna Cotta Sunny Side Up" recipe (Page 468).

Apple Pie Crust Crumbs
(Baci di Dama Cookies Recipe)

Ingredients
8 oz of toasted almonds powdered
8 oz of AP flour sifted
8 oz of butter
8 oz of sugar

Directions
In a small mixer bowl whip the soft butter with the sugar.
Add the powdered almonds and the AP flour, and gently fold.
Mold various pearls of the size of 1 inch each and place on silicone baking mat over a sheet pan.
Bake in hot oven at 325 degrees approximately 12 to 15 minutes.
Hand crush when cold and set aside ready to serve.

To Serve
Set the glass tea candle holder on a long, rectangular serving plate.
From left to right place all the components in the tea candle cavities in this particular order:

A few crumbs of the apple pie crust
Roasted apple sphere rolled in sugar
Lemon sour gelatin circle
A small ball of the green apple sorbet
The orange caramel sauce

Decorate these components as follows:

Place an apple stem on top of each roasted apple and the green apple sorbet giving a realistic visual illusion of miniature real apples

Sprinkle a very small pinch of espresso dust on top of the lemon sour gelatin circle

Place a few cracked chocolate nibs on top of the orange caramel sauce

Torch the cinnamon stick on both ends and rapidly slide it underneath the holder.
Serve immediately while the cinnamon fumes slowly come out of both ends of the glass holder.

Basil Sorbet and Sicilian Chocolate Pepperoncino Gelato

These are two of my favorite gelatos and sorbets.

As a chocolate lover, I always sample, taste and look for the ultimate chocolate rush everywhere I travel. There is a small town in the south of Sicily, not far from where I used to spend my glorious vacation months, called Modica, near Ragusa. It is a very proud little town, set on a cliff carved in a stone mountain, very beautiful and full of history and spectacular at night when lit up. Sicily has always been a prized island for many centuries, and it has been invaded and controlled by great powers. It is the largest island in the Mediterranean Sea and because of its location and natural resources it has been considered crucial and strategic due to its importance for trade routes.

At first Sicily became a Greek colony, then the Romans took over and finally, during the early Middle Ages it was ruled in turn by the Vandals, Byzantines, the Arabs and the Normans. You can imagine how everyone left something of their own in this island over the past 3,000 years. So did the Arabs with their unique chocolate, among many other things. The first time I tasted it, it reminded me of the Mexican one: grainy, coarse, rough in the mouth, but in the end full of flavor and personality. I decided to combine this unique jewel with a local spicy pepperoncino and to craft a tribute to Modica's proud resource in an artisan gelato form.

Do not expect your usual ordinary Sunday morning chocolate ice cream, ladies and gentlemen, but a creamy gelato with deep personality, complex, with many layers in tastes to surprise even the most remote and useless taste buds in your mouth. The spicy pepperoncino is a joy in diversity, a gentle pinch to remind us both ingredients have shared this land for centuries side by side.

A very surprising sorbet is the basil one. For too long, we chefs have attempted to craft any kind of possible sorbets and gelatos by virtually using anything available in the refrigerator to be creative and adventurous. I like the occasional shock value item when it is part of a dish, paired with other ingredients in order to form a whole and complete concept when it helps to transport a specific flavor. I occasionally do that as well in my culinary repertoire, but it is so much harder to appreciate flavors like raw onion gelato, beer or asparagus sorbet or anchovy granita served in a cone or cup, solo. This usually turns out to be a horrific experience for my palate or for any palates in general.

I remember how skeptical and careful I was in selecting plain and simple basil for a new flavor sorbet. Basil is very aromatic, but responds very well to sugar; once I blanched its leaves I was able to produce a silky, light and very aromatic mix with a bright green natural color that did not need to be paired with any other food to be fully appreciated.

As matter of fact, when I first experimented with this sorbet I was in Florida, and I first served it at Atrium restaurant: it was one of the most sold single items on the menu as well as one of the most consumed by kids and adults in a single to-go cup.

Sicilian Chocolate Pepperoncino Gelato

Ingredients
5 cups milk
¾ cup of sugar
¾ cup of cocoa powder
½ tbsp of cornstarch
1 tsp of powdered Sicilian hot pepperoncino
8 oz of coarse chocolate from Modica, crushed

Directions
In a mixer combine sugar, cocoa, corn starch and hot pepper.
Gradually add 4 cups of milk till smooth paste with no lumps.
In a pot bring to boil the remaining 6 cups of milk with the cocoa mix.
Stir in the milk chocolate pastilles until melted and pass in a medium-fine strainer.
Cool and freeze.

Basil Sorbet

Ingredients
1 qt of simple syrup
1 cup of sugar
1 cup of corn syrup
2½ oz of basil leaves
1½ tbsp of lemon juice filtered

Directions
In a high-speed blender combine the corn syrup, the lemon juice, the sugar, and the simple syrup.
In a small pot blanch the basil leaves in boiling water a few seconds only and immediately transfer into the blender with the other ingredients.
Blend at high speed a few minutes to a velvety and smooth mix, and then filter the mix through a fine mesh.
Spin in gelato machine.

Chapter Twelve
The Realities of the Restaurant

A dear friend of mine, Charlie Saah, wrote a memoir about the restaurant business as a result of his personal experiences and real-life situations. In the past 30 years he owned nightclubs and a restaurant, and had a taste of what this industry is all about through good and bad. The book narrows down a frantic and realistic truth. It's called "The best two days of a restaurant owner: the day you open and the day you close."

Enough said.

I often compare the restaurant business to a theater. The similarities are endless: we have actors in the kitchen and in the dining room playing various roles, there are specific lines we memorize for our guests, there are always drama, comedy and action scenarios in our performances in every shift, a great amount of reality improves an addictive sense of nervousness before each play. We strive to deliver a flawless performance for each show, we rehearse in the kitchen and dining room, our uniforms are comparable to costumes, and we all move in symbiosis, orchestrating and producing a wonderful performance. We also spend most of our time behind the scenes on the other side of the curtains, working when everyone else takes a break from their stressful lives to enjoy holidays and festivities.

What about the price of the ticket? Well, it depends on the check: would you like to be seated privately? In that case you are booking a private party. Would you like the best seats in the house, first row center stage? No problem! You have picked well and expensively from the wine list, tasting menus with wine pairings anyone? All I can say is the performance better be worth the price.

After the show restaurants are usually subject to critics and reviews from food connoisseurs, journalists and nowadays regular guests who turn themselves into food bloggers and experts, telling us how our performance was received, experienced, how it was interpreted and at times how it should have been done differently with countless suggestions and inputs. Nowadays everybody is a food critic.

Everyone is armed with digital cameras and password access, many of them have the superb ignorant ability to wrongly describe our work in their own personal opinion, making up scenarios, inventing new ingredients and fabricating theories about chef inspirations, our drive, or our state of mind. A legion of incredibly talented mind-readers. If you ask me they should invest their time guessing the lottery numbers instead.

Many of them make personal suggestions without knowing the facts of the restaurant business or the reasons why specific steps are taken during service to assure quality and proper timing. Therefore, based on an assumption they write at times accurately, but mostly the writing is based on personal state of mind. I love constructive criticisms as they humble me and drive me to correct future problems and mistakes because my number-one priority is to make sure my customers are happy. It is kind of hard, however, to second-guess their thoughts, as often guests reserve their comments for the opportunity to make them public on a blog, and treasure a bad experience with bitter joy without giving us the opportunity to make it right and satisfactory. All they see is a tempting opportunity to voice their opinions in their own words, right or wrong.

To my biggest surprise I found out the majority of online amateur food bloggers write their comments anonymously. How convenient it is to hide behind a cyber door, closing all access for possible and reasonable interpretation of the truth. Giuliano Bottin, a veteran of the Washington, D.C., restaurant scene and the owner of the very popular La Bagatelle Restaurant in the early '80s used to share his words of wisdom with me after consuming a half bottle of Cuddy Sark: "You know, Enzo, guests are people, you just cannot please everyone. Period! They come, they eat, they pay and then they go and according to them we're all professionals and we don't know what to do." I have not seen Giuliano in eight years, sadly, but I wish him good health and peace as he must be pushing into his 80s. I hope to soon see him again with his unmistakable smile, his evergreen perfect tan and his wonderful sense of humor.

The theater of the restaurant industry is so very unique, so stressful, very unpredictable, extremely addictive and comical at times. For sure it is one of the hardest there is. It is a business you must love to be in and if you do not, genuinely, you will eventually hate it.

For a restaurant to be successful one needs to obey the basic hospitality rules, especially when a new project is forming. Developing the concept of the restaurant is comparable to the first laid brick. It is fundamental to define its basics: location, size, menu, service, financial investment, publicity, quality, strategies, beverage program, competition and demographics. Everything starts with the best suitable concept for the chosen location related to the size of the space: do I want to open a trattoria type restaurant or a fine dining establishment, a carry out place or a pizzeria?

Then branch out into details and explore the concept. Once the concept, location and size is decided, apply the "crystal bowl to see into the future" formula, forecasting a dollar figure for the average check and multiply it by the expected number of people patronizing on a daily basis. Subtract the rent, estimated payroll, cost of goods and 15 percent for uncalculated miscellaneous. If the final number is greater than all the expenses, then the idea makes sense and it is worth investing time to further explore. Easy, right?

The restaurant business is one of the lowest in profit margins there is and at the same time one with the highest intensive labor. When a restaurant is profitable it usually draws a margin of about 15 percent on an annual basis. To learn of a restaurant with higher profit is very unusual. The standard is around 8 percent. The amount of expenses involved is just amazing—high payroll, taxes, insurance, rent, and cost of goods alone would make anyone think twice before considering entering into this business.

The concept of the restaurant is extremely important for its success, but what really makes a difference is what people remember by personal experience. Aside from the food and service a respectable restaurateur has to offer something different, an experience to be remembered and talked about, sometimes a simple original idea catapults a business to a different level of acceptance.

For example, my latest restaurant is Osteria Elisir in Washington, D.C. This fine dining establishment is equipped with a high-definition camera located right above the plating station as I wanted my guests to watch us apply the final touches to each plate right before it is served. I wanted them to be involved closely with a virtual "hands-on experience" while having dinner. The live feed is sent to monitors throughout the restaurant and the guests can enjoy watching even if they are dining far from the open kitchen.

Only a few restaurants have attempted to capture the kitchen's live action, but the idea was always offered in the form of partial view or isolated steady screen shots. Take sister restaurants like Per Se in New York and The French Laundry in California, owned by chef Thomas Keller. In the New York kitchen you will find a large-screen TV broadcasting the live kitchen action from California and in the kitchen of The French Laundry the one from Per Se. He linked both restaurants for their qualities and concepts, creating a realistic reminder of the continuous work that goes on behind the curtains.

In the past few years restaurateurs and chefs have been getting obsessed with bringing their guests into the kitchens. They want to share the excitement and get them involved by walking through off limits spaces during service, talking to everyone. I like to keep my guests where they are most comfortable: in the dining room at their table. That is why I created an open kitchen, so everyone can follow the service. The live feed on the monitors brings the action to the guests, avoiding tours of the kitchen on a busy night that could possibly disrupt the service flow delicately based on concentration and timing. (I always welcome kitchen tours, but only at the end of service, short and of course supervised.)

Many details define one restaurant from others. Almost anyone can open a room filled with tables, a few chairs and serve whatever food is listed on a single page, but what really makes the difference is what we decide to do with that and how many details we implement between those four walls. A great culinary journey is based on the whole experience from start to finish. It is hard to produce quality and consistency every single day, but not impossible. The quest for the mythological perfect restaurant is constantly on, but we all know no one will ever achieve it. There are extremely long days and long hours spent on our feet, the stress factor makes us age twice as fast, the trust issues with employees, vendors and a good daily dose of paranoia sets the scene, not to mention any possible problems occurring on a daily basis.

The personal and private life of a restaurant employee is also an unusual one. It is known that one of the highest rates of divorce occur between people in the restaurant business. Long hours away from home, little time available to spend with your family, weekends dedicated to guests is a recipe for trouble. When and if you are eligible for vacation you cannot take more than one week at a time because you are now an asset and the business needs you. But what about your wife, husband, kids or loved ones who have waited so long to finally spend quality time with you? Tough! Unfortunately chances are the first three or four days of your vacation you will be thinking about work, the restaurant, the business you left undone or projects lined up for the upcoming week. Occasionally you will receive surprise phone calls regarding vendors, payroll or specific questions, and by the time you are finally relaxed and set in vacation mode it is time to go back.

When you work six days a week in a busy restaurant, you feel the fatigue settling into your bones. Your feet and back muscles hurt, and you find yourself napping between shifts on a chair with your head down on one of the dining room tables. When your day off finally arrives, it only serves to damage you. A single day hardly helps to recuperate from a tiring week: your internal alarm clock goes off every morning at the same time and it does not know any difference. Our deserved rest day only disrupts our working routine and creates more fatigue when we resume work the following day because our body and minds are slower and unfocused.

You can always spot an employee who has just returned from a day off: he is isolated, not very talkative, moves slower than usual and lacks concentration. If you are honestly willing to accept and understand this bizarre lifestyle, you have better than average chances to make it in this business. There are, however, three basic destructive elements you become exposed to: alcohol, drugs and sex.

No matter how many rules one implements, how many hours of training an employee goes through or how many different legal forms one signs about company regulations, it is virtually impossible to escape these plagues. I have never met anyone whose will is so strong to prevail on all of them. Eventually everyone gives in and falls into the sometimes literal arms of temptation and for some it is the beginning of the end.

The alcohol is present, visible and available in any restaurant or bar. After a long day in the kitchen or on the floor, most people come to desire the so called after-shift drink. In smaller restaurants it is not unusual to grant a free beverage once customers are gone and the staff is sitting around counting money, doing paperwork or resetting tables. Everyone mingles, sharing down time, unwinding, catching up to normalcy, and sharing tales, problems and stories from the just ended shift...and a drink.

Of course in bigger corporate organizations there is no after-shift drink. Even in my restaurants I have always banned this ritual because it can get very expensive for the house and mostly because I do not want to be responsible for those who have the need to consume three or four drinks and drive home intoxicated, endangering their own lives or the lives of others. Some of them meet at a different location to unwind, socialize and often have a late night snack. Once this turns into a ritual it is hard to break the routine and to go home directly from work. It is almost like you are eager to start the final shift of their day, the one you mostly enjoy and deserve, one where you are on the other side of the curtains finally.

I have seen people fall into the habit of drinking heavily, causing all sorts of problems for themselves: picking a fight while drunk, getting arrested while driving, coming home late to their wives and husbands, reporting late for work, not reporting at all, losing their jobs, doing it all over and again at a different restaurant. Very few understand the limits of their own safety and even fewer discipline themselves to obey them.

Same goes for drugs, especially for those who work long hours and need a boost before a busy shift. Having employees hitting a line of cocaine is unfortunately very common. People bring drugs to work, some for personal consumption and others to make a buck reselling them. I once fired a server who was dealing right in the dining room, selling to co-workers right under my nose. My godfather days rarely arise, but when someone intentionally puts my business or others at risk I go crazy and I always cut the problem at the root: leave with your trash, never come back or I baseball bat your head and then I get you arrested. It is very stereotypical Italian, but very effective. Works for me!

The other distraction at most restaurants is the frequency of intense relationships between employees. There are no successful methods to discourage or minimize the closeness that develops with your coworkers in the restaurant business. You can somehow limit the excessive use of drugs and alcohol in the work environment, but relationships are a different story.

As much as possible I do discourage dating between co-workers as it is not good for business; it only creates problems and disrupts a clear and stable state of mind, inhibiting a person to perform the job with professionalism and quality. Employees spend more time together at work than with their spouses at home and therefore learn all about each other's background, hopes, secrets, personal plans and fantasies. It is just a matter of time before the forbidden line gets crossed, mostly as a dare, and at times that dare branches out to divorces, separations, fights and marriages. Here is a common, trendy scenario: Some flirting, a few compliments, an invitation to go for a drink with other co-workers, a bite to eat, one drink too many, the unexpected kiss, the spur of the moment, the follow-up, the inability to stop, the lies, the secrets, the regret, the problems.

I have seen incredible situations develop over the years, incredible matches with the oddest people who have nothing in common, who share no background, culture or ideologies, who cannot even communicate effectively with each other because of the language barrier, people who do not belong together at all. You convince yourself it is OK to cross the line because whatever happens stays between the parameters of work and it does not come home with you. It is indeed exciting! It is all left in an imaginary locker at the end of your shift and taken out for use once you are at work or eventually between shifts in a hotel room or at someone's apartment for a quick rendezvous. One thing remains the same, it always ends in drama.

I hardly drink as I cannot hold my liquor. I do not do drugs, but I have always been a little vulnerable with women. In my first two years of marriage I used to work more than 15 hours a day. Back then I would see my wife only on Sundays on my day off, and by the time I woke up my ex-wife Maury had planned the whole day for us and there was no way to interject unless I wanted to get into a fight. I loved my newborn daughter Chiara very much and no matter how tired I was I would always take care of her with great joy.

I was never too tired for her. I would change diapers in the middle of the night and I would hold her tight but gently, singing Italian songs till she went back to sleep, peacefully at times sucking on my little finger serving as a last minute improvised pacifier. I would spend hours playing with her, teaching her Italian, colors, numbers. It was always a joy to come home and get rewarded with a genuine loving smile. Every time I saw her, even when she was already asleep, the fatigue of a hard day at work would magically vanish into thin air and new refreshed energy would set in, making me realize how much I have been receiving and how little I have been giving. The smell of a newborn, the touch of your own flesh, the materialized and unconditional love of my own blood was enough to make me forget all the problems in my life, or at least momentarily. Unfortunately, even though I was madly in love with my daughter I always had the fear my marriage would not last long. A few months into it and my relationship with Maury was a disaster: I tried to resolve my problems at home, but inevitably we separated, very amicably and very sadly. Today, Maury and I are good friends bounded by respect of our roles in Chiara's life. We have always put our child first before any of our own problems and it has worked out well. It has not always been easy. Actually it has been quite difficult, but it comforts me that we can be there for each other whenever a word of support is needed.

There are also comical situations that accompany our days: starting from the understanding that no one is sane in the service industry. I recall hysterical episodes and situations unique on their own, and always make me laugh—practical jokes played in the kitchen, clueless performances turned into restaurant classics, and real life snapshots that get placed in the restaurant life photo album forever. In my early days as a chef I was supervising a kitchen crew of four young, enthusiastic cooks. I was 20 years old and our days together were very long and very intense. We formed a great and natural friendship in and out of the kitchen, and we would spend time together on our day off with our respective girlfriends enjoying each other's company. We used to play jokes all the time, all day long, as it became an obsession of ours to plan the most malicious and unusual tricks we could think of.

Summers in Washington, D.C., are very hot. Temperatures rise over 100 degrees, and the humidity factor brings temperatures even higher to unbearable levels. Lee was an incredibly fun person who loved to work out and loved to cook. This guy had so much talent he could have become a great chef, but his priorities were set to different directions and his passion for cooking was not as vivid as his free spirit or love for life. I do not think I ever saw him upset once in the 27 years I have known him. Bright and always with a smile on his face, willing to help others, genuinely caring for people: a good friend I really miss and love. We all used to come to work early in the morning, mostly by car, and we would park our vehicles in the back alley of the restaurant all day long. As a respectable Italian restaurant we would work with all sorts of cheeses from back home, different textures and taste, one of those was Gorgonzola cheese with its piercing, pungent aroma.

One of my daily routines was to sneak out from the back door of the kitchen at night and to the parking lot to spread generous amounts of Gorgonzola cheese on Lee's muffler. When driving the muffler would get extremely hot and it would cook the cheese sitting right on top of it, dragging the thick and undesired smell everywhere on hot summer days all over town. Whenever Lee would stop in front of the restaurant at the usual red light on his way home, other cars would often stop next to his. I remember looking at the passengers covering their nose, making faces and comments, turning their heads in search of the source of that horrible stench. It was hilarious! We would stand outside waiting for him to drive by and Lee, always a good sport, would laugh with us, apologizing to cars on his left and right up until the light would change. It was a genius joke because there was no proper way to wash it off completely as the melted cheese would stick on it almost permanently. I remember one morning when he arrived at work laughing, telling us how his date walked out on him while they were making out in his car as the smell of the cheese was way too intense to concentrate on anything else. Upset, she left him there and took a cab home instead. Brilliant!

He would play the same trick on me at times, taking the joke even further when he spread some cheese on the kitchen phone receiver. He would go in the dining room and sneak in a call to the kitchen line. I would answer promptly, pressing a big chunk of Gorgonzola in my ear only to realize he got me good and quick. That smell would stay with me for the rest of the day no matter what I did to get rid of it or how I washed it.

On boring summer nights the whole kitchen crew would step out in the back alley holding at least a dozen eggs each. The very low building separated the alley from the very busy P Street that on prime time evenings would populate with couples and large crowds passing by. Hidden and unseeing they would throw eggs across the roof like in the *Braveheart* movie scene when the English archers would unleash their fury on the enemies. Then they would run immediately inside, pulling the door shut behind them, then into the dining room to the restaurant front door facing P Street to see the results of their actions. I certainly did not condone these actions and I put a stop to them, but it is typical for restaurant workers to let off steam by pulling such pranks. I remember one day in a video store someone next to me was complaining to a friend how he got hit by eggs walking down on his way to a date one night. The very next day we all renamed it Peggs Street.

There are so many fun situations that occurred over the years it is virtually impossible to remember them all. Some of the ones I recall best take place in the kitchen, other memories come from the usual temperamental staff, the older servers facing the end of their careers, the manipulating forced mistakes induced on new employees, the miscommunications with dishwashers, the clueless state of mind of the untrained off the boat Italian waiters and so on...

On a chilly Tuesday morning in late fall I asked a dishwasher to rinse the organic rabbits from the slimy film that developed on them overnight. I was very excited for the upcoming wild game dinner that next evening because I was able to finally purchase buckshot wild hare from Pennsylvania. It was very rare to find such incredibly fresh product and as matter of fact I waited for over a month before I got the green light from the farmer. I cut the veggies and I scaled all the necessary ingredients to make the stew. When I asked the dishwasher if he had cleaned the rabbits, he showed me the most incredible golden smile. He motioned with his hand to follow him into the dish room and begged me to wait one quick minute. I was confused. I turned my head and just like the Thanksgiving Macy's parade here they were coming out slowly from the dishwasher machine—white, cleaned and sanitized. I held my face with both hands and I broke in the most desperate laugh.

A similar situation occurred with the chicken broth one day right after we removed the big stockpot from the stove that had cooked for four hours along with chicken bones, veggies and herbs.

"Please strain this through the fine cone," I said.

"Si, si!" The immediate response rang in the air with excitement. Five minutes later the same guy came over the cooking line and handed me a hotel pan full of bones, herbs and dry vegetables.

"Where's the chicken broth I asked you to strain?" I asked.

"Basura" he replied, translated for trash.

I stood like an idiot holding the hotel pan, looking around the room in disbelief while the rest of the kitchen broke down in the most pitiful laugh. The chicken broth was washed down the drain and the precious bones had been preserved for a rainy day.

Lou, a veteran server in the mid-80s, was tending the table of the famed ABC News correspondent John Scali, who was then a regular in our restaurant. His secret involvement as messenger between the Kennedy administration and the Soviet Union in 1962 made him a pivotal figure in resolving the Cuban Missile Crisis from the brink of nuclear war. Mr. Scali was entertaining important guests and asked ahead of time to make sure the service was top-notch. Lou's new back server was Jamal, a young kid from Eritrea with no experience and on his second day at work. It was Halloween week and I remember the kitchen was armed with masks and costumes for the pre-Halloween party we were supposed to attend that very evening after service.

How did we screw up the dinner of the person responsible to have possibly saved the planet from nuclear disaster? Right this way, please.

We all put our masks on and convinced Jamal that everyone just got ordered to gear up. Serving an important guest wearing a Halloween mask was the best way to show appreciation for the American traditions and for this great country that hosts so many immigrants like us. Jamal did not own either a costume or a mask so we gave him one of the *Star Wars* movie character Darth Vader. We quickly explained, rehearsed and guided him on how to duplicate the character's voice similar to the one in the movie with a low robotic tone, giving life to a realistic and passable impersonation. He was hesitant at first, but then, filled with patriotic excitement he put on the mask and marched to the table holding a water pitcher. He stood table side in silence until Mr. Scali and his guests raised their heads in surprise, confusion and a little fear I am sure.

"Would you like more waaateeerrrrrrr" Jamal asked as instructed, mimicking the character.

Bingo! Lou ran across the dining room and pulled him away from the table, pushed him into the kitchen and threw the mask across the room, ran back to the table and apologized for what just happened. Mr. Scali was speechless and quite embarrassed. He later explained that what had happened was the second most awkward scenario of his life: the first was in 1962 when at the Occidental restaurant near the White House he secretly met the chief of Soviet intelligence, Aleksandr Fomin, the counselor of the Soviet embassy. That day the server accidentally switched orders and Mr. Scali wound up with pork chops instead of his crab cakes. Well, that night at least we got his order right.

Some of the funniest situations I remember with a smile on my face as they are still vivid, real even though they are from 25 years ago. Most of the time our jokes were orchestrated for our own amusement targeting new hires, testing their intelligence, their level of experience and at times just because they seemed clueless. It was no surprise we would ask the new and barely English-speaking food runners to march into the dining room and to scream out loud to all working servers, "86 fellatio! 86 fellatio! We have all the orders in, but from now on no more fellatio!" Of course we would do this only when the dining room was full of guests. We would play constructive jokes on those who did not like us very much and would constantly make comments with disrespect and insults. It is the way most restaurant workers blow off steam and release the stress of a high-pressure environment like a successful restaurant.

Luciano was a gambler, with few morals and little drive in life. He had a good heart, though, and we loved him for that. Tall, skinny with unmistakable white hair, Luciano was about 50 years old when I first arrived in 1986. In the restaurant where we worked the kitchen was smaller than my bedroom. There was a sliding-door beverage refrigerator right behind the small pass across the kitchen line where all sorts of food was stored in absolute disorganization and chaotic mess. Berries, cheeses, meats, fish, vegetables and pastry items, they all shared the same shelves. That refrigerator looked like a failed experiment on the island of Doctor Moreau.

"This guy at table 9 wants some pecorino cheese to finish his wine with," Luciano said in a hurry. We were backed up in the kitchen and on the verge of losing it.

"It's right there on the top shelf in the refrigerator. Help yourself, we're in the weeds!" I said and so he did.

Luciano grabbed a chunk of cheese, placed it on a small plate and served it. A few minutes later the gentleman at table 9 starts waving his hand. Luciano went over.

"This pecorino is very sweet," the guest said.

"Of course! In Italy we have sweet pecorino, cave-aged pecorino, even peppered pecorino," he lectured.

"No! This is really sweet, taste it." And so he did. He was right! This pecorino was unusually very sweet, way too sweet for any cheese.

What are the chances! Dumb, dumb Luciano served a big chunk of white chocolate instead.

Another waiter we really liked was Umberto. A very simple Sicilian man, uneducated, not very professional, but this man did not have a bad bone in his whole body. He was what he was and they hired him just for that: a stable pony. His ways were quite unorthodox and borderline rude, but he really meant well.

When he started working at the restaurant, he was placed under the wings of my dear friend Stefano, a veteran server who is also my daughter's godfather and an incredibly smart and fun person to be with. Still today we share the same sense of humor and the same appreciation for life. Stefano was in charge of guiding Umberto through all aspects of service, selling strategies, wine pairings, server-guest communications and teamwork. Often he would come to the kitchen with tears running down his face, laughing insanely. And so day after day there was always a new story from the adventures of clueless Umberto.

One evening he took the wine order from the host of a small party. The selected Pinot Grigio was priced at $35 and Umberto was visibly not happy with it. So he confronted the host right in front of his guests.

"Sir, why would you order something so inexpensive? That makes you look so cheap in front of everyone else. Order a good bottle like $80, $100. C'mon!"

Umberto did not see anything wrong with his inappropriate comments. He thought he was being funny and entertaining with open and personalized dialogs to his guests.

Between all the dreams and the realities of the restaurant industry, all the expectations and cruel surprises, the good and bad moments, the unpaid sales taxes, the outstanding and unpaid bank loans, the success and the misery, the failing and the succeeding, one might come to ask why do we get ourselves into such demanding, health-declining, family-destructive and mind-losing, life-complicating business?

Two reasons: for those professionals who see the light at the end of the tunnel we are slaves of our own passion, nothing else is more important than our job and everything else becomes secondary and it just gets in our way. For those who have no passion or do not care about finding any light at the end of the tunnel it is a very fast way to generate cash: just as fast as it is made it is spent and blown away even faster, usually all in a matter of hours.

Ironically, Charlie Saah had a very valid point stating the two best days of a restaurant owner may be the day you open and the day you close, but between those two days there is an explosive and passionate rich life only the ones who were born to live it can understand, respect and love.

I, for sure, am one of those, proudly.

Chapter Thirteen
Criticisms, Opinions and Judgments
The Heavy Hand of the Press

All rise!

At times I imagine I am in an overcrowded culinary courtroom where the jury has come to a decision on my behalf. I am wearing a classic, comfortable chef uniform instead of the traditional orange jumpsuit, and I am standing in the middle of the room showing no visible emotions on my face, head high. Proud, no matter what. Today's selected undercover food writer changed his identity to the honorable judge who is about to read the writer's very personal review/sentence for everyone to hear, and I can only hope it to be a fair one.

When I entered this business I was made aware of my culinary rights; I was told I would never have the possibility of appealing any published sentences and to forget any clemencies from the parole board in case I may have an argument. I am the prisoner of my own work. Does my opinion count? Sure, but for me only. In an era when everyone is a food critic I understand a few, I respect fewer and I trust no one, but a personal opinion must be respected.

Growing up professionally in a cosmopolitan town like Washington, D.C., I have learned how important the power of the press really is. As a teenager fresh from Italy I arrived in Washington via San Diego after a disastrous four month gig—green, shy and professionally unaware of culinary journalists or of food critics' existence.

My training in culinary school taught me to love the profession, to carefully select ingredients, to respect them, and mostly to work with pride. The focus for all of us was to graduate and to become one day the best chef we could possibly be. It was our dream to transform the hobby we loved into a working profession. In our culinary program there was no room for specifics on how to attract the attention of the press. It was not an option.

Back in Torino in the mid 1980s there were very few columns in the daily paper, *La Stampa*, about food, only fragments of recipes published here and there, mentions of restaurants or the name of a local culinary professor who had written the usual and expected boring cookbook. The internet did not exist, there was no Twitter, no blogs, no chats and information was limited to the printed version in the 24-hour format.

There was, however, a lot of buzz about the Michelin stars rating for those chefs who back then were considered unapproachable movie stars and from a completely different culinary galaxy, such as Paul Bocuse or Gualtiero Marchesi. The way I remember there was either "nothing or everything" and as a young scholar I grew up in the "nothing" dimension, but as a young cook at the beginning of my career in Washington I got exposed and overwhelmed with "everything".

I remember my very first month in the kitchen of the old Galileo restaurant surrounded by fellow schoolmates flown in from Italy to work and to gather experience: we were absolutely shocked at how much importance was given to any publication. There was so much pressure, fear and alert each time a food critic would walk into the restaurant. The very first time I met the *Washingtonian* magazine food and wine critic's Robert Shoffner was in 1987. Chef Roberto called me to the table where he was sitting with Mr. Shoffner. I was very excited; I thought it was a great honor for him to introduce me to a food critic. I was only 18 and my heart was beating uncontrollably.

"Taste the polenta," Roberto said. "What's the matter with you? Can't you see you forgot to put salt? And the rabbit stew is missing the black olives."

I think I was about to cry when Mr. Shoffner turned to Roberto and said, "Roberto, there is nothing wrong with the polenta, and the stew is absolutely delightful, delicate and very flavorful. Did you make this yourself?" he asked me.

"Yes, sir," I said, exchanging eye contact for a second only.

"What's your name?"

"Enzo Fargione," Roberto said. "He just arrived last month from Torino. We had the same teacher back home in the culinary school, just different years."

I shook Mr. Shoffner's hand, he turned to Roberto and said, "You might want to keep this one; he has a great hand and genuine talent."

"OK, you can go now." Roberto dismissed me.

I went back to the kitchen with a concussion: Wow! That man really liked what I cooked.

That was my very first experience with the press. Each time Mr. Shoffner would eat at Galileo I would always make a point to say hello, with Roberto's permission. Many times he asked me to sit with him and chatted about cooking, Italy, ingredients and about his personal culinary experiences and travels. Other times he simply wanted some company while sharing a glass of grappa (or two) at lunchtime. He indeed was an extraordinary and very charismatic man, who always dressed elegantly and with an unmistakable candid, classy style. I liked him immensely for his friendly and genuine humanitarian approach with people.

His printed recommendations were considered sacred, his comments and point of views were as valuable as blessings from the pope. He created a long trusting and amicable relationship with restaurateurs and chefs in the industry based more on the appreciation for the ingredients and execution other than fearful or forced professional distance.

Of greater importance, in my opinion, were the weekly and much awaited Sunday restaurant reviews from the *Washington Post* by Miss Phyllis Richman. What was meant to be a five-year tryout turned out to be 24 years of passionate work. She delighted us all with her very personal insights, and the quality of her work made her one of the most influential food critics in the nation. She was feared, respected, and surprisingly ruthless at times: "Trust no one" was her motto. Yet she was fair.

Miss Richman was a conservative writer, not very sociable, not very approachable, and at times not very friendly; she always kept a professional safe distance with restaurant owners and chefs and you would rarely see her smile while dining. She was extremely determined, driven and way too direct with those who, like me, were courageous or pretentious enough to go to the table and inquire how her meal was. She would look at you and ask questions with very inquisitive eyes, waiting for a valid and suitable answer worthy of changing her already-set opinion on things.

She would remark that the risotto she had just tasted seemed slightly undercooked.

"How come?" she would ask, looking at you while gently highlighting your mistakes. She would nod and dismiss you after hearing the answer, politely and with class without letting any emotions give away her thoughts or opinions.

She reminds me of the much feared character in the 1995 movie *The Usual Suspects*: Keyser Soze. Screw up Miss Richman's meal and she will write about you, in details and with no reservations.

It was indeed hard to imagine that under such a serious and determined persona was hiding a very gentle and sweet woman. I feel privileged to have had the opportunity and the honor to learn who she really is: after her professional career ended she only slowed down a little, her retirement was a formality related only to her keyboard, file cabinet and deadlines. Her passion for food and wine still drives her to attend numerous food related social events around Washington and she keeps a very close pace with today's industry with the same vivid excitement as ever. When she retired close to 13 years ago, she left an incredible legacy behind that was inherited by today's *Washington Post* food critic, Mr. Tom Sietsema, who had worked with her for many years as an editorial aide.

"She changed my life and taught me standards," Sietsema told me. "What I am today professionally, it's thanks to her."

The days of Mr. Shoffner's and Miss Richman's race to journalistic glory were much different than what they are today. Before the advent of the internet there was a way to write purely from the heart, unconditioned from rumors, preconceived notions of confusing Twitter messages or unfiltered personal reports from diners or food bloggers.

The race to scoop news will always be the same no matter the writer, topic or publication, but over the years there have been dramatic changes in formulating the way the message is sent to readers and mostly the impact it has on chefs and restaurants. The way I remember, in the pre-internet era you would get the turkey without any sides: a single and very direct article describing good and bad, personal opinions, suggestions, in-depth description of the food, service and the overall feeling of a dining experience in an extreme and very personal way. Articles read like they had been written in a tower locked away in isolation, alone only with your thoughts and feelings, unreachable by any possible interference: you never knew what to expect until the article came out. Its impact was just amazing and indescribable on the selected restaurant: the masses would flock and line up for days in order to sample the truth and make their own, and the common interest was vivid and genuine, mostly refreshing for businesses regardless of its outcome. A single writer's opinion could not be questioned, debated or challenged in any way. It was simply accepted and indirectly imposed.

Nowadays I feel the reader receives an editorial turkey with 50 extra sides: the article and its substance is better than ever, details do not only target the restaurant activities or its concept, but go much deeper into personal lives of the chefs, managers, mixologists and restaurant owners, their professional dreams, media activities, blogger notes, celebrity opinions, hype, expectations and celebrity visits.

Readers do not respond to weekly or monthly articles like they used to. Did they lose interest? No! The interest is still very much alive and people feed on culinary news more than ever, but the menu of choices has expanded considerably, maybe too much.

So who do you trust? There is way too much to choose from out there as the truth is hidden by thousands of very different personal opinions, enough to convince even the most sober reader to desperately enter a review rehab. Consequently, if the interest is diversified, so is the patronage. Fewer people are taken by the excitement of trying a newly reviewed restaurant. The economy is unpredictable. Some do not even take the time to buy the printed version anymore as news travels much faster electronically and directly to the palm of your own hand.

A Las Vegas icon of the restaurant and hotel industry once told me: "Enzo, it does not matter what the press says about you, good or bad it's unimportant. The important thing is that they talk about you." There is a fair amount of truth in that statement, but the essence of what transpires by reading an article is nowadays altered by questionable doubts since different and alternative versions are available. The result is often a very big confusion of what to believe.

As the food industry has dramatically changed in the past 30 years so has the way to report its news. Many professionals have redesigned the industry, many writers and chefs have emerged to glory and stardom, and many new restaurants have opened with concepts once considered unimaginable, reshaping the dining scene forever. For example, molecular gastronomy has shaken the food industry the most for the past 15 years.

Emulating one person's interpretation of avant-garde personalized cooking (Ferran Adria, El Bulli restaurant, Spain) so many cooks and chefs are curious, fascinated or tempted to dive into momentary exploration of this new incredible way of cooking, sooner or later. Others adopt this technique and make a career out of it.

Heston Blumenthal, from the decorated restaurant The Fat Duck, just outside London, is the English answer to Ferran Adria, cooking in a way that exceeds even the most unexpected expectations, combining food with the unthinkable: see his dish "Sounds of the Sea," where the diner is given an iPod to hear the sound of the ocean while eating a lookalike moving wave seafood dish. Nowadays more senses are stimulated while dining: the usual vision, taste and smell factors have stretched out to touch and sound as well.

In the States there are two restaurants that have achieved success offering complete and unique molecular gastronomy concepts: Grant Achatz in Chicago at Alinea restaurant and in New York City at WD50 restaurant by Wylie Dufresne. The number one restaurant in the world, according to the annual San Pellegrino list of best 50 restaurants is Noma in Copenhagen, Denmark, where chef Rene Redzepi applies his vision of Nordic cooking in a hardcore molecular gastronomy version with unusual combination of local and seasonal flavors that could be categorized as bizarre: deep-fried moss, sea-buckthorn and birch appear on his menus almost daily.

One thing has not changed: the impact the press can have when judging a restaurant, indirectly reshaping its course of business. How do we restaurateurs deal with that?

I think a single opinion must be respected, but I do not have to agree with it. Incorrect statements lacking basic knowledge or understanding usually drive into negativity when judging someone's work, and when that happens it bothers me a lot. Do you want to write about my work? At least get the facts straight first and educate yourself about items, concepts or ingredients you are not familiar with, then you can tell us what you think.

I have great respect for Mr. Sietsema because even if I do not always agree with his statements and his reviews he is one of the very few reporters, along with James Beard Award winner Mr. Tim Carman, who fact-checks the source by asking proper and related questions about specific dishes, cooking methods, restaurant concept and many more details before he dives into writing. Very few understand the reasons or the drive behind writers' work and I for sure am one of those who is often puzzled and surprised whenever I read a glorious review or a very negative one. Most journalists rate their reviews 50 percent on food and 50 percent on service and ambiance. At times a restaurant is over awarded with compliments and star ratings; others are left in limbo or on cruise control at the very same speed for years when instead they could be celebrated a little more for their consistency, quality, concept and hard work. Writing and dining is very personal, but so is admiration and likeability. It is only logical and normal they can influence a judgment even if any writer would swear journalistic integrity cannot be compromised or influenced in any possible way.

Journalists, reporters, food writers are humans and have real feelings and real personal opinions, likes and dislikes, good days and bad days: journalistic candor is bent, influenced, and at times distorted because of it. It is often tickled, tempted and tested as one can only write based upon his knowledge and his state of mind.

Articles are written once the information is gathered and opinions are formed as a consequence. Often, some of them regret having written articles either too complimentary or too harsh or with sentences that may seem fit at the time, but not really suitable for the story and it is impossible to go back and adjust, retouch or fix.

Mr. Tim Carman, in response to the question, "Did you ever regret writing a piece after it's published?" once told me that when he writes a story he tries to combine facts and opinions based on his personal experience, but at times specific sentences or even the way a story is interpreted by the reader can be quite different from the way it was intended to be received.

He once wrote about a restaurant whose chef had recently departed. A few weeks later he dropped in to scout the work of the new cook in charge. He was not too enthusiastic about his work or the changes he had implemented and so he wrote very bluntly, "He's not worthy to lick the spoon of his predecessor."

You can only imagine what kind of dust storm he created.

I decided to go to the source and consult some of the most prestigious and influential names of culinary journalism, James Beard Award winners, nationwide respected food writers and those who have shaped culinary journalism for the past 30 years in America and beyond.

I compiled a list and I set telephone interviews with very specific and customized questions for each one of them.

To my surprise they all agreed to dedicate their personal time.

Mr. Todd Kliman, from *Washingtonian* magazine, spent almost two hours with me on a Saturday morning, I suspect calling from a playground since I could hear his toddler son in the background throughout the whole interview. I found incredible, welcoming open doors to discuss our complex and demanding industry, the way it has changed and reshaped over time, their personal reasoning behind their writings, memories and of course I tried to find vulnerable and soft spots in all of them in order to stimulate the most honest and personal answers.

Only one high profile journalist of national acclaim turned me down, suggesting me to read one of his "Paesano" books instead as, according to him, all the answers to my (at that point still unasked) questions were stored right in it.

I am still looking.

After many years of distance, fear and forbidden line crossings I finally learned how to feel completely normal and at ease when dealing directly with those who judge me on a daily basis. The professional respect and distance will never fade, but it is refreshing, surprising and quite pleasant to mutually open a window and let out some of the thick air that has stuffed our professional corridors for years. Suddenly as I breathe a cleaner trusting breeze, I cracked the smallest possible smile, and in a small corner I found my very humble culinary peace of mind.

For a large publication a big obstacle in earning readers' trust is the overnight self-declared food bloggers whose work, most of the time, is not edited and therefore the reader is left puzzled, questioning its accuracy as mixed messages confuse the masses. I respect those who have earned their way, reporting out of passion: they mingle with chefs in restaurants, and they are eager to learn and to understand the industry. Their writing, most of the time, reflects dedication and consistency.

There have been times in my career when a respectable food reporter, after conducting an interview with me, has published his story as expected and we all understood the process. The unusual and disturbing part is that a freshly self-appointed writer for a new website decided to comment on the story, feeding on the crumbs of someone else's work, trashing the article, me and my restaurant with harsh words, judgments and unrelated, inappropriate comments in order to shake the system and get noticed.

The writers I interviewed have continuously highlighted the importance of journalistic integrity, and stressed reporters should always pay for their meals and with no exceptions. If they represent a large publication and are paid to report it is only natural an expense account is set up for them to pick and choose restaurants, cities and on occasion countries to report from. However, there are times when a mutual understanding is arranged between the restaurant and those who work for a small publication, a food blog website or a local television station. The restaurant arranges samples of food, cocktails, free dinners, etc. and invites the selected reporter to experience and sample.

While this may seem a little peculiar and off standards, I assure you it is absolutely normal and it is all based on mutual respect and understanding. The difference between big name writers and small local papers or privately owned food sites is limited budgets: they need writing material and restaurants need exposure.

I encourage those who are starting out and trying to genuinely write stories and report food news. Some are very inexperienced, others have done it for years and are excellent at it, and many more do not belong in this industry.

It has happened many times that after a glowing review is published people came up to me and asked me questions such as, "How much did you pay for that?" I just simply smile and shake my head in response. However, occasionally some barriers are attempted to be broken.

I asked Sietsema if in his long career anyone has ever tried to bribe him. "Sure! It has happened several times." He explained he occasionally receives checks from restaurant owners, chefs and enclosed notes in sealed envelopes. He even received a video tape once from a restaurant owner explaining in detail how his business and the wellbeing of his family depended on a review from *The Washington Post*.

He also assured me that each and every attempt is returned to the sender, and no matter whom or what, his professional decisions cannot be influenced, ever. Washington is a very diplomatic city full of embassies and politics, a town driving on cruise control with little ups and downs or excitements, where everybody thinks they are somebody, me first.

Washington is a great town I fell in love with at first sight as it has a very familiar European feel, populated by people from all over the world with their traditions and customs highlighted by their cultures, their folklore and of course by their many different cuisines. As the dining scene constantly changes, new culinary generations settle in, it is constantly evolving and it is already changing to what it is going to be for the next three decades.

In Washington there are eateries offering cuisines from almost every country, the downtown area has exploded with traditional and unusual concept restaurants of any kind at any levels and our suburbs offer some of the best, unprecedented, affordable, and authentic food we ever had. And yet Washington is not considered a respectable food town by many, not if we compare it to New York or Boston, Chicago or San Francisco, to name a few.

Even one of our very own top food writers, Todd Kliman, has said, "Compared to other cities, you just don't get excited about food in D.C.," and he adds, "D.C. does not have too much passion for food. It's a very balanced city and has other interests. Washington needs more fun." I agree with the last part of his statement, but in my opinion Washington has emerged as an incredible food lover place based on the very hard work of people who really care for quality and it shows by its consistency. The recent invasion of celebrity chefs who have opened restaurants and eateries around town confirm this evolutionary phenomenon is clearly projected to the next several years. Even Alain Ducasse decided to come to Washington and stay awhile.

Mr. Tim Carman rightfully says the industry is changing in a way that makes it much harder for the small Mom and Pop restaurants to exist, mostly because of the real estate price increases that force operators to seek locations in the outskirts of the city where it is more economical. "I would love to see more of the affordable international cuisine restaurants in town," he says. Miss Phyllis Richman spoke her mind, saying Washington has been a respectable food city from time to time, but it still needs a stronger representation of artistic international cuisines such as Vietnamese or Scandinavian.

Opinions vary. Even Sietsema bluntly declared, "Washington, D.C., emerged as a food city in 2006 and it's definitely in the top 10 list in this country."

When I first arrived in Washington there were only a handful of good restaurants and many more offering poor imitations of ethnic food.

In the mid 1980s there were no American labeled restaurants, but a string of steak houses and several Continental or Mediterranean eateries of mixed cuisines such as Mexican, Asian, Italian or French. On a given menu one could find quesadillas and pot stickers as appetizers; steaks, hamburgers, grilled and fried fish as main courses, and the occasional overcooked pastas with thick as glue tomato sauce or with cement-like cream and vegetables. Crème brulée, crème caramel and apple pie a la mode were among the most popular desserts at the time.

There was no clear balance for the everyday diner unless the choice of the day was ethnic. Any other restaurant concept was a pure state of confusion. There were also a few over-the-top restaurants such as Le Pavillion by Yannick Cam, Le Lion D'or, Mr. K, The Prime Rib or Jean Louis at the Watergate for those who could afford.

According to each and every prominent food figure I talked to in Washington, the evolution and transformation of the local food culture started with Jean Louis Palladin.

He came to the U.S. as an already decorated and much accomplished chef from France with a suitcase full of hopes and two Michelin stars to helm what would soon become one of the most revolutionary restaurants in the U.S., Jean Louis at the Watergate.

He was a very eccentric man, not always pleasant, not always sociable, so much that someone labeled him Grumpy Frenchman. Today I would label him the revolutionary culinary genius. Even when he publicly apologized for a very animated exchange of opinions in his restaurant with a respectable food writer that made the tour of the town, he did it in a way so typical of him: "I'm an artist and even artists make mistakes."

He gave life and directed professionally some of today's best chefs who proudly continue to share his vision and enthusiasm in the cooking industry, like Eric Ripert or Daniel Boulud, to name a couple. Washington was not ready for him, in any possible way: he got so frustrated with the poor available ingredients, with the lack of flavors of the meat and fish and with the culinary ignorance of the average diner he decided to shake the system and went to war against mediocrity. He started a quest for excellence for both chefs and diners.

He helped to grow food business such as lamb, scallops, organic vegetables and fresh herbs. He made connections with local farmers across America. He encouraged food purveyors and stimulated food import companies to better source their products from overseas, but mostly he shared his resources and techniques with everyone. He created a better industry purely based on quality and stubbornness, and he was always searching for the ultimate, freshest ingredients.

Some, like me, were lucky enough to know him a little better than the average person and spend time with him in and out of the kitchen. I always felt he needed to create a food culture using his beliefs and his magnetic personality: he was always so serious when he talked about food, at any level and at any time.

His early misunderstandings, animated discussions and fights with some of the local food critics are legendary. His uncontrollable temper in the kitchen is legendary, as well as his weakness for beautiful women or his passion for drinking all night and smoking countless cigarettes in the kitchen. It all defined the eccentric person he was. He portrayed a very intimidating image of a tough guy, but indeed he was a very giving and caring man, participating and leading many charity events across the country.

I remember when he went on the Dave Letterman show in 1993 and brought a single giant clam to make a soup with and shocked the audience. He was a unique talent, one of those who could make something exceptional out of leftovers, and over the years I learned you needed to dislike him before you loved him. Unfortunately, he passed away in 2001. However, Jean Louis Palladin is remembered for his eternal passion and respect for food, his will to create and his incredible artistic vision that has modeled and paved the way for so many chefs, cooks, housewives, food critics, and me.

Back then the press had great challenges in understanding and accurately reporting the mind and the drive of this revolutionary rebel. Reporting has never been easy.

And it has never been easy for anyone who has wanted to keep his identity hidden in order to genuinely experience a restaurant without any favoritism or sudden last-minute changes.

Many writers even wear a disguise when dining out, such as fake goatees or mustache, hats and wigs and make reservations under fake names and aliases. They follow these guidelines even when speaking in public: I remember once I saw Miss Richman talking at the Zoofari charity event in D.C., holding a Venetian carnival mask to her face, adorned with ribbons and feathers, for the entire speech. You will never find them on the internet, there are no posted pictures on their Facebook profiles, and if you Google them you will only find their names associated with the publication they represent.

When their face photos occasionally leak out, there is a frantic rush by some restaurateurs to post them in kitchens, hostess stands, bars, etc., and it is passed along to servers and kitchen members just like family pictures, encouraging them to hold on to it for a rainy day. Those who endorse this type of behavior have lost focus of the professional aspect of our job. Some business owners and chefs lose sleep in anticipation of a possible visit, they get nervous, they stress their staff, and they compromise the goal and the concept of their business. Some try to enhance a food critic's experience by adjusting their professional beliefs, modifying the dynamics of service and the vision of their cooking. They are often left questioning their actions and knowledge, stumbling in confusion.

This is a business where ideas must be clear from the start. To implement personal skills into a concept is never easy because there is so much ego and ambition involved in everything we do.

If a system is already running and well-tested why would anyone change it for just one person? I guarantee there is nothing that can be done in 10 minutes to enhance someone's experience. When a harsh review is published, it is not usually related to the mistakes that occurred during a single visit, but of a concept that constantly delivers weakness in food quality and in service execution. Critics usually pay three to four visits to a restaurant for both lunch and dinner before forming a fair opinion. At times, however, the house could perfectly perform and follow every suitable rule and still receive a mediocre review. Judgment is indeed personal.

Critics know about good days and bad days, they are aware of new restaurants working out their kinks, they can spot not-quite-fully-trained staff or easily catch mistakes from the kitchen in just one visit.

Of course, I too get nervous whenever a journalist is dining in my restaurant, but I am a firm believer of a well-implemented system that does not differ between VIP guests and regular patrons: I consider all my guests VIP. This mentality is adopted by upscale restaurants and service industry organizations all over the world that try to make a refined service difference for their guests in an upscale and fine dining environment.

By following these parameters of work I realize it is much easier to minimize common mistakes and it is a more effective way to care for everything we do. Mostly, it is extremely rewarding on a personal level, an ego booster for a job well done and an automatic stimulation to constantly improve.

I would be a liar if I say I always succeed. At times I fail, but the most important thing is to constantly try, every day, graciously.

Occasionally I have received advice and suggestions from random journalists on how to change specific dishes and to possibly alter my cooking. I am a very good listener and I consider myself a moderate and humble man. I accept criticism and suggestions from anyone who has something intelligent to say.

But it does not mean all suggestions I hear are always correct. I have highlighted earlier in this very chapter that doubts frequently arise in the minds of journalists even after articles are written, and at times they are left to ponder on the quality and content of their published work.

Chefs do the same: I occasionally fail when creating new dishes, but I am humbly quick in correcting my work. Dedicated chefs perform following the same beliefs as journalists do: writing and cooking are not too different from each other; furthermore they are so very personal and come from the heart.

As much as I try to put in words where my culinary vision starts and where it ends, there is no realistic way to measure my inspirations, creativity, talent, limits or failures. For sure, I will never change my way of cooking just to meet the approval of any publications or any food critics. The heavy hand of the press comes in cycles and in a very surprising way, mostly unexpected.

Journalists glorify a restaurant or a chef for months and suddenly, when the buzz fades the interest dies with it. Occasionally they dust off old concepts and revisit establishments that have been left in a corner, but food journalism reports the news and it has to create as much interest as possible for the reader.

After all it's called "news" and not "olds."

For ambitious chefs like me, who are constantly trying to accomplish quality, it is so much harder to get established and to be respected. We work at higher risk; we openly expose ourselves and are subject to harsher criticism. In a journalist's mind usually the bigger the name, the bigger the expectations. At times I feel my professional career has been a constant charge elbowing my way in, trying to make room for myself. I cannot thank enough those who over the years have always shown interest for my public work, and I realize that without genuine and passionate interest there would not be criticism.

Every chef and restaurateur dreams of great articles, awards and infinite good press coverage as it all benefits business while elevating awareness, patronage and respect to a completely new level, but unfortunately being only a great chef is not enough to succeed.

A very popular chef friend of mine, who won the James Beard Award for outstanding chef in America, has been giving me two very contradictory pieces of advice in the past few years.

The first is to make sure my guests know I am always in the kitchen cooking and present each time they come in for dinner. The second is to attend as many social events as possible, mingling with bloggers, food writers, press representatives, shaking their hands and making contacts. I have to say that is very good, spot-on advice, but quite hard to implement.

I learned over the years the best thing I can do for myself is to work in a way that makes me professionally happy first and foremost. Chefs and restaurateurs will always be criticized: from a simple sandwich shop to a 3-star Michelin restaurant the main goals are always the same—the ability to create a successful business and the quest to a chef's personal success.

I guess I constantly feel the need to stand in a courtroom and to be judged, to explore my limits, to mature into a profession that has defined me and constantly fills my ego with the hope that one day I could be considered one of the greatest.

Ambition and pride have always crossed the path of success and disappointment driving throughout a chef's career. Some happily arrive at their destination, a few get lost, and others slow down, roll down the window and quietly ask food critics for directions.

The Follow Up

I wrote this Follow Up addition to this chapter out of complete surprise.

After I conducted my interviews and collected information I finally wrote my personal thoughts in the above chapter. Once edited, I felt the moral obligation to send the critics a copy of my manuscript since a few of them had expressed interest in reading it.

I have to be honest when I say for once I felt I was on the other side of the fence: I was somewhat glad and surprised to find out my writing had created a stir of emotions among those I had interviewed, and it involuntarily tested their human factor and made a valid point for my statements above.

I unwillingly provoked their reactions, similar to any other restaurateurs or chefs who have just read an article about their work.

I assure you I have no personal vendetta to settle or personal beef with anyone. The last thing I want is to create enemies with the national press that has elevated and critiqued my work over the years, almost always in a very positive way. My personal and professional relationships with each one of the journalists I interviewed is excellent to this day and based on mutual respect, honesty and admiration. But to me, it is just wonderful to witness a spontaneous reaction with genuine and realistic feelings from those who for once find themselves on the other side of the fence.

My quest remains to better understand those who criticize restaurants and chefs' work, their reasoning and the logic in their writings.

Food critics' responsibility is to their readers only; the job ends once the articles are printed and submitted before deadlines. The consequences that may occur because of their contents are irrelevant to the scope of their work. It is not that they do not care; they do and very much so. They are empathetic when a restaurant fails and extremely supportive when another succeeds, but the nature of their job is what it is: they certainly are not going to write a bad review and then invite a chef to sob on their shoulders. They will not hold a restaurateur's hand throughout therapy sessions or make personal investments in restaurants they harshly criticized in order to help them keep the doors open for business. They probably sleep very well at night and with few particular worries.

But for those who are exposed to public comments and criticism, it is an incredible and uncomfortable place to be: financial investments and life savings are at stake, personal relationships, marriages, college tuitions, personal health, stress and much more. It would be unthinkable to imagine journalists' and food critics' reactions if our roles were reversed.

They have great experience in dealing with those who disagree with their reviews. Numerous telephone calls, email messages and Facebook statements flock in with personal comments, suggestions and demands all the time after an article is published. Occasionally less-than-cordial conversations take place and animated discussions arise with infinite point of views. Bottom line: whatever has been printed cannot be changed, altered, smoothed out or revised, and unfortunately they cannot make everybody happy by giving everyone a 4-star rating.

During an interview a journalist opened up in the above matter, "Why do people get so upset? Don't they understand that it's all part of a process? They should not take it so personal or be so angry about it."

The very next day I sent the manuscript and I have received comments, suggestions, questions and requests from most of them. It seems like I might have struck a nerve, somehow. One prominent reviewer was extremely gracious and polite as well as full of compliments with a few requests and suggestions.

A magazine journalist followed up with an explanation of the facts, offering "needed amplifications" and possible changes for his quotes and statements. I simply replied by saying I felt strong about my beliefs as much as he felt strong about his. By not immediately agreeing with his requests and by assuring I would have considered changing my script to satisfy his request, I involuntary picked a fight that cost me a place in the *Washington's 100 Best*

Restaurant 2013 issue. A cheap shot, childish and way immature by someone I admire so much and consider one of the fairest in the industry. In the end, however, his suggestions were implemented and the manuscript corrected. Another expressed an interest in blogging about my opinions on critics and how I judge their work; mostly he was very sympathetic in bringing to my attention how by doing so I could effectively express my experiences with reviews.

I have come to understand that once stimulated, the human self-defense mechanism engages and turns active when someone's pride is poked or provoked, even with veteran professionals who deal with these sorts of things on a daily basis. How should I have handled their comments, demands, requests or suggestions?

Should I have replied with the same, "Why do people get so upset? Don't they understand it is all part of the process? They should not take it so personal or be so angry about it" statement I was given? I graciously accommodated each request by granting editorial review, and sentences and quotes were changed accordingly to their satisfaction. I realize our situations are hardly comparable.

After all, I am immensely grateful to all of them to have dedicated their time, their care and their interest, but mostly because this process has helped me understand better the dynamics of food journalism.

I will definitely never read a restaurant review the same way, as my level of education in the matter has been elevated to a point of understanding greater than an average reader. It is my hope that we each have a more comprehensive understanding of our roles in the restaurant industry. After all, our goals are very similar—to provide diners with an unforgettable experience and always with a very personal level of interpretation.

But I remain critical…as I am sure they do too.

Index to Recipes

Chicken Broth 31
Veal Stock Reduction 33
Lobster Broth 35
Vegetable Stock 36
Basil Infused Salt 40
Black Olive Infused Salt 41
Chianti Infused Salt 41
Deconstructed Sicilian Green Olive Poppers 41
White Corn and Reggiano Custard with Red Wine Caramel 44
Merlot Red Wine Caramel 45
Anise Dusted Tuna Lollipops 46
Black Peppercorn Anise Dust 46
Bagna Cauda Sauce 47
Gorgonzola Panna Cotta Eggshells 48
Gorgonzola Panna Cotta Cream 49
Candied Celery 50
Polenta Crackers 51
Fava Bean Stuffed Tempura Zucchini Blossoms 52
Fava Bean Stuffing 52
Tempura Batter 53
Cornets of Marinated Salmon and Crispy Fennel 54
Cornets Tulip Mix 55
Salmon Belly and Crunchy Fennel Marinate Mix 56
Salty Goose Liver Spoons and Green Tomato Marmalade 56
Prosecco/Port Wine Stock 58
Goose Liver Roll 58
Chianti Red Infused Salt 59
Deconstructed Dirty Vodka Martini 60
Regional Italian Oyster Shooters 62
Milk Chocolate-Coated Olive Oil Mousse Lollipops 63
Artichoke Mousse 67
Solid Spinach Foam 69
Candied Cherry Tomatoes 69
Ham and Peas in a Toothpaste Tube 71
White Chocolate/Black Olives Square Bites 75
Gorgonzola Cream 76
Poached Veal 84
Tonnato Sauce for Stuffing 84
Roasted Red Pepper Froth 85

Four-Minute Smoked Branzino Carpaccio in a Cigar Box 87
Citrus Dressing 88
Italian Sushi Rolls 91
Balsamic Vinegar Dressing 91
Pickled Shaved Carrots 92
Marinated Goat Cheese 92
Lemon Dressing 94
Chicken Liver Terrine 95
Vin Santo Gelatin 96
Rosemary and Roasted Garlic Bread 97
Marinated Alaskan Wild Salmon 100
Liquorice Froth 100
Arucola Fennel Salad 101
Veal Carpaccio 103
Parmesan Cheese Tulips 103
Black Truffles Lemon Dressing 104
Balsamic Vinegar Glaze 105
Bamboo Cone Stuffing 105
Deconstructed Buffalo Mozzarella Cubes 109
Balsamic Vinegar Gelatin 110
Poached Goose Liver Fantasy 111
Poached Cremona's Mostarda Goose Liver 112
Salty Hazelnut Florentines 113
Toasted Hazelnut Texture 114
Brioche 115
Balsamic Vinegar Gelato 115
Balsamic Vinegar Reduction 116
Tomato and Eggplant Popsicles with Basil Gelatin 117
Basil Gelatin 119
Green Peas Cappuccino 123
Goose Liver Custard 123
Porcini and Fontina Strudel 124
Crunchy Leeks 125
Winter Poached Duck Egg 126
Poaching White Vinegar Water 128
Crunchy Stuffed Sage Leaves 128
Port Wine Reduction Sauce 129
Aromatic Shellfish Broth in an Eggshell 131
Warm Wild Venison Carpaccio 135
Monkfish Liver Custard 140
Sliced Lemons and Chestnut Honey Preserve 141

Artichoke Chips	142
Parsley Powder	144
Butter Roasted Baby Octopus in Spicy Orange Caramel	144
Sweet Raw Polenta Sauce	146
Spicy Orange Caramel	147
Fried Basil Leaves	147
Marinated Roasted Heart of Lamb	149
Goat Cheese Sauce	150
Crispy Potato Rings	151
Gratinée Oysters with Crunchy Pearls by the Sea	152
Mascarpone and Parma Prosciutto Cream	154
Caper's Froth	155
Crunchy Caviar Pearls	155
Vegetarian Caviar Tin	156
Vegetarian Tin	157
Taleggio Fonduta	159
Roasted Artichoke Hearts on Roasted Bell Peppers Carpaccio	163
Black Olives Dressing	166
Baby Arucola White Asparagus Scorzone	167
Black Truffle Hazelnut Balsamic Dressing	168
Grilled Watermelon, Shaved Fennel, Toasted Almonds	169
Almond Oil Dressing	171
Roasted Vidalia Onions Liquorice (and Smoked Tuna Shaves)	172
Golden-Sweet Mustard Dressing	174
Capers Polenta Crackers	174
Deconstructed Ratatouille Honey Lemon Mint	176
Sweet Sour Pearled Onions	179
Honey Lemon Mint Dressing	180
Tomato Velvet Cubes	180
Black Olive Bread	181
Roasted Baby Beets	183
Creamy Goat Cheese Gelato	185
Lacquered Leeks Coins	185
Almonds Morelles Texture	186
Smoked Baby Spinach Crunchy Lobster and Scallops with Fresh Porcini Mushrooms	188
Shallots Vinegar Dressing	191
Creamy Tomino Treviso Radicchio Endive White Truffles	192
Barolo Quince	194
White Anchovies/Walnut Dressing Sauce	194

Creamy Tomino Flan 195
"Electric" Gelatin 195
White Truffle Oil 196
Chilled Honeydew Purée with Roasted Lobster 201
Spicy Sicilian Pepperoncino Gelatin 203
Wet Minestrone 207
Dry Minestrone 208
Crunchy Vidalia Onions 208
Stinging Nettles Pesto 209
For the Coffee Press Pot 209
Pumpkin/Amaretto Soup 212
Chestnut Raviolini 214
Spinach Pasta Dough 214
Chestnuts and Savoiardi Cookie Filling 214
Parmesan Cheese Foam for Siphon 215
Encapsulated Extra Virgin Olive Oil Teardrops 216
White Asparagus Cream Goose Liver Capunet 217
Black Truffle-Tomato Trifle 219
Parma Napoleon 220
Smoked Tomato Bread Soup
with Roasted Shrimp and Crunchy Vidalia Onions in Glass Vase 221
Smoked Tomato Broth 222
Smoked Tomato Paste 223
Focaccia Bread 223
Focaccia Croutons 224
Buffalo Ricotta Flan 227
Duck Sausage 228
Poached Quail Egg 229
Crispy Shallots 230
Artichoke Flan 233
Black Olive Froth 234
Farro and Roasted Garlic Crackers 235
Soft Pecorino di Pienza Croquettes 236
Risotto Gorgonzola Sicilian Pistachio Candied Red Beets 247
Crunchy Yellow Beet Chips 249
Risotto White Truffles and Butter Braised Cardoons 252
Barolo Gel Reduction 254
Risotto with Edible Gold Asparagus Tips Black Truffles 255
Melting Saffron Leaf 257
Risotto with Fresh Tomatoes, Sicilian Frantoio 258
Cherry Tomato Confit 260

Zucchini Blossoms Stuffed with Burrata 261
Basic White Pasta Dough 267
Saffron Pasta Dough 267
Tomato Pasta Dough 267
Black Squid Ink Dough 267
Porcini Pasta Dough 267
Red Beet Pasta Dough 267
Agnolotto Pasta Dough 267
Spinach Pasta Dough 267
Whole Wheat Pasta Dough 267
Red Pepper Pasta Dough 267
Reginette Filled with Smoked Buffalo Mozzarella 268
San Marzano Caviar 270
Basil Froth 271
Saffron Triangles Filled with Burrata 273
Green Peas Emulsion 275
Morel Mushrooms/Parma Prosciutto Ragù 275
Roasted Pancetta with Sage Froth 279
Sweet Breads and Cotechino Sausage Filling 277
Walnut Ricotta Sauce 278
Giant Agnolotto and Running Egg
with White Truffle Shavings and Reggiano Snow 280
Sheep Ricotta/Spinach Filling 281
Crunchy Squid Ink Cannelloni 282
Broccoli Filling 283
Quick Chanterelles Mushrooms Ragù 284
Cherry Tomato and Lobster Confit 285
Porcini Tortelli Filled and Crispy Vidalia Onions
with Black Truffle Shavings 286
Piedmont-Style Veal/Chicken/Cabbage Filling 287
Taleggio Speck Truffle Cream Sauce 288
Red Beet Fagotti and Running Quail Egg 290
Fonduta Cheese Filling 291
Green Asparagus Broth 292
Whole Wheat Pansotti 293
Black Truffle Reduction 295
Black Truffle Zabaglione 295
Artichoke Fondue 296
Pancetta/Porcini Mushrooms/Seared Shrimp Ragù 297
Cavatelli with Smoked Lobster and Porcini
with Green Peas in Sweet Garlic/Mascarpone/Thyme Cream 298

Cavatelli Dough 299
Sweet Garlic/Mascarpone/Thyme Cream 300
Red Peppers Bowties over Sicilian Sword Fish Ragù
with Crunchy Wild Fennel Flowers, Smoked Tuna Prosciutto 300
Sicilian Sword Fish Ragù 302
Artichoke Ragù 306
Modern Spaghetti Chitarra Style
with Instant Carbonara Sauce and Poached Duck Egg 307
Soft Roman Pecorino Fondue Sauce 308
Tomato Ricotta Gnocchi 310
Braised Lamb Ragù 311
Lithograph Pasta/Ink Press 313
Shellfish Stew 314
San Marzano Tomato Emulsion 314
Spicy Broccoli Rabé (or Rapini) Emulsion 315
Spinach Pappardelle in Duck Ragù 316
Pappardelle Pasta 316
Duck Ragù with Duck Livers 317
Liquid Toma Cheese Croquettes 318
Deconstructed Fresh Spaghetti "Aglio Olio" 318
Fresh Spaghetti Pasta 320
Solidified Olive Oil and Roasted Garlic Powder 320
Raw Parsley/Parmesan Cheese Foam 320
Baked Chilean Sea Bass 364
Roasted Norwegian Salmon 368
Sweet Garlic Broth 367
Baked Black Cod 370
Pickling White Vinegar Marinate 372
Spicy Yellow Curry Rub 372
Celery Juice Sauce 373
Charcoal Oil 374
Pan-Seared Striped Bass 374
Fennel Emulsion 375
Candied Lemon Rings 376
Milanese-Style Oyster Mushrooms 377
Crunchy Semolina-Encrusted Soft-Shell Crabs 379
Braised Pig's Ears 380
Tuscan-Style Oven-Baked Cannellini Beans Stew 381
Spicy Raw Tomato Froth 382
Seared Ahi Tuna in Lardo di Colonnata 382
Black Olives/Porcini Stuffing Purée 384

Sicilian Caponata	385
Assorted Dry Vegetable Chips	386
Sweet Water Shrimp and Spicy Salame Stuffing	388
Braised Leeks/Potato/Green Olives Ragù	389
Riesling/Carrot/Thyme Sauce	390
Pastrami-Style Butter-Poached Maine Lobster	391
Pastrami Spice Dust	393
Blood Orange Dressing	393
Italian-Style Crab Cakes	394
Warm Broccoli Emulsion	395
Salt Cured Duck Breast	401
Curing Seasoned Salt	403
Black Olive Sauce	403
Gruviere Cheese/Thyme Turnip Cakes	404
Roasted Veal Fillet and Sweetbreads	406
Blood Orange Mascarpone Cheese Sauce	409
Black Trumpets Mushroom Ragù	410
Rosemary Froth	410
Barolo Marinated Squab in Speck Cage	411
Chestnuts Mashed Purée	414
Caramelized Quince Ragù	415
Barolo Glaze	415
Rabbit Crepinette with Parma/Artichokes	418
Creamy Sage Sauce	420
Savory Ramps	420
Slow Roast Porchetta with Cracked Fennel Seeds	421
Porchetta Spice Marinade	424
Piadina Bread	424
Grappa Marinated Venison Saddle	425
Mashed Cauliflower Purée	427
Balsamic Chocolate Sauce	427
Crunchy Porcini Potato Mat	428
Sour Huckleberries Jam	429
Marinated Pork Ribs	431
Rib's Marinating Wet Dust	432
Italian Sausage	432
Pistou Green Sauce	433
Meatballs "Al Sugo"	434
Soft Black Pepper Polenta	435
Sauté Broccoli Rabé	435
Oven-Cooked Veal Stew	436

Roasted Beef Tenderloin 437
Gorgonzola Pistachio Sauce 440
Morelles Mushrooms and Parma Prosciutto Ragù 441
Stuffed Zucchini Blossoms
with Ricotta and Black Truffles Tempura-Style 441
Balsamic Spray Scent 442
Braised Lamb Shank 444
Gremolata Base Sauce 445
Roasted Bell Peppers 446
Polenta Cage 446
Savory Caramel Sauce 447
Cannolo Cigar in an Ashtray 452
Ricotta Cheese Filling Cream 453
Cigar Tuile Shell 454
Spun Sugar Smoke 455
Mascarpone Cheese Mousse 455
Cigar Ashes 455
Dark, Milk and White Chocolate 458
White Chocolate Flan 459
White Chocolate Mousse 460
White Chocolate Sauce 460
Milk Chocolate Sauce 461
Flexible Chocolate 461
Chocolate Crumb 462
Milk Chocolate Mousse 462
White and Dark Chocolate Cigarettes 463
Vanilla Panna Cotta 468
Simple Syrup 469
Orange Yolk Gelatin Spheres 469
Virtual Bacon 470
Hazelnuts and Lemons 471
Tulip Petals 472
Linzer Dough 472
Hazelnut Cream 473
Hazelnut Brittle 473
Lemon Curd 474
Lemon Sorbet 474
Lemon Chips 475
Gianduja Ganache 475
Barolo Reduction 477
Barolo Crème Brulé 477

Caramel Sauce	478
Saffron Poached Pear Purée	479
Saffron Poached Pear Gelato	479
Vin Brulé (Mulled Red Wine)	480
Warm Zuccottino Cake	480
Gianduja Sauce	483
Quince Vin Santo Gel	484
White Truffle Gelato	485
Deconstructed Caramelized Apple Pie	486
Roasted Apple	487
Orange Caramel	487
Green Apple Sorbet	488
Lemon Sour Gelatin	488
Apple Pie Crust Crumbs	489
Sicilian Chocolate Pepperoncino Gelato	491
Basil Sorbet	492

About the Author

Enzo Fargione grew up in Torino, Italy. He learned to love cooking via his mother's example at a very early age and has never stopped.

At fourteen, he enrolled in The Culinary Institute of Torino, and finished at the top of his class.

In 1986, after having worked in numerous Italian restaurants, fate would play a hand in his future: he packed his bags and became the first head chef at the Little Italy Gourmet in San Diego, CA.

Less than a year later he joined Roberto Donna as sous chef at Roberto's flagship restaurant, Galileo in Washington, D.C.

Between then and now, Enzo has earned success and respect in the culinary world as chef/operating partner and owner of numerous Italian restaurants between the Washington metropolitan area and Florida. Over the years he earned two nominations for Chef of the Year by the Restaurant Association of Metropolitan Washington, and was recognized by magazine and newspaper articles across the country for his personalized approach to modern Italian cooking as well as his playful inventiveness.

Since 2008, Enzo has been showered with impressive local and national media coverage, including being named one of four chefs to watch in the USA in 2008 by *Esquire* magazine. He has garnered multiple star ratings from local and national publications, catapulting him on top of the Italian fine dining scene in Washington D.C.

His latest restaurants, Elisir and Osteria Elisir, have quickly become dining destinations in Washington.

With unflagging energy, Enzo still finds time to teach cooking classes, where he passes on his vision of modern cooking to young talents. He also attends and supports charity events with his fellow chefs, and he is a proud member of the James Beard Foundation, where he often cooks at the Beard House in New York.

Once rated as a rising star, Enzo Fargione has become an asset to the Washington dining scene and to the dining community across the country thanks to his unique personal vision and playful modern Italian cooking.

For more information,
www.osteriaelisir.com
Twitter @EFargioneChef

Find more books from Keith Publications, LLC At www.keithpublications.com

CPSIA information can be obtained at www.ICGtesting.com
Printed in the USA
LVOW01s1003201213

365973LV00007B/46/P

9 781628 820119